INTERNATIONAL LAW IN DOMESTIC COURTS:
RULE OF LAW REFORM IN POST-CONFLICT STATES

SERIES ON TRANSITIONAL JUSTICE

The Series on *Transitional Justice* offers a platform for high-quality research within the rapidly growing field of transitional justice. The research is, of necessity inter-disciplinary in nature, drawing from disciplines such as law, political science, history, sociology, criminology, anthropology and psychology, as well as from various specialised fields of study such as human rights, victimology and peace studies. Furthermore, the research is international in outlook, drawing on the knowledge and experience of academics and other specialists in many different regions of the world.

The series is aimed at a variety of audiences who are either working or interested in fields such as crime and justice; human rights; humanitarian law and human security; conflict resolution and peace building. These audiences include academics, researchers, students, policy makers, practitioners, non-governmental organisations and the media.

All books published within the series are subject to a double-blind peer review by recognised authorities in the field.

Published titles within the series:

1. Stephen Peté and Max Du Plessis, *Repairing the Past? International Perspectives on Reparations for Gross Human Rights Abuses* (2007), 978-90-5095-492-1
2. Laura Stovel, *Long Road Home, Building Reconciliation and Trust in Post-War Sierra Leone* (2010), 978-94-000-0028-5
3. Andy Aitchison, *Making the Transition. International Intervention, State-Building and Criminal Justice Reform in Bosnia and Herzegovina* (2011), 978-94-000-0140-4
4. Stef Vandeginste, *Stones left unturned. Law and Transitional Justice in Burundi* (2010), 978-94-000-0115-2
5. Antoine Buyse (ed.), *Margins of Conflict. The ECHR and Transitions to and from Armed Conflict* (2011), 978-94-000-0157-2
6. Gaby Oré Aguilar and Felipe Gómez Isa (eds.), *Rethinking Transitions. Equality and Social Justice in Societies Emerging from Conflict* (2011), 978-1-78068-003-3
7. Richard Zajac Sannerholm, *Rule of Law after War. Ideologies, Norms and Methods* (2012), 978-1-78068-008-8
8. Nicola Palmer, Phil Clark and Danielle Granville (chief editors), *Critical Perspectives in Transitional Justice* (2011), 978-1-78068-035-4

Series on Transitional Justice, Volume 9

INTERNATIONAL LAW IN DOMESTIC COURTS: RULE OF LAW REFORM IN POST-CONFLICT STATES

Edda Kristjánsdóttir
André Nollkaemper
Cedric Ryngaert
(editors)

intersentia
Cambridge – Antwerp – Portland

Intersentia Publishing Ltd.
Trinity House | Cambridge Business Park | Cowley Road
Cambridge | CB4 0WZ | United Kingdom
Tel.: +44 1223 393 753 | Email: mail@intersentia.co.uk

Distribution for the UK:
Hart Publishing Ltd.
16C Worcester Place
Oxford OX1 2JW
UK
Tel.: +44 1865 517 530
Email: mail@hartpub.co.uk

Distribution for the USA and Canada:
International Specialized Book Services
920 NE 58th Ave. Suite 300
Portland, OR 97213
USA
Tel.: +1 800 944 6190 (toll free)
Email: info@isbs.com

Distribution for Austria:
Neuer Wissenschaftlicher Verlag
Argentinierstraße 42/6
1040 Wien
Austria
Tel.: +43 1 535 61 03 24
Email: office@nwv.at

Distribution for other countries:
Intersentia Publishing nv
Groenstraat 31
2640 Mortsel
Belgium
Tel.: +32 3 680 15 50
Email: mail@intersentia.be

International Law in Domestic Courts: Rule of Law Reform in Post-Conflict States
Edda Kristjánsdóttir, André Nollkaemper and Cedric Ryngaert (editors)

Artwork on cover: Author Jan Jordaan, title 'Hurt', medium Linocut, 1999. From the *Universal Declaration of Human Rights – International Print Portfolio, Article 5*, published by Art for Humanity, South Africa, 1999

GPRC
Guaranteed
Peer Reviewed
Content

ISBN 978-1-78068-041-5
NUR 828

British Library Cataloguing in Publication Data. A catalogue record for this book is available from the British Library.

PREFACE

This volume is the product of a working group on the international rule of law and international law in domestic courts, which commissioned a number of chapters on post-conflict situations.[1]

The editors wish to thank the authors who responded to the invitation to participate in this project, some of whom are promising new voices in their field and others who are established experts, but all of whom have acquired a deep and personal first-hand knowledge of the legal cultures they write about. The Rule of Law Working Group also deserves acknowledgment for the initial conceptual discussions that led to the present collection. Aristotle Constantenides and Cyprus Law School deserve thanks for accommodating the first meeting in Nikosia; Rosemary Byrne, likewise, hosted a meeting at Trinity College in Dublin. Special thanks go to Martine van Trigt for organization and support not only of a meeting in Amsterdam but throughout the life of the project. Sincere thanks also to Belinda Macmahon and Scarlet Wagner for their editorial work on the manuscript.

1 The Working Group was funded by the COST Action ISO602 on International Law in Domestic Courts (*European Cooperation in the field of Scientific and Technical Research*), an intergovernmental framework for European Co-operation in the field of Scientific and Technical Research, allowing the co-ordination of nationally funded research on a European level.

CONTENTS

INTRODUCTION

Edda Kristjánsdóttir, André Nollkaemper
and Cedric Ryngaert

States that are in transition after a violent conflict or an authoritarian past face daunting challenges in (re)establishing the rule of law. The legal system may be in need of rebuilding or reinvention to bring a climate of lawlessness to an end and create the conditions for a more stable future. The culture of impunity, lack of accountability, lack of rights protection, and, more generally, lack of respect for the rule of law that may have been pervasive in societies before undergoing the transition from autocracy to democracy often persist during the transition period itself. To the extent there is law, local 'strongmen' may be above it, or the law is co-opted by power to serve its ends. During the transition from violence or oppression, the pre-existing legal system, in whole or in part, may be temporarily suspended or permanently dismantled, and with it any semblance of the rule of law.

The rule of law challenges that characterize this period may include generalized insensitivity toward the plight of victims of the conflict or the deposed authoritarian regime; major criminals may get away with reduced sentences or outright impunity, ringleaders of criminal enterprises may escape their due because domestic legislation is not adequately equipped to address such modes of responsibility as command responsibility or joint criminal enterprise; the economic and social rights of marginalized groups may be insufficiently protected; judicial review of executive decisions may be non-existent; and the political branches may routinely interfere with the affairs of the judiciary.

During transition from one system to another, different layers of law may moreover be operational at the same time, creating confusion as to which legal standard should apply.[1] Such heterogeneity of law, or legal pluralism, hardly furthers the goal of legal certainty so essential for dealing with past abuses on

1 For instance, in Bosnia, as late as 2003, some local courts continued to apply the former Socialist FRY Criminal Code, whereas others applied the Bosnia and Herzegovina Criminal Code. The BiH Constitutional Court ruled that this lack of uniformity undermined the rule of law and the equal treatment of citizens before the law. See S. Popovic, Prosecution of War Crimes in Bosnian Cantonal and District Courts; the Role of the Rule of Law, in this volume at p. 221.

the basis of the rule of law as opposed to arbitrariness. If there is no continuity of the domestic legal system, the break with the troublesome past may entail impermissible retroactivity of new law. The new regime may also need to grapple with abuses that were committed under color of law in the old regime, by persons obediently doing their duty. Finally, abuses may have been committed in a legal vacuum with no law prohibiting the acts at their time of commission.

This volume examines several recent attempts which states have made to buttress the rule of law by receiving or importing international law into the gaps created in domestic law in a transition period. More particularly, the volume considers the practice of empowering national courts to give effect to international law in order to protect the rule of law in post-conflict settings.[2] Such situations present unique glimpses into 'constitutional moments' that often elevate the role of international law (notably international human rights law and international criminal law) in a domestic legal order. Indeed, the international community hopes that this increased role may help stabilize the legal order, protect fundamental rights, and prevent a return to lawlessness.[3] It forms a key

2 The book primarily focuses on the role of domestic courts as actors of transition in *post-conflict* settings. See in this respect on the emerging concept of *jus post bellum*, amongst others, C. Stahn and J. Kleffner (eds), *Jus Post Bellum*: Towards a Law of Transition from Conflict to Peace (The Hague: TMC Asser Press, 2008); E. De Brabandere, The Responsibility for Post-Conflict Reforms: A Critical Assessment of *Jus Post Bellum* as a Legal Concept, 43 Vanderbilt Journal of Transnational Law 119 (2010). The book primarily conceives 'conflict' as an 'armed conflict' in the sense of international humanitarian law. See on the definition of 'armed conflict' for such purposes ICTY Appeals Chamber 2 October 1995, *Prosecutor v. Dusan "Dusko" Tadic*, Decision on the Defence Motion for Interlocutory Appeal on Jurisdiction, IT-94-AR72, para. 70 (stating that an armed conflict 'exists whenever there is a resort to armed force between States or protracted armed violence between governmental authorities and organized armed groups or between such groups within a State'). Also in such states as South Africa and Russia, which are studied in this book, did an armed conflict take place, as domestic courts in those states have not failed to point out. See in respect of Russia, Constitutional Court of the Russian Federation 31 July 1995, *Sobranie zakonodatelstva Rossiyskoy Federatsii*, 1995, No. 33, Article 3424 (holding that a non-international armed conflict took place in Chechnya), and in respect of South Africa, Cape Provincial Division, South Africa 3 November 1987, *S v. Petane*, 1988 (3) South African Law Reports 51 (rejecting the application of Article 1(4) of Additional Protocol No. II to the Geneva Conventions, but implicitly accepting the existence of an armed conflict between the African National Congress (ANC) and the white minority regime of South Africa). But because the challenges of transition are much more multifaceted in respect of such states, it is probably more accurate to use the broader term 'transitional' or 'post-authoritarian' states. It is however not the ambition of this book to discuss the role of domestic courts in states that are in a time of political or economic transition that is not accompanied by violent conflict (eg Central and Eastern Europe, Brazil, India, China, and so on).

3 See eg H. Durham, From paper to practice: The role of treaty ratification post-conflict, in: B. Bowden, H. Charlesworth and J. Farrall (eds), The Role of International Law in Rebuilding Societies after Conflict. Great Expectations 177 (Cambridge University Press, 2009); R.F. Oppong, Re-imagining International Law: an Examination of Recent Trends in the Reception of International Law in National Legal Systems in Africa', 30 Fordham International Law Journal 323 (2007); D. Feldham, Monism, Dualism and Constitutional Legitimacy, 20 Australian Yearbook of International Law 105, 107 (1999).

element, for instance, of the policy on UN assistance to constitution making,[4] and in UN policies on transitional justice.[5]

In circumstances where old laws are no longer effective or have been discredited, particular possibilities open up for reinvention or overhaul of the legal and constitutional system, even by the very courts that make up the system. In order to fill the rule of law vacuum, courts are increasingly able to summon the aid of international norms. History shows many examples of a pattern of calling on international law in post-conflict settings. The acceptance of international law in the Weimar Constitution of Germany can be traced to the violent period preceding it,[6] and the same can be observed in the post-World War II constitutions of Germany and Italy.[7] This tendency has only increased with the evolution of international law and has come to play a prominent role in the work of domestic courts in the modern post-conflict situations studied in this volume.

The focus of our inquiry into the use of international law to bolster the rule of law required a working definition of the concept of 'the rule of law'. The working group used for this purpose the definition adopted by the UN Secretary-General in his report on *The Rule of Law and Transitional Justice in Conflict and Post-Conflict Societies*, according to which the rule of law refers to:

> A principle of governance in which all persons, institutions and entities, public and private, including the State itself, are accountable to laws that are publicly promulgated, equally enforced and independently adjudicated, and which are consistent with international human rights norms and standards. It requires, as well, measures to ensure adherence to the principles of supremacy of law, equality before the law, accountability to the law, fairness in the application of the law, separation of powers, participation in decision-making, legal certainty, avoidance of arbitrariness and procedural and legal transparency.[8]

This definition is a relatively 'thick' one, including adherence to international human rights standards. In the Concluding Observations at the end of the volume, we address the extent to which thicker or thinner versions have been deemed adequate in the practice of domestic courts in the states discussed in the

---

4 UN, Guidance Note of the Secretary-General – United Nations Assistance to Constitution-making Processes, June 2009.

5 UNSC, Report of the Secretary-General on the rule of law and transitional justice in conflict and post-conflict societies (S/2004/613) (30 July 2004), para 35.

6 Weimar Constitution, Article 13, para 1; A. Cassese, Modern Constitutions and International Law, 192 Recueil des Cours 357 (1985).

7 Article 24(1) of the 1949 German Constitution; Article 10 of the Italian Constitution; A. La Pergola and P. Del Duca, Community Law, International Law and the Italian Constitution, 79(3) American Journal of International Law 602 (July 1985); Cassese, *supra* note 6, p. 371.

8 *Supra* note 5.

individual chapters. *Prima facie*, though, this thicker definition in post-conflict or transitional situations is not without merit, as Beaulac notes in his chapter:

> More importantly, too thin an account of the rule of law, with no basic human rights content for instance, could well be counter-productive as the reforming measures may lack apparent legitimacy and, as a result, might be considered unsatisfactory by people in societies [...], where rule of law performative power ought to contribute to moving away from the old oppressive governance system to a new constitutional structure arrangement acceptable to people.[9]

Attempts to strengthen the rule of law by importing international law often seek to replace the thin conceptions of the rule of law that served the outgoing authorities with a novel, thicker interpretation that is protective of individual rights and the separation of powers. International law as 'thickening agent' may entail giving the individual a right to a remedy for human rights violations, provide for reparations of victims of the conflict, impose responsibility of superiors, reject amnesties or mitigated sentencing, and grant social and economic rights to disenfranchised populations. In times of transition, domestic courts may be able to call upon such international law norms to settle disputes and ensure accountability, thereby perhaps transforming what a society understands as its 'law', and confronting it with how it understands its fundamental values.[10]

The use of the term 'importing international law' does not imply that the use of international norms in national legal orders is a one-way process by which the 'receiving' states choose (or are forced) to import international rules. Often the contrary appears to be the case, and much of the literature on rule of law promotion by states and international institutions takes an 'exporting' rather than 'importing' approach. While we recognize and indeed will, in the chapters that follow, pay ample attention to the activities of international institutions that seek to strengthen the rule of law in particular post-conflict situations, in the final analysis the effect of such strategies, both in legal and practical terms, depends on the 'receiving' state – hence the chosen perspective of the importing state. We will return to this issue in the Concluding Observations.

Our focus on national courts rather than, more broadly, on the importation of international law in national legal orders, comes about by the courts' dynamic involvement in the application of international law in post-conflict and post-authoritarian societies. Through constitutional, legislative, or self-empowered mandates, and often supported by international actors (the UN and other

9 S. Beaulac, Lost in Transition? Domestic Courts, International Law and Rule of Law *'À la Carte'*, in this volume at p 30.

10 Cf R. Teitel, Transitional Justice (Oxford University Press, 2000) (referring to law transforming the prevailing meaning of legality in transitional situations).

intergovernmental organizations, other states, and non-governmental organizations (NGOs)), national courts seem to emerge in situations of transition with an enhanced power to use international law to reconcile the measures that are needed for stabilizing the system with the standards of fairness and reasonable expectations of the citizenry. They can be seen as using this power to keep the political branches in check, notably through the application of human rights law, but also as part of criminal law responses to questions of transitional justice. Such empowerment not only redefines a fundamental constitutional arrangement of the state, but at the same time supports an international rule of law.

International law, traditionally conceived as a set of rules for regulating the relations *between* states, has come also to serve as a set of rules for reconciling new and old versions, or identities, of the same state *inside* its borders. And, just as a state may pass through many constitutional moments in its national history, we in this volume refer to it as an 'international constitutional moment' when international law is imported, or injected, as the instrument for bridging a rule of law gap at domestic level. We focus on the role of the courts as guardians of tradition and as interpreters – in the local legal vernacular – of their own law in transition. We are interested in the cross-influences of domestic law and international law that are highly relevant for international actors in the rule of law field as they continue to build methods and practices to be replicated elsewhere.

In an international constitutional moment, facilitated by granting domestic courts the power to apply international law, international rule of law values may be transmitted from the international to the domestic level, helping to stabilize the legal order, contributing to the protection of fundamental rights, and protecting the separation of powers. An example of such stabilization may be the crowding out of various domestic laws after the Bosnian Constitutional Court, spurred on by the Organization for Security and Co-operation in Europe (OSCE),[11] in 2007 recommended that local courts apply the BiH Criminal Code, which was based on international law.[12] This should bring more legal certainty.[13]

International law itself is also impacted by these local developments, as it depends increasingly on domestic implementation for its effectiveness. However,

---

11 See OSCE, War Crimes Trials before the Domestic Courts of Bosnia and Herzegovina: Progress and Obstacles (March 2005), p. 20, available at www.oscebih.org/documents/1407-eng.pdf (noting 'considerable lack of clarity in relation to which criminal code will apply in pending war crime cases').

12 Constitutional Court, *Abduladhim Maktouf*, AP-1785/06, Decision on Admissibility and Merits (30 March 2007).

13 The relevant bodies of the Federation of Bosnia and Herzegovina have so far not heeded the Constitutional Court's call. The process of harmonization may be accelerated by a 2010 amendment to the Criminal Code of Bosnia and Herzegovina: Article 111 of this Code now provides that the relevant bodies '*shall harmonize* their respective criminal legislation with this Law *within 90* days as of the day when the Law comes into effect' (emphasis added).

optimism should be guarded, as the willingness and ability of domestic courts to apply international law may be limited in various ways, like the chapters in this book show. Their ability may be hampered by lack of full independence, as judges may have been appointed by and served under the old regime, or, if newly appointed, may either have too strong a bias against the participants of the old order, or fear upsetting the still precarious stability.[14] It is precisely for such reasons that the international community has taken an interest in internationalizing national courts and imposing other conditions that aim to insulate them from political pressures; however, such involvement is not always able to overcome domestic obstacles.

The treatment of international law by domestic judges indeed raises many fundamental questions. Should judges with no formal international law training or experience be empowered to introduce it in a volatile power vacuum? Does the empowerment of national courts through the application of international law not risk a backlash as the political power, faced with politically inconvenient international law-informed judicial decisions, may seek to restrict the effectiveness of judicial independence and judicial power, eg by refusing to act upon judicial injunctions, or by curtailing the courts' ability to invoke international law? In some cases, the judiciary may prove far more progressive-minded than the political branches are willing to be, creating a mirage of rights guarantees for individuals on the basis of international conventions, which the executive or legislative branches are unwilling to take measures to enforce. Expectations are raised and dashed swiftly. Where domestic courts are both empowered and willing to apply international law, other hindrances may stand in the way. Willingness is no guarantee that international law will be applied accurately, and an inaccurate application of international law will do little to further its rule of law-enhancing potential. The risk of misinformed application of international law looms particularly large in cases where domestic courts attempt to shoe-horn international law into domestic concepts, for instance in the attempt to safeguard the domestic principle of legality in criminal proceedings relating to international crimes. International law may in such cases be distorted and ineffectual.

In the light of the above-mentioned hopes and potentials, on the one hand, and the various barriers and limitations on the other, the chapters in this volume examine in detail attempts that were made in certain significant post-conflict or post-authoritarian situations to strengthen the domestic rule of law with the aid of international law. We consider such a study to be overdue. While a growing scholarship has examined the role of international law in transitional situations in general,[15] and as part of transitional justice situations in particular, or the role

14 D. Dyzenhaus, Judicial Independence, Transitional Justice and the Rule of Law, 10 Otago Law Review 345, 347 (2003).

15 See eg Bowden et al, *supra* note 3, and the works cited therein.

of international tribunals and commissions, not enough systemic attention has been paid to the empowerment of domestic courts in such situations. The issue is a timely one. As the chapters in this volume neared completion in early 2011, a series of protests and uprisings in North Africa and the Middle East have launched some states into transition – hopefully to a peaceful and stable future. These transitions – or constitutional moments – are occurring under the scrutiny not only of the UN and powerful states, but of the entire world community, interconnected as never before. Urgent questions are arising as to what rules will be applicable and acceptable for courts in those countries to use once they set about to reckon with the past while setting standards for the future. As the case studies in this volume show, international law may serve them as a tool for reconciling the demands for new rights and responsibilities with due process and other rule of law requirements.

The book identifies how attempts at legal empowerment have been carried out and how successful they have been in numerous different situations around the globe. In selecting situations, the book should be seen as eclectic, and not as exhaustive. It is not the aim of the editors to cover every situation in which domestic courts have, or conspicuously have not, relied on international law after a period of violent conflict. There are for instance no contributions regarding Latin America. Efforts at tackling the rule of law deficit in Latin America, and the role of domestic courts in the context of post-conflict and post-authoritarian transitional justice, have however been rather well-documented recently.[16] Notably, after foreign prosecutors and courts targeted former Chilean President Augusto Pinochet, courts throughout Latin America have shown increased willingness to bring former dictators and their henchmen to justice for human rights violations and corruption, thereby heavily relying on international law.[17]

16 J.E. Alvarez, Promoting the 'Rule of Law' in Latin America: Problems and Prospects, 25 George Washington Journal of International Law and Economics 281 (1999); D.M. Brinks, The Judicial Response to Police Killings in Latin America: Inequality and the Rule of Law (Cambridge University Press, 2008); P. Domingo and R. Sieder (eds), Rule of Law in Latin America: The International Promotion of Judicial Reform (London: Institute of Latin American Studies, 2001); J.E. Méndez, G. O'Donnell and P.S. Pinheiro, The Unrule of Law and the Underprivileged in Latin America (University of Notre Dame Press, 1999); L.E. Nagle, On Armed Conflict, Human Rights, and Preserving the Rule of Law in Latin America, 27 Penn State International Law Review 1 (2008); W.C. Prillaman, The Judiciary and Democratic Decay in Latin America: Declining Confidence in the Rule of Law (Praeger, 2000); X, The Judicial System and Rule of Law Reform in Latin America, 25 Arizona Journal of International and Comparative Law 299 (2008).

17 See for a fine account of this 'Pinochet' effect: N. Roht-Arriaza, The Pinochet Effect: Transnational Justice in the Age of Human Rights (University of Pennsylvania Press, 2005). See as regards Peru: K. Ambos, The *Fujimori* Judgment: a President's Responsibility for Crimes Against Humanity as Indirect Perpetrator by Virtue of an Organized Power Apparatus, 9 Journal of International Criminal Justice 137 (2011); L.J. Laplante, The Rule of Law in Transitional Justice: the *Fujimori* Trial in Peru, in: M. Sellers and T. Tomaszewski (eds), The Rule of Law in Comparative Perspective 177–200 (Springer, 2010). See as regards Argentina: J.S. Elias, Constitutional Changes, Transitional Justice, and Legitimacy: the Life

In Colombia, an ambitious 'Justice and Peace Law' was adopted in 2005,[18] which reserves an important role for domestic courts in the Colombian transitional justice process.[19] Also, various Latin American states have recently attempted to partly correct historical wrongs perpetrated against indigenous peoples, by granting them more extensive collective rights based on international (soft) law, that might be justiciable in domestic courts.[20]

Each chapter of this book considers, to the extent relevant, the following questions:

1. What was the constitutional moment that allowed for an increased role for national courts in applying international law?
2. What was the formal manifestation of the constitutional moment? A new constitution? New legislation? New institutions? The same law and institutions, but a new political or judicial will? A new partnership with international institutions?
3. What was the scope of the enhanced practice of local courts to apply all of international law, or only human rights, or some human rights, criminal law, and if so, what parts? What were the sources of international law: only treaty law, or also customary law, general principles, international or foreign legal decisions?
4. How did the possibility to give international law a stronger role come about? Was it a 'bottom-up' change prompted by domestic actors, and if so, which ones? Through the intermediacy of international institutions? Was there a

---

and Death of Argentina's 'Amnesty' Laws', 31 Hastings International and Comparative Law Review 587 (2008); P.F. Parenti, The Prosecution of International Crimes in Argentina, 10 International Criminal Law Review 491 (2010).

18 Law 975, *Ley de Justicia y Paz*, 22 July 2005.

19 The Act notably allows for reduced sentences instead of amnesty for repenting paramilitaries. See for a critical analysis: P. Burbridge, Justice and Peace?: The Role of Law in Resolving Colombia's Civil Conflict, 8 International Criminal Law Review 557 (2008); J.E. Arvelo, International Law and Conflict Resolution in Colombia: Balancing Peace and Justice in the Paramilitary Demobilization Process, 37 Georgetown Journal of International Law 411 (2005).

20 UNGA, UN Declaration on the Rights of Indigenous Peoples, 13 September 2007 (A/RES/61/295) (2007). See for the active role of the Inter-American Commission and Court of Human Rights in respect of the rights of indigenous peoples: IACHR 6 February 2006, *Case of the Indigenous Community Yakye Axa v. Paraguay*, Interpretation of the judgment of merits, reparations and costs, IACHR Series C no 142; IHRL 1526 (IACHR 2006); IACHR 28 November 2007, *Case of the Saramaka People v. Suriname*, Preliminary objections, merits, reparations and costs, IACHR Series C no 172; IHRL 3046 (IACHR 2007); IACHR 23 June 2005, *Case of Yatama v. Nicaragua*, Preliminary objections, merits, reparations and costs, IACHR Series C no 127; IHRL 1511 (IACHR 2005). See for an analysis, amongst others, L. Rodríguez-Piñer, The Inter-American System and the UN Declaration on the Rights of Indigenous Peoples: Mutual Reinforcement, in: S. Allen and A. Xanthaki (eds), Reflections on the UN Declaration on the Rights of Indigenous Peoples 457–483 (Hart, 2011); J. Faundez, Access to Justice and Indigenous Communities in Latin America, in: Y.P. Ghai (ed.) Marginalized Communities and Access to Justice 83–108 (Routledge, 2010).

significant role played by NGOs, for instance, in bringing international law arguments to the courts' attention? To the extent that international actors played a role, what was their agenda?

5. How did domestic courts contextualize international law and adjust it to the particular nature and problems of the situation of transition in question? Did frictions with the national legal context occur (legal transplants)? Did the empowerment of national courts to apply international law change the power relations between the courts, the legislature and the executive? Has there been evidence of backlash from the political branches seeking to recapture power from the courts, thereby limiting the role of international law? Were the courts in question up to the task (in terms of quality, skills) and was the wider legal system and the affected population supportive of an effective application of international law?
6. What was the legacy of the empowerment of the courts in terms of sustained application of international law throughout the legal system, eg norm-penetration into local law? Did changing the place of international law in the domestic sphere achieve the purpose of 'improving the rule of law' or human rights, and can any wider effects be discerned outside the courts? Was/is the application of international law ultimately accompanied by an improvement in the situation of the persons international law purports to protect? Was international law possibly being used to appease the outside world rather than improve matters at home? Or was the reach of norm-entrenchment insufficient to result in concrete improvements?

In Chapter One, Stéphane Beaulac lays the background for the more empirical chapters by considering the performative power of the rule of law that has been at work for some time at the international level, notably in UN promotion efforts, in both development and transition fields. This conceptual chapter explores the possible heuristic models for the rule of law to help discuss the hypothesis of the empowerment of domestic courts, at a 'constitutional moment', through recourse to international law, in post-conflict and post-dictatorial states. The hypothesis involves the relocating of the legal character of normativity, in a separate space, beside the international-national axis. After reviewing the debate around the formal and substantial versions of the rule of law, the argument goes past this thin-thick spectrum. Hence the suggestion of an *à la carte* approach to the concept, which is meant to provide an organizing structure for the relevant rule of law values, actual and aspirational, within a new or true stable constitutional arrangement. In the end, no exhaustive laundry list of values is proposed, but merely tentative non-negotiable elements likely to be appropriate to all societies in transition. Although imperfect, this *à la carte* model constitutes a heuristic tool to guide our reflections on the role that domestic courts in states in transition can and should play by means of international law.

In Chapter Two, Sergei Marochkin examines how domestic courts in Russia implemented and applied rules of international law before and after the end of the former Soviet Union. Russia has undergone substantial changes during the last two decades, mainly triggered by two 'critical moments', as set out by the author. The first one was the dissolution of the Soviet Union in 1991 with Russia emerging as a separate state. The second critical moment was the confrontation between the former parliament and the presidential power in October 1993, leading to the formation of a new government and the adoption of a newly drafted constitution. These events had implications and repercussions for the whole of Russia's political, economic and legal systems, as is also displayed by the practice of domestic courts regarding the application of international law; especially, the rule of law. Based on these observations, the chapter analyses the role taken by international law in the Russian legal order – comparing the Soviet and post-Soviet era.

The chapter by Evelyne Schmid examines the ability of the South African Constitutional Court to apply economic and social rights and its approach towards the definition of the rule of law. When adopting the current impressive Constitution following the Apartheid Regime, the drafters aspired to a substantive conception of the rule of law that would break with the abusive past. The chapter analyzes the effects of empowering domestic courts to apply international legal principles after liberation from an oppressive rule. Especially, it focuses on the success of the constitutional entrenchment of economic and social rights in South Africa's legal system through incorporation in the domestic Bill of Rights, the 'transformative constitutionalism'. The constitutional entrenchment of economic and social rights in the Constitution did display positive results; however, where they were greatest, they have to be seen in conjunction with complementing broader campaigns and cannot be isolated when looking at ground-breaking social transformations as a whole.

In Chapter Four, Rishikesh Wagle explores the Nepalese approach to international law, focusing on human rights obligations. Following the armed rebellion launched by the Communist Party of Nepal (Maoist) from 1996 to 2006, and the subsequent peace accord formally ending the armed conflict, courts increasingly have been confronted with claims concerning the social, economic, and psychological damage caused to Nepalese society. In that respect, the absence of a supportive legal framework – international customary and treaty law being not directly enforceable – has proven difficult for the application of international provisions. The Nepalese Supreme Court, in its groundbreaking judgment in *Dhakal* in 2007, provided for a solution and broke with its previous approach. The author provides an overview of the general applicability of international norms in post-conflict Nepal, and especially focuses on the Supreme Court's answer concerning the applicability of human rights in *Dhakal*. As the author concludes, the Court found that, although treaty norms lack direct enforceability, those instruments – which were very liberally interpreted – can have an indirect influence on the Nepalese legal system.

Haider Ala Hamoudi, in his chapter on International Law and Iraqi Courts, indicates that in some cases, attempts to give international law a more prominent place have failed. When analyzing what appears to be a promising combination for the rise of international law as a source of law in domestic proceedings – the participation in international law-making and implementation, and a largely independent judiciary rising in prominence – one would expect some level of encouragement of national courts to engage in international law; however, both political actors and courts seem to display some reluctance in their manner of resorting to international law. This becomes especially ostensive in areas such as human rights and criminal law. Covering three contrasting eras in Iraqi history, Hamoudi explores the use of international law and the role it played for domestic courts from a historical perspective, for the interim phase under the Coalition Provisional Authority administration, and the approach under the current Constitution.

In Chapter Six, Ebrahim Afsah focuses on the constitutionalism and governance-related aspects of the rule of law in Afghanistan. The increase in rule of law elements as a part of development assistance, particularly in the case of post-conflict stabilization missions, reflects the overall rise in consideration of the legal quality as regards post-conflict societies. This is also true for the international engagement in Afghanistan since December 2001. As the author points out, the general justification for interfering is pointing to a normative conception calling for a uniform application of international standards based on the equality of human beings. The chapter argues that the absence of influence of international legal standards is not primarily caused by cultural or religious impacts, but the lack of effective state institutions. The author examines the juxtaposition of general qualities of statehood and the reality of the Afghan state and infers that constitutionalism is intrinsically linked with effective statehood, denying the possibility of its existence without the latter.

Nicola Palmer's contribution in Chapter Seven explores the contextual examination of the influence that international law, especially international criminal law, has had on the application of law in the Rwandan courts. Subsequent to assessing that the role portrayed by international law in post-conflict Rwanda was a dynamic and varied one, by displaying reciprocal influences, the author argues that acknowledgement of the achievements of domestic courts during a transitional period can usefully strengthen the impact of national law on international law. The aforementioned argument is dissected in three sections: firstly, the rule of law in a transitional period is conditionally connected to its historical, political, and cultural context. The second part examines the constitutional moments in Rwanda following the genocide and civil war, incorporating into domestic law the improved pre-trial detention laws and abolishing capital punishment in 2007; therewith, the standards required by Rule 11*bis* of the Statute of the International Criminal Tribunal for Rwanda (ICTR) were met and transfer for trial under Rwandan law made possible. Thirdly, the author argues that in a concurrent process, international law has shaped the Rwandan approach to post-genocide justice, and the domestic courts' practice has shaped international law in turn. By way of conclusion, it can be extracted that international law in Rwanda, when examined in context, has been both used and resisted; further, omitting to take into account domestic courts' need and purpose might contribute to impairing the strife for stronger national institutions.

The next set of chapters focuses on different aspects of the prosecution of war crimes and the application of human rights in post-conflict Bosnia and Herzegovina. In Chapter Eight, Antoine Buyse discusses the role of the Bosnian Human Rights Chamber, set up under the Dayton Peace Agreement as a mixed institution combining domestic and international elements, in supervising respect for human rights by the parties involved in the conflict. Buyse focuses specifically on how the Chamber applied substantive ECHR rights in relation to property and housing rights, and draws attention to how the Chamber has developed these rights in a flexible manner that was tailor-made to the particular Bosnian post-conflict context, such as post-conflict evictions and the particular concept of 'occupancy rights' under former Yugoslav law. Through directly applying ECHR norms, a similar approach to that of the European Court of Human Rights (ECtHR) could be adopted, and the use of leading cases proved successful for reconciling the requirements of justice, efficiency, and the restoration of the rule of law. Still, after the gradual dissolution of the Human Rights Chamber and integration into the Bosnian Constitutional Court, the Bosnian legal system continues to face challenges in upholding the rule of law.

In Chapter Nine, Katerina Uhlířová examines the process of rebuilding the rule of law in Bosnia and Herzegovina. While the primary role of the local population in that respect is acknowledged, the author also admits that this option may not always be available, and external assistance may be needed. Building on the efforts of the international community in Bosnia and Herzegovina and its major role during the process of reconstruction, the contribution concentrates on the question whether such rule of law efforts were and could have been successful, springing not from local linkage but rather from an external imposition. The chapter especially examines two aspects or goals of the rule of law: providing efficient and impartial justice, and upholding human rights. As international law plays a major role in that regard, both the *process* of empowering domestic institutions to apply international law as well as the actual *application* of international law are analyzed. To this effect, the involvement of the international community in the constitutional process is examined, including developments leading to the conclusion of the Dayton Peace Agreement and the adoption of the current constitutional framework. From this point of departure, the author explores the effects on harmonization of criminal legislation and the implications for prosecution of international crimes, having regard especially to the War Crimes Chamber (WCC). In particular, she focuses on its relationship with the International Criminal Tribunal for the Former Yugoslavia (ICTY) and the domestic application of the concept of Joint Criminal Enterprise (JCE), providing two case studies where the BiH judiciary sought to justify and clarify the application of this 'legal transplant'. The conclusion evaluates the international community's engagement in the application of international law as a means to improve and deliver justice to the victims of the war in BiH.

In her chapter on the prosecution of war crimes in Bosnian cantonal and district courts, Sanja Popovic explores the judicial inadequacies that have become apparent through case law and proposes potential ways for rectification. With the establishment of the ICTY, an international body was set up specifically designed to bring to justice those who committed serious violations of international humanitarian law during the conflict in the former Yugoslavia since 1991. Concurrently, Bosnian local courts were empowered to try those cases that concerned 'less serious' war crimes. The role of the local courts will, however, considerably increase once the ICTY's mandate expires. By taking into account the tangibility of an assessment of local courts' *modi operandi* and the impossibility of an operation of the rule of law – be it a thick or a thin concept – without the desire to be bound by the respective laws, the contribution examines some of the decisions taken by Bosnian cantonal and district courts. Particular attention is paid to the preservation of international criminal law norms and standards, and its impact on the receptiveness of the judicial branch. In some instances the practice of Bosnian courts displays their failure to follow international precedents, and at times it has been proven to be irreconcilable with basic principles of war crimes prosecution.

The last contribution on war crimes prosecution in the former Yugoslavia, by Sharon Weill and Ivan Jovanović, examines the function of the Serbian War Crimes Chamber (WCC) in Serbia. Remarkably, the Chamber – being established within the District Court of Belgrade – constitutes one of the very few courts in the world that, shortly after the ending of a conflict, is prosecuting its own nationals on a systematic scale. The first part of the contribution examines the background of the WCC as another establishment constituting an alternative to the ICTY. The second part provides a critical analysis of the first decisions issued by the Chamber during its first six years of operation, evaluating the WCC's approach to applying international law in practice and its importance as an international player in the wider context of the international rule of law. As the latter is dependent on the Chamber's objective ability to apply international law – which, in practice, seems especially parochial as to the application of international humanitarian law – and its subjective political willingness to do so, the former represents one of its essential elements.

The chapter by Eyal Benvenisti and Michal Saliternik focuses on the jurisprudence of courts in liberated territories concerning the laws and administrative acts that were promulgated and applied by the occupying power. An analysis of a varied range of case law shows that, by tendency, national courts in the aftermath of an occupation prioritize the transitional needs of their societies – at least, in cases of conflict – over addressing questions of international legality. The 'transitional bias' produced by post-occupation courts is examined by reference to case studies originating from several jurisdictions, under occupation during World War I, the Namibian Supreme Court's ruling in the *Cultura 2000* case, the imposition of capital punishment on Saddam Hussein by the Iraqi High Criminal Tribunal, and cases from East Timor and Kosovo in which prescriptive measures of UN territorial administrations were scrutinized by national courts. Inferring from the case studies, the chapter offers insight into the various forms of 'transitional bias', ranging from post-occupation justice and the transitional processes as perceived by domestic institutions over the latter's struggle for reputation to the institutional aspects of post-conflict situations. The chapter concludes by suggesting that, given the countervailing concerns, it would be preferable to distinguish between *ex ante* and *ex post* consideration, and it criticizes the courts for invoking the laws of occupation as the basis for their *ex post* findings, thereby contributing to distorting this law.

Yael Ronen addresses the context of post-conflict restructuring of the legal system, where the use of international law is often perceived as a stabilizing factor, contributing to the protection of fundamental rights and protecting the separation of powers by imposing a more stringent standard for protection of human rights than domestic law does. However, international law operates at various levels and in various contexts, in some cases having a destabilizing effect on the domestic system. Moreover, the courts entrusted with applying international law, no less than other institutions, may abuse their power, and such abuse carries particular weight as it is carried out under the guise of law. This article concerns an incident in which the Court of Appeal of East Timor invoked international legal principles relating to the consequences of illegal annexation when determining the domestic law of East Timor under UN administration and after independence, without due regard to their implications in the field of human rights. Rather than enhancing the post-conflict reconstruction, this invocation risked destabilizing the emerging political and legal apparatus. While this attempt to bring about change was thwarted by the objection of the legal community and the legislature, the incident demonstrates that the recourse to international law must be discriminative so that it does not subvert the very purpose for which this law is invoked. The article describes the dilemma concerning the choice of applicable law in post-conflict East Timor, and the intended and unintended roles that international law has played in shaping that choice, noting the implications for domestic law of unqualified reliance on certain branches of international law. It also places the East Timorese experience in a wider context of post-conflict determinations of applicable law in light of international legal principles.

In the final chapter, the main connecting threads between the chapters are identified, and conclusions are drawn.

LOST IN TRANSITION?

Domestic Courts, International Law and Rule of Law '*À la Carte*'

Stéphane Beaulac*

1. INTRODUCTION

For some time now, we have been told that the rule of law is high on the international agenda for several reasons: it brings political stability and prompts economic growth, and it is also central to sustainable development and contributes to international peace and security.[1] Working around the hypothesis of an international version of the concept, I suggested that 'the "rule of law" is undoubtedly one of the most powerful expressions in the modern world. In a sense, it has become an activity in itself, a mental-social phenomenon which exists within human consciousness and acts independently within physical social realities, like a pat on the back or a slap in the face.'[2] Indeed, it can be argued that the rule of law has become a 'buzzword' ('buzzphrase') in legal theory and political studies.[3] To borrow from Ogden and Richard's philosophy

* Ph.D (*Cantab.*). Professor of Law at the University of Montreal, Canada; 2010 Neil MacCormick fellow at the University of Edinburgh School of Law, Scotland, and visiting scholar at the Amsterdam Center for International Law, University of Amsterdam, the Netherlands. Previous versions of the paper were presented at the conference 'The International Rule of Law Constitutional Moments: The Role of International Law in Domestic Courts in Post-Conflict and Transitional Societies', organized in collaboration with the COST Action Programme International Law in Domestic Courts (ILDC), at Trinity College, Dublin, Ireland, in May 2010, and at the conference 'Globalisation of Law and Legal Professions', organized by the International Association of Legal Methodology, at Aix-en-Provence, France, in June 2010. A shorter version of the paper appears in the proceedings of the latter conference.

1 In particular, see the work by the World Bank, starting with D. Kaufmann, A. Kraay and P. Zoido-Lobatón, Governance Matters, in: World Bank Policy Research Working Papers, no. 2196 (1999), and the more recent updated studies on the subject, available at www.worldbank.org/research.

2 S. Beaulac, The Rule of Law in International Law Today, in: G. Palombella and N. Walker (eds), Relocating the Rule of Law 197 (Oxford: Hart Publishing, 2009) (footnotes omitted).

3 For a point of comparison, where the linguistic sign 'sovereignty' was scrutinized in this fashion, see S. Beaulac, The Power of Language in the Making of International Law – The

of language, the rule of law is a formulation of 'hurrah!' words; that is to say, words that provoke a good feeling in those who voice or hear them.[4]

On the more cynical side, Carothers observed: '[o]ne cannot get through a foreign policy debate these days without someone proposing the rule of law as a solution to the world's troubles.'[5] The United Nations has fuelled such criticism in recent years, including in the context of post-conflict states and other situations of transition. Witness, inter alia, the 2004 UN Secretary-General's report on the rule of law and transitional justice,[6] the outcome document of the 2005 UN World Summit,[7] with a full section on the rule of law,[8] and the uninterrupted string of resolutions by the UN General Assembly, from 2006 to 2010, all entitled 'The Rule of Law at the National and International Levels',[9] as well as the creation of a rule of law unit in the Executive Office of the UN Secretary-General[10] and the many reports by UN officials on the rule of law since 2006.[11] In short, perhaps the rule of law has been a victim of its own success because, as we all know, too much of a good thing can be harmful.

In the context of transition, as in other areas of application of the rule of law, general acceptance does not mean that we know precisely what we are talking about. On the point, Krygier wrote that 'we can more easily state the values it serves, and recognize violations of it, than can specify the particular institutions and practices that will promote it.'[12] Similarly, Peerenboom opined: 'Foreign actors and experts are better at the creation of norms and generating a menu of

---

Word Sovereignty in Bodin and Vattel and the Myth of Westphalia (Leiden & Boston: Martinus Nijhoff, 2004).

4 C.K. Ogden and I.A. Richards, The Meaning of Meaning, 149–150 (London: Kegan Paul, 1927, 2nd ed.), suggest dividing up the functions language can fulfil into two categories: symbolic and emotive. In the latter role, language is used to express or excite feelings or attitudes; language thus used can be referred to as 'hurrah!' words and 'boo!' words, because of the feelings, good or bad, that it generates.

5 T. Carothers, The Rule of Law Revival 77 Foreign Affairs 95 (1998).

6 UNSC, Report of the Secretary-General, The Rule of Law and Transitional Justice in Conflict and Post-Conflict Societies (S/2004/616) (23 August 2004).

7 Endorsed by UN General Assembly Resolution 60/1, 2005 World Summit Outcome (A/RES/60/1) (24 October 2005).

8 *Supra* note 7, section 134.

9 UNGA, The Rule of Law at the National and International Levels (A/RES/61/39) (18 December 2006); (A/RES/62/70) (8 January 2008); (A/RES/63/128) (15 January 2009); (A/RES/64/116) (15 January 2010).

10 Which was recommended as per section 134(e) of the 2005 World Summit Outcome, *supra* note 7, and was established pursuant to Resolution 61/39, *supra* note 9.

11 See, for instance, the Secretary-General's Report, Uniting our Strengths: Enhancing United Nations Support for the Rule of Law (A/61/636-S/2006/980) (2006) and Corr.1.

12 M. Krygier, Rethinking the Rule of Law after Communism, in: A. Czarnota, M. Krygier and W. Sadurski (eds), Rethinking the Rule of Law after Communism 273 (Budapest and New York: Central European University Press, 2005). See also M. Krygier, Transitional Questions About the Rule of Law: Why, What and How?, 28 East Central Europe / L'europe du centre-est 12 (2001).

substantive legal rules than figuring out how they will be implemented.'[13] This being so, one thing is certain though, especially in transition societies: both institutions *and* good practices must be part and parcel of rule of law reforms.[14]

This book is concerned with the possible role of one such institution, namely the national judiciary, in promoting the rule of law domestically through the use of international normativity, particularly in jurisdictions that have gone through violent conflicts or that have moved out of authoritarian regimes. With a view to giving a bit of perspective to the case studies and other discussions in this book, the present chapter dwells upon the heuristic models for the rule of law in relation to the problematics of international law in domestic courts. Avoiding the *lieux communs* of these issues, the goal is to set the tone and help navigate the sometimes obscure waters of these diverse situations of transition toward a structured social organisation based on a new or true stable constitutional arrangement. Before discussing rule of law heuristic models, groundwork questions need to be briefly addressed: what does the UN mean by the 'international rule of law' (section 2), and what do recent debates on interlegality[15] teach us in terms of the rule of law (section 3)? Next, the crux of the paper (section 4), where various formulations of the rule of law are examined, from thin to thick understandings, highlights the difficulties with a spectrum-type of reasoning. The conclusion is that an '*à la carte*' heuristic model is most appropriate for rationalising the rule of law and interlegality.

2. THE UNITED NATIONS AND THE RULE OF LAW

Leaving aside for a moment the actual content of this essentially contested concept[16] – which is analysed in detail later – let us first focus on what the United Nations intends to achieve through the 'international rule of law',[17] pursuant to its proclaimed mission to promote 'The Rule of Law at the National and International Levels'.[18] This is most relevant because, needless to say, the UN is a

---

13 R. Peerenboom, The Future of Rule of Law: Challenges and Prospects for the Field, 1 Hague Journal on the Rule of Law 9 (2009).

14 See R. Kleinfeld, Competing Definitions of the Rule of Law, in: T. Carothers (ed.), Promoting the Rule of Law: In Search of Knowledge 31 (Washington: Carnegie Endowment, 2006). Concentrating on structure and institutions, however, have proven insufficient; see J. Stromseth, Strengthening Demand for the Rule of Law in Post-Conflict Societies, 18 Minnesota Journal of International Law 418 (2009), who speaks of (and deplores) the 'if we build it, they will come' attitude.

15 I use the term *interlegality* to refer to the phenomenon of normative migration among legal orders, in particular the national application of international law by domestic courts.

16 Borrowing from G.A. Gallie, Essentially Contested Concepts, 56 Proceedings of the Aristotelian Society 167 (1955–1956), Jeremy Waldron has suggested that the rule of law is an essentially contested concept; see J. Waldron, Is the Rule of Law an Essentially Contested Concept (in Florida)?, 21 Law and Philosophy 137 (2002).

17 On the international version of the rule of law, generally, see also J. Crawford, International Law and the Rule of Law, 24 Adelaide Law Review 3 (2004).

18 *Supra* note 9.

prominent actor in rule of law promotion around the world, including in transition societies, of course.

Based on the narrative of the UN, I want to underline that referring to the rule of law at the international level can be linked to two different, albeit closely related phenomena.[19] First is what I refer to as the rule of law *internationalized*: that is to say, how rule of law values can be externalized onto and applied within the international legal order. In that regard, one would look at international adjudicative bodies, like the International Court of Justice (ICJ) for instance, in order to assess the extent to which rule of law values are present, be it in terms of legality, equal application of the law, judicial review, etc.[20] The twin phenomenon, or second occurrence, can be called the *internationalization* of the rule of law: that is to say, how the international plane may be used to export the rule of law from domestic spheres and promote its values within other domestic jurisdictions. It acknowledges the fact that the rule of law in domestic law has become an international relations issue and that international normativity and institutions can act as a transit point, in a sense, for rule of law values.[21]

One can observe manifestations of this dual conception of the rule of law from UN policy statements and General Assembly resolutions.[22] One good illustration is the UN Secretary-General 2006 report, 'Uniting our Strengths: Enhancing United Nations Support for the Rule of Law',[23] especially the last part of the document dealing with the future: that is, how to strengthen the UN capacities, coherence, and coordination in regard to the rule of law. The activities under UN auspices pertaining to the rule of law were put into three 'baskets'. The first one is actually labelled the 'rule of law at the international level' and deals with issues linked to the UN Charter, multilateral treaties, international dispute resolution mechanisms, the International Criminal Court (ICC), as well as training and education regarding international law. It is clear that these actions correspond, as per the classification suggested above, to the rule of law internationalized, given that the UN activities pursue rule of law values on the international plane. In other words, these elements are interested in how rule of law values – linked to institutions, normativity, adjudication, human rights – are to be present and embraced within the international legal order.

---

19 This dichotomy was inspired, somewhat, by S. Chesterman, An International Rule of Law?, 56 American Journal of Comparative Law 331 (2008).

20 See S. Beaulac, An Inquiry into the International Rule of Law, European University Institute Working Papers, MWP 2007/14 (2007).

21 These ideas were first articulated at a seminar in January 2008, organized by the Amsterdam Center for International Law and the Leuven Center for Global Governance Studies, where I presented a paper on the recent debates at the United Nations on the meaning of the international rule of law, especially in terms of *accountability*, the theme of the workshop. See A. Nollkaemper, J. Wouters and N. Hachez, Accountability and the Rule of Law at International Level, report available at www.mzes.uni-mannheim.de/projekte/typo3/site/fileadmin/reports/report%20Accountability%20and%20Rule%20of%20Law.pdf.

22 See *supra* notes 6–11.

23 *Supra* note 11.

On the other hand, the second and third baskets of activities in the Secretary-General's report – namely, 'rule of law in the context of conflict and post conflict situations' and 'rule of law in the context of long-term development', respectively – are concerned with the other, twin phenomenon of the internationalization of the rule of law, because they obviously deal with domestic matters, which are promoted via the international law machinery. For example, these rule of law activities relate to the strengthening of justice systems and institutions in domestic jurisdictions (including by means of judicial review), the establishment of truth and reconciliation processes as well as fact-finding and commissions of inquiry, and the improvement of the police and the reform of the penal system, particularly with respect to corruption and organized crime. Such rule of law elements, very much originating from domestic legal orders, are essentially interested in being promoted domestically in other state jurisdictions (not onto the international plane *per se*), especially in the development and transition settings. Thus we would speak of the internationalization of the rule of law when the values do no more than *transit*, so to speak, through the international legal sphere, the final destination being the domestic jurisdictions of states.

Before further developing upon the possible heuristic models for the rule of law, another background issue needs to be injected into the discussion: interlegality.

3. INTERLEGALITY AND INTERNATIONAL RULE OF LAW COMPLEMENTARITY

International law scholarship has spilled much ink in the last century debating the relationship between international law and domestic law.[24] The usual narrative on interlegality refers to the opposition between dualism and monism. It further posits a necessary hierarchy between the international and domestic legal orders,[25] a feature that has recently been challenged.[26] Nijman and Nollkaemper have suggested, for instance, the emergence of a global legal

---

24 See, among the classics, J.G. Starke, Monism and Dualism in the Theory of International Law, 17 British Yearbook of International Law 66 (1936); G. Scelle, *Le phénomène du dédoublement fonctionnel*, in: M. Schätzel and H.J. Schlochauer (eds), *Rechtsfragen der internationalen Organisation, Festschrift für Wehberg* 324 (Cologne: Klostermann, 1956); I. Seidl-Hohenfeldern, Transformation or Adoption of International Law into Municipal Law, 12 International and Comparative Law Quarterly 88 (1963); and L. Ferrari-Bravo, International and Municipal Law: The Complementarity of Legal Systems, in: R.St.J. Macdonald and D.M. Johnston (eds), The Structure and Process of International Law: Essays in Legal Philosophy, Doctrine and Theory 715 (The Hague: Martinus Nijhoff, 1986).

25 See A. von Bogdandy, Pluralism, Direct Effect, and the Ultimate Say: On the Relationship Between International and Domestic Constitutional Law, 6 International Journal of Constitutional Law 397 (2008).

26 See L. Garlicki, Cooperation of Courts: The Role of Supranational Jurisdictions in Europe, 6 International Journal of Constitutional Law 509 (2008).

pluralism, embedded in a community of principles and common values, 'that allow[s] co-existence and cooperation between multiple legal systems.'[27]

It must be pointed out also that we generally accept that there is no one-size-fits-all answer on either side of the dualism-monism fence, for two reasons. First, the effect of international normativity depends, ultimately, on the domestic legal order of each national state.[28] As Greenwood put it, 'the capacity of any institution created by national law and which derived its authority from national law [domestic courts] to apply a rule which emanated from a source outside the nation [is] necessarily confined by rules which circumscribed its jurisdiction.'[29] Note that such an understanding of the interlegality interface is, fundamentally, an application of the dualist logic,[30] used at some *meta-level.* As Kumm wrote: '[t]he very idea that the national constitution is decisive for generating the doctrines that structure the relationship between national and international law is dualist.'[31]

Secondly, there is no universal black-or-white answer to interlegality issues for the simple reason that most national constitutional law and practice show traits of both dualism and monism, which means that the line between them is blurred. Higgins' observation is on point: 'in reality there is usually little explanation or discussion of these large jurisprudential matters in the domestic court hearing. The response of the court to the problem is often instinctive [and], the truth be told, the response is often somewhat confused and lacking in an intellectual coherence.'[32] As a result, she noted, 'not everything is dependent upon whether a country accepts the monist or dualist view, [which] is evidenced by the fact that, even within a given country, different courts may approach differently the problem of the relationship between international and domestic law.'[33]

---

27 J. Nijman and A. Nollkaemper, Beyond the Divide, in: J. Nijman and A. Nollkaemper (eds), New Perspectives on the Divide Between National and International Law 360 (Oxford and New York: Oxford University Press, 2007).

28 See T. Buergenthal, Self-Executing and Non-Self-Executing Treaties in National and International Law, 235 Hague Recueil 317 (1992); and G. Gaja, Dualism – A Review, in: J. Nijman and A. Nollkaemper (eds), New Perspectives on the Divide Between National and International Law 61 (Oxford & New York: Oxford University Press, 2007).

29 C. Greenwood, International Law in National Courts: Discussion, in: J. Crawford and M. Young (eds), The Function of Law in the International Community: An Anniversary Symposium – Proceedings of the 25th Anniversary Conference of the Lauterpacht Centre for International Law (Cambridge, 2008), available at www.lcil.cam.ac.uk?25th_anniversary?book.php.

30 See R. Provost, Judging in Splendid Isolation, 56 American Journal of Comparative Law 125 (2008).

31 M. Kumm, Democratic Constitutionalism Encounters International Law: Terms of Engagement, in: S. Choudhry (ed.), The Migration of Constitutional Ideas 258 (Cambridge: Cambridge University Press, 2006).

32 R. Higgins, Problems and Process: International Law and How We Use It 206 (Oxford: Clarendon Press, 1994).

33 Higgins, *supra* note 32.

As a matter of fact, although many different states make claims to monism in rationalising interlegality at the micro-level,[34] at the meta-level, the interface of the international and the national legal orders is essentially dualist in nature.[35] Indeed, I have suggested in my previous work that,[36] fundamentally, this is so because the matrix within which states operate and international affairs are conducted continues to be based on the Westphalian model of international relations,[37] at the centre of which is the *idée-force* of sovereignty.[38] Accordingly, the traditional stance holds that the Westphalian model of international relations involves an international realm that is distinct and separate from the internal realms.[39]

This apprehension of interlegality, so far, centres on domestic actors and is no doubt very different from the international – or 'internationalist'[40] – point of view, according to which the so-called principle of *supremacy* of international law affirms the superiority of the international legal order *vis-à-vis* domestic normativity. While working within dualism – both at the meta- and micro-levels – Fitzmaurice opined that supremacy is 'one of the great principles of international law, informing the whole system and applying to every branch of it.'[41] In cases of normative conflict, from the international perspective, it is clear that international law must, and in effect does always, trump any incompatible

34 For a forceful example of such a state, the Netherlands; see A. Nollkaemper, The Netherlands, in: D. Sloss (ed.), The Role of Domestic Courts in Treaty Enforcement: A Comparative Study 326 (Cambridge: Cambridge University Press, 2009). Other examples of 'automatic incorporation' of international law are Mexico, Azerbaijan, Namibia, Cambodia, Syria, and Lebanon.

35 See F.G. Jacobs, Introduction, in: F.G. Jacobs and S. Roberts (eds.), The Effect of Treaties in Domestic Law xxiv (London: Sweet & Maxwell, 1987).

36 For my latest contribution on this point, see S. Beaulac, Thinking Outside the 'Westphalian Box': Dualism, Legal Interpretation and the Contextual Argument, in: C.C. Eriksen and M. Emberland (eds), The New International Law – An Anthology 17 (Leiden: Brill Publishers, 2010).

37 Of course, Westphalia is an *aetiological myth*, created by international society to explain the whens, wheres, and hows of its becoming and its being. This acknowledgement, however, does not diminish in any way the extraordinary semiotic effects of Westphalia on the consciousness of international society. See S. Beaulac, The Westphalian Model in Defining International Law: Challenging the Myth, 8 Australian Journal of Legal History 181 (2004) and S. Beaulac, The Westphalian Legal Orthodoxy – Myth or Reality?, 2 Journal of the History of International Law 148 (2000).

38 See A.-M. Slaughter and W. Burke-White, The Future of International Law is Domestic (or, The European Way of Law), in: J. Nijman and A. Nollkaemper (eds), New Perspectives on the Divide Between National and International Law 110–111 (Oxford and New York: Oxford University Press, 2007).

39 I first articulated this view in S. Beaulac, National Application of International Law: The Statutory Interpretation Perspective, 41 Canadian Yearbook of International Law 225 (2003).

40 See, inter alia, B. Kingsbury, N. Krisch and R. Stewart, The Emergence of Global Administrative Law, 68 Law and Contemporary Problems 15 (2005); and, generally, D. Dyzenhaus (ed.), The Unity of Public Law (Oxford: Hart Publishing, 2004).

41 G. Fitzmaurice, The General Principles of International Law Considered from the Standpoint of the Rule of Law, 92 Hague Recueil 85 (1957).

national legal rules.[42] Building on this, Nollkaemper recently suggested that the 'principle of supremacy of international law thus is key to the international rule of law.'[43]

Be that as it may, for the purposes of studying how domestic courts can and should resort to international law, this *dialogue de sourds* between the national and the internationalist perspectives is all but useful. Hence the need to have a sort of *relocating* of the supremacy legal character of normativity along – in fact beside – the international-national axis. This kind of twilight zone of normative supremacy should be located parallel, in a sense, to both the international legal sphere and the domestic legal orders, while at the same time, it ought to be reinforced by the respective claims of superiority of, yet again, both the international legal sphere and the domestic legal orders. In terms of actual rule of law values, this space shall allow for what I call the *reflexive complementarity*[44] of both phenomena discussed in the previous section, ie the rule of law internationalized, on the one hand, and of the internationalization of the rule of law, on the other. The phrase 'reflexive complementarity'[45] is used here to refer to the idea of a circular, mutually self-perfecting relationship between the cause of a phenomenon and the effect upon that same phenomenon. For the present purposes, it means that the occurrence of the rule of law internationalized onto the international plane reverts back and affects not only itself, but also the twin phenomenon of the internationalization of the rule of law in other jurisdictions, and in fact complements the latter. Conversely, the occurrence of the internationalization of the rule of law is not only reflexive onto itself, but is also onto the other phenomenon of the rule of law internationalized, and in fact acts as a complement to it. Hence the suggestion of *reflexive complementarity*, as the twin phenomena are mutually self-perfecting in a circular fashion (onto itself and its twin).

---

42 This application of the principle of supremacy of international law is at the basis of the law of treaties, as per Articles 27 and 46 of the Vienna Convention on the Law of Treaties (1969), 1155 UNTS 331, 8 International Legal Materials 679, as well as the law of international state responsibility, as per Articles 3 and 32 of the Draft Articles on the Responsibility of States for Internationally Wrongful Acts, scheduled to the UNGA Resolution (A/RES/56/83) (28 January 2002).

43 A. Nollkaemper, Rethinking the Supremacy of International Law, Amsterdam Center for International Law Working Papers (2009), available at http://ssrn.com/abstract=1336946. See also A. Watts, The International Rule of Law, 36 German Yearbook of International Law 15 (1993).

44 On *reflexivity* in the social sciences, see the work by Anthony Giddens, and his structuration theory: A. Giddens, The Constitution of Society – Outline of the Theory of Structuration (Cambridge: Polity Press, 1984); that by Pierre Bourdieu, and his sociology of sociology: P. Bourdieu, Homo Academicus (Stanford: Stanford University Press, 1988); and P. Bourdieu and L.J.D. Wacquant, An Invitation to Reflexive Sociology (Cambridge: Polity Press, 1992); as well as that by Ulrich Beck, and his reflexive modernization: U. Beck, Risk Society – Towards a New Modernity (London: Sage Publications, 1992); and U. Beck, A. Giddens and S. Lash, Reflexive Modernization – Politics, Tradition and Aesthetics in the Modern Social Order (Stanford: Stanford University Press, 1994).

45 The terminology of 'reflexive complementarity' is *sui generis* and of my own making.

The other idea, namely of separate, parallel space for normative supremacy as regards interlegality – where reflexive complementarity of the twin phenomena of the international rule of law occurs – draws from Nollkaemper's scholarship, which has suggested 'a third domain between the two levels'.[46] That is to say, I believe, the relocating ought to be between the rule of law at the international level and the rule of law at the domestic level. 'This is the rule of law as it applies to the overlapping sphere of domestic and international law', he wrote; such a sphere 'is characterized by the fact that international law and international institutions can fill rule of law gaps at the domestic law and vice versa, gaps brought about by the very growth of that overlap.'[47] This aspect of rule of law 'complementarity'[48] existing along (in fact, beside) the international legal sphere and the domestic legal orders – accomplished in a reflexive matter – is central to the proposition of an '*à la carte*' heuristic model that follows.

4. THE THIN-THICK RULE OF LAW SPECTRUM AND ITS LIMITS

Speaking in the context of transition, Stromseth, Wippman and Brooks are categorical that one of the main reasons why many rule of law programs have been unsuccessful is '*the failure of many policymakers to examine or fully understand the very concept of "the rule of law"*.'[49] Too many people involved in the field adopt an 'I know it when I see it'[50] attitude toward the content of the rule of law which, though some say might have advantages – easy consensus, for one – raises serious problems, as 'it permits superficiality and obtuseness that has badly limited the efficacy of many rule of law promotion efforts.'[51] Hence the need to look, once again, at the genealogy of the rule of law.[52]

46 A. Nollkaemper, The Internationalized Rule of Law, 1 Hague Journal on the Rule of Law 76 (2009).

47 Nollkaemper, *supra* note 46. The author makes a similar point in A. Nollkaemper, The European Courts and the Security Council: Between Dédoublement Fonctionnel and Balancing of Values: Three Replies to Pasquale De Sena and Maria Chiara Vitucci, 20 European Journal of International Law 868 (2009).

48 See also A. Nollkaemper, Multi-level Accountability in International Law: A Case Study of the Aftermath of Srebrenica, in Y. Shany and T. Broude, The Shifting Allocation of Authority in International Law – Considering Sovereignty, Supremacy and Subsidiarity 345 (Oxford: Hart Publishing, 2008).

49 J. Stromseth, D. Wippman and R. Brooks, Can Might Make Rights?: Building the Rule of Law after Military Interventions 69 (Cambridge: Cambridge University Press, 2006) (italics in original). See also J. Stromseth, Post-Conflict Rule of Law Building: The Need for A Multi-Layered, Synergistic Approach, 49 William and Mary Law Review 1445 (2008).

50 This terminology was also used by M. Krygier, False Dichotomies, True Perplexities, and the Rule of Law, in: A. Sajo (ed.), Human Rights with Modesty: The Problem of Universalism 251 (Leiden & Boston: Martinus Nijhoff, 2004).

51 Stromseth, Wippman and Brooks, *supra* note 49, p. 69.

52 See R. Peerenboom, Varieties of Rule of Law – An Introduction and Provisional Conclusion, in: R. Peerenboom (ed.), Asian Discourses of Rule of Law – Theories and Implementation of

It is generally agreed that, while the various ideas associated with the rule of law are undoubtedly very old[53] – going as far back as Plato and Aristotle[54] – the emergence of the rule of law as a mighty discursive tool within political and legal circles is relatively recent.[55] The expression itself was coined by 19th century author A.V. Dicey,[56] with his 'Introduction to the Study of the Law of the Constitution'.[57] The British scholar wrote that the rule of law had 'three meanings, or may be regarded from three different points of view.'[58] First, it entails 'the absolute supremacy or predominance of regular law as opposed to the influence of arbitrary power.'[59] He further wrote: 'In this sense the rule of law is contrasted with every system of government based on the exercise by persons in authority of wide, arbitrary, or discretionary powers of constraint.'[60]

The second prong in Dicey's rule of law model relates to 'equality before the law, or the equal subjection of all classes to the ordinary law of the law administered by the ordinary law courts.'[61] 'We mean, in the second place, when we speak of the "rule of law" as a characteristic of our country, not only that with us no man is above the law, but (what is a different thing) that here every man, whatever be his rank or condition, is subject to the ordinary law of the realm and amenable to the jurisdiction of the ordinary tribunals.'[62] Thirdly, according to Dicey, the rule of law entails that 'the law of the constitution [...] are not the source but the consequence of the rights of individuals, as defined and enforced by the courts.'[63] Thus, fundamental rights 'are with us the result of judicial decisions determining the rights of private persons in particular cases brought before the Courts.'[64] He suggested that this last element is very much a special attribute of British constitutionalism.

Rule of Law in Twelve Asian Countries, France and the U.S. 1 (London & New York: Routledge, 2004).

53 See J.N. Shklar, Political Theory and the Rule of Law, in: A.C. Hutchinson and P. Monahan (eds), The Rule of Law: Ideal or Ideology 1 (Toronto: Carswell, 1987).

54 Cf. Plato, The Laws, trans. by T.J. Saunders (London: Penguin Classics); and Aristotle, Politics, trans. by T.A. Sinclair (London: Penguin Classics).

55 See J. Rose, The Rule of Law in the Western World: An Overview, 35 Journal of Social Philosophy 457 (2004).

56 See H.W. Arndt, The Origins of Dicey's Concept of the 'Rule of Law', 31 Australian Law Journal 117 (1957).

57 A.V. Dicey, Introduction to the Study of the Law of the Constitution (London: Macmillan, 1885).

58 Dicey, *supra* note 57, p. 202.

59 Dicey, *supra* note 57.

60 Dicey, *supra* note 57, p. 188.

61 Dicey, *supra* note 57, p. 202.

62 Dicey, *supra* note 57, p. 193 (footnotes omitted).

63 Dicey, *supra* note 57, p. 203.

64 Dicey, *supra* note 57, p. 195 (footnotes omitted).A common misreading of the last element in Dicey's model holds that the rule of law requires protection for some substantive rights and freedoms. As Paul Craig pointed out, however, this 'is not what Dicey actually said'; see P. Craig, Formal and Substantive Conception of the Rule of Law: An Analytical Framework, in: Public Law 473 (1997). Rather, his argument was simply that, providing a society wishes to

Accordingly, for Dicey, the rule of law means (1) to be ruled by law, not by discretionary power, (2) to be equal before the law, private individuals as well as government officials, and (3) to be submitted to the general jurisdiction of ordinary courts, the best source of legal protection.[65] These core ideas, in one form or another, are found in the scholarship of most modern authors who write on these issues, both in legal studies and political sciences.[66] It does not follow, however, that there is any kind of consensus or agreement on the meaning and scope of the rule of law: on the contrary, it seems. Some criticisms have been voiced, for instance, on the vagueness and uncertainly of the concept,[67] with Raz famously daring to call the rule of law a mere slogan.[68]

For some time now, legal scholars have attempted to come up with versions or formulations of the concept and to put them into different categories or models. Craig suggested distinguishing between the *formal* conceptions of the rule of law, concerned with how the law is made and its essential attributes (clear, prospective), and the *substantive* conceptions of the rule of law, concerned with these formal precepts but also with some basic content of the law (justice, morality).[69] Tamanaha built on this classification and divided up the formal and substantive models further, making them progressively go from 'thinner' to 'thicker' formulations: that is, from *minimalist* accounts with few requirements to more requirements, each subsequent version including the components of the previous ones, leading to a *maximalist* version of the concept. Thus, starting with

---

give protection to individual rights – that is, if and only if there has been a political will to have such legal guarantees – then, one way of doing it is better than another way, as far as the rule of law is concerned. Namely, the British common law technique ought to be favoured over the Continental written constitutional document technique. That is to say, judge-made-law individual rights would give more effective protection than bills or charters of rights and freedoms, because the latter are easier to abrogate or change by governments.

65 This part of the discussion, in particular Dicey's contribution, draws from Beaulac, *supra* note 20.

66 See J. Stapleton, Dicey and his Legacy, 16 History of Political Thought 234 (1995) and Rose, *supra* note 55, p. 458. For a recent example see, in international law, I. Brownlie, The Rule of Law in International Affairs 212 (The Hague: Martinus Nijhoff, 1998) and, in Anglo-Saxon public law, H. Barnett, Constitutional and Administrative Law, 91 (London: Cavendish Publishing, 2002, 4th ed.), where Dicey's three-prong formulation is reproduced verbatim and analysed in detail.

67 See Shklar, *supra* note 53, p. 1: 'It would not be very difficult to show that the phrase "the Rule of Law" has become meaningless thanks to ideological abuse and general over-use. It may well have become just another one of those self-congratulatory rhetorical devices that grace the public utterances of Anglo-American politicians. No intellectual effort need therefore be wasted on this bit of ruling-class chatter.'

68 J. Raz, The Rule of Law and its Virtue (first published in 93 Law Quarterly Review 195 (1977)), in: J. Raz, The Authority of Law: Essays on Law and Morality 210 (Oxford: Clarendon Press, 1979): 'Not uncommonly when a political ideal captures the imagination of large numbers of people its name becomes a slogan used by supporters of ideals which bear little or no relation to the one it originally designated.'

69 Craig, *supra* note 64. See also P. Craig, Constitutional Foundations, the Rule of Law and Supremacy, in: Public Law 92 (2003).

the formal conceptions of the rule of law, the thinnest is (1) the 'rule-by-law' (law as instrument of government), then (2) 'formal legality' (law that is general, prospective, clear, certain), and the thickest of the formal versions adds (3) 'democracy' to legality (consent determines content of law); then follow substantive conceptions of the rule of law, which all encompass the formal elements, but refer also to other legal features such as (4) 'individuals rights' (property, contract, privacy, autonomy), then a thicker version yet includes (5) 'rights of dignity and/or justice' and, finally, the thickest of the models of the substantive rule of law – of all versions in fact – entails a dimension of (6) 'social welfare' (substantive equality, welfare, community preservation).[70] This scheme I like to call the *sliding scale* of rule of law values, from the minimalist thin end to the maximalist thick end, according to a sort of rule of law 'spectrum'.

A number of scholars in legal studies and political sciences have followed a modest, largely positivist version of the rule of law, advocating limited models that emphasise the formalistic or process-oriented aspects. Fuller, for instance, argues in favour of a system of general rules created and applied consistently with procedural justice and fairness.[71] Eight conditions need to be met: (1) a system of rules; (2) promulgation and publication of the rules; (3) avoidance of retroactive application; (4) clear and intelligible rules; (5) avoidance of contradictory rules; (6) practicable rules; (7) consistency of rules over time; and (8) congruence between official actions and declared rules.[72] A similar enumeration of eight factors essential to the rule of law is given by Finnis.[73] Raz,[74] too, has a list of (yet again) eight elements that should be found in a rule of law system; although slightly differently formulated than Fuller's and Finnis', they considerably overlap and all relate to formal aspects of law, on the thinner side of the scale.[75]

---

70 B.Z. Tamanaha, On the Rule of Law – History, Politics, Theory 91 ff (Cambridge: Cambridge University Press, 2004).

71 L. Fuller, The Morality of Law (New Haven: Yale University Press, 1969, 2nd ed.). On Fuller's, as well as Raz's, formalistic conception of the rule of law, see M. Bennett, 'The "Rule of Law" Means Literally What it Says: The Rule of Law': Fuller and Raz on Formal Legality and the Concept of Law, 32 Australian Journal of Legal Philosophy 90 (2007).

72 Fuller, *supra* note 71, p. 38–39. See also R.P. George, Reason, Freedom, and the Rule of Law: Their Significance in the Natural Law Tradition, 46 American Journal of Jurisprudence 249 (2001).

73 J. Finnis, Natural Law and Natural Rights 270 (Oxford: Clarendon Press, 1980). For his part, R.S. Summers, The Principles of the Rule of Law, 74 Notre Dame Law Review 1691 (1999), stretches the list to eighteen such formal requirements, though only providing a more detailed account of the same basic ideas.

74 Raz, *supra* note 68, p. 214–218. For an interesting assessment of Raz's theory on the rule of law, see Y. Hasebe, The Rule of Law and Its Predicament, 17 Ratio Juris 489 (2004).

75 See also, favouring the formalistic version of the rule of law, J. Waldron, The Concept and the Rule of Law, 43 Georgia Law Review 1 (2008); and M.J. Radin, Reconsidering the Rule of Law, 69 Boston University Law Review 781 (1989).

At the other end of the spectrum, a thicker formulation '*does not necessarily reject the notion that the rule of law has important structural and formal elements – predictability, universality, nonarbitrariness, and so on – but insists that true rule of law also requires particular substantive commitments.*'[76] Now, what are those thick rule of law features? Peerenboom described them as 'elements of political morality such as particular economic arrangements (free market capitalism, central planning, and so on), forms of government (democratic, single party socialist, and so on) or conceptions of human rights (liberal communitarian, collectivist, "Asian Values," and so on).'[77] Some of the well-recognized proponents of a maximalist model of the rule of law are Dworkin,[78] Sunstein,[79] and Shklar.[80] Quite recently, Lord Bingham dwelled upon the meaning of the rule of law in the context of the 2005 constitutional reform in the United Kingdom, offering a definition containing substantive elements, notably fundamental human rights.[81] The thicker formulations of the rule of law have been harshly criticised by several commentators, such as Raz, who notoriously wrote that '[i]f the rule of law is the rule of the good law then to explain its nature is to propound a complete social philosophy.'[82]

Be that as it may, the paradigmatic question becomes: Is the thin-thick sliding scale approach the right methodology to inquire into possible heuristic models for the rule of law in transition and post-conflict societies? To make the point, consider the following. Some argue that we should lean toward the minimalist end of the spectrum and evacuate the substantive rule of law features, with a view to improving support for structural reforms and good governance measures. 'The more the theory of the rule of law is "de-substantivized" to embrace only those institutional forms that as such serve values associated with a formal rule of law', Summers writes, 'the more likely it is that the formal rule of law will receive its due.'[83] Conversely, so goes the argument, thicker versions of the rule

76 Stromseth, Wippman and Brooks, *supra* note 49, p. 71 (italics in original). See also D. Kairys, Searching for the Rule of Law, 36 Suffolk University Law Review 307 (2003).

77 R. Peerenboom, Let One Hundred Flowers Bloom, One Hundred Schools Contend: Debating Rule of Law in China, 23 Michigan Journal of International Law 472 (2002).

78 See R. Dworkin, Political Judges and the Rule of Law, in: R. Dworkin, A Matter of Principle 9 (Cambridge: Harvard University Press, 1985). On Dworkin and the rule of law, see J. Waldron, The Rule of Law as a Theater of Debate, in: J. Burley (ed.), Dworkin and His Critics 319 (Oxford: Blackwell, 2004).

79 See C. Sunstein, Democracy's Constitution (Oxford & New York: Oxford University Press, 2001).

80 See J.N. Shklar, Political Thought and Political Thinkers (Chicago: University of Chicago Press, 1998).

81 T. Bingham, The Rule of Law, Cambridge Law Journal 67 (2006), conference paper presented at the Sixth Sir David Williams Lecture, given at the University of Cambridge on 16 November 2006. See also T. Bingham, The Rule of Law and the Sovereignty of Parliament, 19 King's Law Journal 223 (2008); and, his latest contribution, T. Bingham, The Rule of Law (London: Allen Lane, 2010).

82 Raz, *supra* note 68, p. 211.

83 R.S. Summers, A Formal Theory of the Rule of Law, 6 Ratio Juris 137 (1993).

of law are more likely to be controversial and polarizing in society. Summers, again, contends that 'if the rule of law is taken in general discourse within the society to mean not just governance through rules (and facilitative institutional features) but also capitalism (or socialism), a Bill of Rights (or no Bill of Rights), general democracy (or limited democracy), *et cetera*, then the formal rule of law is not so likely to command the range of *neutral* support it merits (and requires).'[84]

However, this argument seems to be flawed and, as a matter of fact, warrants going past the thin-thick spectrum. Suggesting that, strategically, the better approach is to start with a formal conception of the rule of law, and then (presumably) to move toward a more substantive one, is based on very little hard evidence, if any. Brooks disputed the assumption that the promotion of a thin rule of law version 'will lead reliably and predictably to the emergence of a robust societal commitment to the more substantive aspects of the rule of law.'[85] More importantly, too thin an account of the rule of law, with no basic human rights content for instance, could well be counter-productive, as the reforming measures may lack apparent legitimacy and, as a result, might be considered unsatisfactory by people in societies. On this facet, Trebilcock and Daniels wrote that 'it seems plausible that interested parties are at least as likely to be aggrieved by what is *left out* by a formalistic approach as by what is *brought in* by a more substantive one.'[86] A bare minimalist model, in other words, simply cannot be up to the task given the hype and high aspirations that the rule of law – this formulation of 'hurrah' words[87] – does provoke and generate.

Trebilcock and Daniels are interested in development, of course, but the same observation no doubt applies *mutatis mutandis* to transition situations, where rule of law performative power ought to contribute to moving away from the old oppressive governance system to a new constitutional structure arrangement acceptable to people. Accordingly, a transitional formulation of the concept must take into account formal rule of law values, though maybe not all of them along a spectrum, and it must also include substantive rule of law values, though again not all the way up a spectrum toward a maximalist version. Hence, instead of the typical sliding scale approach, going progressively from thin to thick formulations, what I suggest is an *à la carte* model for the rule of law.

---

84 Summers, *supra* note 83 (italics in original). See also W.C. Whitford, The Rule of Law, Wisconsin Law Review 726 (2000).

85 R.E. Brooks, The New Imperialism: Violence, Norms, and the Rule of Law, 101 Michigan Law Review 2284 (2003).

86 M.J. Trebilcock and R.J. Daniels, Rule of Law Reform and Development – Charting the Fragile Path of Progress 25 (Cheltenham & Northampton: Edward Elgar, 2008) (italics in original).

87 See *supra* note 4 and accompanying text.

5. RULE OF LAW *À LA CARTE* AND RECOMMENDATIONS OF THE *CHEF*

Preliminarily, let us address a concern with the suggestion that an *à la carte* model for the rule of law may not be heuristic at all, be it in general or for the present purposes. It was Palombella who opined that although the rule of law is flexible, 'its normative meaning does not essentially change'; indeed, 'any notion of the rule of law as something relative, its meaning varying from jurisdiction to jurisdiction, is unacceptable.'[88] He referred to some linguistic usages of the concept – namely, rule of law, *Stato di diritto*, *Rechtsstaat*[89] – to support this contention, which he extended to the context of the European Union.[90] While I tend to agree with my distinguished Italian colleague that uniformity in one's model of the rule of law is imperative within the vanguard supra/trans-national legal order in Europe[91] (and perhaps in applying as well an international rule of law reasoning to interlegality issues in general[92]), I do not think that a strict commonality is possible, and is certainly not ontologically required, for the concept to apply to states in transition, particularly in regard to the role their domestic courts can play by means of resorting to international law.

Reflecting upon the future and 'the challenges and prospect for the field' of the rule of law in the 2009 inaugural issue of the Hague Journal on the Rule of Law, Peerenboom identified a clear 'need to disaggregate rule of law and develop more differentiated rule of law promotion plans.'[93] Although efforts are being made in that way, he deplored the continuing overall tendency 'to treat rule of law and rule of law promotion as a single entity or enterprise, and to rely on generally applicable, and hence overly simple, highly reductive and exceedingly abstract, international best practices and off-the-shelf rule of law toolkits.'[94]

88 G. Palombella, The Rule of Law Beyond the State: Failures, Promises, and Theory, 7 International Journal of Constitutional Law 455 (2009).

89 For references on these linguistic manifestations of the rule of law in different European languages, see L. Heuschling, *État de droit*, *Rechtsstaat*, Rule of Law (Paris: Dalloz, 2002); E. Carpano, *État de droit et droits européens* (Paris: L'Harmattan, 2005); and P. Costa and D. Zolo (eds), The Rule of Law – History, Theory and Criticism (Dordrecht: Springer, 2007). See also the following papers: J.-Y. Morin, The Rule of Law and the *Rechtsstaat* Concept: A Comparison, in: E. McWhinney, J. Zaslove and W. Wolf (eds), Federalism-in-the-Making – Contemporary Canadian and German Constitutionalism, National and Translational 60 (Dordrecht: Kluwer, 1992); and R. Grote, Rule of Law, *Rechtsstaat* and '*État de droit*', in: S. Starck (ed.), Constitutionalism, Universalism and Democracy – A Comparative Analysis 269 (Baden-Baden: Nomos Verlagsgesellschaft, 1999).

90 Palombella, *supra* note 88. See also The Rule of Law and Its Core, in: G. Palombella and N. Walker (eds), Relocating the Rule of Law 17 (Oxford: Hart Publishing, 2009).

91 See N. Walker, The Rule of Law and the EU: Necessity's Mixed Virtue, in G. Palombella and N. Walker (eds.), Relocating the Rule of Law 119 (Oxford: Hart Publishing, 2009).

92 Which was at the centre of Palombella's paper, *supra* note 88.

93 Peerenboom, *supra* note 13, p. 7.

94 Peerenboom, *supra* note 13.

Instead, he argued in favour of a 'more refined typology of ideal types or patterns of developing countries and rule of law challenges.'[95] For states in transition, in particular, he opined that each situation 'presents a different set of issues or challenges that requires something more than the standard set of one-size-fits-all prescriptions.'[96] In full agreement with Peerenboom, I would further argue that it is considerably reducing the potential performative power of the concept to compel it to a pre-set menu. In contrast, an *à la carte* approach to the rule of law can prove a most valuable heuristic model, at least in relation to post-conflict and post-dictatorial societies, the circumstances relevant here.

Now, recalling that this book is founded on the hypothesis of an empowerment of domestic courts, at a so-called 'international constitutional moment', through their participatory role in the national application of international law,[97] the proposed *à la carte* approach to the rule of law is meant to provide a model to organize the relevant values, actual and aspirational, within a new or true stable constitutional arrangement. These rule of law values, both formal and substantive, will be at play in the separate, parallel space of supreme normative authority, where they will engage in a process of reflexive complementarity,[98] involving components of the international legal sphere and of the respective transitional domestic legal orders.

Having said that, am I stuck once again with yet another 'sort of laundry list of features that a healthy legal system should have',[99] to borrow from Jeremy Waldron, albeit in transitional *sui generis* settings? For the purposes of the present conceptual chapter, there is no need to speculate on an exhaustive list of rule of law values that the 'perfect' states in transition ought to pick from the *à la carte* menu and include in their parallel space of normative supremacy, within which domestic courts can justify recourse to norms of international law. Other contributors in this book are likely to provide much more useful insights as to the case-by-case content of the *à la carte* model for the rule of law. As far as I am concerned, I shall venture no further than what is likely to gather consensus, among the different actors, in terms of transition society common features and rule of law values: that is, what is likely needed in all jurisdictions that have gone through violent conflicts or have moved out of authoritarian regimes.

95 Peerenboom, *supra* note 13, p. 8.

96 Peerenboom, *supra* note 13.

97 Of course, such participation by domestic courts in transitional processes would certainly amount, in part at least, to a 'judicialization of politics', to borrow from A. Stone Sweet, Governing with Judges: Constitutional Politics in Europe (Oxford & New York: Oxford University Press, 2000). See also R. Hirschl, Toward Juristocracy – The Origins and Consequences of the New Constitutionalism (Cambridge: Harvard University Press, 2004).

98 See *supra* note 44–48 and accompanying text.

99 Waldron, *supra* note 16, p. 154. See also T. Ringer, Development, Reform, and the Rule of Law: Some Prescriptions for a Common Understanding of the 'Rule of Law' and its Place in Development Theory and Practice, 10 Yale Human Rights & Development Law Journal 193 (2007).

Metaphorically, while some courses are indeed *à la carte*, some others are forcefully recommended by the *chef* given his type of cuisine, ie the transition kind.

One such strong recommendation would be the basic rule of law values linked to being ruled by law, meaning that law should constitute the instrument of governance in all transition societies. These values correspond, incidentally, to the first prong in Dicey's conception of the rule of law, namely to be ruled by law, not by discretionary power. Still, on the formal part of the menu come the values associated with legality, requiring that law be general, prospective, clear, and certain. In the circumstances of jurisdictions in transition, however, these features will certainly have to be assessed case-by-case, and are thus fully *à la carte*.[100] Then the next course along, toward more substantive items, are the important democratic values: that is to say, popular consent should dictate the content of the law. Intuitively – and it shall be empirically verified – actors in transition societies, in all of them, will agree that democracy constitutes a non-negotiable *chef* recommendation on the menu *carte*.[101]

Then come the values associated with the more maximalist substantive thick rule of law version, namely fundamental human rights, including human dignity, as well as fairness, equity, justice (restorative, retributive, distributive),[102] and for dessert, social welfare (substantive equality, community preservation). Here, the *à la carte* approach comes in handy, not only for allowing case-by-case analysis (which is not my concern here), but also to assess whether there could be features common to transition societies. Take human rights: we need not go wholesale in identifying what should be viewed as applicable to all states in transition; rather, going piecemeal, we can bring in rights and liberties – criminal legal guarantees, for example – deemed warranted for transition circumstances. One such fundamental right – a must on the selected menu of any society in transition – is the right to equality without discrimination, which incidentally relates to Dicey's second leg of rule of law (equality before the law, for private individuals and for government officials). On the other hand, substantive equality, as well as the type of justice sought – restorative, retributive, distributive – will need to be decided *à la pièce*, for sure.

It is *à propos* to close with the substantive rule of law values linked to judicial decision-making processes, namely fairness and equity,[103] given that the

---

100 Of course, this would be harshly denounced by Justice Antonin Scalia and like-minded authors; see A. Scalia, The Rule of Law as a Law of Rules, 56 University of Chicago Law Review 1175 (1989).

101 See, generally, M. Rosenfeld, The Rule of Law and the Legitimacy of Constitutional Democracy, 74 Southern California Law Review 1307 (2001).

102 See S. Golub, Make Justice the Organizing Principle of the Rule of Law Field, 1 Hague Journal on the Rule of Law 61 (2009).

103 On the necessity of fairness and equity in international adjudicative decision-making, see J.M. Farrall, United Nations Sanctions and the Rule of Law (Cambridge: Cambridge University Press, 2007). See also, on the role domestic courts can play in that regard, E. de

problematics at hand concern the role domestic courts can play in states in transition by resorting to international law. These elements, of course, fall squarely within the third and last category of values identified by Dicey in the 19th century, namely to be subject to the general jurisdiction of ordinary courts, which is the best source of legal protection, including some form of judicial review.[104] Precisely here, at this junction, meet (and in an acute fashion) the matters of interlegality discussed above[105] – ie, the parallel space of supreme normative authority, along with reflexive complementarity of the rule of law internationalized and the internationalization of the rule of law phenomena – and the proposed *à la carte* approach to rule of law values in states in transition.[106] Fairness and equity in decision-making processes of domestic courts are, quite simply, quintessential to the latter role in these societies. Procedural fairness and judicial equity, indeed, go to the core of any transitional rule of law project. Using the same metaphor, one last time, these values constitute the most important course (ie *le plat de résistance*) in the cuisine of transition and, albeit found on the *carte*, they surely are non-negotiable with the *chef.*

Wet, A. Nollkaemper and P. Dijkstra (eds), Review of the Security Council by Member States (Antwerp: Intersentia, 2003).

104 On judicial review and the rule of law, see L.B. Tremblay, Two Models of Constitutionalism and the Legitimacy of Law: Dicey or Marshal?, 6 Oxford University Commonwealth Law Journal 77 (2006). Within a judicial review mechanism, the instrumental role of the idea of *proportionality* should be noted: see D.M. Beatty, The Ultimate Rule of Law (Oxford & New York: Oxford University Press, 2004); and D.M. Beatty, Law's Golden Rule, in: G. Palombella & N. Walker (eds), Relocating the Rule of Law 99 (Oxford: Hart Publishing, 2009).

105 See *supra*, section 3.

106 This is an attempt to answer Randall Peerenboom's invitation, at least in regard to theoretical input; see Peerenboom, *supra* note 13, p. 8: 'Another area where there needs to be more theoretical and empirical work is in the relationship between international rule of law and domestic rule of law.'

INTERNATIONAL LAW IN THE RUSSIAN COURTS IN TRANSITIONAL SITUATIONS

Sergei Yu. Marochkin*

1. INTRODUCTION

This paper analyses and compares the practice of implementation and application of international law rules by the domestic courts in Russia before and after the end of the former Soviet Union.

In the last two decades, Russia has gone through two critical moments which dramatically influenced the change of its political, economic, and legal systems, as well as the role of international law in the practice of domestic courts and in the entrenchment of the rule of law. The first of these critical moments was the disintegration of the Soviet Union and the establishment of Russia as a separate state (December 1991). The second was the confrontation between the Supreme Council (former Parliament) and the presidential power (October 1993), which led to the establishment of a new form of government and adoption of a new constitution (December 1993).

This chapter shows the place of international law in the Russian legal order, the role of Russian courts in implementation and application of international law in the Soviet and post-Soviet periods, and reveals some tendencies in their contribution to the development of the constitutional provisions concerning international law – and to the strengthening of the rule of law.

To offer the reader a sense of all the really radical changes, I first offer a brief look at the constitutional and legislative provisions and the judicial practice in the Soviet period (section 2). Then I review the amendments to the

* Sergei Yu. Marochkin, Doctor of Juridical Sciences, Professor, Honoured Jurist of the Russian Federation (awarded by the President of Russia), Member of the Executive Committee of the Russian Association of International Law and member of the European Society of International Law. Tyumen State University, The City of Tyumen, Russia (email: mar@utmn.ru).
This paper is dedicated to the memory of the distinguished international lawyer, Professor Ian Brownlie.

Constitution of Russia in the transitional period which reflected a step-by-step movement towards more openness to the international community and international law. I also discuss some of the reasons leading to the adoption of a new constitution, and highlight the basic principle of the 1993 Constitution concerning international law and its significance (section 3). The main portion of the chapter is devoted to an analysis and illustration of judicial practice connected with strengthening the role of international law in the domestic legal order. This can be demonstrated from different aspects: international law as a framework for legislation and its implementation, international treaties in determining the applicable law, international norms as a part of the decision on the case, the role of generally recognized principles and norms, of other international instruments (recommendations and decisions of international bodies, etc), of treaties without the participation of Russia, and of rulings of the European Court of Human Rights (ECtHR) (section 4). The chapter concludes with summarizing the general results and achievements, problems, and further tasks of the courts in the entrenchment of international law in the Russian legal system.

2. A BRIEF LOOK AT THE PERIOD PRIOR TO THE BREAKDOWN OF THE USSR

In order to apprehend the changes in Russia's legal system clearly and fully, it is necessary first to recall the role of international law in the legal system of the former Soviet Union.

The last constitution of the socialist period – Constitution of the USSR 1977 (amended 1 December 1988) – in Article 29 of the chapter 'Foreign policy', defined the basis for relations with foreign states. There were ten fundamental principles of international law, among which was the principle of 'fulfillment in good faith of obligations arising from universally recognized principles and norms of international law, from international treaties concluded by the USSR'. This provision was of a general character, however, and the Constitution of the Union did not define the place of international law at the national level, nor did it prescribe its role in the practice of the courts.

Based on the USSR Constitution and with a view to its further development, a law 'On the order of conclusion, implementation and denunciation of the international treaties of the USSR' was adopted in 1978.[1] It contained a short section on implementation of international treaties, which did not establish

1 Bulletin of the Supreme Council of the USSR 28/439 (in Russian) (1978).

detailed procedures or provisions on the performance of treaties, nor did it mention the application of international treaties by the courts.[2]

Meanwhile, some legal and other normative acts did contain more specific provisions. Already in 1961, for the first time in Soviet law, an article providing priority application of international treaty rules over domestic civil law in case of conflict between them was included in the Fundamental Principles of Civil Legislation of the USSR and its Republics. Similar norms were included into the Fundamental Principles of Civil Procedure, Customs Code, Fundamental Principles of Legislation on Marriage and Family, Merchant Marine Code,[3] and other domestic acts, as well as into relevant codes and laws of the Soviet Republics (integral parts of the USSR).

However in general, these norms, being different in their characteristic and content, were not united by a general principle, or by a common concept of correlation and interaction of domestic and international law. The legal system of the state was not adjusted for operation of international law norms at the domestic level. On the contrary, the priority of national ideological interests and of domestic law over international law was typical. In particular, as concerns human rights issues, the Soviet authorities did not recognize the competence of international bodies or accept their decisions concerning violations of human rights treaties, nor did Soviet citizens have the right to refer to such treaties when applying to domestic courts or to international bodies.

Later, the constitutions and legislation of the former Soviet Republics practically copied the legislation of the USSR. For example, the Constitution of the Russian Soviet Federative Socialist Republic (RSFSR) 1978, in an article on foreign policy, provided only that RSFSR 'shall be guided by the purposes, aims and principles of foreign policy, which are defined by the Constitution of the USSR' (Article 28).

The practice of applying international law in domestic courts in those times was not too fragmentary or scanty (or non-existent) as has sometimes been mentioned.[4] This conclusion is based on the author's own examination[5] of the practice of the courts and of the justice authorities (departments of the Ministry of Justice) in different regions of the USSR, as part of an examination of documents on international treaty implementation by a number of the USSR and Russian ministries and departments, as well as on an examination of periodic summaries of case law carried out by the USSR Ministry of Justice.

2 See S. Marochkin, The Problem of Effectiveness of International Law Norms 122–136 (Irkutsk: Irkutsk University Publishing, 1988); S. Marochkin, Application of International Law Norms of the USSR (to Development of the Problem), in: Problems of Realization of International Law Norms 4–11 (Sverdlovsk Law Institute Publishing, 1989) (in Russian).

3 Database 'Consultant Plus'.

4 See eg I. Lukashuk, International Law in the Courts of the States 273 (St. Petersburg, 1993) (in Russian).

5 Marochkin, *supra* notes 2 and 7.

However, it is obvious that in the legal conditions existing during those times, it would not be possible to speak about regular and constant application of international law by the courts. Due to the above-mentioned circumstances (ie the closed character of the constitution and legislation, and the priority of ideology over law), the practice was quite narrow on this matter and not always common or consistent. As with the whole political system, the legal and judicial systems too were closed to the rest of the world. References to international treaties could be made in practice only in quite narrow categories of civil cases. These were bilateral treaties on legal aid for civil, family, and criminal matters, and an Agreement between several socialist states on international railway cargo correspondence.[6]

As for the application of international custom, universally recognized principles and norms, declarations, recommendations of international organizations and conferences, decisions of international courts and other bodies, and international model acts – such questions did not arise at all.[7]

The national doctrine of that period was for many years concentrated around the long-term discussion on 'whether application of international law norms was or was not possible in the area of domestic law'.[8] It did not come any closer than that to enriching the practice by a common conception. No broad system analyses, and no summaries of court practice, were made. Instead, theoretical constructions mostly were not based on practice, did not follow from practice, and, in the end, did not offer any help for the development of practice. Possibly, such theoretical constructions even hid a real side of the problem. Theory and practice developed in parallel.

---

6 There were a few dozens of typical and similar bilateral treaties mostly concluded with other socialist states (eg Bulgaria, Mongolia, Poland, German Democratic Republic, etc) and developing countries.

7 Regarding practical aspects of application of international law norms during the soviet period see eg G. Ignatenko, Relationship of Domestic and International Law (Sverdlovsk, 1981); R. Mullerson, Correlation of International and National Law (Moscow, 1982); G. Ignatenko (ed.), International and Domestic Law: the Problems of Comparative Law, Essays (Sverdlovsk, 1984); S. Marochkin, Legal Grounds and Practice of Application of International Treaties by the Courts in Civil Cases, in: G. Ignatenko (ed.), Implementation of International Treaties in the USSR. Questions of Theory and Practice, Essays (Sverdlovsk, 1986); G. Ignatenko (ed.), Problems of Realization of International Law Norms, Essays (Sverdlovsk, 1989); S. Marochkin, Improvement of Civil Proceedings with Participation of Foreign Citizens, in: The Judicial Reform and Increase of Effectiveness of Justice, Essays (Tyumen, 1991) (in Russian).

8 See eg G. Tunkin, Theory of International Law (Moscow, 1970); E. Usenko and R. Mullerson, Correlation of International and Domestic Law, in: R. Mullerson and G. Tunkin (eds), Course of International Law in 7 Volumes, Vol. 1 272–303 (Moscow, 1989) (in Russian). See also *supra* note 7. Some authors (eg G. Ignatenko, R. Mullerson, G. Danilenko, S. Marochkin) advocated the application of international law in domestic courts.

3. TRANSITION TO A NEW STATE AND LEGAL ORDER AND TO A NEW CONSTITUITON

3.1. FROM "PUTSCH" IN 1991 AND THE BREAKDOWN OF THE USSR TO THE ADOPTION OF THE NEW CONSTITUTION OF RUSSIA

The process of disintegration actively began in the USSR in the beginning of the 1990s. Already on 12 June 1990, Russia adopted a Declaration on Sovereignty of the State[9] and declared its right to exit the USSR. The attempt to perform a state take-over (August 1991), along with other different political and economic reasons, resulted in the breakdown of the USSR. Fifteen Soviet republics on the territory of a single former state became independent states.

During this period, the Constitution of Russia 1978 was amended a number of times (once in 1989, three times in 1990, twice in 1991, and three times in 1992), with some norms of a democratic state and the rule of law. Those amendments related also to provisions regarding international law. Article 32 of the Constitution gave direct effect and priority to international law when dealing with human rights issues: 'Universally recognized international law norms related to human rights have priority over the laws of the Russian Federation and directly result in rights and obligations for the citizens of the Russian Federation'. This norm was new and quite radical for the constitutional development of Russia. It demonstrated an intention of the new Russia to become, through 'importing international law',[10] open to the international community. However, this provision did not live a long life (as we will see below, the current Constitution does not particularly enforce the priority of universally recognized norms over domestic law) and it did not have time to have a substantial effect on judicial practice, or a broad introduction of international law into the work of the courts.

For example, the Constitutional Court of Russia, established in 1991 for the first time and 'paused' in its activities by the President after the events of 3–4 October 1993, delivered just a few judgments and decisions in which it made passing references to the Universal Declaration on Human Rights 1948, the International Covenants on Human Rights 1966, International Labour Organization (ILO) Convention No. 111 1958, International Law Commission (ILC) Recommendations No. 162 1980 and No. 166 1982, the Declaration on Principles of International Law 1970, the Helsinki Final Act 1975, the Final Document of the Vienna Meeting 1986, a Document of the Copenhagen Meeting of the Commission on Security and Cooperation in Europe (CSCE) Human

---

9 Bulletin of the Council of People's Deputies and of the Supreme Council of RSFSR 2/22 (1990).

10 See E. Kristjánsdóttir, A. Nollkaemper and C. Ryngaert, Introduction, in this volume at p. 2.

Dimension Conference 1990, and the Final Document of the Universal Conference on Human Rights 1993.[11]

The armed conflict between the presidential power and the Supreme Council (Parliament) on 3–4 October 1993 resulted in a change of the system and structure of state power, and sped up the working out of a new constitution, which was approved by a popular referendum on 12 December 1993.

3.2. THE CONSTITUTION OF RUSSIA 1993 AND INTERNATIONAL LAW

The 1993 Constitution of Russia contains the following principle in Part 4, Article 15: 'Generally recognized principles and norms of international law and the international treaties of the Russian Federation shall constitute an integral part of its legal system. If an international treaty of the Russian Federation establishes rules other than those provided for by the law, the rules of the international treaty shall apply.'

The draft of the Constitution was discussed during a special session of the Constitutional Meeting. The main subject of the discussion about international law was the place (status) of its norms in the national jurisdiction: was it 'a part of Russian law' or a part of 'the legal system of Russia'? This was a principled question. According to the first approach, international law norms and treaties would be equal in their status to national laws, hence later-adopted laws could abrogate treaties concluded earlier. According to the second approach, the task was to show the specific role of international law, its influence upon all components of the legal system, including national law and judicial practice, and the priority of treaties over the laws in case of contradiction.

Furthermore, the wording 'universally recognized principles and norms' raised objections that it did not subsume 'fundamental principles of international law', and concerning the priority of application: should it be granted to all, but only to ratified international treaties?[12] One could raise some theoretical arguments against these objections but they are a separate subject and outside

---

11 See eg Rulings of the Constitutional Court of Russia: 4 February 1992; 13 March 1992; 23 June 1992; 16 April 1993; 17 September 1993; Determination of the Constitutional Court of Russia, 1 October 1993, in Database 'Consultant Plus'.

12 Some works discussing these provisions: see eg A. Talalaev, Correlation of international and domestic law and the Constitution of the Russian Federation, 4 Moscow Journal of International Law (1995); O. Khlestov, International law and Russia, 4 Moscow Journal of International Law (1994); I. Lukashuk, Constitution of Russia and international law, 2 Moscow Journal of International Law (1995); E. Usenko, Correlation and relationship of international and domestic law and the Russian Constitution, 2 Moscow Journal of International Law (1995); G. Danilenko, The way to the 'kingdom of law and justice', 1 Moscow Journal of International Law (1997) (in Russian).

the purpose of this chapter. Hence, it will not deal with them in detail. What is necessary to note, however, is that during the now almost eighteen years since the adoption of the Constitution, the courts not only have become accustomed to applying this important constitutional principle, but they have also developed its actual content in their practice.

The principle in Article 15 plays an important role. It is aimed at providing an 'external' side of the rule of law state (which is proclaimed in Article 1 of the Constitution) and an openness of the state to the international community and to international law. The article is to ensure and guarantee observance of the international obligations of Russia, first of all human rights obligations. Current legislation is moreover based on unified grounds and approaches to international law that were not typical for Soviet legislation.

The significance of the principle in question can only be ascertained in the context of the above-mentioned international constitutional moments. First, there had never before been an extreme provision like this in the history of Russian constitutional development. The provision unambiguously declares that, on the territory of Russia, international law takes effect without any additional legislative procedures of incorporation. The above-mentioned norm in the 1978 Constitution (as amended in 1992) concerned only human rights, whereas the current principle is of a general character. Not many countries give such effect to international norms in their legal systems.[13] Second, this is not an *ordinary* constitutional norm but one of the basic constitutional principles of Russia formulated in Chapter 1 of its Constitution, which enjoys a special status. It provides the basis of the constitutional order of the state, which in fact includes the characteristics of the rule of law state (human rights as a supreme value, rule of law, separation of powers, political and ideological pluralism, etc). In order to prevent amendment of the foundations of the constitutional order in case political forces change, it is stated in Chapter 9 of the Constitution that Chapter 1 cannot be amended by the Parliament; it can be amended only through a complicated special procedure.

The provision that the rules of international treaties are incorporated into the Russian legal system and prevail over national laws has been included practically in all codes and federal laws adopted since the Constitution, to take into account the peculiarities of different branches of legislation (eg the Civil Code, the Labour Code, the Family Code, etc).

13 The Netherlands, by way of example. See eg A. Nollkaemper, The Netherlands, in: D. Sloss (ed.), The Role of Domestic Courts in Treaty Enforcement: A Comparative Study 327, 368–369 (Cambridge: Cambridge University Press, 2009).

4. THE ROLE OF THE COURTS IN ENTRENCHMENT OF INTERNATIONAL NORMS IN THE LEGAL ORDER OF RUSSIA

During the entire time since the Constitution's entry into force, the appeal to international law norms has become an ordinary event in the work of legislative and law-enforcement bodies, in all subjects of domestic law, affecting both legal persons and individuals.

Judicial practice plays a most significant role in the establishment of international law as an integral part of the legal system of Russia, in changing its legal order, and in maintaining the rule of law. In this sense, judicial practice has a priceless meaning in the understanding and development of the constitutional principle that international law is a component of the legal system of the state.

The special role of the higher courts should be noted. The Constitutional Court of the Russian Federation (RF) deals with cases concerning the constitutionality of federal laws, Presidential decrees, and resolutions of the RF government. The Constitutional Court's rulings and determinations must be taken into account by all the bodies of state power and other subjects of law, as they reveal the constitutional meaning of the existing laws, can declare laws contradictory to the Constitution, and thereby affect the adjustment of legislation and law enforcement.

The Supreme Court of Russia is highest among the courts of general jurisdiction dealing with civil, criminal, and administrative cases. The Supreme Arbitrazh Court of Russia heads arbitrazh courts to hear and decide commercial disputes. Both have judicial review powers with respect to specific cases (supervisory review), evaluate the decisions of the lower courts, and often send cases back for retrial. They also issue documents of general character (generalizations and reviews of judicial practice, Information letters, rulings of the Plenums (Plenary Sessions) with interpretations of existing laws and judicial practice) for the respective systems of the lower courts (ie general jurisdiction and arbitrazh), and provide uniformity in judicial practice, including the application of international law. Therefore, the decisions and acts of the Supreme and Arbitrazh Courts are relevant not only for the particular case and its parties, but also for their judicial systems as a whole (in this sense such decisions and acts have a precedential value). Thus, acts of the higher courts can influence quite specifically the role of international law in the judicial activity of the country and in safeguarding the rule of law.

Let us recall what the Constitution says about one particular situation of the application of international law: if the law contradicts a treaty, the latter must be applied. But the general constitutional principle on international norms and treaties as an integral component of the Russian legal system implies a much wider role for international law. As a result, the courts resort to international law not just for reasoning of judgments and for giving a priority to it over domestic law. They also resort to it for asserting control of the courts vis-à-vis the executive.

In a country in which the political and legal order were closed for many decades and where application of international law was quite rare, the significant role of the courts consists in the increasing insertion and entrenchment of this law in different kinds of cases and legal relationships. This is revealed in several different aspects.

4.1. THE NORMS OF INTERNATIONAL LAW AS A FRAMEWORK FOR LEGISLATION AND FOR ITS IMPLEMENTATION

Trials are based on the fact that, despite the broad scope of discretion of the federal legislator in establishing legal regimes, it is not infinite. The rule of law means, in particular, that the legislative power is itself subjected to the law, and the courts can review acts of Parliament and of the executive in light of law, including international law.

For instance, this is the approach of the Constitutional Court. In the ruling *On constitutionality of the provisions of the Criminal Code and the Criminal Procedure Code*, the Court observed: 'In cases when measures provided by the criminal law do not match social realities, leading to a weakening of the protection of any constitutional values, ... legislator... must bring the criminal law provisions in line with new social realities.' Further: 'This conclusion is consistent with the Universal Declaration of Human Rights...'.[14] In the *Case concerning the constitutionality of the provisions of the Federal Constitutional Law 'On arbitrazh courts in the Russian Federation' and of the Arbitrazh Procedure Code*, the Constitutional Court stressed that federal legislation should provide appropriate regulation on the basis of 'the constitutional goals and values, common principles and norms of international law and international obligations of Russia'.[15]

This approach became a constant legal position which the Court has followed in its most recent cases, in particular *Concerning constitutionality of Articles 392 and 397 of the Civil Procedure Code*.[16] The articles in question did not give an opportunity for reconsidering a final judgment of a domestic court after a decision of the ECtHR on violation of the European Convention on Human

14 Ruling of the Constitutional Court of Russia 20 April 2006, No 18 (2006) Compilation of Legislation of the Russian Federation ('CL RF') 2058.

15 Ruling of the Constitutional Court of Russia 17 January 2008, No 4 (2008) CL RF 300.

16 See rulings: on 26 February 2010, No 11 (2010) CL RF 1255; on 19 March 2010, No 14 (2010) CL RF 1734.

Rights (ECHR). In the first ruling, the Constitutional Court recognized Article 392 as constitutional, but stated that according to Part 4, Article 15 of the Constitution on a priority of international treaties, the courts cannot reject such applications for retrial. It also said that the federal legislator has to make necessary amendments in the Code in order to guarantee such an opportunity. In the second case, the Court found Article 397 unconstitutional and in the operative part of the decision directly obliged the federal legislator to change this provision.

Sometimes, applicants ask the courts to review executive acts by relying on international norms. In some situations such a review would exceed the authority of the judiciary, breach the competence of the executive and, thus, the rule of law. For example, in the *Case on the request of K. challenging the resolution of the Government of the Russian Federation*,[17] the applicant asked the court to invalidate certain provisions of the resolution on financial maintenance of UN military observers. In the applicant's opinion, those provisions were contrary to the federal legislation and the Model Agreement between the UN and Member States contributing personnel to UN peacekeeping operations. He also insisted that the court should oblige the government to establish additional safeguards for these employees. The Russian Supreme Court noted in the decision: 'By the principle of separation of powers enshrined in Article 10 of the Constitution of the Russian Federation, the judiciary has no right to interfere in the rule-making of the legislative and executive bodies and to determine the content of their normative acts'. This decision seems correct in part of 'obliging' the government. But, for some reasons, appealing to this principle, the Supreme Court actually avoided answering another request of the applicant – that it review the legality of the executive act – that was within its competence. And this position of the Court does not appear justified.

Usually, the Constitutional Court has reviewed and does review legality. In decisions of 31 October 2007 and 16 March 2009, it invalidated point 146 of the Regulations of Internal Procedure in Investigatory Isolation Wards passed on 14 October 2005 by the Ministry of Justice of Russia, and point 141 of the Regulations in Isolation Wards for Suspects and Defendants passed on 22 November 2005 by the Ministry of Internal Affairs of Russia.[18] The Supreme Court found in these decisions that the points in question violated provisions of the Constitution, the Criminal Procedure Code, and of the International Covenant on Civil and Political Rights (ICCPR).

---

17 Decision of the Supreme Court of the Russian Federation of 19 April 2007 No GKPI07–142: No 1 (2009) Bulletin 21.

18 Database 'Consultant Plus. Version Prof'.

4.2. THE NORMS OF INTERNATIONAL TREATIES IN DETERMINING THE APPLICABLE LAW AND AS A BASIS OF THE DECISION IN THE CASE

The Constitution provides for the priority of international treaties in case of conflict with the law (part 4, Article 15) in proceedings before domestic courts. Codes and other federal laws mostly repeat this principle.

One can find some cases where the courts resort to prior application of international law norms before the law.[19] In the *Case on constitutionality of the provisions of the Criminal Procedure Code of the RSFSR* (former Russian Soviet Federative Socialist Republic), the Constitutional Court pointed out that Article 14, paragraph 6, of the ICCPR provides for more opportunities to correct judicial mistakes than the criminal procedure legislation of Russia. 'By virtue of Article 15(4) of the Russian Constitution, this international legal norm, being a part of the Russian legal system takes precedence over domestic legislation'. Based on this position, the Court declared unconstitutional point 4, part 2, of Article 384 of the Code, ordered a retrial of the applicants' cases, and directed the legislature to amend the Code.[20]

The Presidium of the Supreme Arbitrazh Court of Russia in an Information letter[21] provided that an arbitrazh court takes for consideration a lawsuit involving a foreign entity if there are rules on its jurisdiction in the international treaty of the Russian Federation. Analysing a particular case, the Presidium concluded that such norms in the Arbitrazh Procedure Code did not coincide with the norms of the Geneva Convention on the Contract for International Carriage of Goods 19 May 1956, and therefore on the basis of part 4, Article 15 of the Constitution the rules of the international treaty were to be applied.

The whole picture is much more diverse, however, and priority is not always accorded to international instruments. In every case, the courts must define the applicable law, and this can be not only international law but also domestic and international law jointly, or just national acts.

---

19 See eg Review of Judicial Practice of the Supreme Court of Russia for IV quarter 2005, No 5 (2006) Bulletin 9–10; ruling and determination of the Constitutional Court: 3 July 1997, No 5 (1997) Herald of the Constitutional Court 31–33; 27 February 2009, No 11 (2009) CL RF 1367; rulings of the Presidium of the Supreme Arbitrazh Court: No 3253/04 of 22 June 2004, No 10 (2004) Herald of the Supreme Arbitrazh Court 67–69; No 10441/05 of 24 January 2006, Database 'Consultant Plus'; ruling of the Federal Arbitrazh Court of the Nothern-Western district No A42–4747/04–13 of 9 December 2004, No 4 (2005) International Commercial Arbitrazh 134–136.

20 Ruling of the Constitutional Court on 2 February 1996, No 7 (1996) CL RF 701; Determination of the Constitutional Court on 10 July 2003, No 42 (2003) CL RF 4106.

21 Information letter of the Presidium of the Supreme Arbitrazh Court of Russia of 18 January 2001 No 58, Review of practice of settlement of disputes by arbitrazh courts connected with defense of foreign investors, 4 Economy and Law 105–106 (2001); see also another example here: 98–99.

In the above-mentioned *Review of legislation and judicial practice*[22] the Supreme Court drew the lower courts' attention to the fact that 'courts shall take into account not only the norms of national legislation in force in this area, but also acts of international law, a party of which is Russia'.

Giving an explanation of legislation on copyright and analysing the practice of its implementation, the Plenum of the Supreme Court in an advisory opinion in Ruling No. 15 of 19 June 2006 *On the issues faced by the courts in civil cases relating to the application of the law on copyright and related rights* specially highlighted the situation where 'a number of provisions contained in international treaties are not enshrined in Russian legislation'. It also gave a comprehensive list of relevant international treaties with Russia and stated that, in proceedings, 'courts must take into account international principles of protection of authors' rights and related rights as enshrined, inter alia, in the Berne Convention for the Protection of Literary and Artistic Works, as well as the International Convention for the Protection of Performers, Producers of Phonograms and Broadcasting Organizations'. Some recommendations as to application of specific topics of the convention have been also given.[23]

Making decisions without proper regard to international treaties often leads to their annulment. Indicative in this respect is the practice of the Supreme Arbitrazh Court on the revision of the decisions of lower courts. When considering, eg, *Case ZAO 'Dzh.T.I. Marketing and Sales' v tax inspection*,[24] the Presidium of the Court pointed out that the lower instances had not applied the Agreement between Russia and Germany 'On avoiding double taxation with respect to taxes on income and assets' which should have been applied in this case. Thus, judgments made without sufficient examination of the treaty violate the uniformity of the interpretation and application of substantive law by the courts.

Appeal to international law has become commonplace in courts of all types and instances in legal reasoning, the formulation of legal positions, determining the applicable law, and deliberation and formulation of a decision on the case. Strictly speaking, all these situations of resort to international law concern not only its application but a much wider implementation. Application means the use of a legal norm in the operative part of the decision, when the case is decided directly on the basis of norm(s) of an international treaty.

One rarely encounters cases where rules of international law are part of the judicial resolution. Indicative in this respect are decisions of the Presidium of the Supreme Arbitrazh Court on a similar question of the recognition and enforcement of decisions of the Arbitration Institute of the Stockholm Chamber

22 No 11 (2008) Bulletin 23–25.

23 No 8 (2006) Bulletin 12–13.

24 Resolution of the Presidium of the Supreme Arbitrazh Court of Russia No 14163/05 18 April 2006, 8 Herald 90–95 (2006).

of Commerce and of the London Court of International Arbitration. The Presidium has constructed a legal argumentation and substantiated its decisions solely on the basis of the provisions of the UN Convention of 10 June 1958 'On the Recognition and Enforcement of Foreign Arbitral Awards'.[25] In the determination of the *Case on the complaint of US citizen in violation of his constitutional rights by part 3 Article 1 and part 1 Article 466 of the Criminal Procedure Code*, the Constitutional Court wrote that part 1 of Article 466 of the Code 'does not suggest – in conjunction with the Convention on Legal Assistance and Legal Relations in Civil, Family and Criminal Matters of 22 January 1993 – to arrest a person on the request of a foreign state for more than 48 hours without a court order... Revealed in the determination the constitutional and legal meaning of the Article is obligatory and excludes any other interpretation of it in law enforcement' (principle of consistent interpretation).[26] In the above-mentioned resolution of 27 November 2007[27] the Presidium of the Supreme Arbitrazh Court concluded: 'The case should be sent to a new trial in the court of first instance to address the issue of compliance inspection solutions... the legislation on taxes and fees without regard to the Agreement.'

4.3. GENERALLY RECOGNIZED PRINCIPLES AND NORMS OF INTERNATIONAL LAW IN JUDICIAL DECISIONS

As was already mentioned, the constitutional principle in Article 15 of the Constitution declares that 'generally recognized principles and norms of international law ... shall constitute an integral part of its legal system'.

The perception is that treaties are more accessible to courts and that treaty application is more widespread in practice. Mostly, this seems to be due to the certain identical characteristics of treaties and domestic laws: the precise and clear form, precision, and certainty of the rules. Exactly the opposite is the situation with regard to generally recognized principles and norms that exist in the form of customary law and do not have such features (unless they are fixed in some international document). It could therefore be assumed that these subjects of law would seldom appeal to judges. But, in fact, evidence suggests quite a bold and regular use of legal argumentation by various state authorities, as well as by natural and legal persons. The courts also regularly rely on generally recognized principles and norms to justify their positions and decisions, but mostly on ones which are contained in treaties and other international instruments (ie exist in written form).

---

25 Resolutions No 14548/04 22 February 2005 in Database 'Consultant Plus', No 10718/08 20 January 2009, No 10613/08 20 January 2009, 5 Herald 287–296 (2009).

26 Determination of the Constitutional Court 1 March 2007, No 28 (2007) CL RF 3478.

27 2 Herald (2008).

These examples[28] can obviously be a response to statements found in the literature about the limited usefulness of universally recognized principles and norms for practical application due to their generalized nature and high level of abstraction. However, perhaps the opposite is true – namely that these features could be seen as an advantage and a special role of such principles and that they form the basic framework, the 'spirit', of international law. And because the courts apply not only the specific and often narrow norms of positive law, but also basic principles, they contribute more balance and reasonableness to their decisions, thus ensuring the rule of law. By contrast, the use of universally recognized norms to justify dubious and positivistic (formalistic) judgments greatly reduces a court's credibility. There are cases to be found that are not purely legal, but more of a political nature, in which so-called political expediency prevails over the legal analysis and the final decision. In such situations, it is obvious that the problem of separation of powers, and especially of independence of the judiciary from the executive, still exists and has not been fully resolved.

Thus, in the obviously politicized ruling in the *Case on the constitutionality of provisions of the federal law 'On general principles of organization of legislative (representative) and executive authorities of entities of the Russian Federation'*[29] the Constitutional Court justified the amendments to the law initiated by the President by virtue of which the elections of senior officials of RF entities were in fact replaced upon their appointment by the President of Russia. These amendments were challenged by a number of citizens as violating their constitutional rights. It seems the court used just casuistic and rhetorical argumentation. Resorting to the aid of international instruments, in particular the Universal Declaration of Human Rights, the court found it convincing enough to write that the Declaration 'does not specify what public authorities and of what level are to be formed exclusively through the holding of such elections, and still does not oblige Member States of the organization to hold only direct elections to the organs of public authority'.

It is clear that the Declaration, by definition, cannot 'specify' this. An attempt to justify the decision on the grounds that general principles do not provide solutions for a specific private matter is actually to substitute legal reasoning by political expediency, motivated by a pre-defined goal, not by the law.

For some reason the courts sometimes avoid legal assessment of executive actions, although they could and should review them by resorting to general international law norms. This position prevents citizens from defending their rights against abuse and does not allow them to expect a fair trial. For example, the Moscow district court dismissed an application by M., who challenged the

28 See eg Determination of the Judicial Division for Civil Cases of the Supreme Court 1 February 2008 No 80-V07-21, No 1 (2009) Bulletin 11–13; determination of the Constitutional Court 4 December 2007, No 52 (2007) CL RF 6533; ruling of the Constitutional Court 11 May 2005, No 22 (2005) CL RF 2194, etc.

29 Ruling of the Constitutional Court 21 December 2005, No 3 (2006) CL RF 336.

action of the Federal Security Service (FSB), which refused to allow her entry into Russia, arguing that it was the exclusive competence of the Service and not subject to judicial interpretation. On appeal, the Moscow City Court left the decision unchanged. M. filed a petition to the Constitutional Court, challenging the constitutionality of the provisions of the federal law on exit from and entry into Russia. The court in its determination of 19 May 2009 № 545-O-O refused to consider the complaint, referring to the fact that verification of the legality and validity of judgments, as well as the applicant's proposal to amend the legislation, did not fall within its competence. Judge A.L. Kononov, in a dissenting opinion, disagreed with the determination and argued that the court should base itself upon the European Convention on Human Rights. Judge Kononov noted that the ECtHR had previously concluded that the challenged law gave the authorities too much discretion in the absence of adequate safeguards against abuse, and that the challenged court decisions did not leave the claimant any chance of effective protection.[30]

The text of part 4, Article 15, of the Constitution and its literal interpretation do not provide grounds for speaking about the order of priority in which the said principles and norms are to be applied before national law, at least principles that exist in unwritten form (such as customary rules).[31] Moreover, the Constitution does not define the role such principles play in law enforcement and their validity in relation to domestic law. This uncertainty has generated conflicting and unstable practices in the development of this particular constitutional provision. Part of the practice creates the impression that courts sometimes are not concerned with the questions of hierarchy and priority. Yet, some courts have gone even further in the development of this constitutional provision and, possibly, in the establishment of recognition, through practice, of the priority of generally recognized principles and norms over the law. This tendency is evident in a very clear ruling of the Constitutional Court on 28 June 2007[32]: 'The right of person to be buried after death according to his will... derives from the Constitution, Articles 21, 22, 28 and 29, guaranteeing the protection of human dignity... and from generally recognized principles and norms of international law, which by virtue of Article 15 (part 4) of the Constitution are part of the legal system of the Russian Federation and *have precedence over domestic law*' (emphasis added). It is here worth mentioning that the Constitutional Court attributed to the Constitution something which it actually does not contain, and it interpreted and developed (perhaps intentionally) its provision by not only a literal, but a wider interpretation.

30 See Database 'Consultant Plus'.

31 See for details S. Marochkin, Action of International Law Norms in the Legal System of the Russian Federation 50–54 (Tyumen: Tyumen University Press, 1998, 2005) (in Russian).

32 No 27 (2007) CL RF 3346; see also the determination 15 January 2009, No 18 (Part II) (2009) CL RF.

4.4. RECOMMENDATIONS AND DECISIONS OF BODIES OF INTERNATIONAL ORGANIZATIONS, ACTS OF INTERNATIONAL CONFERENCES

As is known, the Russian Constitution limits the international component of the legal system of the country by means of two 'elements': on one hand, universally recognized principles and norms, and on the other hand, international treaties. Nevertheless, everything that is not law – such as recommendations of international organizations, acts of international conferences, model acts ('soft' law), binding decisions of international organs – have actively 'invaded' the law-enforcement sphere. In the mid-1990s, when the development and implementation of constitutional principles was going through a period of formation, the appearance in court decisions of non-legal international standards alongside treaties evoked puzzled questions: it was as if, through the courts, and especially the Constitutional Court, rules of a recommendatory nature were being 'declared' as legal ones, contrary to the Constitution.

The general trend is that recourse to international recommendatory acts has not been reduced, but has rather become constant and established practice in all types of courts.[33] Strictly speaking, the courts do not apply such acts, but use them to refine ('reconcile') terms and definitions, and to formulate and justify the position of the court, to confirm or strengthen its legal reasoning. Involvement in the judicial work of this huge 'reservoir' of international norms of recommendation is a solid step in the practical development of the constitutional principle governing the international component of the Russian legal system.

The spectrum and list of international acts of recommendation which courts have used are very broad, demonstrating once again that the courts often turn to them for a variety of issues and areas of the law to strengthen their argumentation in a case. To do this, the courts often resort to 'generally accepted international practice', using recommendatory acts of international organizations in which Russia is not involved. For example, in 1998, the Constitutional Court, in the *Case on constitutionality of the provisions of the Fundamentals of legislation on notaries*, noted that the provisions provided ways to control the activities of notaries in accordance with a European Parliament resolution of 18 January 1994. In another case, the court cited the Code of Conduct for Lawyers in the

[33] See eg rulings and definitions of the Constitutional Court: 23 June 2000, No 33 (2000) CL RF 3431; 8 December 2003, No 51 (2003) CL RF 5026; 5 November 2004, No 51 (2004) CL RF 5264; 1 December 2005, No 6 (2006) CL RF 733; 11 May 2005, No 22 (2005) CL RF 2194; 28 June 2007, No 27 (2007) CL RF 3346; 17 March 2009, No 14 (2009) CL RF 1770; 24 March 2009, No 14 (2009) CL RF 1771; 27 February 2009, No 11 (2009) CL RF 1367; determinations of the Judicial Collegium on Civil Cases of the Supreme Court: No 88-Г05–19 20 December 2005, No 10 (2006) Bulletin 1; No 66-Г08–2 26 February 2008, No 8 (2008) Bulletin 13; No ГКПИ06–54 2 March 2006, No 12 (2007) Bulletin 6–8.

European Community 1988.[34] Courts thus often turn to the enforcement decisions of bodies of international organizations. Sometimes there are links to the European Commission and the European Court of Justice,[35] which, in principle, have no legal significance for Russia. It is obvious that the only role of such examples is to offer a reflection of experiences and approaches in dealing with similar cases, thereby strengthening the argumentation of the court.

4.5. TREATIES WITHOUT PARTICIPATION OF RUSSIA

There are cases in which references are made to international treaties to which Russia is not involved. If such links can be justified, then it is certainly with the proviso that they are not binding for Russia but are provided solely for reference to existing international standards or approaches to the subject matter, and as an additional means of argumentation. Without such reservations, such references may find their way into the main, and perhaps the decisive, means for reaching the conclusions and decision on the case, which negatively affects the validity of the decision. And one may indeed sometimes encounter such situations. But treaties which are not obligatory for Russia have been invoked as examples of foreign or international practice, but they are unlikely to form the legal basis for the recommendations and requirements to the legislator. And the world experience cannot influence the court's conclusion as to whether the law in question is constitutional or not.

In the *Case concerning the constitutionality of articles of the Labour Code and the Federal Law 'On Joint Stock Companies'*, brought by request of the courts and complaints of the citizens,[36] it was argued in particular that the challenged regulation 'is in conflict with the requirements of international legal instruments that prohibit discrimination in employment in any form', and reference was made to ILO Convention No. 158 1982, concerning the termination of employment at the initiative of the employer; to the European Social Charter; and to the Charter of Social Rights and Guarantees of Independent States (approved by the Resolution of the CIS Interparliamentary Assembly on 29 October 1994). None of the mentioned documents was an international treaty for Russia: it was not a party to the first two international treaties at that time (the European Social Charter was ratified by the federal law much later, on 3 June 2009), and the third act is just a recommendation act. But the Constitutional Court did not pay attention to this and only reasoned in the abstract: part of the

34 See ruling and determination of the Constitutional Court: 19 May 1998, No 22 (1998) CL RF 2491; 6 July 2000, No 33 (2000) CL RF 3433, see also determination of judge of the Supreme Court of Russia 25 October 2005 No 33-V05-6, No 7 (2006) Bulletin 6–7.

35 See eg Determinations of the Judicial Collegium on Civil Cases of the Supreme Court 49-Г04-48 21 May 2004, No 11 (2004) Bulletin 4–6.

36 Ruling of the Constitutional Court 15 March 2005, No 13 (2005) CL RF 1209.

challenged provisions cannot be evaluated as being inconsistent 'with the requirements of international law acts ratified by the Russian Federation' (paragraph 4.4). Obviously, the court called these acts treaties, which they were not with respect to Russia, and thus this part of the ruling was flawed from the standpoint of legal reasoning since it was based on abstract acts and did not conform to the principle of the rule of law.

The question of treaties that are not applicable to Russia has also gained an unexpected continuation in connection with the so-called problem of abolishing the death penalty. On 16 April 1997, Russia signed Protocol No. 6 of the ECHR, and imposed a moratorium on the death penalty before the establishment of trials by jury on the whole territory of Russia. This had to be read as meaning that once the courts of jury were established, the question should be raised again. From 1 January 2010, such courts have operated throughout Russia, after their formation in the Chechen republic. The Protocol has not yet been ratified, however, which has created an ambiguous situation as to the possibility of resumption of the death penalty. The Constitutional Court, in its determination of 19 November 2009 No 1344-O-R[37] in the *Case on the request of the Supreme Court*, came to the conclusions that: in international law there is a steady trend towards abolishing the death penalty; the fact that Protocol No. 6 has so far not been ratified cannot be regarded as a legal act of repealing the death penalty in Russia; but this does not preclude recognition of it as an essential element of legal regulation of the right to life. 'As a result of such a long moratorium *in the light of its international legal trends and commitments*, Russia has achieved *a legitimate constitutional legal regime*' (emphasis added) and steady guarantees of the right of a person not to be subjected to the death penalty; there is an irreversible process for its abolition. Evidently, the Court proceeded from one of the principles of the rule of law – the supremacy of human rights. It is also evident that the recognition of the obligation to abolish the death penalty applies to Russia as a norm of customary international law.

4.6. RULINGS OF THE EUROPEAN COURT OF HUMAN RIGHTS (ECTHR)

The solid mass of the international component of the Russian legal system, in addition to its normative part (the generally recognized principles and norms and international treaties), are the rulings of the ECtHR.[38] Of course, there is no

37 No 48 (2009) CL RF 5867; Estimation of this determination, see eg B. Tuzmukhamedov, Dots or nevertheless a dot?, in: *Nezavisimaya Gazeta*, 24 November 2009 (in Russian).

38 See in particular: A. Burkov, The Constitutional Court of the Russian Federation and the case-law of the European Court of Human Rights, 3 Human Rights. Practice of the European Court of Human Rights 18–22 (2009); A. Demeneva, Enforcement by Russia rulings of the European Court of Human Rights: the number, not turning into quality, 4 Comparative

mention of them in the Constitution, since Russia joined the Council of Europe and recognized the jurisdiction of the ECtHR after the adoption of the Constitution. Nevertheless, over the past years, this jurisprudence quite noticeably, and even powerfully, 'invaded' the legal system, mainly as to its practical part (enforcement), thanks primarily to the courts.

In this sense, the courts have once again had a great influence on the development of the constitutional principle governing the international law component of the legal system. The federal law on the ratification of the ECHR outlined quite concrete limits on the jurisdiction of the ECtHR: its rulings are binding for Russia on the interpretation and application of the Convention and its Protocols, in cases of alleged violation by Russia of the provisions of these acts, when the alleged violation took place after their entry into force for Russia.[39] Significantly, after years of 'work' of the Russian courts with the rulings of the ECtHR, the Constitutional Court, interpreting this provision of the law, issued a landmark assessment of their role in the legal system of Russia: 'Thus, as well as the Convention on the Protection of Human Rights and Fundamental Freedoms, rulings of the European Court of Human Rights when they interpret the contents of the Convention on the basis of universally recognized principles and norms of international law… – *are part of the Russian legal system…*' (emphasis added).[40] In fact, the Court has interpreted not only legislation, but also Article 15 of the Constitution – which speaks only of international law norms (not judicial decisions) more broadly – as being a part of the domestic legal system. Again we see the role of the judiciary in the development of the content of the constitutional principle.

In fact, the quantity of ECtHR decisions used by the Russian courts has turned out to be much greater than what was outlined by the law on ratification. As the judicial practice shows, the courts do not wonder whether they can take into account decisions of the ECtHR that are compulsory only for Russia (if the law were interpreted formally and legally) or also decisions compulsory for other countries. They accept and cite every decision which they find relevant to the particular domestic case.

Courts accept the ECtHR decisions (ie refer to them) in various contexts: in the assessment of specific terms or situations; the reflection of the legal position of the ECtHR and its case law; and as grounds for review of judicial decisions. It should be noted that the legal positions and the ECtHR decisions have had a noticeable effect on Russian judicial practice and on establishing the rule of law. The courts also often consider the ECtHR's rulings as an authoritative

Constitutional Review 63–80 (2009) (in Russian). See for the influence of the ECtHR in post-conflict situations also A. Buyse, Virtuous Flexibility – The Application of International Human Rights Norms by the Bosnian Human Rights Chamber, in this volume at p. 175.

39 Federal Law 30 March 1998 No 54-FZ 'On ratification of the Convention on the Protection of Human Rights and Fundamental Freedoms and its Protocols', No 14 (1998) CL RF 1514.

40 Ruling of the Constitutional Court 5 February 2007, No 7 (2007) CL RF 932.

interpretation of the Convention and use them to justify their positions and decisions. Because such interpretation enriches the content of the rule, one can assume that the relevant parts of the regulations are elements of law-making.

Russian courts have worked out the practice of comparing (correlating) their legal positions with the positions of the ECtHR. This helps the perception and understanding of the meaning of the provisions of the ECHR, its adjustment, the development of jurisprudence in line with the norms of the Convention, and with the decisions of the ECtHR, sometimes even the correction of legislation. In ruling on *A challenge to the constitutionality of the provisions of the Civil Procedure Code*,[41] the Constitutional Court ordered that 'federal legislator should, taking into account the legal position of the European Court of Human Rights... provide the legal regulation of supervisory review... in accordance with recognized Russia's international legal standards.'

The importance of legal positions is periodically a matter of the attention of the Plenum of the Supreme Court: in a ruling on 10 October 2003 on the application of universally recognized principles and norms and international treaties (paragraph 12) and in the rulings on different aspects of the judicial practice.[42]

Appeal to the precedents of the ECtHR has indeed become usual in the courts' activities.[43] In addition to interpretation of the provisions of the ECHR, the legal positions and precedents of the ECtHR help the Russian courts to clarify the legal reasoning of the case, and create their own sustainable practices on similar or overlapping issues. From the formal legal point of view, the rulings of the ECtHR play a subsidiary role: the courts cite them to confirm and reinforce their assessments and findings (eg 'this position is confirmed by the practice of the ECtHR', 'from the practice of the European Court follows', 'this conclusion corresponds practice of the Court', 'the same approach followed by the ECtHR', etc). In fact, they often 'lead' the courts to validate and make their own decisions in a given case. At times, however, the ECtHR's rulings also play a 'negative role', when they are used as a 'worthless' form of reasoning. In the above-mentioned ruling *On the federal law on general principles of organization of the authorities of the entities of the Federation* (see above, footnote 29) the Constitutional Court, in order to justify of its position, drew upon the ECtHR's ruling in *Gitonas v Greece* of 1 July 1997 as an example of the application of Article 3 of Protocol 1 to the

---

41 *Supra* note 40.

42 See eg rulings: 24 February 2005 No 3 'On judicial practice in cases of defamation of citizens, as well as the goodwill of citizens and legal persons', No 4 (2005) Bulletin; 6 February 2007 No 6 'On amending and supplementing certain provisions of Supreme Court of Russia in civil cases', No 5 (2007) Bulletin.

43 See, in particular: the rulings and determinations of the Constitutional Court of Russia: 25 April 2001, No 23 (2001) CL RF. 2001 2408; 24 January 2002, No 7 (2002) CL RF 745; 21 December 2005, No 3 (2006) CL RF 336; 20 February 2006, No 10 (2006) CL RF 1145; 4 December 2007, No 52 (2007) CL RF 6533; 17 January 2008, No 4 (2008) CL RF 300; 3 July 2008, No 5 (2009) CL RF 678; 27 February 2009, No 11 (2009) CL RF 1367; etc.

ECHR. But the ruling and article talk about elections only to legislative bodies, while the complaints of citizens and the matter of the Russian case related to the elections of senior officials of the RF entities. The Court also used it for other matters and based on the wrong argument of correspondence of the changes in the law to the Constitution.

Significantly, the Russian courts appeal not only to positive law and legal positions of the ECtHR, but also to the general principles of law and universally recognized principles of international law used by it. Due to this, such principles are actively introduced into the domestic legal system, especially law enforcement, and are becoming 'habitual' (usual) normative bases for decision-making, along with legislation.

In one case, the Judicial Collegium for civil cases of the Supreme Court expressly applied the principle of the rule of law, citing an excerpt from the decision of the ECtHR in the case of *Ryabykh v the Russian Federation* of 24 July 2003 for the interpretation of the Convention: the rule of law is recognized as a part of the common heritage of contracting states. One of the fundamental aspects of the rule of law is the principle of legal certainty.[44] Based on this principle, the Collegium endorsed the decisions of the first and appellate courts concerning the illegal involvement of T. as criminally responsible (as a result of the sentence the court justified T.), and abolished the regulation of the supervisory instance, which sent the case back for retrial.[45] Thus, from the point of view of the principle of legal certainty, the Collegium considered as final the decisions of the lower courts but not of the higher (supervisory) one.

Recognition of the Court's compulsory jurisdiction on the interpretation and application of the Convention, if a decision has been issued against Russia, means not only a duty of compensation, but may also lead to revision of judicial decisions. This is clearly illustrated by a recent ruling of the Constitutional Court on 26 February 2010 No 4-P[46] in the case *On constitutionality of Article 392 of the Civil Procedure Code*. In several prior rulings, the ECtHR found violations of Article 6 of the ECHR and Article 1 of Protocol No. 1.[47] The courts of general jurisdiction dismissed the applications to revise earlier court decisions on new circumstances, referring to Article 392, which in those circumstances does not call for a ruling of the ECtHR. The petitioners filed complaints before the Constitutional Court challenging the constitutionality of this article. The court found the article constitutional, but noted in the decision that according to the rule set forth in Article 15 of the Constitution on the priority of international

44 Complaint No 52854/99, available at www.espch.ru/content/view/16/25/.

45 Determination on the case No 18-B08–55, No 9 (2009) Bulletin 31–32; on the principle of legal certainty as an aspect of the rule of law, see also determination of the Supreme Court on the case No 18-B08–56, No 10 (2009) Bulletin 21–22; ruling of the Constitutional Court 13 June 2010, No 29 (2010) CL RF 3983.

46 No 11 (2010) CL RF 1255.

47 Rulings of the Ect.HR 13 April 2006, 18 January 2007, 8 January 2009.

treaties, Article 392 could not be interpreted as allowing refusals to review cases in connection with decisions of the ECtHR.

5. CONCLUSION

In the almost 20 years since the adoption of the 1993 Constitution of Russia, a broad, diverse, and sustainable practice of use and application (by courts, prosecutors, and other types of law enforcement officials, lawyers, citizens, and legal entities) of international law norms has developed. The judiciary plays a leading role in this development. Appeals to international standards have become routine in the courts of all types and levels.

Enshrined in the Constitution as one of the foundations of the country's constitutional system, the provision on universally recognized principles and norms of international law and international treaties of Russia as a component of the country's legal system (part 4 of Article 15) radically changed the place and role of international obligations in the sphere of domestic jurisdiction.

As evidenced by the present chapter, jurisprudence plays a most significant role in promoting international law in the domestic sphere in Russia, in changing the legal order in its period of transition, and in strengthening the rule of law. Relying not only on the Constitution, but also on international law, the courts have ensured the implementation of principles of the rule of law state (separation of powers, human rights as the supreme value, the rule of law, etc).

The constitutional principle that makes international norms and treaties an integral part of the domestic legal order entails a wide role of courts in that order. In a country in which the political and legal order was closed for many decades and where application of international law was quite rare, the significant role of the courts consists in the increasing insertion and entrenchment of this law into different kinds of cases and legal relations. Courts resort to international law for their legal reasoning, formulation of legal positions, the determination of applicable law, and the deliberation and formulation of a final decision in the case.

That said, there are not so many cases in which the courts expressly rely on international law for reasoning of judgments and give it a priority over domestic law. There also are not many cases that have political relevance and in which international law serves as an instrument for control of the courts *vis-à-vis* the executive. As for the legislative branch, one can mention constant and continuing practice of the Constitutional Court on the matter of the constitutionality of statutes in which international law is being involved for review of the legislature. Nevertheless, in some cases, it is obvious that the problem of separation of powers, and especially of the independence of the judiciary from the political branches, still exists and has not been fully resolved.

At the same time, the courts do not treat and realize this constitutional principle in a formalistic manner (ie according to just its literal meaning). They have developed and enriched its content, and strengthened the domestic rule of law by resorting to international law: basing themselves not only on the legal component (generally recognized principles and norms and international treaties), but on virtually all elements of the international normative system – such as the resolutions and recommendations of international organizations, the decisions of international bodies, model acts, and the legal positions and decisions of international judicial institutions. Such acts, being of a non-binding legal or normative nature, have been used by the Russian courts for legal reasoning, for confirmation of their findings and assessments, development of legal positions, rationale and decision-making. As for the decisions of international courts that are compulsory on Russia – also for reviewing the acts of the Russian courts to comply with international obligations. It is also necessary to note a new element: the role of the judiciary (the Constitutional Court in particular) in the recognition of international obligations in treaties that are non-binding for Russia on the basis of the existing practice of domestic courts (in fact, as norms of customary international law).

Thus, the courts have actually ensured the position that in reality, the international component of the Russian legal system is much broader than that envisaged by the letter of the Constitution.

THICKENING THE RULE OF LAW IN TRANSITION: THE CONSTITUTIONAL ENTRENCHMENT OF ECONOMIC AND SOCIAL RIGHTS IN SOUTH AFRICA

Evelyne SCHMID*

1. INTRODUCTION

This chapter examines the ability of the South African Constitutional Court to apply economic and social rights (ESR) and whether the constitutionalization of ESR represents a mechanism capable of entrenching a substantive or 'thick'[1] conception of the rule of law. After apartheid, South Africa adopted an impressive Constitution which considers international law and justiciable human rights as pillars of the new democracy. The negotiators of the new constitutional framework acknowledged that the decades of economic and social exclusion of a large proportion of South Africa's population had to end if the rule of law was to be established in a meaningful way.[2] A mere retraction of discriminatory laws and an adherence to a formal ('thin')[3] notion of the rule of law was viewed as insufficient to break with the abusive past of the apartheid era. Instead, the

* Lecturer in Law at the University of Bangor, Wales, UK. The author thanks the editors of this volume as well as the members of the COST working group on International Law in Domestic Courts for their helpful comments.

1 A 'thick' or substantive conception of the rule of law is one which not only deals with formalist attributes of a legal framework, but also with substantive notions of justice, such as equality or dignity. In the Dworkinian conception, proponents of a 'thick' understanding of the rule of law emphasize that the formal legal rules should capture and enforce substantive rights. See J. Stromseth, R. Brooks and D. Wippman, Can Might Make Rights? Building the Rule of Law after Military Interventions ch 3 (Cambridge: Cambridge University Press, 2006).

2 A. Sachs, Advancing Human Rights in South Africa xii (Cape Town: Oxford University Press, 1992).

3 A 'thin' or minimal conception of the rule of law is one which emphasizes the rule of law's formal and structural components, such as rules, legal processes and procedures regularly followed. In the Aristotelian view, a 'government of laws, not men' protects people against anarchy and allows the predictability of legal consequences. See Stromseth, Brooks and Wippman, *supra* note 1, ch 3.

drafters adopted a 'thick' account of the rule of law. The aspiration of this substantive conception of the rule of law is characterized by the commitment to the values enshrined in South Africa's Bill of Rights, including justiciable economic and social rights.[4] The preamble of the 1996 South African Constitution states that the country modified its constitutional framework in order to '[h]eal the divisions of the past and establish a society based on democratic values, social justice and fundamental human rights.'[5]

The present volume studies the effects of empowering domestic courts to apply international legal principles after countries emerge from conflict or oppressive rule. South Africa is an example of an attempt to empower domestic courts to consider international law. Perhaps even more importantly, South Africa is an example of a domestification of the international rule of law: whereas the previous Constitutions of 1910, 1961, and 1983 had no bill of rights, the drafters of the current, 1996 Constitution made a deliberate effort to harmonize the new Bill of Rights with international law. The reliance on international human rights norms was not confined to civil and political rights, but the 1996 Constitution includes a wide range of justiciable socio-economic rights and adopts language from the International Covenant on Economic, Social and Cultural Rights (ICESCR) and from General Comments of the UN Committee on Economic, Social and Cultural Rights ('the UN Committee').

This chapter examines the success of the constitutional entrenchment of ESR in South Africa's legal system. The chapter considers 'transformative constitutionalism'[6] and its ability to fulfil the ambitions, expressed in the new constitutional preamble, of setting out to establish a society based on social justice and fundamental human rights. The South African jurisprudence after the constitutionalization of human rights, in particular ESR, has been praised by the international community. Nevertheless, the central tenets of the chapter are two cautionary findings. First, the analysis cautions against using constitutional change alone to enhance the rule of law after conflict or oppressive rule. Although constitutional adjudication in South Africa has had positive outcomes, modifying the place accorded to international law in the domestic legal system is largely

4 On the varieties of substantive conceptions of the rule of law see Stromseth, Brooks and Wippman, *supra* note 1, ch 3.

5 Constitution of the Republic of South Africa, Act 108 of 1996 preamble, available at www.info.gov.za/documents/constitution/1996/index.htm ('1996 Constitution').

6 S. Liebenberg, South Africa: Adjudicating Socio-Economic Rights under a Transformative Constitution, in: M. Langford (ed.), Social Rights Jurisprudence: Emerging Trends in International and Comparative Law 75 (Cambridge University Press, 2009). According to Liebenberg, a transformative constitution is one which is to 'facilitate a fundamental change in the legacy of injustice produced over three centuries of colonial and apartheid rule.' The term goes back to K. Klare, Legal Culture and Transformative Constitutionalism, 14 South African Journal on Human Rights 146 (1998). The Constitutional Court emphasized that the new Constitution was to effect social change. *S v. Makwanyane*, 1995 (6) BCLR 665 (CC), para. 261 f; *Bato Star Fishing (Pty) Ltd v. Minister of Environmental Affairs and Tourism and Others*, 2004 (7) BCLR 687 (CC) para. 74.

insufficient for the realization of ESR and the 'thick' conception of the rule of law envisioned by the drafters of the 1996 Constitution. Second, the chapter finds that a domestic belief in the relevance of international and national legal norms was decisive in the South African experience. The constitutional empowerment of domestic courts to apply international legal principles would not, by itself, explain the practice of national courts insisting on the implementation of rights recognized in international law. Moreover, a number of unique factors related to the actors and process leading to the constitutional transformation in South Africa contribute to explain the remarkable transition towards an international law-friendly constitution. While the empowerment of domestic courts in South Africa provides lessons for other states, those lessons are primarily ones regarding limitations, complexities, and context-specific issues that arise in the empowerment of domestic courts to apply international legal principles in situations of transition.

Section 2 describes the role of international law in the domestic legal system before and after the end of apartheid. Section 3 presents the most important constitutional cases that have arisen from the ESR provisions in the 1996 Constitution. It assesses the ability of courts to deal with socio-economic rights according to two alternative criteria: the degree of formal entrenchment of international norms, and concrete improvements in the realization of the socio-economic rights litigated before the Constitutional Court. Section 4 endeavours to identify some lessons as to what can reasonably be expected from modifications of the prominence given to international law and the role of domestic courts when it comes to the vindication of economic and social human rights. Section 5 offers conclusions.

2. SOUTH AFRICAN CONSTITUTIONAL LAW DURING AND AFTER APARTHEID

The emphasis on international law and human rights in domestic proceedings in South Africa was minimal before the end of apartheid. This section delineates historical changes following South Africa's transition from apartheid.

2.1. THE 'THIN' RULE OF LAW DURING APARTHEID

The apartheid regime was built on widespread violations of social, economic, civil, and political rights.[7] Since the accession of the National Party (NP) to

7 M. Pieterse, Possibilities and Pitfalls in the Domestic Enforcement of Social Rights: Contemplating the South African Experience, 26 Human Rights Quarterly 882, 883 (2004). International Commission of Jurists (ICJ) and G. Bindman, South Africa: Human Rights and the Rule of Law (London: Pinter, 1988).

power in 1948, rights to freedom of movement, employment, electoral, education, and many others were severely restricted. Forced evictions were carried out on a massive scale.[8] In the absence of an instrument delineating constitutional human rights, the courts could not discuss or determine issues regarding potential violations of human rights by the Parliament.[9] The conception of judicial review was very narrow and courts were deferential to the (unrepresentative) legislative branch.[10] No law enacted by Parliament could be invalidated by the courts, except in relation to the 'entrenched clauses' which protected the equality of English and Afrikaans as the two official languages.[11] Judges gave effect to discriminatory and unjust laws and generally refused to interfere with administrative orders.[12] Was South Africa therefore lacking the rule of law? The answer of course depends on one's notion of the rule of law. While the apartheid regime was considered woefully illegitimate by the domestic majority and the international community,[13] apartheid was framed within a minimalist, formal rule of law regime.

South Africa's experience differs from the situation of many other transitioning countries because its courts continued to function throughout apartheid. Oppressive practices were implemented according to laws promulgated by Parliament pursuant to formal legal rules. If one would define the rule of law as mere obedience to laws adopted through formal procedures – irrespective of the substance of those laws – then apartheid was a regime implemented according to a minimal ('thin') rule of law. But not even Steven Kautz, adherent of a 'thin' notion of the rule of law, would qualify the apartheid regime as one of the rule of law. According to Kautz, it is only '*reasonable* obedience to laws that respect the natural *equality* of human beings' which constitutes the rule of law.[14]

---

8 ICJ and Bindman, *supra* note 7, p. 9.

9 Constitution of the Republic of South Africa, Act 110 of 1983, s 34(3) ('1983 Constitution').

10 D. Penna, Apartheid, the Law and Reform in South Africa, 37(2) Africa Today 5, 7 (1990). South Africa has a mixed legal system based on Roman-Dutch substantive law and English procedural law. For an introduction, see R. Zimmermann and D. Visser, Southern Cross: Civil Law and Common Law in South Africa (Oxford: Clarendon Press, 1996).

11 1983Constitution, *supra* note 9.

12 D. Ipp, Ethical Problems with Judicial Activism: Edited Version of a Paper Given at a Conference in Beijing Organised by the National Judicial College, Beijing, 12 October 2004, available at www.lawlink.nsw.gov.au/lawlink/Supreme_Court/ll_sc.nsf/pages/SCO_ipp12_191004 n 30. See also the final report of the Truth and Reconciliation Commission (TRC), analysing the role of the legal profession during apartheid: South Africa TRC, Report of the Truth and Reconciliation Commission Vol. 4 (Cape Town: The Truth and Reconciliation Commission, 2002).

13 See for instance UNGA Resolution 2202 (1966) GAOR 21st Session (16 December 1966), stating that apartheid constituted a crime against humanity.

14 Kautz defines the rule of law as reasonable obedience to laws 'to remedy our natural human condition of insecurity'. Law has to be followed, 'for its own sake and not as a means to justice.' S. Kautz, Liberty, Justice, and the Rule of Law, 11 Yale Journal of Law and the Humanities 435, 438, 468 (1999) (emphasis in original).

After closed door negotiations had been underway for some time, the 1990 release from prison of Nelson Mandela of the African National Congress (ANC) started the process towards a 'thicker' notion of the rule of law. Not without violence,[15] a long and well-documented bargaining process between the protagonists of the main parties ensued.[16] A record of understanding, signed in 1992, formed the essential core of the broader and detailed agreement finalized in June 1993 – the 'Interim Constitution'. The Interim Constitution contained 34 principles and provided for a Constitutional Court to have wide jurisdiction. The Interim Constitution also entrusted to the new Court to 'certify' the final constitution to ensure that it complied with the agreed 34 principles. In 1996, the new, amended Constitution was adopted.

2.2. INTERNATIONAL LAW IN THE NEW CONSTITUTION

In the early 1990s, the attitude in South Africa towards international law shifted profoundly. During apartheid, South Africa had not been a party to any UN or regional human rights conventions. Dugard notes how South Africa had become 'a pariah state within the international community; a delinquent state in the context of the "new" international law of human rights. Domestically, international law fared little better.'[17] The lengthy process of formalizing a new constitution was used as an opportunity to establish anew what its drafters considered the most appropriate relationships between the different branches and levels of government, as well as between domestic law and international law. The two major political forces participating in the negotiations, the governing NP and the ANC, both appeared to agree that human rights law was a necessary element of the new order. In the fall of 1992, the NP and the ANC established that the new constitution to be drafted 'shall incorporate guaranteed justiciable fundamental rights and freedoms'.[18] The 1993 Interim Constitution included a first bill of rights and provisions on the place of international law in the domestic

15 It is estimated that more than 14,000 people lost their lives in political violence. P. Du Toit, South Africa's Brittle Peace 31 (Palgrave, 2001).

16 See in particular M. Newitt and M. Bennun, Negotiating Justice: A New Constitution for South Africa (University of Exeter Press, 1995); R. Spitz and M. Chaskalson, The Politics of Transition: A Hidden History of South Africa's Negotiated Settlement (Hart Publishing, 2000); B. De Villiers, Birth of a Constitution (Kenwyn: Juta, 1994); S. Friedman and D. Atkinson, The Small Miracle: South Africa's Negotiated Settlement, 7 South African Review (1994); H. Cobban, Mozambique, Rwanda and South Africa Assessed, in: W. Schabas, R. Thakur and E. Hughes (eds), Atrocities and International Accountability: Beyond Transitional Justice 42 (Tokyo: UN University Press, 2007).

17 J. Dugard, International Law and the South African Constitution, 8 European Journal of International Law 77 (1997).

18 Record of Understanding, Concluded at a Meeting Between the State President of the Republic of South Africa and the President of the African National Congress Held at the World Trade Centre on the 26 September 1992, available at www.anc.org.za/show.php?id=4206.

legal system. The Interim Constitution was therefore conceived as 'a historic bridge between the past of a deeply divided society and a future founded on the recognition of human rights and opportunities for all South Africans'.[19]

The 1996 Constitution consolidated the interest in human rights and international law. There are four reasons for describing the 1996 Constitution as an instrument friendly to international law.[20] First, self-executing international treaty provisions can be directly implemented without prior legislative action.[21] Second, the Constitution provides that international law is a guide to judicial interpretation and must be considered by the adjudicators, and law of other national jurisdictions may be considered.[22] Third, courts are required to give priority to any interpretation consistent with international law.[23] Finally, 'when interpreting any legislation, and when developing the common law or customary law, every court, tribunal or forum must promote the spirit, purport and objects of the Bill of Rights.'[24] This clause illustrates the conception of a 'thicker' notion of the rule of law and the willingness to empower courts to transform society in a way that would 'establish a society based on democratic values, social justice and fundamental human rights.'[25] In addition, section 232 constitutionalizes the rule that customary international law is part of South African law unless it is inconsistent with the Constitution or an Act of Parliament. By entrenching international norms in the legal system, the drafters of the new Bill of Rights deliberately sought to harmonize the Constitution with international law. Furthermore, they facilitated South Africa's accession to human rights treaties and promoted reintegration of South Africa in the 'family of nations'.[26]

While the human rights provisions of the Interim Constitution were largely confined to civil and political rights,[27] the 1996 Bill of Rights extends protection to ESR. All six UN human rights conventions existing at that time were relied upon in the drafting process.[28] Interestingly, the ICESCR served as a normative guide despite South Africa's failure to ratify it.[29] According to Dugard, the importance given to international human rights norms is evident in the first case

---

19 (Interim) Constitution of the Republic of South Africa Act 200 of 1993 'postamble', available at www.info.gov.za/documents/constitution/93cons.htm ('1993 (Interim) Constitution').

20 C. Heyns and F. Viljoen, The Impact of the United Nations Human Rights Treaties on the Domestic Level 542 (The Hague: Kluwer, 2002).

21 1996 Constitution, *supra* note 5.

22 1996 Constitution, *supra* note 5, s 39(1)b.

23 1996 Constitution, *supra* note 5, s 233.

24 1996 Constitution, *supra* note 5, s 39(2).

25 1996 Constitution, *supra* note 5, preamble.

26 1996 Constitution, *supra* note 5, preamble.

27 Heyns and Viljoen, *supra* note 20, p. 553. The main exception is the right to education, which was already contained in the Interim Constitution.

28 Heyns and Viljoen, *supra* note 20, p. 552.

29 See *In Re Certification of the Constitution of the Republic of South Africa*, 1996 (10) BCLR 1253 (CC) n 46. Paradoxically, South Africa signed the treaty on 3 October 1994, but, after repeated promises, it has yet to ratify the treaty.

heard by the new Court: in 1995, in a decision on the death penalty, the Constitutional Court dispelled fears that the term 'international law' might be narrowly construed to cover only undisputed customary international law and conventions ratified by South Africa. Courts are obliged to consider public international law when interpreting the Bill of Rights,[30] and the Court insisted that this provision must be read to refer to international law broadly, including to international treaties not ratified by the Republic and soft law such as declarations or resolutions by the UN General Assembly.[31]

2.3. THE BILL OF RIGHTS AND REASONS FOR A 'THICK' CONCEPTION OF RULE OF LAW

During the negotiations of the 1996 Constitution, the widely perceived need to break with the past caused many to argue for a comprehensive Bill of Rights. This position was in the end adopted and it led to the eventual constitutionalization of ESR.[32] For the negotiators, a retraction of explicitly discriminatory laws was insufficient for building a legitimate and substantive rule of law and to consolidate a new and more equitable order.

2.3.1. Justiciable Economic and Social Rights

The core provisions regarding socio-economic rights are contained in sections 26, 27, 28(1)(c), 29, and 35(2)(e) of the 1996 Constitution.[33] Sections 26(1) and 27(1) contain the right of everyone to have access to adequate housing, health care services, sufficient food and water, and social security. The state must, under sections 26(2) and 27(2), 'take reasonable legislative and other measures, within its available resources, to achieve the progressive realisation of each of these rights'. With minor differences, these subsections mirror Article 2(1) of the ICESCR.[34] The drafters of the 1996 Constitution adopted the wording of that article and section 7 of the Constitution also embraced the tripartite typology of

30 1993 (Interim) Constitution, *supra* note 19, s 35(1) and 1983 Constitution, *supra* note 9, s 39(1)b.

31 *S v. Makwanyane*, *supra* note 6, para 35. The case concerned the death penalty; the ICCPR and foreign law were extensively used by the Court.

32 T Maluwa, International Human Rights Norms and the South African Interim Constitution 1993, 19 South African Yearbook of International Law 14 (1994).

33 1996 Constitution, *supra* note 5.

34 There are two subtle differences between the wording of the second sub-section of s 26 and 27 in the South African Constitution and Article 2(1) of the ICESCR: first, the South African provision uses 'reasonable measures' instead of 'appropriate', and the ICESCR speaks of the 'maximum of available resources', while s 26 and 27 use the standard 'within available resources'.

interdependent duties. Theoretically developed first by Shue[35] and later, by the jurisprudence of the supervisory UN Committee,[36] the state has three-dimensional obligations to respect, protect, and fulfil human rights. Sections 26 and 27 have attracted the most attention from commentators because it was on the basis of them that the Constitutional Court developed its socio-economic rights jurisprudence.[37]

The Constitution gives South African courts the power to interpret socio-economic rights, to resolve disputes by relying on the principles of socio-economic rights, and to make a just and equitable order, including the ability to award 'appropriate relief'.[38] Brand describes South African courts' impressive array of remedial powers: they can enforce constitutional socio-economic rights directly by hearing constitutional challenges to any legislation;[39] by hearing challenges that state or private conduct is inconsistent with socio-economic rights;[40] or by accepting an argument by the litigant that the law is inconsistent with the 'objective value system' underlying the particular provisions of the Bill of Rights.[41] At levels below the Constitutional Court, judges can also enforce socio-economic rights. The ability of lower courts to adjudicate these matters is significant, since these courts are more accessible and often less constrained in their ability to enforce rights, particularly if legislative, executive, or administrative action has already defined them. South Africa's law on standing is broad, such that persons can also enforce statutory commitments against the state on behalf of a group of persons or in the public interest.[42]

2.3.2. Inspiration from International Law

The constitutionalization of justiciable ESR was controversial. Those opposed to the inclusion of ESR argued that empowering courts to enforce them would breach the separation of powers and would interfere with the budgetary and

35 H. Shue, Rights in the Light of Duties, in: P. Brown and D. MacLean (eds), Human Rights and US Foreign Policy (Lexington: Lexington Books, 1979).

36 UN Committee on Economic, Social and Cultural Rights, General Comment No. 12 on the Right to Adequate Food (E/C.12/1999/5) (12 May 1999), para. 15; and UN Committee on Economic, Social and Cultural Rights, General Comment No. 14 on the Right to the Highest Attainable Standard of Health (E/CN.12/2000/4) (11 August 2000), para. 33.

37 See S. Liebenberg, Protecting Economic, Social and Cultural Rights under Bills of Rights: The South African Experience, 16 Human Rights Defender 2 (2007).

38 1996 Constitution, *supra* note 5, s 38.

39 See D. Brand, Socio-Economic Rights and Courts in South Africa: Justiciability on a Sliding Scale, in: F. Coomans (ed.), Justiciability of Economic and Social Rights: Experiences from Domestic Systems 207 (Antwerpen: 5 Maastricht Series in Human Rights, Intersentia, 2006).

40 The Court could overturn such conduct and draft a constitutional remedy.

41 If the court would accept this argument, it could interpret the statutory provision in question, or develop the common law rule so as to give effect to the spirit, purport, and objects of the Bill of Rights.

42 1996 Constitution, *supra* note 5, s 38.

policy competences of the legislative branch.[43] Furthermore, they considered that ESR were difficult to adjudicate due to the perception that they were of an exclusively 'positive nature', and 'unclearly defined'.[44] The discussions largely mirrored the international debates on the justiciability of socio-economic rights. However, concerns of overly powerful courts or an infringement of the separation of powers eventually gave way to a thicker conception of the rule of law based on the values enshrined in the Bill of Rights.[45]

Civil society and supporters of a comprehensive Bill of Rights relied heavily on the ICESCR to campaign for the inclusion of ESR.[46] According to Liebenberg, three arguments proved particularly persuasive.[47] First, the Bill of Rights – the reflection of the highest normative commitments of the nation – should explicitly outline provisions for redressing the systemic socio-economic deprivation experienced by the black population under colonial and apartheid rule.[48] Second, without access to basic services and resources, it would be difficult to enjoy many of the civil and political rights.[49] Third, socio-economic rights were regarded as integral to the creation of a more equitable society. In the *First Certification* judgment, the Constitutional Court dismissed arguments that it was infringing on the legislature's powers when it adjudicates socio-economic matters having budgetary implications.[50] The Court held that it had the power to determine accountability of the government with respect to all rights included in the Bill of Rights and thus also the enforcement of ESR.[51] The road was thus paved for constitutional litigation of ESR provisions which are, according to the

43 See D. Davis, The Case against the Inclusion of Socio-Economic Demands in a Bill of Rights except as Directive Principles, 8 South African Journal on Human Rights 475 (1992); A. Sachs, Concluding Comments on the Panel Discussion, 8 ESR Review 17 (2007) (describing opponents' arguments).

44 South African Law Commission, Group and Human Rights: Interim Report (Pretoria: The Law Commission, 1991).

45 See, for instance, ANC Submission to the Theme Committee, 23 September 1995, and Lawyers for Human Rights Submission, 30 July 1995; both discussed in Heyns and Viljoen, *supra* note 20, p. 553.

46 Heyns and Viljoen, *supra* note 20, p. 553.

47 Liebenberg, *supra* note 37.

48 For the arguments of proponents: N. Haysom, Constitutionalism, Majoritarian Democracy and Socio-Economic Rights, 8 South African Journal on Human Rights 451 (1992); E. Mureinik, Beyond a Charter of Luxuries: Economic Rights in the Constitution, 8 South African Journal on Human Rights 464 (1992); C. Scott and P. Macklem, Constitutional Ropes of Sand or Justiciable Guarantees Social Rights in a New South African Constitution, 141 University of Pennsylvania Law Review 1 (1992).

49 In Mandela's words, 'we do not want freedom without bread, nor do we want bread without freedom'. N. Mandela, Address on the Occasion of the ANC's Bill of Rights Conference 12 (A Bill of Rights for a Democratic South Africa: Papers and Report of a Conference Convened by the ANC Constitutional Committee, 1991).

50 In *Re Certification of the Constitution of the Republic of South Africa*, *supra* note 29.

51 In *Re Certification of the Constitution of the Republic of South Africa*, *supra* note 29, paras 76–78.

Constitutional Court, 'clearly modelled'[52] on the most relevant international instrument in this respect – the ICESCR.

3. EVALUATING THE EMPOWERMENT OF COURTS TO ADDRESS ESR

The Constitutional Court has developed extensive jurisprudence on socio-economic rights and in so doing has relied upon international norms. This section outlines the Court's approach to some of the socio-economic rights enshrined in the Bill of Rights.

3.1. IF AND HOW INTERNATIONAL NORMS HAVE BEEN USED

References to international ESR norms serve as potential indicators of the extent to which these norms are entrenched at the domestic level. Another possible indicator is the emphasis given to ESR by the highest instance court; in other words, whether the Constitutional Court uses its constitutional powers to review ESR related cases.

The first case on ESR following the certification of the 1996 Constitution involved an application for an order directing a hospital to provide the appellant with ongoing renal dialysis. The Court held that, given the limited resources and the patient's poor health condition, the denial of the treatment, even if life-sustaining, did not breach constitutional rights.[53] While it was factually a difficult first case, the Court was able to confirm its role as an adjudicator of socio-economic rights claims. In several subsequent cases, the Court has refused the government's arguments that resource constraints were the sole reason for a lack of progress in the realm of ESR, holding that the government failed to demonstrate that every reasonable effort had been made to use all resources at its disposition. Cases such as *Government of the Republic of South Africa v. Grootboom*,[54] *Minister of Health v. Treatment Action Campaign*,[55] *Khosa v. Minister of Social Development*,[56] *Port Elizabeth Municipality v. Various Occupiers*,[57] or the more

[52] *Residents of Bon Vista Mansions v. Southern Metropolitan Local Council*, 2002 (6) BCLR 625 (Witwatersrand Local Division), para 15.

[53] *Soobramoney v. Minister of Health (Kwazulu-Natal)*, 1997 (12) BCLR 1696 (CC).

[54] *Government of the Republic of South Africa et al v. Grootboom et al*, 2001 (11) BCLR 1169 (CC).

[55] *Minister of Health v. Treatment Action Campaign (TAC)*, 2002 (5) SA 721 (CC).

[56] *Khosa and Others v. Minister of Social Development and Others, Mahlaule and Another v. Minister of Social Development*, 2004 (6) BCLR 569 (CC).

[57] *Port Elizabeth Municipality v. Various Occupiers*, 2004 (12) BCLR 1268 (CC).

recent cases *Occupiers of 51 Olivia Road v. City of Johannesburg*,[58] *Joe Slovo Community v. Thubelisha Homes & Others*,[59] and *Mazibuko v. City of Johannesburg*,[60] all underscore the reality of the judicial enforcement of ESR. Cases on purely negative duties, which are not subject to the qualifications of progressive realization and resource constraints, have also been successfully litigated by claimants.[61] In the *Treatment Action Campaign (TAC)* case, the Court requested the government to provide anti-retroviral drugs to reduce the rate of HIV transmission from mothers to children. The *TAC* case stands for the unequivocal dismissal of the government's argument that courts are not empowered to grant remedies other than declarations in complex ERS cases.[62]

In these landmark decisions on rights, mostly qualified by progressive realization and resource constraints,[63] the Court has adopted a standard of 'reasonableness'.[64] A particularly interesting decision is *President v. Modderklip*, in which the Constitutional Court expressly linked the implementation of constitutional ESR with the rule of law. The Court found that the state's failure to avoid the eviction of a community with no alternative housing secured was a violation of section 1(c) of the Constitution, which states that South Africa is a democratic state founded on the 'supremacy of the constitution and the rule of law'.[65] In the view of the Court, the rule of law therefore requires substantive steps taken by the state to actively protect ESR. By holding that the failure to avoid the homelessness of the community amounted to an infringement of the rule of law, the Court thus indicated that the constitutional framework favours a 'thick' account of the rule of law characterized by the commitment to the values enshrined in the Bill of Rights.

---

58 *Occupiers of 51 Olivia Road, Berea Township and 197 Main Street Johannesburg v. City of Johannesburg and Others*, 2008 (5) BCLR 475 (CC).

59 *Residents of Joe Slovo Community, Western Cape v. Thubelisha Homes & Others*, CCT 22/08 [2009] ZACC 16.

60 *Lindiwe Mazibuko and Others v. City of Johannesburg and Others*, Case CCT 39/09, 2009 ZACC 28.

61 The case of *Jaftha v. Schoeman and Others, Van Rooyen v. Stoltz and Others*, 2005 (1) BCLR 78 (CC), involved a successful challenge to an Act that permitted the sale in execution of people's homes in order to satisfy debts without judicial oversight.

62 Pieterse, *supra* note 7, p. 894 and the *TAC* case, *supra* note 55, para. 38.

63 Not all economic and social rights are qualified by progressive realization. Exceptions are for instance children's ESR, the right not to be refused emergency treatment, or the right not to be evicted without a court order.

64 The *Soobramoney* Court, *supra* note 53, started to establish criteria for assessing reasonableness, and these criteria have since been elaborated. A government program must be comprehensive, coherent, coordinated; appropriate financial and human resources must be made available; it must be balanced and flexible and make appropriate provision for short, medium, and long-term needs; it must be reasonably conceived and implemented; it must be transparent, and its contents must be made known to the public. In *Grootboom*, *supra* note 54, the Court mentioned that those whose needs are most urgent must not be ignored by the measures.

65 *President of the Republic of South Africa and Another v. Modderklip Boerdery (Pty) Ltd*, 2005 (8) BCLR 786 (CC), para. 47.

The new constitutional era has led to the inclusion of international law principles in the decisions of the Constitutional Court. The practice of construing the term 'international law' broadly to include soft law instruments was reaffirmed in a 2009 decision on the right to housing. In *Joe Slovo Community v. Thubelisha Homes*, the Court affirmed an eviction order but referred to General Comment No. 7 of the UN Committee supervising the implementation of the ICESCR to make the point that evictions should not result in people being rendered homeless.[66] According to de Wet, the Court however lacks a uniform and consistent strategy in considering non-applicable human rights instruments and soft law; it is often reluctant to consider international law norms other than those contained in human rights instruments.[67] Other commentators have noted that the Justices sometimes have failed to carefully ascertain the existence of an international rule before concluding whether its interpretations were consistent with international law.[68]

3.2. SIMILARITIES AND DIFFERENCES BETWEEN THE SOUTH AFRICAN ESR JURISPRUDENCE AND INTERNATIONAL NORMATIVE DEVELOPMENTS

Three aspects of the South African jurisprudence reveal similarities and differences in the ways ESR have been interpreted by the South African Constitutional Court and at the international level. As the sub-sections below describe, first, there are examples of the Court in the past overlooking the applicability of relevant ESR provisions. Second, the Court has refused to apply the controversial minimum core concept developed by the UN Committee. Third, the interaction between international and domestic norms is two-directional and South African jurisprudence was incorporated into one of the newest international human rights law treaties, the Optional Protocol to the ICESCR.

3.2.1. Non-Application of Relevant ESR Provisions

Commentators have raised concerns that the Constitutional Court has sometimes denied applicability of the provision on ESR most specifically dealing with the core of a claim.[69] For instance, despite the clear language in section 28 of the Bill

66 *Residents of Joe Slovo Community, Western Cape v. Thubelisha Homes and Others*, 2009 (9) BCLR 847 (CC), para. 232. The Court insisted on meaningful engagement between public authorities and the persons to be evicted.

67 E. de Wet, The 'Friendly but Cautious' Reception of International Law in the Jurisprudence of the South African Constitutional Court: Some Critical Remarks, 28 Fordham International Law Journal 1529 (2005).

68 See eg Dugard, *supra* note 17, p. 90, discussing the use of amnesties in *Azanian Peoples Organisation and Others v. President of the Republic*, 1996 (8) BCLR 1015 (CC).

69 See C. Scott, Reaching Beyond (without Abandoning) the Category of Economic, Social and Cultural Rights, 21 Human Rights Quarterly 633, 639 (1999).

of Rights that children's rights to basic food, shelter, and health are not subject to progressive realization,[70] the Court's openness to international law did not result in the prioritization of economic and social rights obligations contained in the Convention on the Rights of the Child.[71] Instead of applying section 28, which relates to children's ESR, the Court held in *Grootboom* that section 26, subject to progressive realization, was the only applicable right in that case.[72] Despite the generally progressive approach by the Court of ESR interpretation, here, its interpretation appears more limited than the text of the Constitution would require it to be.

3.2.2. *Rejection of the Minimum Core Concept*

There is at least one area in which the South African jurisprudence differs from concepts developed at the international level. Although not uncontroversial at the international level,[73] the UN Committee has developed a 'minimum core standard' of socio-economic rights as a means of delineating the most basic state obligations under the ICESCR. These minimum levels of rights are, according to the Committee, not subjected to progressive realization.[74] The South African Constitutional Court did not adopt this concept. Claimants in the *Grootboom* case were about to be evicted from slums with no alternative housing solution. The Constitutional Court ruled that the individuals could not be evicted until an acceptable housing alternative had been provided for them, but it explicitly rejected the existence of a minimum core obligation underlying sections 26 and 27.[75] The Court confirmed this stance in the *Mazibuko* case, in which poor residents in Soweto challenged the authorities' plan for a new water policy to curb water losses, leaking pipes, and unpaid bills. The question of whether the Court should adopt a minimum core approach (in this case, a certain number of litres of free water per person) was at the centre of the decision. The unanimous Court underscored that while international law, including soft law, was relevant and helpful for the resolution of constitutional disputes, it would not adopt the

---

70 1996 Constitution, *supra* note 5, s 28(1)c, providing that 'every child has the right to basic nutrition, shelter, basic health care services and social services'.

71 South Africa ratified the Convention on the Rights of the Child in 1995.

72 *Grootboom*, *supra* note 54, para. 71. Discussed in Pieterse, *supra* note 7, p. 900 and C. Scott and P. Alston, Adjudicating Constitutional Priorities in a Transnational Context: A Comment on *Soobramoney*'s Legacy and *Grootboom*'s Promise, 16 South African Journal on Human Rights (2000).

73 K. Young, The Minimum Core of Economic and Social Rights: A Concept in Search of Content, 33 Yale Journal of International Law 113 (2008).

74 The concept first appears in UN Committee on Economic, Social and Cultural Rights, General Comment No. 3 on the nature of states parties obligations (E/1991/23) (14 December 1992), para. 10.

75 *Grootboom*, *supra* note 54, paras 30–33. For an analysis of the implications of the refusal to acknowledge the existence of minimum core obligations, see Pieterse, *supra* note 7, p. 898.

minimum core approach as posited by the UN Committee.[76] Rather, as already held in *Grootboom* and *TAC*, the Court repeated that the appropriate test for assessing whether ESR are 'progressively realised within available resources' was one of 'reasonableness'. This standard of review has been criticized as being deferential and failing to engage with the substance of the rights in question. However, recourse to the principle of reasonableness allowed the Court to find a policy unreasonable without having to prescribe to the other branches of government what they must do in order to act reasonably.[77] Pieterse has sceptically appraised that standard, comparing it to the standard of reasonableness in administrative law,[78] a principle of common law that also applied during apartheid.[79] According to Pieterse, '[b]y retreating to the comfort zone of administrative law, the *Grootboom* Court has made an important conceptual gain – it has mapped out a (what it considers appropriate) role for the judiciary in adjudicating the often polycentric issues raised by social rights claims. In doing so, *Grootboom* illustrates that vindicating social rights is not as far removed from courts' "ordinary" review function as is often contended.'[80]

There are, however, three reasons why the rejection of the minimum core test in the South African jurisprudence should not be overemphasized. First, reasonableness is a standard found in the South African Constitution and as such, it is natural that the Court invokes it over the unsettled concepts developed by the UN Committee. Second, the idea of a minimum core is actually similar to the South African reasonableness test. Fredman, for instance, has convincingly likened the minimum core with a right to action from the state and right to require the state to take immediate steps according to a plan that has to be designed taking equality and public participation into account.[81] This understanding of the minimum core concept, as opposed to an approach interested in a predetermined baseline of a bundle of goods, indeed closely resembles the South African reasonableness test. Third, regardless of whether the Court refers to a minimum core or a test of reasonableness, the more important question is whether deference has gone too far, so that the test employed no longer provides for practical meaning of constitutional rights. The recent *Mazibuko* decision indeed illustrates the implications of turning the reasonableness standard into a very deferential test. As Fredman explains, while the Court considered it appropriate to demand justification for government

76 *Mazibuko*, *supra* note 60, paras 52–61.

77 Brand, *supra* note 39, p. 227 and Liebenberg, *supra* note 37, p. 5.

78 Pieterse, *supra* note 7, p. 893.

79 J. Meierhenrich, The Legacies of Law: Long-Run Consequences of Legal Development in South Africa 1652–2000 287 (Cambridge: Cambridge University Press, 2008).

80 Pieterse, *supra* note 7, p. 893. See also C.R. Sunstein, Designing Democracy: What Constitutions Do 234 (New York: Oxford University Press, 2001).

81 S. Fredman, Socio-Economic Rights in the South African Constitutional Court: Is the Honeymoon Over? (Oxford Transitional Justice Research, 8 March 2010), available at media.podcasts.ox.ac.uk/socleg/otjr_seminars/michalowski-fredman-medium-audio.mp3.

policies,[82] it was overly forthcoming in accepting the justification advanced by the authorities.[83] While the *Mazibuko* case was litigated in South African courts, the conceptual approach of reasonableness review turned out to be the one which resolved the last remaining issue in the negotiation of the Optional Protocol to the ICESCR, as the next section illustrates.

3.2.3. South African Jurisprudence Influences the Optional Protocol to the ICESCR

The Optional Protocol (OP) to the ICESCR is the procedural instrument that will, once entered into force, allow the supervisory body to receive individual communications on rights contained in the ICESCR.[84] The appropriate standard of review of communications was resolved only in the last moments of the drafting. The Gordian knot was cut with language borrowed from the jurisprudence of the South African Constitutional Court. Article 8(4) of the OP directs the Committee 'to consider the reasonableness of the steps taken by the State Party in accordance with part II of the Covenant.'[85] Porter appropriately summarizes that 'just as the South African Constitutional Court has incorporated jurisprudence from the ICESCR into its own domestic jurisprudence, so has South African jurisprudence now informed the text of an international human rights instrument.'[86] Thus, although South Africa is still not a state party to the Covenant,[87] it has influenced the relevant normative reference to assess a state's compliance with the obligations contained in the ICESCR.

So far, this chapter has discussed the jurisprudence of the South African Constitutional Court in light of the references it has made to international norms on ESR, affirming international principles pertaining to socio-economic rights on multiple occasions. It has dismissed arguments denying its institutional competence to deal with ESR and it has shown a notable openness to a variety of international legal sources. At the same time, discomforting signs of a potentially deferential use of the reasonableness review and a rejection of the applicability of some ESR provisions indicate that the Court's comfort zone has its limits. Measured against the legal situation prevailing two decades ago, the country has shown remarkable capacity to transform its legal system and the place it accords

82 Fredman, *supra* note 81.

83 For instance, the Court accepted a legalistic interpretation that residents who cannot afford additional water credit do not suffer 'discontinuation' of water unlawful under the Water Services Act, but merely a 'suspension in water services'. *Mazibuko*, *supra* note 60, para. 115.

84 UNGA, Optional Protocol to the International Covenant on Economic, Social and Cultural Rights (A/Res/63/117) (adopted 10 December 2008) (OP to the ICESCR).

85 OP to the ICESCR, *supra* note 84, art. 8(4).

86 B. Porter, The Reasonableness of Article 8(4) – Adjudicating Claims from the Margins, 27 Nordisk Tidsskrift for Menneskerettigheter 39, 50 (2009).

87 See Heyns and Viljoen, *supra* note 20, p. 46 and n 29.

to international law and human rights law in particular. But to what extent has the entrenchment of ESR norms led to concrete improvements in the realization of human rights? An assessment of purely formal aspects, such as whether the Court cites international human rights treaties or General Comments, does not answer the question whether progress has been made towards realizing the ends of human rights law and, by extension, of the rule of law.

3.3. WHETHER ENTRENCHING INTERNATIONAL ESR NORMS HAS LED TO CONCRETE IMPROVEMENTS

Kleinfeld is justifiably critical of the fact that the current rule of law literature is overly focused on institutions and formal legal outcomes, rather than on what she calls 'the ends of rule of law'.[88] Ends of the rule of law include substantive criteria, such as concrete protection of human rights and equality.[89] To evaluate success in realizing such ends, the analysis must go beyond an assessment of the interactions between international legal norms of ESR and the case law of courts. The preamble of the 1996 Constitution describes unabashedly ambitious ends-based criteria: that the entrenchment of ESR in the Bill of Rights would lead to 'a society based on democratic values, social justice and fundamental human rights'.[90]

For a former Chief Justice of the South African Constitutional Court, 'what counts is the effect on the ground. Judicial protection of human rights must ultimately translate into a utility that is real and accessible to those that need it the most.'[91] Despite the international praise of *Grootboom* and other decisions, the actual impact of that judgment on the housing situation of the litigants and those who find themselves in a similar situation has been very limited.[92] In 2008, Irene Grootboom, the main litigant in the 2001 landmark case, died homeless.[93] A study completed a few months prior to her death found that the decision of the Court did not translate into effective implementation, essentially because of a 'failure to plan proactively, lack of co-operative governance and inadequate

88 R. Kleinfeld, Competing Definitions of the Rule of Law, in: T. Carothers (ed.), Promoting the Rule of Law Abroad: In Search of Knowledge 34 (Carnegie Endowment for International Peace, 2006).

89 Kleinfeld, *supra* note 88, p. 35.

90 1996 Constitution, *supra* note 5, preamble.

91 P. Langa, Taking Dignity Seriously – Judicial Reflections on the Optional Protocol to the ICESCR, 27 Nordisk Tidsskrift for Menneskerettigheter 29, 31 (2009).

92 K. Pillay, Implementing *Grootboom* – Supervision Needed, 3 ESR Review: Economic and Social Rights in South Africa 1, 3 (2002).

93 P. Joubert, Grootboom Dies Homeless and Penniless, Mail & Guardian (Johannesburg, 8 August 2008), available at www.mg.co.za/article/2008-08-08-grootboom-dies-homeless-and-penniless.

controls over financial and human resources' at the level of local government.[94] From a constitutional law perspective, the *Grootboom* judgment propelled the jurisprudence on ESR and even influenced the wording of a new international treaty. But the picture is rather bleak if one measures the success according to ends-based criteria about the concrete realization of the economic and social rights of the litigants and others similarly placed.

Apart from sometimes weakly implemented decisions, the wider effects of the constitutionalization of ESR have also fallen short of achieving the ambitious transformative goals expressed in the Constitution's preamble, which envisages 'a society based on democratic values, social justice and fundamental human rights'.[95] In the decade after the adoption of the new Constitution, the country has improved in the protection of civil and political rights,[96] but despite significant economic growth, South Africa remains a country where large parts of society *de facto* continue to be denied access to work, health, or education.[97] Paradoxically, fifteen years after this remarkable negotiated transition, socio-economic inequalities have increased in South Africa.[98]

The effects of constitutionalizing ESR norms have been modest both on a formal and a practical level. Further complicating the picture are a number of factors specific to South Africa. These contextual factors cast doubt on the independent value of textual transformations of a constitution. Some of the assumptions behind transformative constitutionalism as a rule of law strategy may thus have to be rethought. Yet, we do not have to end on an entirely pessimistic note.

4. IDENTIFYING LESSONS FROM A GLASS HALF EMPTY

The literature discusses a number of factors which may have made South Africa a unique case and which may explain the relative success of its formal transition. As discussed below, these factors include special characteristics of the process and actors through which the 1996 Constitution came into being, as well as a shared belief among the stakeholders in the relevance of law.[99]

94 H. Kruuse, Life in the Suburbs After '*Grootboom*': The Role of Local Government in Realising Housing Rights in the Eastern Cape (LLM thesis, Rhodes University, 2008).

95 1996 Constitution, *supra* note 5, preamble.

96 Two available measurements are Freedom House, Freedom in the World 2009: South Africa (Washington DC: Freedom House, 2009). M. Gibney, L. Cornett and R. Wood, Political Terror Scale 1976–2008, available at www.politicalterrorscale.org.

97 M. Leibbrandt et al, Trends in South African Income Distribution and Poverty since the Fall of Apartheid 67 (OECD, Paris 2010).

98 Leibbrandt, *supra* note 97, p. 4.

99 Other unique aspects not discussed here were the ability of the leadership to overcome inter-group enmity, other elements which helped to legitimize the state (such as the Truth and

4.1. PROCESS AND ACTORS

One unique factor of South Africa's transition is that most, if not all, of the protagonists negotiating the new constitutional framework were domestic actors. While there was international pressure to end apartheid,[100] and a number of foreign academics played a role in informing the debate,[101] the actual negotiation process was domestically driven: domestic civil society lobbied for the new Bill of Rights in general and for the inclusion of ESR in particular,[102] and law clinics at non-white universities drew attention to abuses during the apartheid era.[103] While international pressure and the years of naming and shaming likely influenced the constitutional negotiations, it was the government itself that, to the surprise of most jurists, changed its attitude to the Bill of Rights and abandoned its original opposition to human rights.[104] Domestic ownership of such a process heavily influences the degree of legitimacy afforded to the new constitution.[105] Equally important is the degree of public involvement in the process of constitution-making. Posters, pop songs, television debates and cartoons explained the process and urged people to share their thoughts on the new constitutional order. This unparalleled degree of public involvement meant that 1.9 million people offered their ideas on the new Constitution.[106]

The constitutional process in South Africa differed from recent experiences in other transitional countries. Despite the rhetoric of 'local ownership', international actors and foreign states often impose impetus, resources, and timetables. Since its transition was domestically driven, South Africa had no external time restrictions in its constitutional process, engaging in a five to seven-year transformation project.[107] Conversely, Kosovo's recent constitutional process took hardly more than a year,[108] and Iraq is a textbook example of a

---

Reconciliation Commission), economic interdependency, and the country's ability to move from an initial period of formal, guaranteed power sharing (consociationalism) to a more integrative approach of power-sharing.

100 D. Rothchild, Managing Ethnic Conflict in Africa (Washington DC: Brookings Institution Press, 1997).

101 Aucoin recommends that outside actors should confine their role in constitution-making to form the debate and to create a participatory process. L. Aucoin, The Role of International Experts in Constitution-Making-Myth and Reality, 5 Georgetown Journal of International Affairs 89, 90 (2004).

102 For an overview of civil society in South Africa, see J. Stremlau and H. Zille, A House No Longer Divided: Progress and Prospects for Democratic Peace in South Africa (Washington DC: Carnegie Commission on Preventing Deadly Conflict, 1997).

103 Stromseth, Brooks and Wippman, *supra* note 1, p. 334.

104 ICJ and Bindman, *supra* note 7, p. 142.

105 T. Carothers, Aiding Democracy Abroad: The Learning Curve 260 (Carnegie Endowment for International Peace, 1999).

106 T. Sisk, International Mediation in Civil Wars 104 (Routledge, London, 2009).

107 Stromseth, Brooks and Wippman, *supra* note 1, p. 96.

108 J. Tunheim, Rule of Law and the Kosovo Constitution, 18 Minnesota Journal of International Law 371, 365 (2009).

rushed process driven by international timetables.[109] It is likely that the domestic ownership over the process and its timing helps explain the largely positive attitude of South Africans towards this document.[110] Commentaries also suggest that a separation of the process into different phases, namely the record of understanding in 1992 and the 1993 Interim Constitution, helped to facilitate transparency and credibility over time.[111]

4.2. LEGAL TRADITION AND A SHARED BELIEF IN THE RELEVANCE OF LAW

Meierhenrich has examined another significant distinctiveness of the South African example: the shared belief in the centrality of law. His main argument is that in South Africa, law assisted the negotiators in the framing of complex problems and contributed to the enforcement of credible commitments. While he insists that his analysis is in no way apologetic about apartheid, he points out that even the illiberal legal norms and institutions of the apartheid era had an important structuring effect on democratic outcomes.[112] Meierhenrich argues that path-dependent confidence in the utility of law in the transition from authoritarian rule created the conditions for the emergence of trust between democracy-demanding and democracy-resisting elites.[113] Mandela and De Klerk – lawyers themselves – both acknowledged the legacy of South Africa's legal tradition. The perceived capacity of the legal order to positively matter for the purposes of social change is eloquently described by former Justice Albie Sachs:

> In the case of South Africa, the rules that govern purchase and sale and insurance and companies and cheques, that deal with self-defence and dishonesty and with when people should be held responsible for injuries to others, happened to have come from Europe. Like the railways and trousers and dresses and Bibles and the English language, they came in the context of dispossession and domination, but like the railways and trousers and dresses and the Bible and the English language, they [...] have now become South Africanised. [...] Shorn of their associations with domination, there is no reason why these institutions should not be taken over and infused with a new spirit so as to serve the people as a whole rather than just a minority.[114]

---

109 J. Morrow, Iraq's Constitutional Process II an Opportunity Lost 8 f (Washington DC: United States Institute of Peace, 2005).

110 Stromseth, Brooks and Wippman, *supra* note 1, p. 343.

111 Stromseth, Brooks and Wippman, *supra* note 1, p. 92 and United States Institute of Peace, Iraq's Constitutional Process: Shaping a Vision for the Country's Future (Washington DC: United States Institute of Peace, 2005).

112 Meierhenrich, *supra* note 79, p. 3.

113 Meierhenrich, *supra* note 79, p. 4 (footnotes omitted).

114 A. Sachs, The Future of Roman Dutch Law in a Non-Racial Democratic South Africa: Some Preliminary Observations, 1 Social and Legal Studies 217, 223 (1992).

In South Africa, there was a shared conception that law matters. Unfortunately, there is no reason to assume that such a belief is ubiquitous in other states emerging from a repressive regime or from an armed conflict. Courts cannot invent such belief in the relevance of law. As Stromseth explains, 'when people believe law matters, it will matter; when people think law does not matter, it rarely can, and few rule of law programs pay explicit attention to the conundrum of how to go from the latter stage to the former'.[115] With regard to ESR in South Africa, the formal status of the ICCPR was not of decisive importance for its relevance in the domestic jurisprudence.[116] Rather, the ICCPR was relevant due to the attitude of the judiciary and their opinion about the division of power between the legislature and the judiciary.[117]

The recommendation that follows is that the South African experience should not be considered as a model that can be readily replicated in other situations. The belief in the relevance of international human rights norms and the perceived jurisdictional authority of the South African courts appear to have been a precondition for the entrenchment of ESR in the domestic legal system – and even under those fertile conditions, the practical success so far has been relative. Considering that these contextual factors present in South Africa differ radically from many other transitioning states, should we therefore be pessimistic about the effects of entrenching international norms in the domestic legal system? The concluding section offers broader considerations on the benefits that the South African experience with ESR may offer to assist assessing the merits and pitfalls of constitutional engineering.

5. CONCLUSION

This chapter has dealt with South Africa's efforts to entrench a thicker conception of the rule of law by constitutionalising ESR rights within the domestic Bill of Rights. Severe poverty, inequality, and discrimination were key features and consequences of apartheid. Rather than 'merely' clarifying the role of different branches of government and restraining the state's power from interfering with citizens' lives, the South African Bill of Rights was envisioned as assisting in the creation of a more equal society based on respect for human rights. By delineating the inclusion of ESR and therefore the new emphasis placed upon international law in the domestic legal system, this chapter has provided a mixed picture of the

115 Stromseth, Brooks and Wippman, *supra* note 1, p. 312.

116 A similar argument is made by Heyns and Viljoen, *supra* note 20, p. 569 f.

117 P. Van Dijk, Domestic Status of Human Rights Treaties and the Attitude of the Judiciary – the Dutch Case, in: M. Nowak, D. Steurer and H. Tretter (eds), Progress in the Spirit of Human Rights: Festschrift für Felix Ermacora 631 (Kehl: Engel, 1988); M. Craven, The Domestic Application of the International Covenant on Economic, Social and Cultural Rights, 403 Netherlands International Law Review 367, 389 (1993).

success of the transformative constitutionalist ambitions. While the judicial system has demonstrated a significant increase in the adoption of international legal principles, the practical impact of the Constitutional Court's decisions on socio-economic rights are insufficient in themselves to establish a society based on social justice and fundamental human rights. The effects of constitutionalism can only be considered as one, albeit crucial, aspect of a much larger societal project. This chapter therefore cautions that rule of law programming that tries to entrench ESR in a domestic legal system should consider the South African experience as a reminder of the complexities involved in a such project, rather than an example of a fast-track solution to redress past and present inequalities.

Arthurs exposes assumptions underlying contemporary models of transformative constitutionalism that are based on a belief in constitutional adjudication as a way of transforming economies and polities, societies, and cultures. He points out that 'written texts, entrenched rights and constitutional litigation do not and cannot actually contribute much to fundamental social and political transformations'.[118] Examining India, South Africa, and Germany as countries that adopted a new constitutional regime in the aftermath of conflict, colonialism, and authoritarianism, Arthurs observes that in all three cases the judiciary 'often, if not always, applied [human, political and social rights] energetically and imaginatively'.[119] Ultimately however, as suggested in this chapter, the most relevant question is one which inquires as to the actual contribution of this new constitution to social, political, or economic transformation. In Arthurs' view, 'constitutional litigation has only a marginal effect on public policy, practical governance and the allocation of public goods'.[120]

There are nevertheless good reasons to be somewhat more optimistic. By affirming human rights, courts legitimate their practice and advocacy, which in turn contributes to the wider legitimization of claims based on socio-economic rights language.[121] It seems that in South Africa, the best outcomes were achieved where constitutional litigation was not an alternative strategy to social mobilization, but rather an essential element of a wider campaign.[122] In other words, where civil society was able to combine the court-based litigation strategy

118 H. Arthurs, Constitutionalism: An Idea Whose Time Has Come...And Gone?, 75 Amicus Curiae 4 (2008).

119 Arthurs, *supra* note 118, p. 6.

120 Arthurs, *supra* note 118, p. 6.

121 Arthurs, *supra* note 118, p. 8.

122 S. Robins, From Revolution to Rights in South Africa: Social Movements, NGOs & Popular Politics after Apartheid (Woodbridge: University of Kwazulu-Natal Press, 2008); J. Squires et al (eds), The Road to a Remedy: Current Issues in the Litigation of Economic, Social, and Cultural Rights, 2005 233 (Sydney: University of New South Wales Press, 2006); D. Davis, Socio-Economic Rights: The Promise and Limitation: The South African Experience, in: D. Barak-Erez and A.M. Gross (eds), Exploring Social Rights: Between Theory and Practice 211 (Oxford: Hart, 2007).

rights with a broader mobilization, as in the *TAC* case, the new Bill of Rights had good prospects of contributing to practical changes. The *TAC* judgment probably saved thousands of lives by ordering that the government act 'without delay' to provide antiretroviral drugs and that it undertake reasonable measures to provide testing and counselling facilities.[123] Moreover, unlike the *Grootboom* decision, *TAC* was much better implemented in practice.[124] The *Mazibuko* water case was another example of a case which was pursued in tandem with social mobilization efforts. Even if the Court ultimately rejected the applicants' arguments, it emphasized that the constitutional obligation to ensure progressive realization of ESR entails that any policies must be continually monitored.[125] It has been argued that at least some engagement by the authorities was spurred by the litigation in the case itself.[126] Hence, even unsuccessful cases can sometimes lead to changes in policies during the process of litigation, while successful but unimplemented cases like *Grootboom* can lay the foundation for effective future decisions.[127] Wickeri explains that 'despite the absence of sweeping change for South Africans living in informal settlements, *Grootboom* provided a powerful tool for communities involved in evictions proceedings, building a growing body of right-to-housing case-law based on discrete victories for various communities.'[128]

Many countries emerging from conflict or oppressive rule face daunting challenges as a result of denials of socio-economic rights for large parts of their populations. Even if several crucial aspects made South Africa's transition unique, its constitutional moment enables us to think anew of the complexities facing actors promoting the rule of law. The drafters of the 1996 Constitution acknowledged that a substantive or 'thick' understanding of the rule of law must be established if the structural injustices were to be addressed. They hoped that the constitutionalization of socio-economic rights would contribute to the country's social transformation. Fifteen years later, it can be said that entrusting

---

123 *TAC* case, *supra* note 55, para. 135.

124 See also Centre on Housing Rights and Evictions, Litigating Economic, Social and Cultural Rights: Achievements, Challenges and Strategies ch 11 (Geneva: COHRE, 2004). Implementation has been much better than in *Grootboom*, *supra* note 54, but not entirely without problems. See, for instance, TAC submits complaint to Human Rights Commission Against Minister of Health and MEC for Health of Mpumalanga (2 December 2002), available at www.tac.org.za/community/node/2478.

125 *Mazibuko*, *supra* note 60, para. 40.

126 P. Danchin, A Human Right to Water? The South African Constitutional Court's Decision in the Mazibuko Case, European Journal of International Law Reports (2010), available at www.ejiltalk.org/a-human-right-to-water-the-south-african-constitutional-court%E2%80%99s-decision-in-the-mazibuko-case/.

127 The Road to a Remedy, *supra* note 122, p. 231 ff. The *TAC* case, *supra* note 55, for instance, undoubtedly benefited from the earlier jurisprudence in *Grootboom*, *supra* note 54.

128 E. Wickeri, *Grootboom*'s Legacy: Securing the Right to Access to Adequate Housing in South Africa, Center for Human Rights and Global Justice Working Paper No 5 (2004), available at www.chrgj.org/publications/docs/wp/Wickeri%20Grootboom%27s%20Legacy.pdf.

courts to enforce ESR norms was a partial, but modest, success in South Africa and results were strongest where court-based strategies were complemented as part of broader campaigns. In short, the constitutional entrenchment of ESR did have positive effects, but we should not expect that constitutionalism, in isolation, will necessarily lead to ground-breaking social transformations in every situation.

JUDICIAL ACTIVISM AND THE USE OF INTERNATIONAL LAW AS GAP-FILLER IN DOMESTIC LAW: THE CASE OF FORCED DISAPPEARANCES COMMITTED DURING THE ARMED CONFLICT IN NEPAL*

Rishikesh WAGLE**

1. INTRODUCTION

The degree of social, economic, and psychological damage caused to Nepalese society by the armed conflict between the government and the Communist Party of Nepal (Maoist) during 1996–2006 is yet to be fully measured. However, there are some indicators. The armed conflict is said to have claimed more than 13,000 Nepali lives and about 1,500 people were involuntarily disappeared and thousands remain displaced.[1] There were several other serious violations of human rights, including widespread practice of torture[2] and use of child soldiers.[3] The Comprehensive Peace Accord (CPA),[4] signed in November 2006, formally ended the armed conflict. It paved the way for the promulgation of the

* I wish to thank Prof. Suzannah Linton for her invaluable suggestions in the course of writing this paper.

** District Court Judge, Syangja, Nepal. PhD candidate at the University of Hong Kong.

1 UNHCR, Report of the United Nations High Commissioner for Human Rights on the human rights situation and the activities of her office, including technical cooperation in Nepal (March 2009).

2 See Advocacy Forum, Sharing Experience with Torture Survivors (Kathmandu: Advocacy Forum, 2006); Advocacy Forum, Hope and Frustration: Assessing the Impact of Nepal's Torture Compensation Act, 1996 (Kathmandu: Advocacy Forum, 2008).

3 See www.unmin.org.np/?d=activities&p=arms (visited 1 June 2009). The United Nations Mission in Nepal verification has found 2,973 child soldiers in CPN (M) PLA cantonment.

4 Comprehensive Peace Accord entered between the Government of Nepal and the Communist Party of Nepal (Maoist), 1 November 2006, Kathmandu ('CPA').

Interim Constitution[5] and election for the Constituent Assembly.[6] However, the Constituent Assembly failed to meet the two-year deadline to promulgate a new constitution in May 2010, and extended its tenure for one more year. A political impasse has contributed to the failure of the Constituent Assembly to select the Premier in its Parliamentary capacity and it has further delayed the constitution drafting process. Ultimately, it has also delayed the formation and implementation of a comprehensive post-conflict justice scheme for Nepal.

At the time of writing, Nepal faces many complex challenges for the consolidation of the rule of law that was brought to its lowest ebb during the conflict, and for the establishment of a stable democratic regime. For this purpose, among other things, it is necessary to deal with the human rights violations committed during the armed conflict. Even after the end of the conflict, the failure of the Nepalese state system to prevent or end the culture of impunity perpetuated during the armed conflict has not been ameliorated, and nor have the provisions of the CPA relating to the post-conflict justice measures[7] aimed at remedying past abuses been implemented. Among the reasons for the difficulty facing the domestic legal system in dealing with past human rights abuses may be the absence of a strong legal framework and the role for the principle of legality in dealing with past cases (prohibition of retroactive application of the law). International experience shows that international law may in such a situation provide a workable foundation for bridging a gap in the law.[8] Nepalese practice also follows this line. To fill a clear gap in the domestic law's ability to deal with past cases of forced disappearance, the Supreme Court of Nepal in June 2007 handed down a ground-breaking judgment[9] in which it

---

5 The Interim Constitution of Nepal, 2007. It was promulgated on 15 January 2007 and shall remain in force until a new constitution is promulgated by the Constituent Assembly.

6 Election for the Constituent Assembly was held on April 2008. As per the Interim Constitution, the Constituent Assembly was required to draft and promulgate a new constitution within May 2010. However, it could not promulgate a new constitution, but extended its tenure for one more year through an amendment of the Interim Constitution in May 2010.

7 Some of the important provisions relating to the post-conflict justice included in the CPA were: (i) the formation of a truth and reconciliation commission in order to investigate the truth about those who have seriously violated human rights and those who were involved in crimes against humanity in the course of the war and to create an environment for reconciliation in the society (Article 5.2.5); (ii) to make public the information about the real name, surname, and address of the people who were disappeared by both sides and who were killed during the war and also to inform the family about it within 60 days from the date of signing of the Accord (Article 5.2.3); and (iii) the formation of a National Peace and Rehabilitation Commission to carry out relief work for the people victimized and displaced by the war and to rehabilitate them (Article 5.2.4). There is no provision in respect of amnesty for past human rights abuses.

8 R. Teitel, Transitional Jurisprudence: The Role of Law in Political Transformation, 106 Yale Law Journal 2009–2080 (1996–1997), citing the cases from Greece and Hungary.

9 *Rabindra Prasad Dhakal on behalf of his brother Advocate Rajendra Prasad Dhakal and Others v. Government of Nepal, Ministry of Home Affairs and Others*, Supreme Court Bulletin (Special Issue, Jestha 2064) 1–86; ILDC 756 (NP 2007).

invoked the Disappearance Convention[10] to deal with past cases of forced disappearances. This judicial activism paved the way for the transmission of international law to the domestic sphere as a means for dealing with past abuses of human rights. This chapter examines the role of the Supreme Court of Nepal in adopting the international rule of law value in post-conflict situations by breaking with its previous cautious approach toward the internalization of international law.

The *Dhakal* case,[11] decided by the Supreme Court of Nepal against this backdrop, introduced various international justice norms into the Nepalese legal system. Its main contributions are: recognition of the right to know the whereabouts of a disappeared person as an integral part of the right to a judicial remedy; recognition of the right to compensation to the family of the disappeared person; and ordering the government to initiate legal action against the perpetrators of past human rights violations and providing an adequate legal framework for addressing the issue of enforced disappearances of persons on the basis of the Disappearance Convention.[12] The *Dhakal* judgment has contributed to the internalization of international law norms in dealing with past human rights violations by interpreting domestic constitutional provisions and drawing on the persuasive force of the principles laid down in the judgments of the regional human rights courts and the Indian Supreme Court. However, the case did not settle the deficiencies prevailing in current judicial practice in respect of the status of international treaty norms in the Nepalese legal system. Moreover, to some extent, the case created a further problem in respect of determining an obligation of the state arising under a treaty. The Court's emphasis on internalizing the provisions of the Disappearance Convention blurred the distinction between obligations arising out of a treaty to which the state is a party and to which it is not. Despite those problems, however, the general acceptance of this judgment by different stakeholders has paved the way for internalization of international norms in dealing with past human rights violations, despite the lack of a principled and coherent judicial practice to internalize international legal norms in the Nepalese legal system.

Section 2 of this chapter offers a brief explanation of the place of international law in the Nepalese legal system to provide context for Nepalese practice in this area. Section 3 sets out the background of the *Dhakal* case, followed by a critical analysis of the judgment and an evaluation of the role played by the several actors in the lead-up to the judgment. It also examines the way the judiciary asserted judicial power pursuant to the Constitution to fulfil obligations under international human rights law in case of failure of the executive, and provided

10 International Convention for the Protection of All Persons from Enforced Disappearance, adopted at New York, 12 December 2006, GA Resolution 61/177 (A/RES/61/177) (2006) (entered into force on 23 December 2010) ('Disappearance Convention').

11 *Rabindra Prasad Dhakal v. Government of Nepal*, *supra* note 9.

12 Disappearance Convention, *supra* note 10.

remedies to the victims of forced disappearance by invoking innovative investigative mechanisms. The chapter concludes with an evaluation of the judgment's contributions to domesticating the international rule of law and dealing with past human rights abuses in Nepal.

2. PLACE OF INTERNATIONAL LAW IN THE NEPALESE LEGAL SYSTEM

Historically, the Nepalese legal system developed on the basis of Hindu texts, without a direct influence of the common law or civil law systems. Since the 1950s, however, it has been greatly influenced by the Indian legal system, which follows the common law tradition.[13] Thus, some features of the common law system, such as the adversarial trial and the doctrine of precedent, are adopted in the Nepalese legal system through legislative enactments. Still, there is no common law as such enforceable by the Nepalese courts. Thus the customary rules of international law which are accepted as a part of common law in the common law system are not a part of Nepalese law as such. Despite having worked in the courts of Nepal since 1993, this author has knowledge of neither a question raised in a court of law for the application of the rules of customary international law, nor of any state action taken on that basis.

In the case of treaties, it has not yet been clearly settled whether a treaty requires incorporation into domestic law, or whether it forms a part of the Nepalese legal system when the state becomes party to a treaty. The post-1990 era witnessed both the enactment of statutory provisions for giving effect to a treaty in the domestic sphere, as well as judicial practice settling issues that have elements of international law. It seems that the statutory codification and judicial practice are not moving in the same line.

Before 1990, there was no legal provision pertaining to matters raising issues of international law.[14] Section 126 of the 1990 Constitution designated the authority of the state in respect of becoming a party to a treaty. It required, inter alia, treaties dealing with certain important national issues to be ratified by a two-thirds majority of the members present at the joint session of Parliament.[15] This provision was incorporated into the Constitution primarily for subjecting the executive's treaty-making power to strict parliamentary scrutiny. It was done because there was an apprehension among the Nepalese people that India had

13 Cf. R. Stith, Unconstitutional Constitutional Amendment: The Extraordinary Power of the Nepal's Supreme Court, 11(1) American University Journal of International Law and Policy 47 (1996).

14 Section 2 (m) of the Nepal Law Interpretation Act, 1953 gives an extensive list of what is law. But it does not include international law in this category.

15 Article 126, the Constitution of the Kingdom of Nepal, 1990. This provision is incorporated, *in verbatim*, in Article 156 of the Interim Constitution of Nepal, 2007.

been securing unfair advantages to the detriment of Nepal under treaties between them in harnessing water resources flowing from Nepal to India. Thus, a stricter provision for ratification of treaties was incorporated in the Constitution.[16] Within two months of the date of promulgation of the Constitution, the Nepal Treaty Act, 1990 was enacted by the interim cabinet in its legislative capacity to give effect to this constitutional provision.[17] In addition to prescribing procedures for becoming a party to a treaty, the Act granted superior status to treaty provisions over parliamentary legislation in the domestic sphere in case of any inconsistencies between them, although this provision does not categorically state that a treaty is an integral part of the domestic legal system.[18]

2.1. DIFFICULTY IN RECOGNIZING A TREATY AS A PART OF THE DOMESTIC LAW

Although the Supreme Court indicated in *obiter dicta* that it has jurisdiction to test the constitutionality of a treaty provision under the judicial review of legislation jurisdiction[19] and the superior status of a treaty provision over the domestic law,[20] in concrete disputes, the Court has refrained from recognizing a treaty provision enforceable as a part of domestic law. In effect, this has watered down the supremacy clause of the Treaty Act.

The Court's refusal to conduct a constitutional validity test of a treaty on the ground that a treaty is not law on par with parliamentary legislation contributed to this situation. In *Gyanraj Rai*,[21]a tripartite agreement of 1947 between Nepal, India, and the United Kingdom[22] was challenged on the ground that it created unequal treatment between British citizens and Nepalese citizens working in the British Army in contravention of the Constitution. The Court held that the provision of the Treaty Act which stipulates that a treaty shall have equal effect of law did not mean that it also possessed all other characteristics of a Parliamentary Act. It ruled that it could not test the validity of the treaty which

---

16 S.P. Subedi, When a Treaty is a Treaty in Law? An Analysis of the Views of the Supreme Court of Nepal on a Bilateral Agreement between India and Nepal, 5 Asian Yearbook of International Law 201–209 (1997).

17 Preamble to the Treaty Act, 1990.

18 Section 9, the Treaty Act, 1990.

19 *Balakrishna Neupane v. Ministry of Water Resources and Others*, NKP 2054 (3) 77.

20 Eg *Tilotama Poudel v. Government of Nepal*, NKP 2058 (7/8) 423; *Jyoti Poudel v. Government of Nepal*, NKP 2066 (12) 2001.

21 *Gyanraj Rai v. Cabinet Secretariat and Others*, Writ no. 2651 of the Year 2057, 21 March 2002.

22 Tripartite Agreement Between the Government of the United Kingdom, the Government of Dominion of India and the Government of Nepal, Memorandum of Agreement, 9 November 1947, Kathmandu. For full text, see B.C. Upreti, India and Nepal: Treaties Agreements Understandings 66–75 (Delhi: Kalinga Publication, 2009).

had been challenged for unfair treatment of Nepalese citizens in another country. This was a question about the jurisdiction of the Court, but the Court went beyond that and made some significant observations. It is submitted that this has created difficulties in establishing a general rule for the application of treaty law in Nepal.

To distinguish a treaty provision from a provision of a Parliamentary Act, the Court emphasized their differences in the process of creation. It noted that, unlike in the case of an Act, Parliament was not competent to amend a treaty provision. Thus, the law mentioned in Article 88(1) of the Constitution, which authorizes the Court to declare a law void in case of inconsistency with the Constitution, is the Parliamentary Act: 'A treaty applicable as a law pursuant to Section 9(1) of the Treaty Act cannot be understood as that it has been authorized to a court of law to directly enforce any treaty or a provision thereof as a law in force.'[23] This ruling leads to the conclusion that a treaty is not applicable as law unless incorporated by a Parliamentary Act, implying that section 9(1) of the Treaty Act is completely inoperative.

The Court's approach of abstaining from recognizing a treaty provision as part of the domestic legal system reached a climax in *Dinesh Kumar.*[24] In that case, the petitioner claimed that a provision of the Finance Ordinance to impose additional custom duties on the import of vehicles from India should be declared inoperative, as the imposition of such duties was contrary a provision of the Trade Treaty[25] entered between Nepal and India. Although the Court did not explicitly rely on the reasons given in *Gyanraj* to distinguish between a treaty provision and a Parliamentary Act, it ruled that a treaty provision applicable as law does not mean that it has equal force of law for all purposes. It ruled thus that a treaty applicable as law does not stand on par with a law made through a legislative process. Consequently, the Court refrained from exercising jurisdiction under Article 88(1) of the Constitution to settle an issue of whether a domestic law contravenes a treaty provision. As a result, there is a void of jurisdiction in Nepal to settle an issue of inconsistency between domestic legislation and a treaty provision. By default, therefore, domestic law applies.

The general rule that evolved out of these practices is that an international treaty to which Nepal is party is not enforceable as a legal rule in Nepal. On that basis, it may be argued that the over-emphasis on treaties over domestic law in the Nepal Treaty Act led to this situation: had the Act, first, simply provided that treaty provisions would be on equal footing with an Act of Parliament, this would have led, in effect, to general internalization of treaty norms in the

---

23 *Gyanraj Rai v. Cabinet Secretariat, supra* note 21.

24 *Dinesh Kumar Sharma v. Cabinet Secretariat,* NKP 2063 (9) 1136. Cf. *Rama Panta Kharel v. Government of Nepal,* NKP 2065 (4) 398.

25 Treaty of Trade Between His Majesty's Government of Nepal and the Government of India, 6 December 1991, New Delhi: Nepal Gazette, Part V, Section 41, Additional Issue 55(C), 6 December 1991.

domestic legal system. Then the supremacy clause, in the second place, would be workable. In this situation, the general rules of statutory interpretation would have solved questions of inconsistency between a Parliamentary Act and a treaty.

2.2. INFLUENCE OF INTERNATIONAL HUMAN RIGHTS LAW IN THE NEPALESE LEGAL SYSTEM

As discussed in the preceding paragraphs, in a concrete dispute, the Court has not recognized a treaty provision as an enforceable law in Nepal. Yet, international human rights instruments have deep influence in the Nepalese legal system, albeit indirectly. The Supreme Court has recognized international human rights norms in a very liberal fashion.

The influence of international human rights law in the Nepalese system started in 1990 with the adoption of the new Constitution with an extensive list of fundamental rights. Moreover, Nepal became a party to seven core international human rights instruments during the 1990s.[26] Those international human rights instruments became fertile ground for bringing public interest litigations directly before the Supreme Court, especially on issues of gender justice, demanding the striking down of various laws as being contrary to the treaty provisions. However, this opportunity for establishing a clear relationship between domestic law and treaty law in the Nepalese legal system has not been fully utilized by the Supreme Court. That being said, although the question of direct application of international treaty law remains obscure, judicial practice shows three positive trends in respect of the influence of international human rights treaties in Nepal.

First, the laws in question were challenged not only for being contrary to a treaty provision, but also as inconsistent with the fundamental rights guaranteed under the Constitution. The Court settled this issue on the basis of a law's consistency or inconsistency with the Constitution without addressing the issue

---

26 Nepal became a party to the United Nations Convention on the Rights of Child, 20 November 1989, 1577 UNTS 3 (entered into force 2 September 1990) on 14 September 1990; the Convention on the Elimination of All Forms of Discrimination against Women, 18 December 1979, 1249 UNTS 13 (entered into force on 18 December 1979) (CEDAW) on 22 April 1991; the International Covenant on Economic, Social and Cultural Rights, 16 December 1966, 993 UNTS 3 (entered into force on 3 January 1976); the International Covenant on Civil and Political Rights, 16 December 1966, 999 UNTS 171 (entered into force on 23 March 1976) (ICCPR); the Optional Protocol to the International Covenant on Civil and Political Rights, 16 December 1966, 999 UNTS 302 (entered into force on 23 March 1976); and the Convention Against Torture and Other Cruel, Inhuman or Degrading Treatment or Punishment, 10 December 1984, 1465 UNTS 85 (entered into force on 26 June 1987) (CAT) on 14 May 1991; and on 4 March 1998 to the Second Optional Protocol to the International Covenant on Civil and Political Rights, Aiming at the Abolition of Death Penalty (A/RES/ 44/128) (15 December 1989) (entered into force on 11 July 1991).

of the law's direct inconsistency with a treaty provision. In *Reena Bajaracharya*,[27] a provision of the Employee Service Regulation of Royal Nepal Airlines, a state-owned flight-operating corporation that fixed different compulsory retirement ages for air hostesses and air stewards, was challenged for violating women's rights under the Convention on the Elimination of All Forms of Discrimination against Women (CEDAW) and the Convention on Political Rights of Women,[28] as well as the right to equality under the Constitution. Holding that Article 11 of the Constitution had internalized the spirit of Article 15 of CEDAW, the Court struck down the impugned provision for being discriminatory against women and for being contrary to the constitutional provision of equality.

Second, where the Court finds a legal provision to be inconsistent with a treaty provision and a constitutional provision, it issues a directive order to the government to initiate a process for amending the law to address those issues. In *Mira Dhungana*,[29] clause number 16 of the Chapter on Partition [of ancestral property] of the *Muluki Ain*[30] was challenged as being inconsistent with Article 15 of CEDAW as well as with the equality provisions of the Constitution. This provision, the petitioner claimed, was discriminatory to a daughter on securing her portion of ancestral property since it ensured a son's right to ancestral property at birth, but a daughter should remain unmarried until 35 years of age in order to get that right. The Court found this provision discriminatory against women. But it observed that merely declaring the provision void would further create discrimination against men, since under the law in force, a woman acquired this right from her husband at marriage. If a woman is also entitled to this right to parental property, she secures this right from two families. Thus, the Court ordered the government to introduce a bill in Parliament addressing various issues associated with this problem as a whole. While disposing of two other cases which challenged various legal provisions on similar grounds,[31] the Court referred the issues of those cases to be addressed while introducing a bill

27 *Reena Bajracharya and Others v. Cabinet Secretariat and Others*, NKP 2057 (7) 537. See also *Devendra Ale and Others v. Cabinet Secretariat and Others*, NKP 2061 (6) 1156; *Lily Thapa and Others v. Office of the Prime Minister and Others*, NKP 2062 (9) 1054; *Rajuprasad Chapagain and Others v. Office of the Prime Minister and Others*, NKP 2065 (10) 1180.

28 Convention on the Political Rights of Women, adopted at New York, 31 March 1953, 193 UNTS 135 (entered into force 7 July 1954).

29 *Mira Kumari Dhungana and Others v. Ministry of Law Justice and Parliamentary Affairs and Others*, NKP 2052 (6) 468. See also *Sapana Malla Pradhan and Others v. Office of the Prime Minister and Others*, NKP 2065 (8) 917.

30 The *Muluki Ain* was originally promulgated in 1863 as the first comprehensive legal code of Nepal. It has undergone various amendments since then. In spite of enactment of various Parliamentary Acts, it still remains the basic law in the matters relating to court procedures, family law, and criminal law. For its historical development, see A. Sever, Aspects of Modern Nepalese History 42–62 (New Delhi: Vikash Publishing, 1996).

31 *Sapana Malla Pradhan v. Ministry of Law Justice and Parliamentary Affairs and Others*. NKP 2053 (2) 2; *Dr. Chanda Bajracharya v. Parliamentary Secretariat and Others*, NKP 2053 (7) 537.

in Parliament as per the directive order issued on the previous case. Parliament enacted legislation for maintaining gender equality incorporating the issues expressed in the Court's directive orders.[32] This practice also indicates that incorporation of a treaty provision into domestic law is necessary for judicial enforcement of rights guaranteed under an international treaty.

Third, the Supreme Court has started relying heavily on international human rights instruments to which Nepal is a party to interpret domestic legal provisions. In *Mira Dhungana*,[33] the petitioner prayed for declaring clause number 1 of the Chapter on Rape of the *Muluki Ain* void since it criminalizes rape but not marital rape, arguing that this classification is unreasonable and contrary to the right to equality guaranteed under the Constitution as well as international human rights instruments. It is because non-criminalization of marital rape is based only on the marital status of a woman. Reviewing various provisions of those instruments, the Court stated 'the Treaty Act, 1990 categorically requires the international treaty of which Nepal is a party to be accepted as Nepal law. The status of international treaty and convention is superior since they prevail in case of inconsistency with Nepal law. Those human rights treaties are *sastras*[34] of modern age. It is necessary to enact and interpret national law in accordance with those provisions. In the present context, while defining rape, the constitutional sprit as well as the background and the context of those international treaties should be kept in mind.'[35] Referring to the judgments of courts of other jurisdictions and the history of the enactment of the impugned provisions and rules of statutory interpretation, it further stated that 'with reference to the right to equality under the Constitution, international human rights instruments ratified by Nepal, and changed values in criminal and family laws it is reasonable, appropriate, and contextual to define marital rape also as a criminal offence.'[36] Thus, the Court defined marital rape as included in the impugned statute and found it unnecessary to declare that provision void. It has been observed that the judiciary here assumed the role of the legislature in the creation of a criminal offence.[37] Despite the ruling that marital rape is included in the ordinary definition of rape, the Court did not dare to equate it with a rape committed by an outsider for the purpose of punishment. It observed

32 *The Muluki Ain* (Eleven Amendment Act), 2002; The Act To Amend Some Nepal Acts For Maintaining Gender Equality, 2006.

33 *Mira Dhungana v. Ministry of Law Justice and Parliamentary Affairs and Others*, NKP 2059 (2) 26.

34 *Sastra* is a Sanskrit word. In Hinduism, it means a sacred text. Here, it may be understood as an analogy of the Bible used in the Western literature for authority.

35 *Mira Dhungana v. Ministry of Law Justice and Parliamentary Affairs*, *supra* note 33.

36 *Mira Dhungana*, *supra* note 33.

37 Dr. Rajit Bhakta Pradhananga, *Aajako Paribartit Sandharvama Hamro Jabarjastikarani Sambandhi Kanoon: Eak Aadhayan* (Our Laws Relating to Rape in the Changed Context: A Study) Nyayadeep: Criminal Law Issue 2062 p. 92 (An Occasional Journal of the Society of the Government Attorneys of Nepal).

that the penal provision under the law in force envisioned only rape committed by an outsider, which implied that a husband cannot be punished for committing rape against his wife like an ordinary rapist. Then it issued a directive order to the Ministry of Law and Justice to initiate amendment to the penal provision for punishing a rapist husband, taking into account, inter alia, marital relations between victim and perpetrator. The penal provision was subsequently amended, providing lenient punishment for marital rape.[38]

As these examples illustrate, post-1990 Nepalese judicial practice is greatly influenced by international human rights instruments. Although the Supreme Court has not enforced provisions of those instruments directly, it gives them high respect when interpreting domestic legal provisions and uses them as a catalyst for law reform. The *Dhakal* case can be seen as the culmination of the liberal approach towards international human rights law in the courts of Nepal beginning in the 1990s. However, the main issue of direct enforceability of international treaties in the domestic legal regime still remains obscure.

3. THE *DHAKAL* CASE

3.1. BACKGROUND

The petitioners brought some of the abuses of human rights committed during the armed conflict between the government and the Communist Party of Nepal (Maoist, CPN (M)) before the Supreme Court, claiming the enforcement of fundamental rights guaranteed under the Constitution.[39] On 1 June 2007, the Supreme Court of Nepal dealt with a batch of 28 *habeas corpus* petitions, the oldest one filed in 1999, that originally prayed for the release of 83 individuals who had allegedly been arrested and disappeared by the state forces following an armed rebellion by the CPN (M) in 1996, and supplementary petitions of mandamus that the status of the detainees be made public. The supplementary petitions also prayed that legal actions be taken against the officers responsible for the gross and systematic violations of human rights and financial relief be provided to the families of the victims. The government agencies, in response to the Show Cause Notices issued by the Court, contended that most of the named persons had never been arrested; some had been questioned and released immediately, one escaped from custody, and one died of illness.

---

38 The Act to Amend Some Nepal Acts For Maintaining Gender Equality, 2006. Cf. *Jitkumari Pangeni (Neupane) v. Office of the Prime Minister and Others*, NKP 2065(6) 664.

39 Originally the petitions were filed pursuant to the Article 88 of the Constitution of the Kingdom of Nepal for the enforcement of rights guaranteed under that Constitution. At the time of disposal of the cases, that Constitution was abrogated by the Interim Constitution of Nepal, 2007, and the Court exercised judicial power for the enforcement of fundamental rights pursuant to Article 107 of the Interim Constitution, which is an *in verbatim* incorporation of Article 88 of the 1990 Constitution.

Before all the petitions were joined together for the final hearing, the Supreme Court formed a Detainee Investigation Task Force (DITF)[40] under the convenorship of an Appeals Court Judge to inquire into the status of three arrested persons, and later ordered the inclusion of one more person named under another petition in the list of the detainees. Upon investigation, the DITF reported that one of the arrested persons had died of torture during detention and three had been disappeared by the security personnel. No such judicial inquiries were held in the case of the remaining detainees. The United Nations Office of the High Commissioner for Human Rights – Nepal Office in May 2006 also made public an investigative report about the arrest, torture, and disappearances of 49 persons in an army barrack in Kathmandu.[41] Many individuals named under the writ petitions were included in the list of disappeared persons in this report.

The Court in the judgment accepted its responsibility to fulfil obligations under international human rights law in case of the failure of other state organs. It went on to order the government to criminalize forced disappearance, provide remedies to the victims, and take legal action against the perpetrators. In so doing, it heavily relied on international human rights law. That may be seen as a break with the cautious approach regarding the internalization of international law in Nepal. However, a clear distinction is seen between the previous cases and the present case. In the past cases discussed above, there was a claim regarding inconsistencies of international law and domestic law, but in the present case, international law was invoked to fill a gap in domestic law. Thus it may be inferred that the *Dhakal* judgment has paved the way for direct application of international law, if there is no question of inconsistency with domestic law. The various aspects of the judgment are examined in the following sub-sections.

3.2. JUDICIAL ACTIVISM TO FULFIL THE OBLIGATIONS UNDER INTERNATIONAL HUMAN RIGHTS LAW

The formation of the DITF was the result of judicial activism to fulfil the obligation under international human rights law. The Court faced unprecedented challenges in handling those cases at the procedural stages. It was quite difficult to locate the whereabouts of the detainees, despite the Court's best efforts. In the Nepalese legal system, neither the judiciary nor any agency under its direct supervision conducts fact-finding inquiries or criminal investigations. However, in this case the Court questioned the truthfulness of the answers furnished by

40 Order of the Supreme Court at procedural stage, 28 August 2006.

41 United Nations Office of the High Commissioner for Human Rights Nepal, Report of investigation into arbitrary detention, torture and disappearances at Maharajgunj RNA barracks, Kathmandu, in 2003–2004 (May 2006) ('UNOHCHR-Nepal Report').

the state authorities and sought avenues for finding the truth.[42] It felt that strict adherence to procedural formalities and dismissal of a *habeas corpus* petition in the absence of proof of the detainees in the custody of the respondent would lead the Court towards failure in rendering justice. It observed: 'if [this] court disposes of the cases without locating the whereabouts of the persons who are claimed as detained it would amount to the judiciary, like the state [executive] failing to discharge its judicial obligation honestly.'[43]

Thus, the Court categorically accepted the judicial obligation under the international human rights instruments, and argued that this justified adopting unusual measures to conduct a judicial inquiry. 'Since Nepal has expressed her commitment to fulfill responsibilities under ICCPR and other international human rights treaties at the national and international levels by being a party to those instruments, the Court itself should be ready to discharge those responsibilities, require other [state] institutions as well supervise and monitor them. Thus, the Court should not hesitate to adopt any measure for the protection of human rights and the rule of law'.[44] And the Supreme Court, by an order constituted by the DITF, set forth its mandate and working procedures. The Court's reliance on international human rights laws justified its finding of the whereabouts of the disappeared persons on its own initiative.

The Court's reference to the rule of law, in this order of August 2006, may be interpreted as a reference to the fulfilment of the obligations arising out of the international human rights instruments. Thus, it opened the way for transferring the international rule of law to the domestic sphere. It can plausibly be inferred that this observation has empowered the Court to rely heavily on international law when passing the final judgment in June 2007.

3.3. OBLIGATION OF THE STATE UNDER DOMESTIC AND INTERNATIONAL LAW IN POST-CONFLICT SITUATIONS AND THE ROLE OF COURTS

Acknowledging the whereabouts of many persons were unknown, the Court discussed the responsibilities of the state towards its citizens in general terms. It observed that, next to the protection of its frontiers, it is the obligation of the state to protect life and property of its citizens. It further highlighted that this obligation extends throughout the period of armed conflict, since civil rights are at greater risk in such adverse situations.[45] The Court noted the seriousness of the incidences of enforced disappearances during the armed conflict and

42 Order of the Supreme Court, *supra* note 40.
43 Order of the Supreme Court, *supra* note 40.
44 Order of the Supreme Court, *supra* note 40.
45 *Rabindra Prasad Dhakal v. Government of Nepal*, *supra* note 9, p. 58.

cautioned the state to be extra vigilant to prevent the flourishing of the culture of impunity during the armed conflict.[46]

With respect to the disappeared citizens, the Court established three obligations of the state: (1) to determine the factual conditions of the disappeared persons; (2) to initiate proceedings against the persons responsible for disappearances; and (3) to provide appropriate relief to the victims. Those responsibilities arise out of international [human rights] instruments, judgments of foreign courts and human rights-related regional courts,[47] and Nepalese constitutional provisions.[48] However, it seems that it is problematic to establish each of those responsibilities categorically under a particular normative foundation. This created difficulty with identifying under which normative source and how the state is under the obligation to fulfil them in the present case.

With respect to the obligations arising from international law, the Court referred to the obligation of states under Article 2 of the ICCPR to ensure effective remedy against violations of rights, to General Comment No. 31 of the Human Rights Committee, which states that enforced disappearances violate rights guaranteed under Articles 6, 7, and 9 of the ICCPR, and to the prohibition of torture of a person in detention under the Convention Against Torture. Then, the Court explicitly observed that '[p]ursuant to Section 9 of the Treaty Act, 1990 treaties or agreements shall be applicable as Nepal law. Thus, there is no ground for the state to get itself free from the obligations created by these instruments to which Nepal is a party.'[49] However, this ruling could not explicitly settle the issue of direct application of international treaties in Nepal, since the Court did not directly apply any international treaty provision in the case, nor was there a contention of inconsistency between a treaty provision and a domestic legal provision. Instead, the Court held that, in respect of the fulfilment of Nepal's international obligations, it has a responsibility to ensure those obligations in case of failure of the executive branch to do so. It observed that '[t]he primary obligation to ensure the protection of rights of the citizens rests on the state [executive]. Since the Constitution has endowed the Court with the responsibility of the guardian and watchdog of civil liberties, when other organs of the state fail to fulfill their obligations, the Court can issue an appropriate and necessary order to require them to do so.'[50] Although the judgment does not directly refer

---

46 *Rabindra Prasad Dhakal v. Government of Nepal, supra* note 9, p. 68.

47 Judgments of the Supreme Court of India: *Rudl Sha v. State of Bihar* (1983) 4 SCC 141; *Sebastian M. Hungary v. Union of India* (1984) 3 SCC 83; *Nilabati Behara v. State of Orissa* (1993) 2 SCC 746. Judgments of the Inter-American Court of Human Rights: *Velasquez Rodriguez v. Honduras* Petition No. 2970/1981; *Trujillo Oroja v. Bolivia*, Judgment of 29 July 1988; Judgment of 26 January 2000. Judgment of the European Court of Human Rights: *Kurt v. Turkey*, Application no 2476/94, Judgment of 24 May 1998.

48 *Rabindra Prasad Dhakal v Government of Nepal, supra* note 9, p. 61.

49 *Rabindra Prasad Dhakal v Government of Nepal, supra* note 9, p. 54.

50 *Rabindra Prasad Dhakal v Government of Nepal, supra* note 9, p. 62.

to it, it seems that the term 'appropriate and necessary order' is taken in the same sense as it is used in Article 107(2) of the Interim Constitution.[51] It is because the remedial order was issued under the authority of Articles 100 and 107(2) of the Constitution. This term gives ample latitude for judicial discretion to issue any type of order for effective enforcement of the fundamental rights and legal rights. Upon its determination that those obligations were not fulfilled by the state, the Court issued a comprehensive directive order for adopting various measures, including new legislation to deal with the systematic practice of enforced disappearances committed in the recent past.

3.3.1. Recognition of 'Right to Truth' as a Fundamental Right

The *Dhakal* judgment recognized the 'right to truth' as one of the components of the fundamental right to justice. It interpreted the incidence of disappearance as violations of the right to life, liberty, and justice guaranteed under the Constitution. 'Since the incidence of disappearance is taken as a violation of the fundamental rights to life, liberty and justice of a citizen, the legal investigations and proceedings on disappearance are taken as a part of the fundamental right to justice. Thus, finding the truth can be taken as a part of the enforcement of the right to justice.'[52] It referred to the provisions of the Comprehensive Peace Accord[53] that are related to making the whereabouts of the disappeared persons public, as well as the incorporation of those provisions within the framework of State Policy in the Interim Constitution. The Court, by interpretation, ruled that provisions under the State Policy are subordinate to the 'right to truth' and categorically established that the state has no discretion but a strict obligation to provide a remedy to the victims of enforced disappearances. Thus, the Court took a very liberal attitude to elaborating the scope of the right to justice, and established an obligation on the state, on the basis of that right, to form a disappearance commission as a part of enforcing this right with respect to the disappeared citizens.[54]

---

51 The Interim Constitution, *supra* note 5.

52 *Rabindra Prasad Dhakal v. Government of Nepal*, *supra* note 9, p. 60.

53 Articles 5.2.3 and 5.2.5, Comprehensive Peace Accord, *supra* note 4.

54 *Rabindra Prasad Dhakal v. Government of Nepal*, *supra* note 9, p. 60. The reasoning of the Court in this issue seems rather confused, with the obligation of the state to conduct criminal investigations and proceedings against the perpetrators of enforced disappearance. It has not been clearly stated whether the 'right to truth' is independent of criminal investigation and proceedings against the perpetrators or whether it means only to know the truth through criminal trial. The contextual linkages of those parts of the judgment give a reasonable sense to understanding that 'right to truth' is recognized as an independent right that is not necessarily linked to criminal trials, since these parts of the judgment follow the question related to finding the truth about the disappeared persons, and subsequent paragraphs also categorically talk about the obligation of the state to make public the status of the disappeared persons.

For the evaluation of the situation of the enforcement of 'the right to truth', in addition to the Report of the DITF, the Court acknowledged the inquiries separately conducted by one member committee constituted by the Ministry of Home, the OHCHR Nepal Office, and the National Human Rights Commission. However, those efforts were found to be incomplete, and the Court found it necessary to conduct extensive and effective investigations into disappearances committed during the armed conflict.

For the purpose of formation of a disappearance commission, to give effect to 'the right to truth', the Court found the legislation in force, namely the Commission of Inquiry Act, 1969, inadequate since, at the time of its enactment, incidents such as mass disappearances had not been envisioned. Thus, the Court felt it necessary to order the enactment of a new legal provision to form a disappearance commission – either as a separate Act or included as a part of the Act to be enacted for the protection of persons from enforced disappearance – that would conduct an independent and effective inquiry.

3.3.2. Obligation of the State to Provide Relief to the Victims

The Court referred to the jurisprudence developed by the Supreme Court of India on awarding compensation to the victims of illegal detention and enforced disappearances, as well as the jurisprudence developed by the Inter-American Court of Human Rights and the European Court of Human Rights regarding the obligation of the state to compensate the victims of enforced disappearances.[55] For this purpose, the Court relied on the constitutional provision that the judicial authority of Nepal shall be exercised, inter alia, on the basis of recognized principles of justice.[56] Thus, this judgment clearly opened the way for internalization, by implication, in the Nepalese legal system of the jurisprudence developed through the judgments of foreign and regional human rights courts.

Since the opportunity for making claims against the state for compensation under the Civil Liberties Act, 1955 or the Torture Compensation Act, 1996 could not be utilized effectively because of the still unknown status of the disappeared citizens, a separate law was required to address this issue.[57] Thus, the Court ordered the state to include, inter alia, the right of the disappeared persons or family members to receive compensation in the legislation to be enacted for the protection of persons from enforced disappearances.[58] Further, it was ordered to formulate and act upon a suitable relief package that would include appropriate

55 *Rabindra Prasad Dhakal v. Government of Nepal, supra* note 9, p. 54–56. *Rudl Sha v. State of Bihar; Sebastian M. Hungary v. Union of India; Nilabati Behara v. State of Orissa; Velasquez Rodriguez v. Honduras; Trujillo Oroja v. Bolivia; Kurt v. Turkey, supra* note 47.

56 Article 100(1), Interim Constitution, *supra* note 5.

57 For further discussion about the retroactivity of the legislation, see section 3.3.3, below.

58 *Rabindra Prasad Dhakal v. Government of Nepal, supra* note 9, p. 81.

economic, educational, and employment measures, taking into account the continuous adverse effects caused by enforced disappearances.[59]

Considering the pain and trauma suffered, and the time and labour spent to clarify the status of the disappeared persons by the family members, the Court found it appropriate to award symbolic monetary compensation to them. The government was ordered to provide Rupees (Rs) 200,000, Rs 150,000, and Rs 100,000, respectively, to the nearest relative of the person who died in detention, whose arrest had been established, and whose status was still unknown, as interim relief.[60]

3.3.3. Obligation to Initiate Legal Proceedings Against Perpetrators

The Court relied heavily on Article 2 of the ICCPR for the state's obligation to initiate legal proceedings against the perpetrators of disappearances. An adequate discussion on how and what rights were violated by enforced disappearances, and how it was linked to the obligation of the state to initiate legal proceedings as part of ensuring an effective remedy for the enjoyment of those rights, was lacking, however. A simple reference to General Comment No. 31 of the Human Rights Committee, which provides that enforced disappearance violates rights guaranteed under Articles 6, 7, and 9, and amounts to a crime against humanity, fails to create a strong legal ground for establishing the obligation of the state to initiate a criminal investigation into the enforced disappearance. Further, the Court's recognition of *per se* criminal liability for the act of enforced disappearance is somewhat problematic. Indeed, the Court's reliance on General Comment No. 31 of the ICCPR, which recognizes that enforced disappearance violates a number of rights guaranteed under the Covenant, does not justify the *ex post facto* criminalization of enforced disappearance in the absence of other binding rules.

To fill the legal gap for criminal prosecution that exists due to the absence of criminalization of enforced disappearances, the Court ordered the government to initiate a process for enacting new legislation, taking as guidance the Disappearance Convention, to protect citizens from enforced disappearances and criminalize enforced disappearance accordingly. The Court also gave extensive guidelines for this purpose.[61]

As for the perpetrators identified in the present case by the DITF, the government was ordered to initiate legal proceedings immediately against the responsible officers for causing the death of Mr. Chakra Bahadur Katwal in custody. No specific crimes for which they were to be indicted were mentioned in the judgment. It seems plausible to infer that the proceedings were possible

---

59 *Rabindra Prasad Dhakal v. Government of Nepal, supra* note 9, p. 86.

60 *Rabindra Prasad Dhakal v. Government of Nepal, supra* note 9, p. 85–86.

61 *Rabindra Prasad Dhakal v. Government of Nepal, supra* note 9, p. 80–83.

under the existing penal law with respect to murder. However, for the perpetrators identified by the DITF as responsible for arresting and causing disappearances of three victims, the Court could not order immediate legal proceedings in the absence of specific legislation. Thus, the government was ordered to take immediate departmental action and initiate legal proceedings as per the law to be enacted to criminalize enforced disappearance pursuant to the Court's order. This order of the Court clearly authorized the government to initiate legal proceedings on the basis of *ex post facto* penal legislation. As the Court failed to pay attention to how this legislation could be permissible under the constitutional guarantee[62] against retroactive criminalization of an act, a serious legal problem could arise when an action is taken on the basis of any law enacted for *ex post facto* criminalization of disappearance pursuant to this court order.

3.4. ORDER FOR INTRODUCING SEPARATE LEGISLATION TO DEAL WITH ENFORCED DISAPPEARANCES

On one hand, the existing legal framework to render justice to the victims of enforced disappearance was not effective. Thus, any order of the Court in the absence of a workable legal framework would only amount to lip service to the victims. On the other hand, the Court had no jurisdiction to order the enactment of legislation in a certain fashion. This is the sole business of Parliament under the Constitution and the constitutional doctrine of separation of powers. However, as discussed above, there is a practice developed by the Court whereby in a case where the Court finds a legal provision *prima facie* inconsistent with the Constitution or a treaty but faces practical difficulties in declaring it void, it could direct the executive branch to initiate a process for law reform addressing the questions raised on the constitutionality test.[63] In the *Dhakal* case, however, there was no question of unconstitutionality of a law, but rather a problem created by a void of law in a specific area. Upon concluding that separate legislation was necessary to provide a remedy to the victims of mass enforced disappearances, the Court proceeded: '[the Court] takes the view that to suggest such a law on this subject as needed is not to interfere with or encroach upon the jurisdiction of the Parliament, rather it should be taken as a legitimate expression

---

62 Article 24(4) of the Interim Constitution of Nepal 2007 reads as: 'No person shall be punished for an act which was not punishable by law when the act was committed, and no person shall be subjected to a punishment greater than that prescribed by the law in force at the time of the offence.'

63 *Mira Dhungana v. Ministry of Law Justice and Parliamentary Affairs*, *supra* note 29; *Sapana Pradhan Malla v. Office of the Prime Minister*, *supra* note 29; *Sapana Malla Pradhan v. Ministry of Law Justice and Parliamentary Affairs*, *supra* note 31; *Dr. Chandra Bajracharya v. Parliamentary Secretariat*, *supra* note 31.

of judicial concern to make additionally effective law keeping in mind the international standards to protect civil liberties for which the state has expressed commitment.'[64]

It seems that this judicial innovation – requiring separate new legislation – has been easily accepted in the Nepalese political system. It is because the executive and legislative branches of the state did not express their discomfort with the judicial order. There are two possible reasons for going easy on this scheme of judicial activism to require legislation in respect of enforced disappearance. First, political commitment expressed in the Comprehensive Peace Accord[65] to make the status of disappeared persons known within 60 days was already overdue. In line with this commitment, a constitutional provision, under the heading of obligation of the state, called for awarding compensation to the disappeared persons on the basis of findings of a commission constituted in respect of disappeared persons,[66] which could not be fulfilled unless a strong legal framework was created for the functioning of the commission. Second, the government did not take the issue seriously, since it never intended to act on the judgment of the Court. A study highlighted the trend of ignoring implementation of the directive orders of the Court.[67] Also in this case the order of the Court was not adhered to by the government: after the decision of the Court, it formed a commission to inquire into the incidences of disappearance on the basis of the old law, the Commission of Inquiry Act, 1969, which was condemned by the Supreme Court for its inadequacy to cover the cases of mass enforced disappearance. This commission was ultimately aborted due to strong objections from human rights groups on the grounds that it undermined the Court's order that the Commission of Inquiry Act was not adequate to deal with the cases of mass disappearance of persons.[68]

3.5. APPLICATION OF THE DISAPPEARANCE CONVENTION FOR DEALING WITH THE PAST IN NEPAL

The Court in *Dhakal* expressed its strong desire for the full implementation of the provisions of the Disappearance Convention in the Nepalese context. However, one can observe a palpable strain in the judgment to stand this desire

64 *Rabindra Prasad Dhakal v. Government of Nepal*, *supra* note 9, p. 69.

65 Article 5.2.3, Comprehensive Peace Accord, *supra* note 4.

66 Article 33(q), Interim Constitution, *supra* note 5.

67 Shyamkumar Bhattarai and Umesh Koirala, *Sarbochha Adalatbata Jari Bhayaka Nirdeshatmak Aadheshharuko Karynayanko Abasta (Status of Execution of the Directive Orders Issued by the Supreme Court)* (National Judicial Academy, Kathmandu, 2063 Magh).

68 Ghanashyam Ojha, *Govt. confusion delays disappearance commission*, Katntipuronline, 25 September 2008, available at www.kantipuronline.com/kolnews.php?nid=161791 (visited 27 July 2009).

on a strong legal foundation. It did not seem appropriate for the Court to consider the Convention as a normative and binding instrument, since it had not yet entered into force. Moreover, Nepal was not a signatory to the Convention. Instead, the Court sought to bring the contents of the Convention into the Nepalese legal system in two ways.

First, it viewed its contents as accepted standards of international law: 'Even as [it] has not come to force till date and neither has Nepal ratified it [sic], this convention has set a fundamental standard concerning the obligation of the State with respect to the security of disappeared persons; and also in the condition that the convention has been accepted by the international community, it is expedient to accept the standards of the conventions as the standards of international law and thereby carry out activities by the state pursuant to the same.'[69] It would be appropriate and desirable to apply those standards in Nepal where enforced disappearance had been practiced on a mass scale in a systematic manner. But from a legal perspective, the logic behind the judgment is hardly convincing. Unless it has already been crystallized as a customary rule of international law or it is the codification of an already existing customary rule, a treaty provision does not possess binding legal force for a state that is not a party to it. None of these conditions are applicable with respect to criminalization of forced disappearance in the case of the Disappearance Convention.

Second, the judgment linked the provisions of the Convention with the current international human rights treaty framework. The Court referred to, without discussing their contents, three international human rights soft law instruments,[70] and observed that they are meant to implement the International Covenant on Civil and Political Rights, the International Covenant on Economic, Social and Cultural Rights, and the Convention against Torture, of which Nepal is a state party. Then it observed, 'the convention … should also be seen on the same footing,'[71] without differentiating soft law instruments from an international convention.

The Court further added that '[t]his convention has not established separate values other than that of prevailing international human rights laws rather it has reinforced the values enshrined in the mainstream human rights laws, and therefore, the fact of non-ratification of this convention does not provide any ground to consider that the state obligation created by mainstream human rights instrument are minimized to any extent.'[72] This leads to the inference that the Court did not take notice of the gaps prevailing in the international legal framework to deal with the cases of enforced disappearances which the

69 *Rabindra Prasad Dhakal v. Government of Nepal*, *supra* note 9, p. 50.

70 The Basic Principles on the Use of Force and Firearms by Law Enforcement Officials, 1990; the Declaration of Basic Principles of Justice for Victims of Crime and Abuse of Power, 1985; and the Standard Minimum Rules for the Treatment of Prisoners, 1977.

71 *Rabindra Prasad Dhakal v. Government of Nepal*, *supra* note 9, p. 51.

72 *Rabindra Prasad Dhakal v. Government of Nepal*, *supra* note 9, p. 51.

Convention is intended to fulfil.[73] In this respect, the Manfred Nowak Report had identified the absence of recognition of the specific right not to be subjected to enforced disappearance, the lack of a legally binding universal obligation to combat enforced disappearance under domestic criminal law, and the absence of effective remedy and right to reparation to the victims of disappearance and their families as some of the gaps in the prevailing international human rights and international criminal law framework for the protection of persons from enforced disappearance.[74] Thus, one of the most important contributions of the Convention is the establishment of an independent right not to be subjected to involuntarily disappearance.[75] Moreover, this statement of the Court does not seem compatible with its own earlier assessment in respect of the development of an international legal regime against enforced disappearances where it recognized insufficiency of international legal norms as to this subject prior to the Convention.[76]

The problem faced by the Court is again expressed in its reasoning on the necessity to implement the Convention: '[it] is yet to be ratified, there are no barriers to take but it is necessary to take the provisions of the convention theoretically as a guiding element on the basis of the obligation created out of conventions ratified by Nepal together with the principles of prevailing international human rights law for the protection of human rights.'[77] Thus, it has been made clear that even in the absence of direct obligations arising out of international law, it is desirable to apply them in the domestic sphere. However, it is difficult to justify the obligation on the normative ground.

While the Court was convinced of the need to incorporate the Convention into the Nepalese legal system (it even ordered that most of the provisions of the Convention be included in an Act to be enacted pursuant to the order),[78] in the absence of a theoretical foundation of the ruling of the Court in respect of giving effect to the provisions of non-ratified treaties, it will be difficult to follow this ruling consistently in future cases: which international conventions need to be incorporated into domestic law in the absence of Nepal being party to the convention?

---

73 Report submitted by Mr. Manfred Nowak, independent expert charged with examining the existing international criminal and human rights framework for the protection of persons from enforced or involuntary disappearances, pursuant to paragraph 11 of Commission resolution 2001/46 (E/CN.4/2002/71) (8 January 2002).

74 Report, *supra* note 73.

75 See S. McCrory, The International Convention for the Protection of all Persons from Enforced Disappearance, 7(3) Human Rights Law Review 545–56 (2007).

76 *Rabindra Prasad Dhakal v. Government of Nepal*, *supra* note 9, p. 49.

77 *Rabindra Prasad Dhakal v. Government of Nepal*, *supra* note 9, p. 51.

78 *Rabindra Prasad Dhakal v. Government of Nepal*, *supra* note 9, p. 51.

3.6. FACTORS THAT EMPOWERED THE COURT TO COME TO THE DECISION

In spite of the theoretical problems raised by the judgment, the craft and courage of the justices in handing down this ground-breaking judgment should be commended. It is noted, however, that in the present case other factors also played important roles in empowering the Court to deliver this judgment that rests so heavily on international law.

One cluster of factors is the collapse of the active monarchy in April 2006, the formal end of the armed conflict in November 2006, the promulgation of the Interim Constitution in January 2007, and the consensus-oriented political environment in which the election of the Constituent Assembly took place, all of which created a conducive environment for the Court to hold the government responsible for violations of human rights committed during the armed conflict.

Another important factor empowering the Court was made by the DITF. There is a strong reason to believe that, in addition to fact-finding, the DITF understood its mandate widely, since it made extensive recommendations on legal issues.[79] Thus, in the second part of the final chapter entitled 'recommendations', it suggested a number of legal recommendations to the Court for disposing of those cases referred to the DITF and other cases involving similar issues. The Court endorsed the fact-findings of the DITF without speaking about the recommendations. But those recommendations, with certain exceptions, are clearly reflected in the judgment.[80]

It seems that the United Nations Office of the High Commissioner for Human Rights (OHCHR) Nepal Office's report[81] also contributed immensely to the Court's understanding of the systematic pattern of disappearance. The report made public in May 2006 claimed that 49 persons were tortured in, and disappeared from, an army barracks in Kathmandu. Out of them, 35 persons[82]

---

79 In paragraph no. 1 of the order constituting the DITF, the Court stated 'to submit concluding opinion in respect of the persons mentioned in the writ petition whether they were taken into custody or not, to find out their updated and factual status and what is appropriate to do in the cases involving the similar questions… '. Under the heading mandate of the DITF, in the same order, the Court has mentioned only to find out the factual situations. See Order of the Supreme Court of 28 August 2006, *supra* note 40.This author understands that the mandate of the DITF is only to find out facts, and any reference of opinion is limited to establish fact. It does not include the advice to the Court on legal issues to be settled by the Court in handing down the judgment.

80 The DITF produced recommendations in the following headings: 6.1 Recommendations; 6.1.1 Formation of an Investigative Committee; 6.1.2 Criteria for Formation of the Investigative Commission; 6.2.3 Formulation of New Legislation; 6.6.4 Judicial Directive; 6.1.5 On Person under the Writ Petitions. Under each sub-heading there are a number of recommendations. See Report of the Detainee Investigation Task Force 2063, original with case file (copy on file with author).

81 UNOHCHR-Nepal Report, *supra* note 41.

82 On checking the names mentioned at p. 21 of the judgment against the list of the disappeared persons mentioned in the UNOHCHR-Nepal investigative report, the names of 35 persons were repeated.

were named in the *habeas corpus* petitions that were *sub judice* before the Court. In addition to reliable investigative information about the persons who were praying for the authority of the Court for their relief, the report highlighted the systematic pattern of enforced disappearance practices by the state forces. The Court not only found the investigation credible, but it also suggested the use of the Criteria for the Commission on Enforced Disappearance, developed by the OHCHR Nepal Office,[83] as guidelines for designing a framework for the disappearance commission in the legislation to be introduced pursuant to the Court's order. Naming the perpetrators[84] gave impetus to the feasibility of identifying the perpetrators and the possibility of bringing them to justice, eg on the basis of the liability mode of command responsibility, which is not known in Nepalese legal practice.

Finally, the attorneys appearing on behalf of the disappeared persons empowered the Court in two ways. First, they based their arguments mainly on international law, since there was no clear domestic legal framework for providing a remedy to the victims of disappearances. They strongly emphasized the obligation of the state, under international human rights instruments, to protect those rights and provide an effective remedy in case of their violation. Secondly, it seems that, in addition to the original *habeas corpus* petitions, the supplementary applications of mandamus for seeking actions against the perpetrators and remedies to the families of the victims were filed to allow the Court to give enough room to consider the issues in a broader perspective on the basis of international human rights law, rather than limiting itself to the *habeas corpus* issue.

4. CONCLUSION

In a post-conflict society, the complex challenge of establishing the rule of law requires multiple interventions. In addition to strong political will and international support for that purpose, the central role of the judiciary is critical for dealing with the issues of post-conflict justice. The transmission of international rule of law norms through judicial practice helps rebuild the domestic rule of law. In this respect, the *Dhakal* case may be seen as a constitutional moment for enforcing international rule of law in Nepal. The juridical will for the invocation of the Disappearance Convention and the internalization of jurisprudence developed by foreign courts and international human rights courts bodes well for the transmission of other international norms in the future. It is noted that the Nepalese judiciary is taking the lead in developing law-based post-conflict justice initiatives in Nepal, and that this empowerment process seems to be home-grown, without direct influence from international actors.

---

83 *Rabindra Prasad Dhakal v. Government of Nepal*, *supra* note 9, p. 54.

84 UNOHCHR-Nepal Report, *supra* note 41, p. 66.

The Nepalese Supreme Court's bold effort to enforce the responsibilities of the state under international human rights instruments has sent a message that the failure of the executive would not be excused by the judiciary. The message of the *Dhakal* case is that the judiciary is ready to take into account international norms in dealing with past human rights abuses if the executive has failed to do so.

However, judicial activism alone is not sufficient to deal with past human rights violations in a comprehensive manner. The executive itself should initiate and lead the process. One may observe in this respect that it seems that the Court's order to initiate new legislation to criminalize forced disappearances has been accepted by the executive branch. However, a law in this regard has still not been enacted, although it needs to be mentioned that the enactment process appears to be in progress. The executive, led by the CPN (M), the rebel force turned into the largest political party after the election of the Constituent Assembly, promulgated a law through an executive order,[85] which unfortunately lapsed due to the failure to introduce it for parliamentary approval. But subsequently, the executive formed in May 2009 after the fall of the CPN (M)-led government also introduced a bill for that purpose in December 2009.[86] Both of these instruments criminalize forced disappearance, pave the way for the prosecution of the perpetrators of disappearance committed during the armed conflict, and provide for the establishment of a disappearance commission to find out the whereabouts of the disappeared persons. Although the objectives and reasons for the introduction of the bill in Parliament do not state that it was aimed to give effect to the *Dhakal* judgment, the government has stated in a hearing conducted by the Court that the bill was indeed introduced for that purpose.[87] In addition to the disappearance bill, forced disappearance of a person has been included as a crime in the draft penal code proposed by a committee formed by the government.[88] That being said, as long as the current political impasse continues, and the Constituent Assembly does not draft and promulgate a new constitution, it does not seem plausible to infer that new legislation in dealing with the past will be enacted soon.

---

85 The Enforced Disappearance of Person (Crime and Punishment) Ordinance, 2009.

86 The Enforced Disappearance of Person (Crime and Punishment) Bill, 2009.

87 In the course of hearing in *Rammaya Nakarmi v. Office of the Prime Minister and Others*, decision date 26 August 2010, *The Nagarik* 10, 28 August 2010 (full text of the judgment yet to be prepared), the Supreme Court asked the government about what was done in respect of some cases of forced disappearance investigated by the National Human Rights Commission. Although the Court did not ask directly about the progress for the enactment of legislation pursuant to the *Dhakal* judgment, the Office of the Prime Minister and Council of Ministers sent a letter to the Court stating that the bills in respect of the disappearance commission and the truth and reconciliation commission were introduced for the purpose of giving effect to the order of the Court in that case. It is important to note that the Court did not order to initiate the process of enactment of truth and reconciliation legislation in the *Dhakal* judgment. See A letter from the Office of the Prime Minister and Council of Ministers to the Supreme Court, August, 2010, original with case file (copy on file with author).

88 Chapter 16, the Proposed Penal Code, 2067.

In the absence of domestic legal provisions in the matter of international law crimes, reparation to and protections of the victims, truth and reconciliation, and amnesty in respect of atrocities committed during the armed conflict, any future legislation dealing with these matters will work in the void of the past domestic experience. Many complex issues would arise in the courts of law if actions could be brought on the basis of such legislation. Reliance on the principles laid down by the foreign and international courts would help Nepal to handle those cases and strengthen the rule of law. Thus, the *Dhakal* case empowered the courts to internalize those principles as 'recognized principles of justice' in the Nepalese legal system.

It appears that the *Dhakal* case is recently gaining more authority, through judicial practice as well as victim relief packages formulated by the government. In dealing with similar cases of the past disappearances, the Supreme Court has relied on the *Dhakal* case on the issue of the desirability of the acceptance of the Disappearance Convention as a standard of international law.[89] In addition to providing monetary relief to the victims identified in the *Dhakal* case, the government has formulated a plan to provide the same amount of money to the relatives of all persons disappeared during the armed conflict. It seems that the government has taken the amount fixed by the Court as a benchmark for interim relief.[90]

Despite these positive signs, the most complicated issue of the prosecution of the perpetrators of enforced disappearance is not gaining momentum. On the surface, all main political forces seem ready to enact a law for that purpose and take action accordingly. But in reality, *Realpolitik* is playing an adverse role. Political forces have not only been unable to deal with past human rights abuses; they have also failed to reach agreement on other major political issues. In fact, it seems that unless a comprehensive political settlement is agreed upon, the issue of prosecution will remain unsettled. The judiciary, for its part, apparently believes that such a comprehensive scheme will come: after all, the Supreme Court refused to issue an order to the government to take action on a particular case of disappearance and subsequent death, on the ground that those issues would be dealt with in a comprehensive scheme which would include truth and reconciliation legislation[91] and disappearance legislation. Yet for the time being, the judiciary appears to be far more progressive than the government is willing or able to be.

---

89 *Baburam Giri and Others v. Cabinet Secretariat and Others*, NKP 2066 (3) 413.

90 Directive to Provide Relief to the Relatives of the Disappeared Persons, 2065.

91 *Rammaya Nakarmi v. Office of the Prime Minister*, *supra* note 87. In addition to the Disappearance Bill, *supra* note 86, the Truth and Reconciliation Bill, 2010, was introduced in the Parliament on 18 March 2010. The CPA does not speak about amnesty for serious violations of human rights law and grave breaches of humanitarian law. There is no provision of amnesty in the Disappearance Bill. The Truth and Reconciliation Bill provides for conditional amnesty for crimes except for killing after taking into custody, killing an unarmed person, torture, rape, forced disappearance, and abduction.

INTERNATIONAL LAW AND IRAQI COURTS

Haider Ala Hamoudi*

1. INTRODUCTION – PROMISING CONDITIONS AND UNFULFILLED PROMISE

In a book that contains so many laudable chapters detailing the rising importance of international law applied directly in domestic courts, Iraq stands as a stark anomaly. Following the departure of the US and UK administered Coalition Provisional Authority (CPA) and the restoration of Iraqi sovereignty to a democratically elected government, Iraq's authorities seem to be at best equivocal and at worst somewhat hostile to the notion that Iraq's domestic courts should play a role in ensuring that Iraq abide by its international legal commitments, in particular as concerns the matters of human rights and criminal law that attract much scholarly attention.

This is rather surprising for two reasons. First of all, Iraq is not a nation that is wary of international commitments. This was very much the case historically, and even more so following the fall of the Saddam regime. Prior to 2003, Iraq was a signatory to most major human rights treaties, among them the Genocide Convention (acceded to in 1959), the International Covenant on Civil and Political Rights (ICCPR) as well as the International Covenant on Economic, Social and Cultural Rights (ICESCR) (both ratified by Law 193 of 1970), the International Convention on the Elimination of All Forms of Racial Discrimination (ratified 1970), the International Convention on the Elimination of All Forms of Discrimination Against Women (ratified 1986), and the Convention on the Rights of the Child (ratified 1994).

If anything, the commitment to international law as a formal matter has grown more robust. Even a cursory glance at Iraq's legislative achievements over the past legislative term, running from 2006 to 2010, demonstrates a decided commitment to enter into international obligations and treaties of various sorts rather than, as regrettably happens all too often in the United States, to avoid

* Assistant Professor of Law, University of Pittsburgh School of Law.

them on the grounds that they are some sort of pernicious 'entanglement'.[1] In 2008 and 2009 alone, for example, Iraq's Council of Representatives, which serves as its legislature,[2] ratified or acceded to twenty-two separate international treaties or covenants, a number that I surmise would compare well with ratification rates in nearly any other nation over the same time period. In addition, Iraqi political leaders routinely speak proudly of their commitment to adhere to international law, eschewing the histrionic antics of some of the more colourful Middle Eastern leaders who prefer to rail at the United Nations as being some sort of imperialist project.

Moreover, the call to adherence to international law and international relations is very often grounded at least in part in the desire to adhere to broader global commitments and understandings respecting human rights in particular. Thus, in his address to the General Assembly in 2008, Iraqi President Jalal Talabani called for the assistance of 'countries around the world' in building Iraq into a 'modern nation which ensures justice, equality, the strengthening of the rule of law, the respect for human rights, and women's participation in all spheres of life.'[3] Later in the same speech President Talabani speaks with pride of the number of international legal instruments to which Iraq was recently signatory, as well as an unspecified 'international compact to achieve economic growth and social justice in partnership with the international community.' These are not sentiments which would suggest any hostility to the conception of international law as domestic constraint, particularly inasmuch as human rights, women's rights, and even social justice are concerned.

Secondly, and equally importantly, Iraq's judiciary is robust and increasingly outspoken, willing to address core legal questions that constrain executive power. For example, in June of 2010, the Federal Supreme Court certified electoral results that reflected a parliamentary victory for the rival of the sitting Prime

---

1 In fact, Iraq has even approved treaties that the United States has opposed under both Democratic and Republican Administrations. The first treaty approved by the previous Council of Representatives, in 2006, was the Convention on the Prohibition of the Use, Stockpiling, Production and Transfer of Anti-Personnel Mines and on Their Destruction (1997). To much international criticism, the United States did not sign the treaty under President Clinton when it was negotiated, and has not signed it to date, citing security guarantees to South Korea, and the need for mines to repel a North Korean invasion, as the basis for its refusal. S. Safrin, The Unexceptionalism of U.S. Exceptionalism, 41 Vanderbilt Journal of Transnational Law 1307–54 (2008) (arguing that the United States was not acting in an 'exceptional' fashion by refusing to sign the treaty given its existing international commitments on the Korean peninsula).

2 Under Article 47 of the Iraqi Constitution, Iraq's legislative power is divided into two bodies – the Council of Representatives and the Federation Council. However, under Article 65, the Federation Council is to be created by legislation enacted by the Council of Representatives, and no such legislation has been enacted. This leaves the Council of Representatives as the sole legislative body for the time being.

3 Statement of H.E. Mr. Jalal Talabani, President of the Republic of Iraq, at the 63rd Session of the General Assembly Hall (25 September 2008), available at www.un.org/en/ga/63/generaldebate/pdf/iraq_en.pdf.

Minister,[4] even as the Prime Minister had been contesting the results for weeks prior to this.[5] The Prime Minister may have been disappointed in the results, but he made no public objection to the certification.

In a separate ruling, the Court declared that a key ally of the Prime Minister, the Provincial Governor of Salahuddin province, was validly removed after a vote of its Provincial Council, the Prime Minister's opposition to this decision notwithstanding.[6] The most remarkable aspect of this episode was the Prime Minister's reaction to the Court ruling, and to subsequent and previous events related thereto. He refused to acknowledge the Provincial Council's vote dismissing the Provincial Governor initially, yielded only after the Court issued its decision, and then proceeded to take over the Governor's premises by military force, accepting the Court's judgment respecting dismissal, yet not allowing a replacement selected by the Provincial Council itself to be seated who did not meet with his approval.[7] Stated differently, *everything that the Prime Minister did with respect to this episode seemed tainted with illegality, some of it rather blatant, except adherence to the order of the Court to remove his political ally.* That the Prime Minister finds it unobjectionable to occupy a local government building by force against the wishes of the local government and its Provincial Council, and yet still yields to Court orders that order the dismissal of his ally, speaks volumes respecting the legitimacy and authority of the Court. The Prime Minister thought nothing of dismissing the demands of the Provincial Council,

---

4 A. Shadid, Iraqi Court Ratifies Parliamentary Election Results, New York Times A7 (2 June 2010).

5 T. Williams and Z. Thaker, Iraq's Premier, Trailing His Main Rival, Endorses a Recount of the Vote, New York Times A4 (22 March 2010). Admittedly, and as others have pointed out, the Court in a separate ruling indicated that the electoral list that earned the most candidates (in this case, that of the Prime Minister's rival) was not necessarily the one that would be asked to form a government first, as one could imagine a post-election coalition of two electoral lists whose numbers combined exceed those of the winning list. See Iraq Federal Supreme Court, Decision 25 of 2010, available (in Arabic) at www.iraqja.iq/ifm.php?recordID=102. This decision is not unprecedented, as precisely the same conclusion was reached in Israel after the previous elections, where Netanyahu, a second place finisher, was charged with the task of government formation when it was clear that his bloc was able to secure more parliamentary allies than the first place finisher, Tzipi Livni. I. Kershner, Netanyahu to Form New Israel Government, New York Times A7 (21 February 2009).
More relevant for our purposes, a court captive to the interests of a sitting executive would not confirm electoral results that declare the sitting Prime Minister a second place finisher and then suggest that he might be able to retain his position and form a government if he finds sufficient numbers of allies among other electoral contenders with representatives. Rather, if the sole basis of decision-making was to keep the Prime Minister in his current position, the court rulings would be precisely reversed – the Prime Minister's party would be declared the winner due to some sort of alleged electoral fraud *and* the court would rule that by necessity his party would have to be given the first opportunity to form the government. That the Court did not adopt such an approach does suggest its willingness to separate itself from the Prime Minister in significant ways.

6 Iraq Federal Supreme Court Decision No. 58 of 2009.

7 S.L. Myers and A. Shadid, Leader Faulted on Using Army in Iraqi Politics, New York Times A1 (11 February 2011).

even when issued pursuant to constitutional authority, yet was willing to adhere to Court orders that contravened his interests.

This is not to say that judicial institutions in Iraq have *never* had their independence impugned in the post Saddam era – the disqualifications of hundreds of candidates prior to the March 2010 elections, and the approval thereof by the Court, are probably the most egregious example of executive interference. After a commission disqualified nearly 500 potential candidates for alleged ties to the Ba'ath, and the matter was brought before the judiciary for review, the relevant court set aside the ruling. Reasoning that it could not possibly review in a period of weeks before a pending election the evidence for so many putative candidates, it held that the more sensible course was to let all of them stand for office, where a vast majority seemed destined to lose in an election involving 7,500 candidates seeking 325 seats, and the courts could then revisit the matter after the elections. Following an outcry, demonstrations, and even a meeting between political leaders (and most prominently the Prime Minister) and the Chief Justice, the court reversed itself and agreed to review the matter. In the end, only 26 candidates were reinstated.[8] Clearly, this was not a shining example of judicial independence, and cannot be defended as such. My point is only that, Iraq's own dysfunctions aside, over the process of dizzying transformation from totalitarian dictatorship to messy and imperfect democratic rule, the Federal Supreme Court, and supporting judicial institutions, have risen in prestige, importance, and legitimacy, such that their rulings are routinely followed by political actors even when contrary to their interests.

There is thus what appears to be a promising combination for the rise of international law as a source of law within domestic courts. On the one hand, Iraq is a nation favourably disposed to integrating itself further into the international community, and expanding its level of international commitments, particularly with respect to the matters of economic development, human rights, and social justice. On the other, it enjoys a largely independent judiciary rising in prominence. Given this, one would expect some level of encouragement of national courts to engage international law, and some willingness on the part of the courts to do just that. That nothing of the sort has happened, that in fact *both* political actors are not interested in widespread use of international law in domestic courts, *and* that the courts themselves seem quite reluctant to use it in any event, is worthy of some consideration.

I have divided the balance of this chapter, designed to explain this odd result, into three parts. The first discusses the use of international law historically within Iraqi courts. The second describes an interim phase, between the fall of the Saddam regime and the ratification of the current Constitution, where promising indications could be located that appeared to give recognition to a

8 S.L. Myers, Few Barred Candidates Are Restored to the Iraqi Ballot, New York Times A19 (14 February 2010).

new legal order wherein international law would play a more important role in domestic judicial practice, and the third part describes the manner in which that practice largely receded with the ratification of the current Constitution, rendering the position of international law, as a source of law in domestic courts, of marginal importance at best.

2. TRADITIONAL APPROACHES

At a formal level, there is no reason that the Iraqi judiciary could not use international law, or perhaps better stated, some number of sources within international law, as a basis for decision-making in the proper context. All of Iraq's treaties, after having been ratified, are given the force of law by being issued as 'laws' and published in full in the Official Gazette – copied, essentially, into a domestic act. Thus, for example, both the ICCPR and the ICESCR appear as Law 193 of 1970, as any other law would, and appear as if they had been enacted as an ordinary domestic law.[9] Nothing would seem to prevent a judge from accessing and applying this law as she would any other. Such an approach could not be used for customary international law admittedly (nor for any treaty that had not been approved by the legislature or for any other reason had not been republished in the Official Gazette as domestic law), but the reference of the judge to a treaty which appears as a law in the Official Gazette *should be* no more and no less controversial than reference to any other law. Importantly, this was as true, as a formal matter, in the era of Saddam Hussein as it is now.

Moving from *formal* judicial empowerment to the *actual* application of international law in a domestic setting, however, has proven more difficult. It is starkly in contrast to Iraqi judicial *culture and practice* as it has developed over the past several decades. There are a number of reasons for this. First of all, there is the fact that Iraqi judges would be, during the Saddam era in particular, somewhat reticent to refer to international legal instruments that might offer additional procedural protections beyond those set forth in the relevant domestic codes. Even the idea of *domestic, constitutional* constraint on enacted law was highly disfavoured at the time, as current Minister of Justice Dara Nuruddin discovered when during the Ba'ath era, when he was a judge, he declared a particular piece of legislation unconstitutional. After refusing to reconsider his ruling, Judge Dara spent two years in prison for his offense.[10]

Nevertheless, this ground for judicial reluctance, while quite significant, can hardly serve as adequate grounds in all instances, in particular in those cases in which the regime had no obvious interest in the outcome. The reality is that

9 The Official Gazette can be accessed via the website of the Global Justice Project Iraq, www.gjpi.org/2009/02/02/official-gazette-of-iraq/ (last accessed 28 January 2011).

10 A Look at the New Iraqi Leaders, Baltimore Sun (16 July 2003).

political prisoners and other real or perceived opponents of the regime were never processed through the ordinary court system – to the extent that any courts were involved, they were part of a separate system known as the Revolutionary Courts, which were organized specifically to deal with security threats against the state.[11] The Saddam regime did not generally interfere in how the courts might deal with an ordinary defendant accused of an ordinary crime. As a result, the real protections afforded in the Criminal Procedure Code during this era, including a right to silence, the prohibition against the use of coercive methods to obtain a confession, and a right to be questioned within 24 hours of appearing before a judge, could be and were invoked, albeit intermittently in the opinions of some.[12] If this was the case for the rights contained in the Criminal Procedure Code, it is difficult to see why the regime would object, again with respect to these ordinary cases, to the application of rights contained in international law. International law provides more by way of protection, but the law *already* constrains particular police actions, and thus reference to international law as a *further constraint* might well be disfavoured by the regime, though it is not entirely clear by how much.

In addition, however, there was the broader resistance of Iraqi judges to look beyond a procedural code that they tended to view (in keeping with popular civilian mythology on the subject) as comprehensive, determinative, and complete. This is not to say that judges necessarily viewed any amendment to the Code as unthinkable or even unnecessary, but rather to the extent that some level of legal reform was necessary, it needed to be undertaken, in their view, in the instrument itself rather than through the extraneous use of material beyond the provisions of the Code. Certainly this is the view that immediately became apparent to me in my discussions with judges who were tasked by the Higher Judicial Council to work with international experts to produce suggested amendments to the Criminal Procedure Code.[13]

In any event, whether on account of either of these two factors, or any other factor that one might consider, the reluctance to employ international law was a very strong one, and in fact continues in force in large part to this day. Iraqi judges have never at any significant level relied upon international commitments to inform, much less supplant, relevant provisions of domestic law.[14] Iraqi judges

11 M. Cherif Bassiouni, Post-Conflict Justice in Iraq: An Appraisal of the Iraq Special Tribunal, 38 Cornell International Law Journal 360 n 170 (2005).

12 Law of Criminal Procedure of Iraq, No. 23 of 1971 ('Criminal Procedure Code'), at arts. 123, 127, 179.

13 This particular project was undertaken by the University of Utah S.J. Quinney School of Law in cooperation with the Iraq Higher Judicial Council from the spring of 2009 through March of 2010. The project was led on the international side by Andrew Allen and Sara Abdullah. I served as Deputy Chief of Party for the broader program organized by the S.J. Quinney School of Law and in that capacity had some limited interactions with the committee involved in developing the suggested amendments.

14 Naturally it would be impossible to state with any degree of certainty that domestic courts *never* applied a right contained in an international legal instrument to which Iraq is signatory

do not consider it their role to disregard the Code in favour of the ICCPR. In fact in my experience, even those judges who would prefer to see respect for the ICCPR's more protective positions in Iraqi courts frame their demands in the form of an amendment to the Code, not independent judicial recognition of the ICCPR.

In light of this background, in order to render meaningful the applicability of international law in domestic courts, forceful changes in both the law and the broader judicial culture would prove to be necessary. As is shown in the next two sections, an effort to exact such changes was made in the interim period, but ultimately abandoned by the time that the final constitution came to be negotiated and ratified.

3. THE CPA AND INTERNATIONAL LAW

The CPA administered Iraq from just after the fall of the Saddam regime, in April of 2003, until the end of June of 2004, when it turned over sovereignty to a transitional Iraqi government constituted through an interim constitution known as the Transitional Administrative Law (TAL). The TAL then created a mechanism through which a Transitional National Assembly would be elected, and would draft a constitution submitted for popular referendum.[15]

The CPA has been much criticized for being largely distant from the population it claimed to administer, and there is certainly much truth to this.[16] Yet for all of the criticisms leveled against the CPA during the period that it ruled Iraq as the occupation authority, its own efforts, however fitful and in vain, to incorporate greater human rights protections guaranteed in international law into Iraqi judicial proceedings can scarcely be doubted. This was achieved in various ways. One of these was the enactment of CPA orders and memoranda which amended Iraqi law in various ways, some of dubious legality,[17] and which incorporated the substance of international legal protections into existing Iraqi

in a domestic setting. However, based on my own extensive observations of Iraqi courts, as well as my many encounters and interviews with Iraqi criminal judges, I can say with some level of certainty that any such references are, to the extent they exist at all, exceedingly rare.

15 Transitional Administrative Law of Iraq (2004), Art. 2(B) (TAL).

16 See generally R. Chandrasekaran, Imperial Life in the Emerald City (Knopf: New York, 2007).

17 The CPA claimed that it had international legal authority to engage in the type of lawmaking that it did on the basis of Security Council Resolution 1483, which among other things called upon the CPA to 'promote the welfare of the Iraqi people through effective administration' of Iraq. SC Resolution 1483, para. 4 (S/RES/1483) (22 May 2003). Most legal experts have dismissed this reasoning as dubious, given that the next paragraph of the same Security Council Resolution requires conformity with the Hague Regulations IV, which require an occupying force to respect existing law 'unless absolutely prevented'. Hague Convention IV, 18 October 1907, 36 Stat. 2277, TS No. 539, art. 43. See also H.A. Hamoudi, Money Laundering Amidst Mortars: Legislative Process and State Authority in Post Invasion Iraq, 16

law. Hence, to take the simplest example, CPA Memorandum 3 amended the Criminal Procedure Code by granting to an accused the right to counsel during questioning (including paid counsel if the accused was indigent).[18] This is not the use of international law in domestic proceedings so much as the conforming of domestic law to the substance of existing obligations as set forth in international instruments. It is worthy of much consideration, but unfortunately beyond the scope of this chapter. Fair treatment of the complex and nuanced relationship of Iraqi *domestic* law to evolving human rights norms requires far more attention than I am able to devote in these few pages.

The other means to ensure broader judicial recognition of international legal obligations, and the more significant one for our purposes, arose in the TAL. The TAL was drafted by a group of Iraqi leaders that the CPA had formed to advise it, known as the Iraq Governing Council, and approved by the CPA just prior to the transfer of sovereignty back to Iraq. Article 23 of the TAL marks a significant and in many ways remarkable departure from traditional Iraqi positions respecting the use of international law in domestic proceedings. It reads in relevant part:

> The enumeration of the foregoing rights must not be interpreted to mean that they are the only rights enjoyed by the Iraqi people. They enjoy all the rights that befit a free people possessed of their human dignity, *including the rights stipulated in international treaties and agreements, other instruments of international law that Iraq has signed and to which it has acceded, and others that are deemed binding upon it, and in the law of nations* (emphasis supplied).[19]

In some way, this appears to extend even beyond international legal obligations, strictly defined. That is to say, the rights are those 'that befit a free people possessed of their human dignity', which *include* international obligations, but do not seem to be limited by them. Moreover, the rights to which Iraq is obligated to adhere in addition to those that befit a free people may be divided into four categories:

1. Those 'stipulated in international treaties and agreements';
2. Those contained in *other* instruments of international law to which Iraq has acceded;
3. Those otherwise deemed binding upon it;
4. Those contained in the law of nations.

Transnational Law and Contemporary Problems 523, 528 n 22 and references cited therein respecting legality of CPA activities.

18 CPA Memorandum 3, Section 4(c) (2003).

19 Article 23 TAL, *supra* note 15.

Assuming that category 1 is not entirely subsumed by category 2 would mean that the rights contained in 'international treaties and agreements' would be beyond those in treaties *that Iraq had signed.* Assuming that category 1 is not entirely subsumed by category 3 would mean that such rights were also those that might otherwise be deemed binding on Iraq through custom or otherwise. Category 4 appears to be some sort of 'catch-all', though precisely what it might include that category 3 does not is unclear.

In any event, taken together, Iraqi judges were effectively called upon to add, to whatever rights might be contained in Iraqi domestic law, the following material:

1. Those contained in treaties Iraq had signed;
2. Those contained in treaties Iraq had not signed;
3. Customary international law;
4. Those that 'befit a free people possessed of their human dignity.'

The breadth is astonishing for a few reasons. First of all, it is baffling how the CPA, whose personnel in some cases were specifically vetted on the basis of *their opposition in the American context to the type of progressive judicial policymaking which such language specifically invites,*[20] could have any role in the promulgation of a clause of this sort. This is to say nothing of the fact that senior CPA personnel were themselves openly contemptuous of international law at times, in some ways in keeping with broad US exceptionalism, in this context of a more pathological variety.[21] The only sensible explanation appears to be that the CPA placed much more faith in the secular Iraqi judiciary than the more generally Islamist Iraqi political classes who were likely to win an election. Allowing the judiciary to create rights and impose obligations in the Iraqi context may have therefore seemed appealing to the CPA personnel, even if they might have decried it as fundamentally undemocratic if attempted in the American context.

Unfortunately, however, the breadth of Article 23 seems to take almost no account of Iraq's legal history, where international law was given almost no recognition in domestic proceedings at all. To alter this would require something

20 Specifically, two CPA personnel were asked how they felt about the American case of *Roe v. Wade*, the US Supreme Court decision constitutionalizing the right to abortion, as part of their interview process, presumably to ensure their adherence to Republican Party orthodoxy opposing that decision. Chandrasekaran, *supra* note 16, p. 91. The common criticism of *Roe* from American conservatives – that it extends the conception of constitutional rights well beyond those specifically enumerated in the US Constitution – would be obliterated under a theory pursuant to which judges were asked to recognize any and all rights 'befitting a free people possessed of their human dignity.'

21 Chandrasekaran, *supra* note 16, p. 142–43 (describing Thomas Foley, in charge of private sector development for the CPA, as indicating that he did not care about international law, and that his sole commitment was to fulfill the US President's directive to privatize Iraqi businesses).

of a cultural revolution within the judiciary, one that would be more likely to be successful the less it required by way of substantive change. Encouraging judges to apply treaty law to the extent enacted in Iraq and published in the Official Gazette would have been difficult, but potentially sustainable. Encouraging them to use customary international law as well would have been yet more difficult, and of questionable long term viability. However, a judge reluctant to use as the basis for decision-making source material beyond that presented in a domestic code is almost surely not going to readily incorporate rights 'befitting a free people' or rights contained in international agreements that Iraq has not signed, *to the potential derogation of domestic law.* Even to hope for the gradual realization of such a result, in a document enacted as the CPA was ceding authority to the Iraqis, seems fanciful and naïve.

Nevertheless, upon the departure of the CPA in June of 2004,[22] such was the applicable law. I am not aware of any instance where a judge thought to apply it, though it is possible Article 23 was used somewhere, by someone, at some time. To the extent called upon, however, the references were never significant enough to merit public attention. In any event, the real issue would not be the use of any particular provision of an interim document which was only applicable law for a period only slightly exceeding fifteen months.[23] Rather, the matter would depend on the extent to which the *final* constitution, drafted not by handpicked Iraqi advisors but rather an elected National Assembly, and approved not by the CPA but by the Iraqi people in a general referendum, would adopt the formulation of the TAL respecting rights set forth in international law. This is the subject of the next and final section of this chapter.

4. THE FINAL CONSTITUTION AND THE REJECTION OF INTERNATIONAL LAW IN DOMESTIC PROCEEDINGS

I have indicated that one reason that the CPA may have been willing to countenance a rather broad conception of judicial policymaking as concerns the establishment of fundamental rights, with such a liberal reference to international law, is because it trusted the secular judiciary more than it did the Islamist politicians who were evidently poised to win the first election that Iraq held, in January of 2005.[24] Whether or not this is the case, it seems abundantly clear that

22 While the TAL was drafted in March of 2004, it did not take effect according to its terms until the departure of the CPA, in June of 2004. See Iraq Constitutions, Global Justice Project (Iraq), www.gjpi.org/library/primary/iraqi-constitution/ (last visited 25 October 2010).

23 The final Iraqi Constitution was approved by a popular referendum on 15 October 2005.

24 H.A. Hamoudi, Identitarian Violence and Identitarian Politics: Elections and Governance in Iraq, 51 Harvard International Law Journal (Online) 86 (2010).

the Islamic parties, who won these elections in the numbers that were expected,[25] were deeply and fundamentally distrustful of international law as a source of rights, particularly in the broadly articulated form set forth in the TAL. The matter was viewed as a means by a black robed elite to thwart the will and desire of the people to organize society by whatever religious or moral principles they deemed appropriate. Ironically, opponents of *Roe v. Wade* in the American context often adopt the same position, and it was *Roe v. Wade* itself that was a litmus test for at least some members of the CPA to obtain their positions.[26]

In the Iraqi context, the religious or moral principles being referred to necessarily included the *shari'a*, that vast body of norms and rules developed by jurists from Muslim sacred text, some of which, at least as traditionally understood, does conflict with contemporary understandings of human rights. That international law was at least potentially hostile to *shari'a*, and that judges as a result must not be permitted to have recourse to it to make rulings in derogation of *shari'a*, was a perception that would prove to be of fundamental importance.

As a result, when the Islamist dominated interim National Assembly came to convene, and select a Constitutional Committee, and when that Constitutional Committee came to have its meetings to draft the final constitution, it was abundantly clear from the minutes of the meetings (to which I have been given access by the former chair of the Committee as part of ongoing research for a book respecting the drafting of the Constitution)[27] that nothing of the breadth of Article 23 of the TAL would be seriously contemplated. The Shi'i Islamic parties in particular voiced such serious and grave doubts that more secular forces on the Committee, most notably the Kurdish contingent, did not even try to revive Article 23 as originally formulated. Even a proposed compromise formulation that repeated the language of Article 23 in large part but limited its applicability to circumstances where the provisions did not contravene the principles of Islam was rejected, by both sides. The Islamists were concerned about the scope of the legal obligations that Article 23 might entail, and the Kurds were concerned that too many legal obligations would be curtailed by the *shari'a* proviso.

The discussion quickly narrowed to focus instead on *existing international legal commitments* that Iraq had already undertaken. Here, the secularist argument carried more force. The Islamist objection, as we have seen, had been

25 A. Arato, Constitution Making Under Occupation: The Politics of Imposed Revolution in Iraq 208 (New York: Columbia University Press, 2009) (showing election results).

26 Chandrasekaran, *supra* note 16, p. 97.

27 Specifically, I was permitted to review the documents *in the offices at the Council of Representatives* at my leisure, to take any notes I wished, but not to make any copies of the documents themselves. I spent weeks in the offices taking notes so as to comply both with the imposed limitations on access and with my own scholarly need to ensure proper attribution. I should also note in full disclosure that the former chair of the Constitutional Committee is my paternal uncle.

that Article 23 could very well reference rights and obligations that run counter to the settled matters (*thawabit*) of the *shari'a*. In meeting minutes, Islamist Jalaluddin Al-Saghir listed three examples – non-marital sex, homosexuality, and usury. Surely, however, the same concern could not apply, the secular forces countered, as for treaties to which Iraq was *already* signatory, and which it had *already* ratified. These are existing legal obligations, after all, and it could not be reasonably said that they include provisions unknown to the drafters and repugnant to the *shari'a*.

These arguments, supported by the US Embassy as well, turned out to be strong enough to result in inclusion of an article in a relatively late draft of the constitution that read largely as follows:

> To each individual is the right to enjoy all of the freedoms contained in the conventions and relevant international treaties respecting human rights which Iraq has signed.[28]

This is admittedly narrower than the TAL's Article 23, and refers exclusively to international legal material that has been approved by Iraq. Nevertheless, when combined with the Article 2 prohibition against the enactment of law that violates 'fundamental rights and freedoms' and the Article 94 grant of authority to the Federal Supreme Court to interpret constitutional text, the implication would have been, seemingly, to empower domestic courts broadly in the application of international law in the areas of human rights and criminal law in particular, if not so broadly as to grant them recourse to rights beyond those contained in the substantial number of treaties to which Iraq is signatory.[29]

The provision, however, was ultimately removed, in a very late stage of negotiations known as the 'political kitchen', wherein a final text with a series of disputed provisions was provided to Iraq's chief political leaders, and they were tasked with making necessary amendments. Though this particular article was never slated as 'disputed' by the leaders, it was nonetheless removed in the process of these late negotiations. The meeting minutes contain little information concerning the cause of the late removal, even if earlier reports suggested some level of Islamist misgivings over the matter.

According to Ashley Deeks and Matthew Burton, who have written quite an informative piece on the drafting of the Iraq Constitution, the objection to the

28 Article 44 Draft Consitution of Iraq, dated 21 August 2005.

29 To be clear, and for purposes of emphasis, Iraq's Criminal Procedure Code *does* contain reference to human rights protections, albeit in different forms and using different language than that contained in prevailing human rights treaties. Judges making recourse to such material is uncontroversial. What is more controversial is the application of human rights provisions from international treaties, even those printed as domestic law in the Gazette, in a manner not specifically contemplated in Iraq's domestic procedural codes.

proposed article came from Najaf, the site of the seminaries and the home of Grand Ayatollah Sistani, who had insisted that if it were kept, there would have to be a limiting clause indicating that the rights so incorporated could not contravene other provisions of the Constitution.[30] (The provision of the Constitution the Grand Ayatollah had in mind would no doubt be Article 2, which prohibits the enactment of law that conflicts with the 'settled rulings' of Islam.) Unwilling to include any caveat as to the applicability of international law on Iraqi territory, the secularists preferred its removal to the inclusion of the limitation, and hence, according to Deeks and Burton, the article was removed.[31]

There are other provisions of the Constitution referencing international law as well. However, they are hardly encouraging as concerns domestic court application of international law. Article 8, for example – the one article that addresses Iraq's international obligations as a general matter – reads as follows:

> Iraq shall observe the principles of good neighborliness, adhere to the principle of non-interference in the internal affairs of other states, seek to settle disputes by peaceful means, establish relations on the basis of mutual interests and reciprocity, and *respect its international obligations* (emphasis supplied).[32]

In the first place, this hardly seems to be the basis for a broad assumption of international law within the domestic judicial context, in that the provision addresses primarily foreign relations with other nations rather than matters such as human rights or criminal protections afforded defendants. Admittedly, however, the language 'international obligations' could be read broadly enough to encompass both questions of relations with other nations and substantive international human rights obligations if a judiciary were so inclined to interpret it.

A second problem is that the term 'respect' (*tahtarimu*) is far more significant in the context of Middle East politics than has been recognized by commentators like Deeks and Burton, who seem to equate it with 'comply'. In fact, it arguably means something less. In particular, the Palestinian militant Islamist organization Hamas has made it clear that it will not accede to any framework with its more secular Palestinian competitor Fatah that involves it 'being bound by' (*taltazimu*) previous agreements with Israel, though it will agree to 'respect'

---

30 A. Deeks and M. Burton, Iraq's Constitution: A Drafting History, 40 Cornell International Law Journal 37 (2007).

31 Deeks and Burton, *supra* note 30.

32 Article 8 Constitution of Iraq, available at www.uniraq.org/documents/iraqi_constitution.pdf (last visited 28 January 2011).

them.[33] The wordplay received a great deal of attention in the Arab world and on Arab television, and the term 'respect', when combined with legal obligation, was understood to suggest something short of a full commitment.

The linguistic nuance was not lost on the drafters themselves, who proved more than capable of strengthening the language when they found it expedient to do so. Article 9(e), for example, a late addition to the text, indicates that Iraq will 'respect' *and* 'implement' its obligations as concerns non-proliferation of chemical, biological, and nuclear weapons, implying that to 'respect' an international commitment is not quite to 'implement' it.[34] That weapons of mass destruction were a matter of significant concern to the United States, indeed at least a putative *casus belli* of the war with Iraq, and that comments were made on a draft in Arabic by a non-native speaker urging a stronger formulation, suggests that the United States may have been as aware as any of the potential limitations implicit in the term 'respect'.[35]

To be clear, it certainly is *possible* to equate, in the original Arabic, the term 'respect' with the term 'abide by', just as it is *possible* to read Article 8 broadly to encompass all obligations imposed on Iraq by international law. Taken together, these would empower the judiciary to incorporate international obligations in the context of domestic proceedings. All hope for the use of international law by a local judiciary is not, therefore, lost. Yet against this reading lies a deep professional culture within the judiciary that does *not* involve reference to international law, a political reality wherein references to international law have been *reduced* as Iraqi sovereignty and democratic praxis has expanded, rather than the reverse, and a largely implacable (at least over the short term) belief that international law could be used as some sort of subversive attempt to thwart the core of the *shari'a*, however that core might be defined. It would seem unlikely to say the least that under the current circumstances one would expect very much by way of reference to international law in domestic courts.[36]

---

33 See eg K.A. Toameh, Pals at War, Jerusalem Post (24 April 2009).

34 Article 9(e) reads as follows: 'The Iraqi Government shall respect and implement Iraq's international obligations regarding the non-proliferation, non-development, non-production, and non-use of nuclear, chemical, and biological weapons, and shall prohibit associated equipment, materiel, technologies, and delivery systems for use in the development, manufacture, production, and use of such weapons' (see *supra* note 32).

35 Deeks and Burton indicate that the most likely party to have insisted upon this provision were the Kurds. Deeks and Burton, *supra* note 30. p. 34–35. Their own reporting indicates nevertheless that the United States did emphasize the importance the United States ascribed to Iraq's adherence to treaty obligations.

36 It would be wrong to suggest that Iraqi courts will *never* make reference to international law under current conditions. In some instances, the Constitution requires it. Article 21 for example does not permit the granting of asylum to one who committed 'international crimes', and presumably a court would need to make that determination to deny asylum. However, the use of international law will, I suspect, be fleeting, limited, and for the most part, quite marginal.

5. CONCLUSION

Having established the relatively limited role that international law seems to play in domestic courts, and the seemingly deliberate decision on the part of the Constitution's drafters to keep it that way, it might behoove us to consider precisely what happened. That is, how did a nation seemingly willing, both before regime change and after, to undertake any number of international legal obligations through treaty and convention, and willing to entrust its judiciary with a fair amount of independence and legitimacy, end up reacting so coolly to the possibility that international law might become a part of the domestic judicial process?

The concerns, I suspect, might well be narrowed to two. The first is broader in nature and recurs throughout the Islamic world, and the second is unique to Iraq's anomalous circumstances immediately following an American occupation. Respecting the first concern, it appears that competing commitments on the part of the Constitution to Islam and Islamic law on the one hand, and largely transplanted constitutional rights and freedoms on the other, led to the decision to remove the reference to rights and freedoms contained in international law. All parties seemed relatively comfortable with the panoply of rights and freedoms offered in the Constitution, which included the standard set that one expects in any constitution. The concern, however, on the part of Islamist groups in particular, was that adding a reference to international law might enable a secular minded judiciary to *thwart* Islamic goals because there might be rights found within international law that might be to the derogation of what the Constitution refers to as the 'settled rulings' of Islam. This demonstrates an abiding suspicion of international law, and international human rights law in particular, as being some sort of Western imposed set of norms not necessarily applicable in the Iraqi context.

Naturally, given this concern, references to international law as a general matter, or to international custom, were the most suspect, precisely because the contours of those rights are potentially harder to identify and delimit. Somewhat less controversial were treaty provisions, particularly from treaties to which Iraq was signatory. Yet the concern was still present as it is difficult, absent exhaustive research, or so it was maintained, to know precisely the scope of even the existing international obligations, and thus important to make such rights *subsidiary to and not concomitant with* the 'settled rulings' of Islam. The failure of the parties to agree on that delimiting language led to the excision of the entire article.

Given this background, it seems that the CPA and the Iraq Governing Council may have committed what turned out to be, at least in hindsight, a grave strategic error in seeking such a forceful and radical change from existing judicial practice, where international law was all but unrecognized. This position only fuelled suspicions further. The fact is that whether pleased with the departure of Saddam Hussein or not – and most politicians in Iraq's new political structure are necessarily pleased, given their opportunity to participate in the state in a manner that would scarcely have been imaginable less than a decade ago – there is understandable suspicion when there is substantial external participation in Iraqi affairs on the part of foreign governments, the United States in particular. Even the presence of the American ambassador at the Iraqi legislature on the eve of a crucial vote on amendments to the Electoral Law was viewed with some level of hostility on the part of one significant Shi'i Islamist parliamentarian, who came close to threatening physical violence.[37] That this same parliamentarian elsewhere objected to an NGO law because it did not account sufficiently for the fact that NGO's could be used as a front for foreign espionage[38] only demonstrates the rather extensive level of suspicion.

The wiser course it seems would have been to adopt a milder formulation, one that did not empower the judiciary to find rights to the extent that they 'befit a free people possessed of their human dignity', as that only furthered Islamist suspicions that what was being attempted was an undemocratic coup on the *shari'a* organized by the United States and its secularist allies. A less revolutionary (in the context of Iraq) approach might have yielded more success, or so it seems, given the near ability of the Kurdish secular forces allied with the United States to negotiate with the Islamists a provision respecting existing treaty obligations that was only removed at the last minute. One can only wonder whether or not, in the absence of TAL Article 23, Islamist opposition might have been less implacable and the Constitution thus more amenable than it is to the possibility of international law being used in domestic proceedings.

It is always best, however, to end not with regret but instead on an optimistic note. The constitutional language is sufficiently elastic to permit a reading

37 On 9 November 2009, Naji interrupted a parliamentary session to raise what he declared was a 'point of order', which was in fact not a point of order at all (as he was told by Deputy Speaker and fellow Shi'i Khaled Al-Attiya, though it did not quiet him). Instead, it was a diatribe against the US and UK Ambassadors for helping to negotiate an election law without seeking prior authorization from the Presidency Council of the Council of Representatives, thereby subjecting Iraq to what Naji perceived was an attack on its sovereignty. Naji was willing to concede that in fact the Ambassadors may have done some good, but that their blatant disregard of protocol was inexcusable and that the Council of Representatives Presidency Council would be responsible if angry members zealously protective of Iraq's sovereignty, starting with Naji himself, decided to 'react' to any foreigner who approached him without prior approval of the Council of Representatives Presidency Council. As the entire episode took place in open session, much of it on television, and in full view of US Embassy observers, it was widely reported within political circles in Baghdad at the time.

38 The law was ultimately enacted as Law No. 12 of 2009 but not before the accomplished and erudite (female) drafter of the bill, Maysoon Al-Damaluci, was treated to the humiliating spectacle of Mohammad Naji insisting that the bill be sent to the Committee of Security and Defense, with its, to use his words, 'mostly male' members who could then ensure that it was sufficiently protective of national security interests.

granting a more robust understanding of what the judiciary might use by way of international law to reach determinations in domestic courts. Equally importantly, the sensitivities respecting American imposition that work to limit the broad use of international law are somewhat limited as to their duration, and are likely to abate as US influence grows less pronounced following its military withdrawal. One can only hope that over time, as Iraq's judiciary develops its independence further and as Iraq itself grows in as a fully sovereign member within the family of nations, the broad reluctance to involve domestic courts in the application of international law will turn into a relic of the past.

CONSTITUTIONALISM WITHOUT GOVERNANCE: INTERNATIONAL STANDARDS IN THE AFGHAN LEGAL SYSTEM

Ebrahim Afsah*

1. INTRODUCTION: THE ROLE OF LAW IN STABILISING CONFLICT

There has been a lot of attention in recent years about improving the quality of legal systems in overseas jurisdictions. This is reflected in the growing proportion of rule of law components in development assistance[1] and, especially, in post-conflict stabilisation missions.[2] External actors endeavour to strengthen the role of international legal standards in the courts and, more broadly, the political life of societies emerging from violent conflict. Virtually all stabilisation missions contain today important rule of law components, a shift in emphasis that is mirrored in bilateral financial assistance.[3] The international engagement in Afghanistan since December 2001 has been no exception, having placed a heavy emphasis on introducing international legal norms into the Afghan legal and political system.

---

* Associate Professor of International Law, University of Copenhagen. The views presented here are solely those of the author and should not be attributed to the organisations or governments which currently or in the past funded his work. Correspondence can be addressed to ebi@post.harvard.edu.

1 A workable definition of the concept has been provided by the United Nations which describes the 'rule of law' broadly as 'a principle of governance in which all persons, institutions and entities, public and private, including the State itself, are accountable to laws that are publicly promulgated, equally enforced and independently adjudicated, and which are consistent with international human rights norms and standards.' UN, Report of the Secretary-General, Rule of Law and Transitional Justice in Conflict and Post-Conflict Societies (S/2004/616) (23 August 2004), p. 4, para. 6.

2 United Nations, Justice Components in United Nations Peace Operations, Ref. 2009.30 (New York: United Nations DPKO/DFS, 2009).

3 For details on this shift in emphasis, see K. Hamilton, K. Bolt and G. Ruta, Where is the Wealth of Nations? Measuring Capital for the 21st Century (Washington DC: World Bank, 2006).

This concerted interest in the rule of law in peripheral overseas societies is generally justified by reference to the *normative* conviction that human beings are equal and deserve equal protection, thus calling for the application of uniform international standards.[4] This essentially moral position is sometimes cloaked in the language of enlightened self-interest, claiming that the protection of equal norms abroad will prevent negative spill-over in the future:

> For we live in a world in which apathy about what happens in 'far away countries of which we know nothing' can all too easily lead – through contagion, through the message such moral passivity sends to troublemakers, would-be tyrants, and ethnic cleansers elsewhere – not to the kind of Armageddon we feared during the Cold War but to a creeping escalation of disorder and beastliness that will, sooner or later, reach the shores of the complacent, the rich, and the indifferent.[5]

To many, the veracity of this causal chain was powerfully affirmed by the painful experience of the attacks of September 2001, which directly led to the costly and on-going military intervention in Afghanistan.[6] According to this popular reading of history, societal collapse can never be contained, but will eventually reverberate through the international system.

The emphasis on law as a tool for societal stabilisation is owed to two distinct but related phenomena.[7] First, the majority of international stabilisation missions are undertaken by Western societies which share common functional set-ups and normative commitments. Their administrative procedures and political decision-making are centred on public law and constitutional principles. These normative commitments and procedural constraints cannot easily be ignored when the polity acts externally.[8] This is particularly pronounced in 'wars of choice' which do not respond to an immediate existential threat.[9]

---

4 A convincing critical treatment of this school of thought can be found in J. Kokott, *Souveräne Gleichheit und Demokratie im Völkerrecht*, 64 (3) *Zeitschrift für ausländisches öffentliches Recht und Völkerrecht* 520–21, 533 (2004).

5 S. Hoffmann, In Defense of Mother Teresa, 75(2) Foreign Affairs 75 (March-April 1996). Hoffmann is paraphrasing here British Prime Minister Chamberlain's 1938 remarks about Czechoslovakia.

6 'Then came 9/11, a reminder that there are no far away places. ... [We need to understand] the deep instability in many parts of the globe, including Afghanistan, and that this instability – and the hatreds associated with it – *pose a risk not only to people in a region but to us*. This is where the Vietnam analogy breaks down: the West can't afford to lose.' B. Rae, Why Afghanistan is not Vietnam, The Star (Toronto, 2 August 2010) (emphasis added).

7 For a defence of this role, see the well-argued R. Teitel, Transitional Jurisprudence: The Role of Law in Political Transformation, 106 Yale Law Journal 2009 et seq (1997).

8 For a theoretical exploration of these dynamics, see V.A. Baird, Building Institutional Legitimacy: The Role of Procedural Justice, 54(2) Political Research Quarterly 333–54 (June 2001).

9 M. Ottaway, Promoting Democracy after Conflict: The Difficult Choices, 4(3) International Studies Perspectives 314–22 (2003); T.M. Sandler and K. Hartley, The Political Economy of NATO: Past, Present, and into the 21st Century (Cambridge: Cambridge University Press, 1999).

Put bluntly, the tax-paying, conscription-bearing public in democratic societies demands a certain degree of democratic idealism if it is to accept the costs of facultative overseas engagements.[10] Recourse to democratic ideals thus serves primarily domestic psychological reasons, namely the need to maintain a cherished self-image of a rule-bound, majoritarian, deliberative society remaining true to itself when acting abroad.[11]

According to these normative beliefs there would be little sense in accepting the costs of foreign intervention only to replace anarchy with dictatorship. In this vein, an impressive list of countries[12] have during the past decade assumed considerable costs[13] to not only stabilise but transform Afghanistan into a democracy governed by the rule of law.[14]

There is a second set of reasons for the emphasis on democracy and the rule of law in the pacification of fractured societies. It is believed that the creation of rule-bound institutions has powerful benefits for the internal and external behaviour of societies,[15] in other words that democracies are more *peaceful* than autocracies.[16] While the empirical evidence for this proposition of *political* stability is complex and mixed,[17] evidence for the domestic *economic* benefits of

---

10 F. Fukuyama, America at the Crossroads – Democracy, Power and the Neoconservative Legacy (New Haven: Yale University Press, 2006); S.N. Katz, Gun Barrel Democracy? Democratic Constitutionalism Following Military Occupation: Reflections on the U.S. Experience in Japan, Germany, Afghanistan and Iraq, Princeton Law and Public Affairs Working Paper No. 04–010 (Princeton Law and Public Affairs Working Paper Series, 2004).

11 B. Spector, Memory, Myth, and the National Mall, 2(3) Culture and Psyche 73–97 (Summer 2008).

12 For a list see NATO, NATO/ISAF Contributions by Country, Mons, Belgium, NATO Headquarters, 2010, available at www.isaf.nato.int/en/troop-contributing-nations/index.php (visited 30 April 2010).

13 *Ein toter Soldat kostet 2,3 Millionen Euro, Süddeutsche Zeitung* (München, 21 May 2010); Deutsches Institut für Wirtschaftsforschung, *Die Kosten des Afghanistan-Einsatzes müssen auf breiterer Basis berechnet werden*, Wochenbericht des DIW Berlin Nr 21/2010 (Berlin: DIW, 26 May 2010).

14 Comprehensive overviews of these efforts can be found in United Nations Development Programme, Afghanistan Human Development Report 2007. Bridging Modernity and Tradition: Rule of Law and the Search for Justice (Kabul: UNDP, 2007), available at www.undp.org.af/publications/KeyDocuments/nhdr07_complete.pdf (visited 7 May 2010); United States Institute of Peace, Establishing the Rule of Law in Afghanistan, Special Report 117 (Washington DC: USIP, March 2004).

15 M.H. Halperin, M.M. Weinstein and J. Siegle, The Democracy Advantage: How Democracies Promote Peace and Prosperity (London: Routledge/Council for Foreign Relation, 2004).

16 While superficially persuasive, the proposition is empirically considerably more complex than is commonly acknowledged: see inter alia C. Layne, Kant or Cant: The Myth of the Democratic Peace, 19(2) International Security 5–49 (1994).

17 E.A. Henderson, The Slow Roasting of Sacred Cows: J. David Singer and the Democratic Peace, in: Paul Diehl (ed.) The Scourge of War: New Extensions on an Old Problem 169–88 (Ann Arbor: University of Michigan Press, 2004): C. Davenport, State Repression and the Domestic Democratic Peace (Cambridge: Cambridge University Press, 2007).

the rule of law is overwhelming.[18] As the World Bank has noted, '[e]conomic growth, political modernization, the protection of human rights, and other worthy objectives are all believed to hinge, at least in part, on "the rule of law."'[19]

These normative and functional preferences for the rule of law have guided international efforts to transform the Afghan conflict by building stable statehood. While the normative re-alignment of the Afghan state with the international legal mainstream has, at least partially, been effected in constitutive legal texts, the practical reality remains largely at odds with these pronouncements.

This chapter argues that the failure of international legal standards to have a marked impact is not primarily grounded in countervailing cultural or religious norms, but the lack of effective state institutions, including courts and law enforcement agencies. The next section therefore describes the political climate in which the international community conferred chief responsibility on a largely fictitious Afghan state. The third section explores the implications of this approach in the institutional context of dysfunctional, merely nominal state organs. The fourth section examines the functional assumptions and cultural norms implicit in prevailing notions of constitutionalism, premises which are largely inapplicable in Afghanistan. The fifth section looks at the disjuncture between general qualities of statehood and the very different reality of the Afghan state. The sixth section thus examines the importance of functioning state structures for the rule of law, raising, in the seventh section, the question whether constitutionalism can exist without effective statehood. The concluding section denies this is possible.

2. POLITICAL CONTEXT OF RECONSTRUCTION

Self-serving descriptions by its protagonists notwithstanding,[20] the Afghan conflict was only marginally a national defence against a foreign aggressor. Primarily, it was a civil war fought between those who favoured accelerated modernisation and those who resisted this change with reference to an atavistic understanding of religion.[21] This underlying conflict both predated and survived the Soviet intervention, ossifying by 2001 into a murderous stalemate of perennially shifting alliances of self-interested armed groups. The tragedy of the

18 For an overview of the field, see D.M. Trubek and A. Santos, The New Law and Economic Development: A Critical Appraisal (Cambridge: Cambridge University Press, 2006); Y.P. Ghai, R. Luckham and F.G. Snyder (eds), The Political Economy of Law. A Third World Reader (Delhi: Oxford University Press, 1987).

19 World Bank, Rule of Law and Development (Washington DC: World Bank 2009), available at http://tinyurl.com/dfyymq (visited 29 October 2010).

20 See note 343.

21 G. Dorronsoro, Revolution Unending: Afghanistan, 1979 to the Present (London: C. Hurst & Co. Publishers, 2005); G. Kepel, The Roots of Radical Islam (London: Saqi, 2005).

September 2001 attacks on the United States had the unintended *positive* effect of breaking up that stalemate. Following the refusal of the Taliban *de facto* government to hand over al-Qaeda suspects believed to have been responsible for the attacks,[22] the United States initiated military action against Afghanistan. Two aspects of this intervention are noteworthy.

Operationally, the US military action differed from interventions explicitly done for humanitarian purposes by eschewing any pretext of neutrality and openly taking sides in the on-going civil war by utilising the predominantly Tajik Northern Alliance as the ground troops of the invasion.[23] The military preponderance of the United States led to the quick disintegration of the Taliban government and the subsequent takeover of the capital and the physical centres of government by the Northern Alliance.[24]

Politically, the intervention occurred (unlike later in Iraq[25]) with the endorsement of the United Nations Security Council and the almost universal approval of the international community.[26] The attacks were condemned by both the General Assembly[27] and the Security Council.[28] It was broadly recognised that these attacks triggered the inherent right of self-defence of the United States.[29]

The broad legitimacy of the military intervention and the unwillingness of the United States to create an occupation government[30] led to internationally meditated negotiations towards an inclusive peace agreement that enjoyed

22 The Taliban had failed to respond to earlier requests to take actions against preparatory activities by terrorists: S/RES/1214 (1998) of 8 December 1998; S/RES/1267 (1999) of 15 October 1999; S/RES/1333 (2000) of 19 December 2000; S/RES/1378 (2001) of 14 November 2001), or to the requests to turn over Osama bin Laden and his associates in S/RES/1267 (1999) of 15 October 1999 and S/RES/1333 (2000) of 19 December 2000.

23 International Crisis Group, Afghanistan: The Problem of Pashtun Alienation, Asia Report, No. 62 (Brussels/Kabul: ICG, 2003).

24 S. Chesterman, Walking Softly in Afghanistan: The Future of UN State-building, 44(3) Survival 37–46 (Autumn 2002).

25 P.J. Katzenstein, Same War – Different Views: Germany, Japan, and Counterterrorism, 57(4) International Organization 731–60 (2003).

26 For an overview of the copious literature confirming this position, see E. Afsah and A. Hilal Guhr, Afghanistan: Building a State to Keep the Peace, 9 Max Planck Yearbook of United Nations Law p. 406, n 127 (2005).

27 A/RES/56/1 of 12 September 2001.

28 S/RES/1368 (2001) of 12 September 2001. The curt statement made on 19 September 2001 by the President of the Security Council, Jean-David Levitte (France), is highly indicative in this regard: Today there is one, and only one, message the Security Council has for the Taliban: implement United Nations Security Council resolutions, in particular resolution 1333, immediately and unconditionally.' Available at <www.un.org.pk/latest-dev/hq-pre-010918.htm>.

29 R. Wolfrum, The Attack of September 11, 2001, the Wars Against the Taliban and Iraq: Is There a Need to Reconsider International Law on the Recourse to Force and the Rules in Armed Conflict?, 7 Max Planck Yearbook of United Nations Law 1–52 (2003).

30 Again, the contrast to the war in Iraq is striking: see E. Afsah, Limits and Limitations of Power: The Continued Relevance of Occupation Law, 7(6) German Law Journal p. 569, 573–4 (June 2006).

considerable domestic, regional, and global legitimacy.[31] The extremely fractious nature of Afghan politics and countless failed prior mediation efforts did not bode well for the outcome of the negotiations held in Bonn.[32] That these succeeded against such odds is primarily due to the willingness and ability of the United States to coerce compliance in addition to the enticing prospect of international assistance.[33]

The negations yielded an agreement that was more a road-map than a comprehensive peace settlement. It is noteworthy that the Bonn Agreement contained no stipulations to deal with transitional justice.[34] This impunity for past abuses reflects the composition of the negotiating groups which contained many Afghan leaders widely believed to have been responsible for war crimes.[35] This shortcoming was acknowledged by the chief United Nations negotiator Lakhdar Brahimi in his report to the Security Council:

> The provisional institutions whose creation is suggested will not include every one who should be there and it may include some whose credentials many in Afghanistan may have doubts about. Please remember that what is hopefully to be achieved is the elusive peace ... the broad based interim administration is the beginning, not the end of the road.[36]

The Agreement established the character of the international involvement in Afghanistan as merely supportive, with control lying in the hands of the Afghan authorities. It reaffirmed 'the independence, national sovereignty and territorial integrity of Afghanistan'[37] and stipulated that power would be transferred to an

---

31 UN, Agreement on Provisional Arrangements in Afghanistan Pending the Re-establishment of Permanent Government Institutions (Bonn Agreement) (S/2001/1154) (5 December 2001), available at www.un.org/News/dh/latest/afghan/afghan-agree.htm (visited 6 February 2011).

32 The rather long and sad history of failed United Nations mediation efforts is well explained in Chapter 2 of A. Rasanayagam, Afghanistan: A Modern History – Monarchy, Despotism or Democracy?, The Problems of Governance in the Muslim Tradition (London: I.B. Tauris, 2005).

33 Afsah and Guhr, *supra* note 26, p. 410–16, especially p. 412.

34 Quite to the contrary, the Agreement went out of its way to praise the coterie of warlords as 'heroes of jihad and champions of peace, stability and reconstruction of their beloved homeland' and seeking international financial assistance for them 'in recognition of the heroic role played by the mujahidin in protecting the independence of Afghanistan and the dignity of its people.' Bonn Agreement, *supra* note 31, Preamble, para. 4; Annex III (4).

35 ICG, Asia Report No 45, Afghanistan: Judicial Reform and Transitional Justice 17 (28 January 2003); P.G. Danchin, Transitional Justice in Afghanistan. Confronting Violations of International Humanitarian and Human Rights Law, 4 Yearbook of International Humanitarian Law 3–51 (2004).

36 Lakhdar Brahimi, Briefing to the Security Council, Transcript from 13 November 2001, available at www.un.org/News/dh/latest/afghan/brahimi-sc- briefing.htm (visited 31 March 2005).

37 Bonn Agreement, *supra* note 31, Preamble, para. 2.

Interim Authority only two weeks after the talks in Bonn,[38] confirming that 'the Interim Authority shall be the repository of Afghan sovereignty, with immediate effect.'[39] It laid down a very ambitious time frame for the further establishment of state institutions.

The Agreement in essence did three things: first, it attributed sovereignty to an unelected, ad hoc Interim Authority;[40] second, it stipulated the convening of an Emergency *Loya Jirga* (grand national assembly) to elect a more representative Transitional Authority;[41] and third, it clarified the law of the land[42] and re-endowed the court system.[43] It also postulated a constitutional process involving drafting, popular consultation, review, and representative adoption.[44] Annex I outlined support by the international community for the maintenance of security; Annex II laid out the role of the United Nations during the transitional process; Annex III contained the request to the international community for financial support; and Annex IV laid out the composition of the Interim Administration.

Without restating in detail its substantive and procedural content and the three-year transitional period it outlined,[45] the Agreement's approach to the rule of law was characterised by pragmatism. The Afghan legal landscape resembled a palimpsest of layers of overlapping, sometimes contradictory laws introduced by successive political regimes. To disentangle this statutory mess was not only impossible due to the shortage of time and skilled lawyers, but, more prosaically, because most physical trace of these laws had been destroyed in the country. The process of piecing together the mosaic of the Afghan law of the land from scattered isolated holdings in private collections and libraries abroad has been painfully slow, difficult, and remains an on-going endeavour.[46] The only realistic option in this situation was to reinstate the 1964

---

38 Bonn Agreement, *supra* note 31, Section I (1). Sovereignty was transferred to the Afghan Interim Authority on 22 December 2003.

39 Bonn Agreement, *supra* note 31, Section I (3).

40 Bonn Agreement, *supra* note 31, Section III.

41 Bonn Agreement, *supra* note 31, Section I (5) and Section IV.

42 Bonn Agreement, *supra* note 31, Section II (1) (ii).

43 Bonn Agreement, *supra* note 31, Section II (2).

44 Bonn Agreement, *supra* note 31, Section I (6).

45 Comprehensive treatments can be found in Afsah and Guhr, *supra* note 26, p. 419–38; M. Schoiswohl, Constitution-making and International Law in post-conflict Afghanistan, 39(3) Vanderbilt Journal of Transnational Law 819–63 (2006).

46 Some success has been made in this respect in the intervening years and some, perfunctory, collections have been placed online. A good collection can be found at Asian Legal Information Institute, Afghan Laws 1933–2008, Sydney, Australia, ALII, 2008, available at www.asianlii.org/af/legis/laws/ (visited 29 October 2010). A good collection of links to resources on government and law can be found at New York University Law School and Omar Sial, GlobaLex: Islamic Republic of Afghanistan Legal System and Research, New York, New York University, December 2006, available at www.nyulawglobal.org/globalex/Afghanistan.htm (visited 29 October 2010).

Constitution[47] and declare all prior laws without distinction as remaining in force unless otherwise provided:

> (1) The following legal framework shall be applicable on an interim basis until the adoption of the new Constitution referred to above:
> (i) The Constitution of 1964, (a) to the extent that its provisions are not inconsistent with those contained in this agreement, and (b) with the exception of those provisions relating to the monarchy and to the executive and legislative bodies provided in the Constitution; and
> (ii) existing laws and regulations, to the extent that they are *not inconsistent with this agreement or with international legal obligations to which Afghanistan is a party*, or with those applicable provisions contained in the Constitution of 1964, provided that the Interim Authority shall have the power to repeal or amend those laws and regulations.
>
> (2) The judicial power of Afghanistan shall be independent and shall be vested in a Supreme Court of Afghanistan, and such other courts as may be established by the Interim Administration. The Interim Administration shall establish, with the assistance of the United Nations, a Judicial Commission to rebuild the domestic justice system in accordance with Islamic principles, international standards, the rule of law and Afghan legal traditions.[48]

From a purely textual point of view these decisions were appropriate, but, as will shortly become apparent, the real challenge laid with the non-existing administrative capacity without which laws remain ineffective. Furthermore, the references to international law were made in response to foreign insistence, not any perceptible Afghan desire to anchor their new state to fundamental norms.[49] Consequently, international legal standards continue to be largely perceived as foreign impositions with only limited political or bureaucratic traction.

The affirmation of Afghan control left only a supportive role for the international community,[50] described by Brahimi as a 'light foot approach' of

47 This document was chosen because it was widely considered to have been technically proven and ideologically neutral, as well as being emblematic of the perceived 'golden age' of relative stability and prosperity.
For a discussion of the country's other constitutions, see Afsah and Guhr, *supra* note 26, p. 424, n 219. In-depth treatments can be found in R. Bachardoust, *Afghanistan – droit constitutionnel, histoire, régimes politiques et relations diplomatiques depuis 1747* (Paris: L'Harmattan, 2003); Gerhard Moltmann, *Die Verfassungsentwicklung Afghanistans von 1901 bis 1986*, 35 *Jahrbuch des Öffentlichen Rechts* 509–74 (1986).

48 Bonn Agreement, *supra* note 31, Section II (1)(i).

49 This was, by contrast, a very strong motivating factor in the development of the post-war European human rights mechanisms: see for instance A. Moravcsik, Explaining International Human Rights Regimes: Liberal Theory and Western Europe, 1(2) European Journal of International Relations 157–89 (1995); A. Moravcsik, The Origins of Human Rights Regimes: Democratic Delegation in Postwar Europe, 54(2) International Organization 217–52 (2000).

50 Report of the Secretary General, The situation in Afghanistan and its implications for international peace and security, para. 98 (A/56/875-S/2002/278) (18 March 2002).

the international community's assistance efforts.[51] The principle sought to make a virtue of the political and operational constraints that defined the Afghan conflict. Despite its obvious unreality, it is highly questionable whether an alternative to 'Afghan ownership' existed because it would have necessitated a degree of foreign 'vice-regency' that was fiscally, militarily, and politically just not feasible.

Nonetheless, in the face of the inability of Afghan institutions to actually govern, the stipulation of 'Afghan ownership' failed to designate an *effective* decision-making authority. The Afghan warlords who took over nominal control after Bonn were at best inexperienced and lacking requisite legal, managerial, and administrative skills. At worst, they pursued determined policies of personal enrichment to the detriment of society at large.[52]

3. INSTITUTIONAL CONTEXT OF RECONSTRUCTION

One of the most striking characteristics of the Afghan situation is the degree of formalism with which state agencies are created and maintained, with only the flimsiest connection to any administrative output, let alone service delivery to the public. Already in Bonn no fewer than 29 ministries were identified,[53] and the number has since grown substantially, augmented by countless independent agencies, commissions, and other government bodies. With the possible exception of the Ministries of Finance, Interior and Defence, none of these institutions centre around *functions* but exclusively around *structures*. The creation and maintenance of these bodies follows a patron-client logic and a

---

51 The conceptual outlines of this approach had been laid down by Brahimi already some time earlier in the influential document Lakhdar Brahimi, Report of the Panel on United Nations Peace Operations ('Brahimi Report'), United Nations, New York (21 August 2000), available at www.un.org/peace/reports/peace_operations/. Its application to the Afghan conflict is described at some length in Afsah and Guhr, *supra* note 26, p. 383, 404–05; see also Chesterman, *supra* note 24.

52 The collapse of Kabul Bank has become a symbol for the extreme degree of graft exhibited by the country's 'elite' and bank-rolled by the international community. About a dozen 'shareholders' of this bank, who were members of the Afghan cabinet or related to the President, stole almost a billion dollars. Not only did this act have virtually no criminal or civil repercussion for these individuals, but the Central Bank, ie the international community, replenished Kabul Bank's coffers with an additional US$450 m.: see A.J. Rubin and J. Risen, Losses at Afghan Bank Could Be $900 Million, New York Times (30 January 2011).

53 It should be stressed that it can actually make sense during peace negotiations to create administratively useless structures simply to have enough perks and post to include possible spoilers in the process, rather than have them undermined it if left out. See also C. Bell, Peace Agreements: Their Nature and Legal Status, 100(2) American Journal of International Law 373–412 (2006); S.J. Stedman, D. Rothchild and E.M. Cousens (eds.), Ending Civil Wars: The Implementation of Peace Agreements (Boulder: Lynne Rienner, 2002).

vague idea of what it means to be a 'real' state, not any tangible functional necessity.[54]

In consequence, many bodies have overlapping mandates and generally only the most remote connection to the living realities of the population they are meant to serve. In short, most agencies of the Afghan state have an almost exclusively nominal existence, employing large numbers of people, elaborate administrative structures and byzantine procedures, yet producing very little in terms of administrative output.

But while state institutions are largely dysfunctional, they *do* have concrete institutional and personal reality. Perhaps paradoxically, this shell of a state exhibits considerable resilience and administrative inertia.[55] The judiciary has here been representative of the wider Afghan state. The country's Supreme Court had remained in existence throughout the period of turmoil and enjoyed a remarkable degree of personal continuity, at least throughout the period of the mujahidin civil war, Taliban takeover, and post 2001. The Court administered and paid a nominally comprehensive system of district, provincial, and appeal courts[56] and it had reasonably effective lines of communication with the judges and clerks throughout the country.[57]

This relative institutional stability was recognised by the Interim and Transitional Authority after 2001 which left the existing, heavily Pashtu dominated and pro-Taliban judiciary virtually unperturbed.[58] But like most of the other nominal structures of the Afghan state, these bureaucratic structures were largely inward-looking conduits of patronage to the members of the organisation, rather than oriented towards delivering judicial decisions for society. Not surprisingly, the formal justice system remains largely ignored by society and plays a minor role in dispute resolution.[59]

---

54 One of the most instructive examples is the Afghan Atomic Energy Commission, centred around a friend of President Karzai who lives in retirement from the IAEA in Vienna and employing no less than 126 staff, none of whom is a physicist. Needless to say that the country has not even the most rudimentary basis for nuclear energy.

55 This, again, is not peculiar to the Afghan experience: see F. Fukuyama, Why is there no Science of Public Administration?, 58(1) Journal of International Affairs 192 (Fall 2004).

56 These structures have subsequently been codified in the Law on the Organization and Jurisdiction of Courts, Official Gazette No. 851.

57 The author worked from 2004–2005 embedded with the Supreme Court, the Ministry of Justice and the Attorney General's Office in support of the country's Priority Reform and Restructuring programme. As such he obtained a fairly accurate view of existing structures and administrative capabilities.

58 T. Barfield, On Local Justice and Culture in Post-Taliban Afghanistan, 17 Connecticut Journal of International Law 437 (2002).

59 Hard figures are difficult to come by due to the country's inaccessibility and volatility, but reasonable estimates see only between 5–10% of disputes being resolved in the formal system, with the remainder being addressed by traditional justice mechanisms; ignoring the substantial percentage of disputes where no forum exists at all due to the military, economic, or political strength of the perpetrator. See inter alia T. Barfield, Afghan Customary Law and Its Relationship to Formal Judicial Institutions (Washington DC: United States Institute for

Likewise, existing state structures remain unable to provide essential services and carry out administrative orders. The picture that emerges is that of a *nominally* sound regulatory and administrative framework,[60] but which *functionally* is not able to do very much of anything.[61] While it is therefore correct to state, as the World Bank has done, that the basic structure of governance and legal system 'provide a coherent management and accountability framework for government',[62] the main bottleneck for the establishment of the rule of law was and remains bureaucratic capacity, not least in the judiciary.

Much diplomatic and academic attention has been given to the character of the applicable legal framework in Afghanistan, in particular its commitment to upholding international legal standards as referenced in Sections II (1)(ii), II (2), III (C) (7), and V (2) and (3) of the Bonn Agreement, and Article 7 of the 2004 Afghan Constitution.[63] These are important debates and, in time, it is conceivable that domestic audiences will use international law as a lever to protect their interests in domestic debates and before judicial fora. But during the past decade and for the foreseeable future, Afghan society has remained normatively divided about the utility of Western concepts of law and human rights and their complementarity with local notions of the Islamic good life.[64] More importantly, the country's institutions, notably its courts, have been both unwilling and unable to live up to the functional necessities to make these overarching legal commitments a practical reality.[65]

The Bonn Agreement does constitute in many respects a genuine constitutional moment, defined in the context of this book as specific situations in which attempts have been made to strengthen the domestic rule of law by resorting to international law as an aid.[66] But the relationship with international law has by no means been simply one of empowerment of domestic defenders of the rule of law. Due to the general weakness of formal institutions, the strength

---

Peace, 26 June 2003); Whit Mason (ed.), The Rule of Law in Afghanistan. Missing in Inaction (Cambridge: Cambridge University Press, 2011).

60 World Bank, Afghanistan: State Building, Sustaining Growth, and Reducing Poverty, World Bank Country Study (Washington DC: World Bank, 2005).

61 B.R. Rubin, (Re)Building Afghanistan: The Folly of Stateless Democracy, in: Current History 165–70 (April 2004).

62 See World Bank, Afghanistan Building an Effective State Priorities for Public Administration Reform ch. 1 (Washington, DC: World Bank, 2008), available at http://tinyurl.com/25agjkd (visited 7 May 2010).

63 Article 7, para. 1: 'The state shall abide by the UN charter, international treaties, international conventions that Afghanistan has signed, and the Universal Declaration of Human Rights.'

64 H. Travis, Freedom or Theocracy: Constitutionalism in Afghanistan and Iraq, 3(1) Northwestern University Journal of International Human Rights 1–52 (2005).

65 The importance of institutional capacity for the effectiveness of public law is explored in depth by T. Ginsburg and R.A. Kagan, Institutions & Public Law: Comparative Approaches (New York: P. Lang, 2005); see also R. Hirschl, Juristocracy vs. Theocracy: Constitutional Courts and the Containment of Sacred Law, 1(2) Middle East Law and Governance 129–65 (2009).

66 From the Editors' Introduction in this volume.

of unprincipled power brokers, and atavistic notions of culture, the attitude of Afghan state and society towards international law has remained a 'love hate relationship'.[67] It is widely understood that adherence to international standards defines *bona fide* statehood and there is considerable pride in the country's Constitution as having received international recognition as a state of the art legal text.[68] Yet, paradoxically and schizophrenically, there is simultaneous outrage at the perception of foreign interference and moral lecturing when the gaping discrepancy between actual conditions in the country are contrasted with the lofty commitments the country has made.[69]

4. FUNCTIONAL ASSUMPTIONS AND CULTURAL NORMS

Questions about the relative power of courts, the constitutional allocation of functions or the role of institutional actors are necessarily comparative and assume a shared understanding of certain key concepts of constitutional law, political science, and organisational theory. Many of these assumptions, however, are deeply problematic in much of the developing world characterised by a truncated reception of modernity.[70]

Despite the all-pervasive influence of religion, the main determinant of Afghanistan's current and future outlook is not Islam but the weakness of its political institutions. It is the lack of a functioning state and the absence of suitable ingredients for building one that has throughout Afghanistan's history determined the livelihood of its people and its relations with the outside.

67 M. Schoiswohl, The New Afghanistan Constitution and International Law: A Love-Hate Affair, 4 International Journal of Constitutional Law 664–76 (2006).

68 For an interesting comparison with the 1905 Iranian Constitution, which likewise symbolised popular yearning for outside recognition of one's 'respectability', see S.A. Arjomand, Constitutional Developments in Afghanistan: A Comparative and Historical Perspective, 53(4) Drake Law Review 943–63 (2005). For a wider still context see R.P. Anand, Family of 'Civilised' States and Japan: A Story of Humiliation, Assimilation, Defiance and Confrontation, 5 Journal of the History of International Law 1–75 (2003) and Y. Onuma, When was the Law of International Society Born? An Inquiry of the History of International Law from an Intercivilizational Perspective, 2(1) Journal of the History of International Law 1–66 (July 2000).

69 So, for instance, the Minister for Labour and Social Affairs, Ms Amina Afzali, who defended the government's attempt to close down women's shelters with reference to the highly publicised case of an eloped girl whose husband had cut off her nose and ears in punishment. In her view the main problem was neither the atrocity nor the underlying social mores, but international *media* coverage, because such publicity 'humiliates us in the eyes of the world.' A.J. Rubin, Afghan Proposal Would Clamp Down on Women's Shelters, New York Times (10 February 2011).

70 I have explored these issues at some length elsewhere: E. Afsah, Contested Universalities of International Law. Islam's Struggle with Modernity, 10 Journal of the History of International Law 259–307 (2008).

However aggressive, intolerant, and backward widely prevailing notions of Islam in this country have been, it is the lack of effective governance, not religious parochialism, that brings about chaos and poverty.

The role of Islam in public and private life in Afghanistan remains highly contentious,[71] a point that has become starkly apparent in the context of the constitutional drafting process where international pressures for the incorporation of universal normative commitments clashed sharply with an Afghan political elite beholden to the dominant Islamist discourse.[72] Already the Bonn Agreement had made clear commitments to upholding international legal standards, not least with respect to human rights. These stipulations were included at the behest of the international mediators facilitating the negotiations. While resistance by the Afghan political factions to the incorporations of these norms had been relatively muted in Bonn, it became extremely vociferous during the constitutional drafting and adoption process in Kabul.[73]

Neither the Constitutional Drafting nor the Constitutional Review Commissions contained any foreign legal experts and the general quality of legal expertise going into the process must be described as poor.[74] Outside technical assistance was available in principle but was utilised only very haphazardly and incoherently; by and large outside legal expertise was seen at best as an irritant to inter-factual horse-trading and at worst an attempt at cultural domination. In the end, the review process and, especially, the debate at the Constitutional *Loya Jirga* exposed the tremendous gap between the international legal *acquis* as understood even by other Muslim nations, and the prevailing social and legal norms espoused by the dominant strata of Afghan society.

It is often forgotten in the deliberate dichotomy between the Taliban and the Western-supported current regime that moderate Islam, let alone secularism, had been one of the earliest victims of the decades of conflict. Virtually all of the factions yielding influence during the years of *jihad*, civil war and now in Bonn and Kabul adhered to some of the most radical interpretations of Islamist ideology.[75] Their overall financial and military dependence on Western largesse post 2001 ensured, albeit under severe external pressure, a certain modicum of lip service being paid to universal legal norms. But there is little doubt that

---

71 K. Mendoza, Islam and Islamism in Afghanistan, Afghanistan Legal History Project, Islamic Legal Studies Program, Harvard Law School, available at www.law.harvard.edu/programs/ilsp/research/mendoza.pdf (visited 7 May 2010); G. Vercellin, What is an 'Islamic State': The Factor: 'Islam' in the Constitutions of Afghanistan, 9(1) Nomos 35–64 (2004); S. Mahmoudi, The Sharî'a in the new Afghan Constitution: Contradiction or Compliment?, 64(4) *Zeitschrift für ausländisches öffentliches Recht und Völkerrecht* 867–80 (2004).

72 See with respect to human rights norms in the Constitution, inter alia, Schoiswohl, *supra* note 67; Travis, *supra* note 64.

73 The process is described at length in Afsah and Guhr, *supra* note 26, p. 423–434.

74 Schoiswohl, *supra* note 67, p. 832 ff.

75 J.A. Thier, The Crescent and the Gavel, New York Times (26 March 2006); O. Roy and O. Mongin, *Généalogie de l'islamisme* (Paris: Hachette, 2001).

international legal norms carried neither great persuasive force nor liberating potential for those who wielded influence in the process.

While resisting the temptation of seeing Afghanistan in an essentialist light,[76] it is nevertheless accurate to state that Islam – or more accurately, customary practices and cultural norms which are *believed* to be Islamic[77] – play an overwhelming role in the contemporary political life of that nation. This is not so much a result of any inherent dogmatic characteristic of Islamic law but the product of the peculiar socio-political experience of fragmentation, radicalisation, displacement, and massive institutional erosion. Given the endemic weakness of the Afghan state ever since its tentative foundation in 1747, it would be misleading to look here merely at formal governance institutions.

Recalling that the state, even during the period of its greatest strength in the 1920s and 1960s,[78] never achieved more than the most fleeting impact on the life of its subjects,[79] one must accept that those 'stable, valued, recurring patterns of behaviour'[80] that could be discerned in Afghanistan were generally *not* linked to the state. Most of the institutions that formed the rudiments of a beginning civil society in the modern sense, such as schools,[81] universities,[82] political parties,[83] trade unions, etc[84] disintegrated during the upheaval of civil war and exile, leaving little more than tribal and religious institutions relatively intact.[85]

76 As justly criticised in general by S. Zubaida, Law and Power in the Islamic World 3 (London: I.B. Tauris, 2005.

77 Jon Lee Anderson, How Afghans Define Themselves in Relation to Islam, in Revolutions and Rebellions in Afghanistan, M. Nazif Shahrani and Robert L. Canfield (eds) (Berkeley: University of California Press, 1984); B. Glatzer, Being Pashtun – Being Muslim: Concepts of Person and War in Afghanistan, in: Essays on South Asian Society: Culture and Politics, Zentrum Moderner Orient, Arbeitshefte, Nr. 9 (Berlin: Das Arabische Buch, 1998).

78 Arjomand, *supra* note 68, p. 945, 951.

79 O. Roy, *La formation de l'armée en Afghanistan*, in: Y. Richard (ed.) *Entre l'Iran et l'Occident: adaptation et assimilation des idées et techniques occidentales en Iran* 61–67 (Paris: Editions MSH, 1989); C. Noelle-Karimi, C.J. Schetter and R. Schlagintweit, Afghanistan: A Country Without a State, Vol. 2, *Schriftenreihe der Mediothek für Afghanistan* (Frankfurt am Main: IKO, 2002).

80 Huntington's broader definition is helpful in this regard: 'Institutions are stable, valued, recurring patterns of behaviour. Organisations and procedures vary in their degree of institutionalisation. Harvard University and the newly opened suburban high school are both organisations, but Harvard is much more of an institution than the high school.' S.P. Huntington, Political Order in Changing Societies 12 (New Haven: Yale University Press, 1968).

81 C. Davis, 'A' Is for Allah, 'J' Is for Jihad, 19(1) World Policy Journal 90–94 (2002).

82 S.R. Samady, Modern Education in Afghanistan, 31(4) Prospects 587–602 (2001).

83 T. Ruttig, Islamists, Leftists – and a Void in the Center. Afghanistan's Political Parties and where they come from (1902–2006) (Kabul: Konrad-Adenauer-Stiftung, 2006); A. Giustozzi, Between Patronage and Rebellion: Student Politics in Afghanistan (Kabul: AREU Briefing Paper Series, Afghanistan Research and Evaluation Unit, February 2010).

84 A Giustozzi, War, Politics and Society in Afghanistan, 1978–1992 (London: C. Hurst & Co. Publishers, 2000).

85 C.J Schetter, *Ethnizität und ethnische Konflikte in Afghanistan* (Berlin: Reimer, 2003).

5. IDEAL AND REALITY OF STATEHOOD

The Afghan state that throughout its history possessed only the most threadbare material existence[86] emerged from the civil war without functioning governance institutions and was largely reduced to the *idea* of a territorial and political entity. As such it paradoxically acquired through the shared experience of common struggle against the Soviets and communal exile a psychological hold over the national imagination that it had never enjoyed in peacetime.[87] Given the difficult terrain, most Afghans had traditionally led very localised lives, both physically and in terms of political loyalty.[88] The conflict that erupted in 1978 and the mass exodus that ensued brought Afghans into contact with other Afghans from different parts of the country and ethnic backgrounds, often for the first time in living memory.

Prior to 1978, membership in the Afghan state meant little to an ethnically and geographically divided population,[89] as loyalties and identities were mainly based on kinship ties which had only a very tenuous link to territorial units. The dual impact of the foreign invasion and the subsequent extreme political fragmentation among the *mujahideen* forces, which threatened the dismemberment of the country, changed the perception of the national territory among ordinary Afghans.[90]

It was only through the experience of exile and resistance that the idea of the nation as a '*communauté de destin*'[91] gained ground. While ethnic divisions persist, most Afghans today strongly identify with the Afghan nation. To be sure, in the absence of other meaningful political units, distributional struggles over power and resources continue to be expressed in ethnic terms, but membership in the nation as such is no longer disputed. What successive Afghan governments failed to accomplish has thus been achieved by default: the forging of a national identity, albeit at the cost of a long and painful conflict.

The fact that the *idea* of an Afghan nation is no longer contested is a positive development. But it cannot obscure the fact that there exists absolutely no consensus about *how* this nation should constitute itself and order its public life. While the adoption of a new Constitution in 2004 as part of the Bonn Process

---

86 Good accounts of its history include V. Gregorian, The Emergence of Modern Afghanistan: Politics of Reform and Modernization, 1880 – 1946 (Stanford: Stanford University Press, 1969); M. Hasan Kakar, Government and Society in Afghanistan: The Reign of Amir Abdur Rahman Khan (Austin: University of Texas Press, 1979).

87 C. Schetter, *Die Territorialisierung nationaler und ethnischer Vorstellungen in Afghanistan*, 44(1) 75 Orient (2003).

88 See Chapter 1, The Sociogenesis of the Afghan State, in: G. Dorronsoro, Revolution Unending: Afghanistan, 1979 to the Present 23–61 (London: C. Hurst & Co. Publishers, 2005).

89 B.R. Rubin, The Fragmentation of Afghanistan: State Formation and Collapse in the International System 22 (New Haven, Conn.: Yale University Press, 2002, 2nd ed.).

90 Schetter, *supra* note 87.

91 Bachardoust, *supra* note 47, p. 21.

agreed in December 2001 has certainly been a remarkable achievement in light of the scores of failed earlier mediation efforts, few would argue that the Constitution substantially settled many divisive political issues.[92] More damaging still, as a poorly drafted piece of law it does not even provide robust procedural guidelines about how to settle these issues in a reasonably peaceful manner.[93]

Chief among the disputed provisions of the Constitution have been the debate about the nature of the state as a parliamentary or presidential system and between a central or federal system. As just one example among many to illustrate the *technically* inferior quality of the drafting, one can refer to Article 60, which sets out to define the role of the President in a polity ostensibly dedicated to the separation of powers, but ending up fundamentally missing the point of an independent judiciary or representative democracy: 'The President is the head of state of the Islamic Republic of Afghanistan, and *conducts his authorities in executive, legislative, and judiciary branches* in accordance with the provisions of this Constitution.'[94] The poor technical quality of this and similar provisions has subsequently been reflected in the incoherent and unworkable *Basic Organisational Law* currently under review, which seeks to translate the Constitution into the daily reality of government, but of course cannot resolve these inherent contradictions.[95]

Likewise, the role of religion has been controversial and it cannot be argued that the Constitution has satisfactorily settled these debates. Its Article 3 provides laconically that '[i]n Afghanistan, no law can be contrary to the beliefs and provisions of the sacred religion of Islam.' Such stipulations can be found in a large number of Muslim states, notably in Egypt and Pakistan,[96] and there is a vigorous debate about the utility and desirability of such efforts in terms of legal policy.[97] Whatever normative position one might want to take with respect to the (re-)introduction of divine law into a modern state machinery, the Afghan example is particularly ill-conceived because it ignores the methodical tools,

---

92 This is, for instance, explicitly admitted in the otherwise critical commentary by International Crisis Group, Afghanistan's Flawed Constitutional Process.

93 It is not necessary to describe here in detail the drafting history and content of the Constitution, as good accounts are plentiful in the literature. See inter alia Schoiswohl, *supra* note 72, p. 675, 678.

94 Afghan Constitution 2004, Article 60, sentence 1 (emphasis added).

95 The author has been involved in reviewing this law for the Civil Service Commission.

96 B. Johansen, The Relationship between the Constitution, the Sharî'a and the Figh in the Jurisprudence of Egypt's Supreme Constitutional Court, 64(4) *Zeitschrift für ausländisches öffentliches Recht und Völkerrecht* 881–96 (2004); C.B. Lombardi, Note: Islamic Law as a Source of Constitutional Law in Egypt: The Constitutionalization of the Shari'a in a Modern Arab State, 37 Columbia Journal of Transnational Law 81 et seq (1998).

97 E. Afsah, Constitution-Making in Islamic Countries – A Theoretical Framework, in: R. Grote and T. Röder (eds), Constitutional Law in Islamic Countries (Oxford: Oxford University Press, 2010).

such as a clear hierarchy of norms, to resolve inevitable conflicts of laws.[98] Similarly impractical has been the reference in Article 131 to the applicability of their personal law to followers of the Shia sect.[99] Heralded at the time as a great step towards minority protection, the provision has since proven to be singularly abrasive and open to political abuse, not least as a tool to suppress the rights of women and children protected elsewhere in the Constitution.[100]

6. STATEHOOD AS A PREREQUISITE OF CONSTITUTIONALISM

Before looking at some of the more problematic elements of the constitutional bargain and its interpretation by the Supreme Court, attention must be drawn to the underlying problem of the continued malaise in Afghanistan. Too much can be made of a purely textual critique of the constitutional provisions reserving an elevated role for Islam,[101] the insincere lip-service being paid to international law and the human rights obligations the country assumed through its adherence to international covenants in Article 7 of its Constitution,[102] the insufficient protection of women,[103] etc. Lawyers are trained to work with texts and therefore find it most convenient to focus their attention on the quotable constitutional provisions and the few properly drafted pieces of legislation that have been promulgated since.[104] The problem is that such textual exegesis tells us little if anything about the legal reality[105] in a country where the state, even after almost

98 See inter alia S. Tellenbach, Fair Trial Guarantees in Criminal Proceedings Under Islamic, Afghan Constitutional and International Law, 64(4) *Zeitschrift für ausländisches öffentliches Recht und Völkerrecht* 929–41 (2004); Schoiswohl, *supra* note 45, p. 836–8.

99 'Courts shall apply Shia school of law in cases dealing with personal matters involving the followers of Shia Sect in accordance with the provisions of law. In other cases if no clarification by this constitution and other laws exist and both sides of the case are followers of the Shia Sect, courts will resolve the matter according to laws of this Sect.' Afghan Constitution 2004, Article 131.

100 J. Boone, 'Worse than the Taliban' – new law rolls back rights for Afghan women, The Guardian, (London, 31 March 2009).

101 El Fadl, *et al*, Democracy and Islam in the New Constitution of Afghanistan (California: Rand Corporation, 2004).

102 Schoiswohl, *supra* note 45, p. 851–60.

103 M.H. Kamali, References to Islam and Women in the Afghan Constitution, 22 Arab Law Quarterly 270–306 (2008).

104 Good analyses of the constitutional provisions can be found in R. Grote, Separation of Powers in the New Afghan Constitution, 64(4) *Zeitschrift für ausländisches öffentliches Recht und Völkerrecht* 897–915 (2004); Mahmoudi, *supra* note 71.

105 This is the main problem of purely textual approaches such as M. Hamed Saboory, The Progress of Constitutionalism in Afghanistan, in: Nadjma Yassari (ed.) The Sharī'a in the Constitutions of Afghanistan, Iran, and Egypt 5–22 (Hamburg: Mohr Siebeck, 2005); R. Moschtaghi, Organisation and Jurisdiction of the Newly Established Afghan Courts – The Compliance of the Formal System of Justice with the Bonn Agreement, 10 Max Planck Yearbook of United Nations Law 531–90 (2006).

ten years of sustained Western financial, military, and technical support, exists for all intents and purposes *in name only*. Here we do well to remember Samuel Huntington's opening lines of his seminal *Political Order in Changing Societies*: 'The most important political distinction among countries concerns not their *form* of government but their *degree* of government.'[106]

The contemporary debate about the constitutional protection of individual and group rights and the attendant emphasis on the necessity of vigorous constitutional jurisprudence has been premised on the negative experience with Eastern European states that, if anything, functioned *too* well. These states followed the Leninist model of using the state apparatus as an instrument of forceful social engineering and suppression. Consequently, following the collapse of the old order it was generally seen as necessary to defuse the state's coercive machinery and emasculate its instruments of repression through the creation of effective means of interpellation. In short, the protection of the citizen *from* the state was and continues to be seen as the primary goal of constitutional law and jurisprudence.

In this light, most analysis of the Afghan Constitution has focused exclusively on the procedure of its adoption and its textual exegesis,[107] critiquing whether consultations were inclusionary enough,[108] whether those tasked with drafting it requested and received sufficient technical drafting expertise,[109] whether the

106 Huntington, *supra* note 80, p. 1 (emphasis added).

107 For a comprehensive and insightful account, see J.A. Thier, The Making of a Constitution in Afghanistan, 51(3) New York Law School Law Review 557–80 (2006).

108 K. Papagianni, Transitional Politics in Afghanistan and Iraq: Inclusion, Consultation, and Public Participation, 15(6) Development in Practice 747–59 (2005). For the official view heavily emphasising the inclusiveness of the prior consultation and subsequent public education process, see Secretariat of the Constitutional Commission of Afghanistan, The Constitution-making Process in Afghanistan (Kabul: Constitutional Commission, 10 March 2003).

109 In short, they did neither. See the pertinent critique by Schoiswohl who, like the author, was personally involved in the process: 'The Draft Constitution, largely based on the 1964 ancestor, similarly suffered from yet insufficient legal considerations in view of the overshadowing major political issues that needed to be resolved. Emphasis had primarily been given to meeting the deadlines stipulated in the Bonn Agreement, rather than to develop a legally sound and consistent document. The composition of the Constitutional Drafting and Review Commissions was not driven by legal (constitutional) considerations (expertise), but rather by the need for establishing a balanced platform for the conception of the basic structure of the future State of Afghanistan. Perhaps a function of the "light foot" approach and its emphasis on national ownership, neither the Drafting Commission nor the Review Commission perceived the technical assistance offered by the international community as more than advisory. Nor was the technical assistance geared towards the legal technicalities of constitutional drafting, but remained largely preoccupied with the provision of broad conceptual choices on the basis of comparative studies. It should be added, that little constitutional expertise was available within the United Nations on the ground, which mostly relied on consultancies and the commissioning of (comparative) studies abroad. The few attempts to highlight technical concerns were either not taken seriously or simply lacked understanding.' Schoiswohl, *supra* note 67, p. 670.

distribution of the political organs of the state was equitable or effective,[110] whether the bill of rights it contained was sufficient and in conformity with international human rights standards,[111] and whether the role of Islam in the text was likely to portent future problems for rights protection and effective governance.[112] These are very important issues, not least with respect to their implications for future stabilisation missions in other post-conflict scenarios.[113]

But in the peculiar Afghan context – and arguably in most other failed states as well – there is an even more important issue, namely the actual capacity of the state to act. While public law prescribes *how* the state is to use its power, the real question is *what* power the state has at its disposal.[114]

Whatever the lessons of the post-Communist renaissance of liberal democracy,[115] recent experience in countries as diverse as Somalia, Afghanistan, Chechnya, Sudan, etc teaches that however dangerous overbearing, strong states can be for individual liberty, the absence of statehood does not necessarily portent greater personal freedom.[116] As the destruction and subsequent implosion of Iraq has shown, an erstwhile strong and repressive state cannot necessarily be seen as an unmitigated evil if the alternative is chaos.[117] If the early 1990s could be characterised by a growing public appreciation of the wisdom of John Locke, Jean-Jacques Rousseau or Baron Montesquieu, the early 21st century has undoubtedly forced us to recognise how pertinent Thomas

110 Especially the extreme American pressure in favour of a presidential as opposed to a parliamentary or a mixed system with a prime minister has been criticised extensively. See inter alia L.P. Goodson, Bullets, Ballots, and Poppies in Afghanistan, 16(1) Journal of Democracy 24–38 (January 2005).

111 Schoiswohl, *supra* note 45; B.R. Rubin, Transitional Justice and Human Rights in Afghanistan, 79(3) International Affairs 567–81 (2003); Amnesty International, Afghanistan: Re-establishing the Rule of Law (London: Amnesty International, International Secretariat, 2003); S. Tellenbach, Fair Trial Guarantees in Criminal Proceedings Under Islamic, Afghan Constitutional and International Law, 64(4) *Zeitschrift für ausländisches öffentliches Recht und Völkerrecht* 929–41 (2004).

112 S.A. Arjomand (ed.), Constitutional Politics in the Middle East – With Special Reference to Turkey, Iraq, Iran, and Afghanistan (Portland: Hart Publishing, 2008); Kamali, *supra* note 103; R. Hirschl, The Rise of Constitutional Theocracy, 49 Harvard International Law Journal 72–82 (2008); Travis, *supra* note 64; Mahmoudi, *supra* note 71.

113 S. Chesterman, Imposed Constitutions, Imposed Constitutionalism, and Ownership, 37(4) Connecticut Law Review 947–54 (Summer 2005); N. Feldman, Imposed Constitutionalism, 37(4) Connecticut Law Review 857–91 (Summer 2005); D.S. Lutz, Thinking about Constitutionalism at the Start of the Twenty-First Century, 30(4) Publius, Essays in Memory of Daniel J. Elazar 115–35 (2000).

114 B.R. Rubin, *supra* note 61, p. 165–70.

115 A. Lijphart and C.H. Waisman, Institutional Design in New Democracies: Eastern Europe and Latin America (Boulder: Westview Press, 1996).

116 L. Diamond, Promoting Democracy in Post-Conflict and Failed States: Lessons and Challenges, in: National Policy Forum on Terrorism, Security, and America's Purpose (6–7 September 2005); J.L. Hirsch and R.B. Oakley, Somalia and Operation Restore Hope (Washington DC: US Institute of Peace Press, 1995).

117 J. Benomar, Constitution-Making after Conflict: Lessons for Iraq, 15(2) Journal of Democracy 81–95 (April 2004).

Hobbes continues to be. In a place like Afghanistan, governmental repression is the least of personal worries because it is the *absence* of governance of any sort that makes life 'nasty, brutish and short'. The current nostalgia felt for the Communist president Najibullah or the persistent latent sympathy with Taliban shadow governance structures show that *some* predictability and stability, even at the price of repression, is widely perceived to be better than *no* authority.[118]

The Afghan state had been weak to begin with, but since the fall of the Communist regime in 1992 it is questionable whether it continued in anything more than nominal form. As a weak state built on personal and ethnic loyalties rather than any of the abstract principles Weber described for the rational bureaucratic state,[119] law never played a very prominent role in the administration and governance of Afghanistan.[120] During the height of the civil war of 1992–1996 it appears almost obscene to speak of a state at all. During the Islamic Emirate set up by the Taliban from 1996–2001, reasonably effective governance was indeed established, but no attempt was made to formalise this structure, let alone create a legal foundation for this edifice.[121] Whatever the ideological claims brought forward by the Taliban about the 'authenticity' of their form of government and their way of administering justice, it does not appear that it lived up to the standards of procedural and substantive clarity and predictability required by Islamic law, whether in its historical[122] or in contemporary form.[123]

It is important to recall that the Bonn Process did *not* come at the end of an inconclusive civil war in which the participants had exhausted their physical and psychological means of fighting.[124] Rather, the various losers of the previous conflagration were brought together by an external actor who had interfered and

118 International Crisis Group, Afghanistan: Elections and the Crisis of Governance.

119 Max Weber, *Wirtschaft und Gesellschaft: Grundriss der Verstehenden Soziologie* (Frankfurt am Main: Zweitausendeins, 2005), pp. 157–164, 715–716.

120 O. Roy, *De la stabilité de l'État en Afghanistan*, 59(5/6) *Annales Histoire, Sciences Sociales* 1183–202 (Asie centrale 2004); M.H. Kamali, Law in Afghanistan: A Study of the Constitutions, Matrimonial Law and the Judiciary, 36 Social, Economic and Political Studies of the Middle East (Leiden: Brill, 1985); Leon B. Poullada, Reform and Rebellion in Afghanistan, 1919–1929: King Amanullah's Failure to Modernize a Tribal Society (Ithaca: Cornell University Press, 1973).

121 The ruthless but relatively effective, if haphazard, manner of the Taliban regime is described in A. Rashid, Taliban: Islam, Oil, and the New Great Game in Central Asia (London: I.B. Tauris, 2000).

122 Baber Johansen, *Staat, Recht und Religion im sunnitischen Islam*, in Contingency in a Sacred Law – Legal and Ethical Norms in the Muslim Fiqh`, Baber Johansen (ed), Studies in Islamic Law and Society (Leiden: Brill, 1999), 263–348; M. Khadduri and H.J. Liebesny (eds), Law in the Middle East, Vol. 1. Origin and Development of Islamic Law (Washington DC: The Middle East Institute, 1955).

123 Probably the closest approximation of a contemporary legal system with its historical model can be found in Saudi Arabia, ably described in F.E. Vogel, Islamic Law and Legal System: Studies of Saudi Arabia (Leiden: Brill, 2000).

124 The importance of this factor for lasting peace is stressed in Edward N. Luttwak, Give War a Chance, 4 Foreign Affairs (1999), 36 et seq.

taken sides in an ongoing civil war.[125] Without denigrating either process or outcome, it is necessary to underline that the parties in Bonn and later during the Emergency and Constitutional *Loya Jirgas* did *not* share a common normative or practical vision for the (re-)establishment of governance in Afghanistan.[126] The resulting arrangement, while miraculous for the sheer feat of having been concluded within the extremely tight timeframe, neither resolved most of the lingering divisions over the normative direction of society nor the distribution of power between the envisaged organs.

More importantly, the constitutional *form* simply assumed, as the entire Bonn Process had done, that the Afghan state was not only a purely nominal entity but existed in a tangible manner. It is this assumption which is most problematic and which renders most constitutional discussions in the Afghan context ultimately moot. The dilemma was aptly summarised by the current Chief Justice of the Supreme Court when asked by a claimant what to do with the verdict in his favour that was simply ignored by the powerful defendant: 'If there was any problem in our procedure, you come to us,' he said. 'But we do not have any soldiers. We have no force to use. There are so many cases where decisions are made but not enforced. In these cases, there is nothing we can do.'[127]

7. CONSTITUTIONALISM WITHOUT A STATE?

The Afghan state has throughout its history depended on foreign largesse by competing foreign powers – first the Russian and British empires, later the Soviet Union and United States[128] – supplemented by a recovering Germany after each of the two World Wars.[129] The Cold War provided Afghanistan with ample opportunities to play off the superpowers against each other and extract significant rents from both sides in the form of military and economic aid.[130] Not surprisingly, the Afghan state acquired the outward *appearance* of modern

125 L. Lombart, *La reconstruction politique de l'Afghanistan post-taliban: de la chute de l'Émirat islamique à la proclamation de la République islamique* (2001–2004), 60 *Revue française de droit constitutionnel* 861–82 (2004).

126 Comprehensive accounts can be found in Thier, *supra* note 107; Afsah and Guhr, *supra* note 26; International Crisis Group, Afghanistan: The Constitutional Loya Jirga, ICG (Brussels/Kabul, 12 December 2003).

127 K. Barker, At the Supreme Court, an unlikely new hero. Afghanistan's chief justice has launched a quiet revolution, targeting corrupt judges and demanding accountability in the country's long-inept judiciary, Chicago Tribune (21 January 2007).

128 B.R. Rubin, The Search for Peace in Afghanistan: From Buffer State to Failed State (New Haven: Yale University Press, 1995).

129 The close link between the Weimar Republic and King Amanullah's Afghanistan is described inter alia in B. Chiari and M. Forschungsamt (eds), Afghanistan: Wegweiser zur Geschichte (Paderborn: Schöningh, 2006).

130 This was supplemented by support given by superpower satellites such as Britain, West and East Germany. The type of projects and the enormous relative scope of these external transfer

statehood, including ministries, a court system, a diplomatic service, etc. But as a rentier state,[131] Afghanistan dispensed with the need to establish a monopoly of force and to extract enough resources to pay for this security,[132] as state formation historically has been characterised.[133]

Instead, Afghan leaders used foreign money to build weak institutions that could neither raise revenue nor effectively carry out decisions of the state. In a sense, the Afghan state existed like a Potemkin village only in outward appearance, and these façades were then further eroded during the decades of civil war. The situation in December 2001 presented the outside world with a fiercely proud, violently defiant, and internally divided Afghan society in the midst of severe unrest.

7.1. INSTITUTIONS MATTER

Recalling the earlier definition of an institution as a 'stable, valued, recurrent pattern of behaviour',[134] legal institutions in Afghanistan are few and far between. There is nothing stable about the manner in which disputes are settled, which generally depends on the balance of physical force rather than normative commitments, Islamic, tribal, or otherwise. There is nothing valued about the way warlords, tribal chiefs, and war entrepreneurs have managed to entrench their hold on society.[135] Those norms that do enjoy legitimacy, be they traditional or religious, largely exist outside formal structures. And apart from endemic corruption, violence, and despotism there is little recurrent about the pervasive insecurity that prevails in the country and the way politics is conducted there.[136]

The political pact reached in Bonn could not create institutions but relied instead on resurrecting old ones which nominally had continued to exist. Crucial

payments for the Afghan budget are described, if somewhat uncritically, in L. Dupree, Afghanistan (Princeton, N.J.: Princeton University Press, 1973).

131 States that derive a significant portion of their budget from unproductive endeavours, essentially windfalls, are described as rentier economies. The ideal type are those enjoying income from oil and gas, Panama or Egypt from canal fees, but also poor states where foreign aid essentially fulfils the same function. For a discussion, see H. Katouzian, The Political Economy of Modern Iran: Despotism and Pseudo-modernism, 1926–1979 (London: Macmillan, 1981).

132 C. Tilly, The Formation of Nation States in Western Europe (Princeton: Princeton University Press, 1975); C. Tilly, Coercion, Capital and European States, AD 990–1990 (Cambridge: Basil Blackwell, 1990).

133 Huntington, *supra* note 80, chapter 1.

134 See above n. 80.

135 Goodson, *supra* note 110; J. Goodhand, From War Economy to Peace Economy? Reconstruction and State Building in Afghanistan, 58(1) Journal of International Affairs 155–74 (Fall 2004); B.R. Rubin, The Political Economy of War and Peace in Afghanistan, 28(10) World Development 1789–803 (2000).

136 C.J. Riphenburg, Afghanistan: Out of the Globalisation Mainstream?, 27(3) Third World Quarterly, 507–24 (2006).

questions about who should govern and what direction the polity was to take were postponed and relegated to future elections. But elections require a set of political institutions to be effective and not divisive, namely '[t]he development of a pattern, and ultimately a culture, of *moderation, accommodation, cooperation*, and *bargaining* among political elites' which is increasingly stressed in process-oriented thinking on democratic transition and consolidation.[137]

At the heart of any constitutional compact lies the commitment by *all* societal actors towards a 'security community in which there is real assurance that the members of that community will not fight each other *physically* but will settle their disputes in some other way.'[138] Constitutionalism is therefore premised on the ability of the state to credibly police this commitment and thus rests on a particular notion of law. In this Weberian sense, law is a quintessential ingredient of the rationally organised *Anstaltsstaat*[139] because 'law was necessary for the conduct and discipline of diplomatic and military administration in the new territorial states priding themselves on their efficiency.'[140] In any constitutional state – whether committed to an expansive, 'thick' notion of liberalism or to a restrictive, 'thin' version[141] – there is an implicit acceptance that power resides *primarily* in the bureaucracies that administer it, not necessarily in the person that formally holds it:

> In a modern state, actual power is manifested neither in parliamentary speeches nor in royal pronouncements, but in the bureaucratic dealings of everyday life. Power thus inevitably lies in the hands of civil servants, both military and civilian.[142]

Law is the tool by which rational bureaucracies communicate and act. While it is possible to imagine the dispensation of justice, ie the application of law, without a formal bureaucracy,[143] it is difficult to imagine a modern bureaucracy in the Weberian sense without rational, predictable, standard operating procedures, in other words without law.[144]

---

137 L. Diamond, Developing Democracy – Towards Consolidation 166 (Baltimore: John Hopkins University Press, 1999) (emphasis in the original).

138 K.W. Deutsch, Political Community and the North Atlantic Area 5 (Princeton: Princeton University Press, 1957) (emphasis added).

139 Weber, *supra* note 119, p. 157–222, particularly p. 159–160, 164.

140 Q. Wright, A Study of War 332 (Chicago: University of Chicago Press, 1965, 2nd ed. [1st ed. 1942]).

141 See the contribution by S. Beaulac, Lost in Transition? Domestic Courts, International Law and Rule of Law '*À la Carte*', in this volume at p. 17.

142 Weber, *supra* note 119, p. 1047 (translation by the author).

143 See for instance T. Barfield, Afghan Customary Law and Its Relationship to Formal Judicial Institutions, United States Institute for Peace (Washington DC, 26 June 2003).

144 Weber, *supra* note 119, p. 162–65, 716–23; see also J.-C. Spender, Organizational Knowledge, Learning and Memory: Three Concepts in Search of a Theory, 9(1) Journal of Organizational Change Management 63–78 (February 1996); M.D. Cohen and P. Bacdayan, Organizational Routines Are Stored As Procedural Memory: Evidence from a Laboratory Study, 5(4) Organization Science 554–68 (November 1994).

This, however, is clearly *not* an adequate description of contemporary Afghanistan, nor has it ever been true throughout its history. As a quintessentially *pre-modern*[145] state, power in Afghanistan has always been personal, and formal institutional arrangements meant little beyond the individuals, their convictions, and their connections. This is amply demonstrated in the Afghan court system and most pertinently, in its Supreme Court.

7.2. DECREPIT JUSTICE SYSTEM

There is a regrettable Manichean tendency in the public perception of the ongoing Afghan intervention, much of it the result of deliberate political statements by troop-sending nations. There are the vilified Taliban representing an atavistic, inhuman ideology on one side, and a reasonably coherent broad public and elite alliance yearning for 'freedom' on the other. Both the monolithic vision of the Taliban is inaccurate, as is the postulation that there exists even a modicum of agreement among the other power brokers about the desirable direction of the country.[146] The transitional process set off by the Bonn Agreement has not been an effective 'constitutional moment' for at least two reasons. First, there was an overwhelming continuity of armed elites from the civil war into the new era, albeit without any commitment to ideological or physical disarmament.[147] Second, no political agreement was ever reached about a common normative vision. The absence of such a shared vision meant that the institutional and normative set-up of the state was not realigned to produce a workable edifice. Instead, the existing state apparatus, however dysfunctional, was retained and all attention focused on the division of spoils. Accordingly, the distribution of institutional power in the constitutional set-up was not based on a logical balance of power or checks and balances, but responded unabashedly to the jockeying and horse-trading for personal influence.[148]

This has been particularly apparent in the formal judicial system. The existing court structure remained in place and continued to be staffed by the very same individuals who had been put into their judgeships by previous governments, most notably during the Taliban emirate. A minute fraction of these individuals

---

145 It is important to stress that the term 'modernity' is used here in a technical, Weberian sense, ie it refers to a particular institutional alignment. It is not meant to convey necessarily a value judgment in the sense that popular discourse often equates modernity with progress, liberation, etc. For an elaboration see Afsah, *supra* note 70; M. Berman, All That is Solid Melts into Air: The Experience of Modernity (New York: Penguin, 1988).

146 J.F. Tierney (ed.), Warlord, Inc. Extortion and Corruption Along the U.S. Supply Chain in Afghanistan, Report of the Majority Staff, Subcommittee on National Security and Foreign Affairs, Committee on Oversight and Government Reform (Washington DC: US House of Representatives, June 2010).

147 Roy, *supra* note 120.

148 International Crisis Group, Afghanistan: Elections and the Crisis of Governance; Barfield, *supra* note 58.

possessed any legal training at all, and the vast majority did not even possess a secondary school leaving certificate.[149] As a result of considerable pressure during the Constitutional *Loya Jirga* by very powerful warlords, notably Abdul Rasul Sayyaf,[150] an extremely conservative Pashtun cleric, Faisal Ahmad Shinwari, without any formal legal training, was appointed by President Karzai as Chief Justice to head the Supreme Court.[151]

While nominally not associated with the previous regime, Mr Shinwari was in cultural, political, ethical, and ethnic outlook extremely close to Taliban positions. He staffed the Supreme Court exclusively with elderly Pashtun clerics and showed an astounding disregard for any procedural rules laid down in the Constitution or elsewhere.[152] The Supreme Court thus approximated the other organs of the state, which were seen more in terms of ethnic fiefs than in terms of institutional functions.[153] While he and the members of the bench appointed by him certainly shared a commitment to an extreme version of political Islam very much like that propagated by the Taliban or other extremist groups,[154] the most startling aspect of his tenure has been his utter ignorance and, more disquieting still, disinterest in the formal requirements of legal process, whether constitutional or Islamic.[155]

This is particularly surprising and revealing in light of the well-documented commitment by him and his backers to Wahabist Islam.[156] Legal opinions were rarely, if ever, couched in legal terms, let alone following established procedures. A number of highly controversial legal opinions were issued, none of which paid much heed to legal subtleties such as methodically sound statutory interpretation or levels of jurisdiction, beyond paying lip service to 'Afghan legal sovereignty' and undefined references to 'national mores'.[157]

---

149 Data collected while working 2004–2005 on the Priority Reform and Restructuring (PRR) programme in the Supreme Court, Ministry of Justice, and Attorney General's Office on contract from the World Bank and UNDP.

150 Ustad Abdul Rasul Sayyaf, Global Security, n.d, available at www.globalsecurity.org/military/world/ afghanistan/sayyaf.htm (visited 19 May 2010).

151 For a personal account of a colleague who worked with me during this time on administrative reform at the Supreme Court, see A. Schwarz, *Justizreform und Islam in Afghanistan*, 65(1) *Zeitschrift für ausländisches öffentliches Recht und Völkerrecht* 257–68 (2005).

152 Instead of the constitutionally mandated nine members of the Supreme Court (including himself), he appointed for instance more than 130 (!) Supreme Court judges, overwhelmingly Pashtun and without legal qualification.

153 Schetter, *supra* note 85; A. Banuazizi et al, The State, Religion, and Ethnic Politics: Afghanistan, Iran, and Pakistan (Syracuse: Syracuse University Press, 1986).

154 Despite the demonization of the Taliban, their particular worldview is by no means an isolated, or even particularly extreme iteration of a wider phenomenon. See Sadiq Jalal al-Azm, Islam, Terrorism, and the West Today, 44(1) *Die Welt des Islams* 114–28 (2004).

155 This is, after all, one if not *the* key characteristic of orthodox Islamic law. For a discussion of the literature and historical examples see inter alia B. Johansen, Casuistry: Between Legal Concept and Social Praxis, 2 Islamic Law and Society 135–56 (1995).

156 N.J. DeLong-Bas, Wahhabi Islam: From Revival and Reform to Global Jihad (New York: Oxford University Press, 2004).

157 He drew particular opprobrium for reinstating the hated Taliban-era Ministry for the Promotion of Virtue and Prevention of Vice, renamed as the Ministry for Haj and Religious

Despite being re-nominated by President Karzai amidst much international opposition, Mr Shinwari failed to obtain the necessary parliamentary approval in May 2006. This opened the way for the appointment of a dramatically different bench. The new bench is largely technocratic, far better educated and ethnically more diverse. The new Chief Justice, Abdul Salam Azimi, and most of the other justices have proper law degrees, sometimes from foreign institutions. The new court is dramatically more attuned to a reasonably liberal social vision, as well as for the first time in decades actually being able to draft proper legal opinions.

The most controversial decisions taken by the court since then have concerned the distribution of power between the various organs of the state, thereby exposing the technical limitations of the Constitution as a legal text. The first dramatic instance concerned the interpellation of then Foreign Minister Rangin Dadfar Spanta by parliament.[158] The Supreme Court delivered a surprisingly well reasoned opinion, predictably siding with President Karzai and reinstating Minister Spanta.[159] The most recent controversy surrounded the certification of the disputed presidential elections won under allegations of fraud by President Karzai. The Court has likewise concerned itself with a number of international crises affecting the government, such as the repeated expulsion of Afghan refugees by Iran, but it is questionable to what extent the Court had standing to express itself on these matters.

8. CONCLUSION

While the composition of the new Supreme Court is certainly an enormous advance over the previous court, and despite the commitment and personal integrity of many of its members, the overall institutional set-up does not permit us to speak of credible constitutionalism, let alone a constitutional moment inspired by international law. The state continues to be endemically weak to non-existent, and the very concept of an objective, impersonal civil service in the

Affairs. The dubious *formal* authority of such an essentially executive act is apparent. Further controversial decisions concerned for instance the banning of cable TV, coeducation, broadcasts of female singers, etc. See inter alia Reporters Sans Frontières, Afghanistan: Supreme Court bans cable TV, International Secretariat, Asia-Pacific Desk, RSF (Paris, 21 January 2003), available at www.hrea.org/ lists/huridocs-tech/markup/msg00917.html.; C. Franco, Despite Karzai Election, Afghan Conservatives Soldier On, Eurasia (6 December 2004), available at www.eurasianet.org/departments/insight/articles/ eav120704.shtml (visited 19 May 2010).

158 Under Articles 77 and 92, Afghan Constitution of 2004. Parliament was incensed at Spanta's perceived inaction when Iran expelled several thousand Afghan refugees. Additionally, the issue concerned Spanta's additional German citizenship obtained while living in exile there and presumably contrary to Article 72.

159 Supreme Court of Afghanistan 4 June 2007, *In re. Spanta*, Opinion of High Council of the Supreme Court of Islamic Republic of Afghanistan, Kabul (on file with author).

service of the state remains strongly contested.[160] The very idea of heeding international law remains deeply controversial and unpopular, seen as an infringement of national sovereignty, religious stipulations, or both.

The insistence by the international community during the Bonn negotiations, and ever since, of including formal commitments to international legal standards into the constitutive legal documents have not led to the empowerment of the judiciary or of other societal groups. While there are a small number of non-governmental organisations and official institutions[161] which refer actively to legal commitments to push for a version of social liberation through law, it seems fair to state that popular and elite attitudes towards international law remain deeply ambivalent. By and large, international standards of good governance and human rights are ill-understood and seen as culturally alien impositions. The distribution of bureaucratic posts and political power does not follow functional imperatives and the general bureaucratic commitment to written rules remains extremely tenuous. The somewhat idealistic vision of national courts and social actors emerging from a period of domestic unrest turning to international law as a way of 'anchoring' normative commitments against a reversal of political fortunes is not applicable in Afghanistan. Unlike post-war Europe,[162] there does not exist in Afghanistan today a broad social commitment to the idea of judicial control, let alone to the idea of international law as the yardstick of domestic social and governmental practices,[163] quite apart from the obvious fact that the very stability of the state continues to be very much under siege.[164]

---

160 E. Afsah, P. LeJeune and K. Zimmermann, Feasibility Study for a Civil Service Training Institute for Afghanistan, European Commission (Kabul, September 2005); World Bank, Fighting Corruption in Afghanistan Summaries of Vulnerabilities to Corruption Assessments (Washington DC: World Bank, May 2009), available at http://tinyurl.com/257askt (visited 7 May 2010); World Bank, Afghanistan Building an Effective State Priorities for Public Administration Reform, *supra* note 62; World Bank, Afghanistan: State Building, Sustaining Growth, and Reducing Poverty, *supra* note 60.

161 Notably the Independent Afghan Human Rights Commission, which continues to be the recipient of disproportionate international financial and technical support and is much envied and resented for this.

162 See Moravcik's insightful examination of the diplomatic record leading up to the adoption of the European Convention on Human Rights, where he showed conclusively that it was *not* the traditionally liberal, democratic states that pushed for the Convention, but the erstwhile authoritarian states of Italy, Germany, and others which sought to cement their new-found commitment towards individual rights and constitutional protections by establishing international normative supervision. A. Moravcsik, The Origins of Human Rights Regimes: Democratic Delegation in Postwar Europe, 54(2) International Organization 217–52 (2000).

163 John Dempsey and J. Alexander Thier, Resolving the Crisis over Constitutional Interpretation in Afghanistan, USIP Peace Briefing, United States Institute for Peace, Washington, D.C. (March 2009), available at http://beta.usip.org/files/resources/USIP_0309_2.PDF.

164 U.S. Department of Defence, Report on Progress Toward Security and Stability in Afghanistan and United States Plan for Sustaining the Afghanistan National Security Forces.

UNDERSTANDINGS OF INTERNATIONAL LAW IN RWANDA: A CONTEXTUAL APPROACH

Nicola PALMER*

1. INTRODUCTION

The Rwandan Prosecutor General, Martin Ngoga, leant forward to emphasize his point, 'Justice in this country has been contextual. What they call double standards is justice in a contextual environment.'[1] He was responding to the 2007 decision by the International Criminal Tribunal for Rwanda (ICTR) not to transfer genocide-related cases to the Rwandan domestic courts. Rule 11 *bis* of the Rules of Evidence and Procedure of the ICTR governs the transfer, to competent national jurisdictions, of individuals indicted but not yet tried by the ICTR. This rule was intended to create a bridge between the practice of international criminal law and domestic criminal justice processes, by ensuring that domestic courts had an adequate legal framework to try international crimes and provide suitable fair trial guarantees. However, on 8 October 2008, the Appeals Chamber of the ICTR[2] upheld the decision not to transfer the case of Yussuf Munyakazi[3] from the jurisdiction of the ICTR to the Rwandan national courts. This was followed by two consistent decisions relating to Gaspard Kanyarukiga[4] and Ildephonse Hategekimana,[5] respectively.

---

* Nicola Palmer is Global Justice Research Fellow at St Anne's College and convenor of the Oxford Transitional Justice Research (OTJR) group.

1 Interview with Martin Ngoga, Prosecutor General for Rwanda, Parquet Général (Kigali Rwanda, 5 September 2008) (notes on file with author).

2 UNSC Res. 955 (S/RES/955) (8 November 1994).

3 ICTR Appeals Chamber 8 October 2008, *Prosecutor v. Yussuf Munyakazi*, Decision on the Prosecutor's Appeal against Decision on Referral under Rule 11 *bis*, No. ICTR-97–36-R11*bis*.

4 ICTR Appeals Chamber 30 October 2008, *Prosecutor v. Gaspard Kanyarukiga*, Decision on the Prosecutor's Appeal against Decision on Referral under Rule 11 *bis*, No. ICTR-2002–78-R11*bis*.

5 ICTR Appeals Chamber 4 December 2008, *Prosecutor v. Ildephonse Hategekimana*, Decision on the Prosecutor's Appeal against Decision on Referral under Rule 11 *bis*, No. ICTR-00–55B-R11*bis*. The transfer of Jean-Baptiste Gatete was also refused by the Trial Chamber and was not appealed: ICTR Trial Chamber 17 November 2008, *Prosecutor v. Jean-Baptiste Gatete*,

The Trial Chambers were not persuaded that the accused would receive a fair trial in Rwanda. Supported by an influential *amicus curiae* brief from Human Rights Watch (HRW), it was successfully argued that the accused would be unable to raise an effective defence before the Rwandan national courts. This occurred despite the promulgation of specific legislation in Rwanda governing the transfer of cases from the ICTR[6] and the extensive domestic prosecution of the international crimes of genocide, crimes against humanity, and war crimes at a national level through the formal criminal courts, both civilian and military,[7] and on every hill across the country through the *gacaca* courts.[8] Given Rwanda's use of international criminal law within its own legal structures, the decision by the ICTR judges not to transfer cases to the national courts suggests that, from the Tribunal's perspective, the promulgation and application of such laws has not secured the country's domestic rule of law. Meanwhile, inside Rwanda, these decisions raise the important question as to what role *has* international law played in their domestic setting?

This chapter pursues a contextual examination of the impact of international law on the Rwandan courts. The chapter argues that international law has played a dynamic and varied role in post-genocide Rwanda. The process has been dialectic: international law has shaped Rwanda's domestic law, while domestic understandings of international law have also been shaped by the actual practice of the national courts. Through focusing on the national courts as discrete and important institutions in their own right, this chapter illustrates how international law has been both used and resisted in ways that are less predictable than what many international legal proponents may expect. How the courts understand their own practice is consistent with how they assess international law. Current Rwandan judges and lawyers focus on improved domestic judicial

---

Decision on the Prosecutor's Request for Referral to the Republic of Rwanda, No. ICTR-2000-61-1.

6 Organic Law No. 11/2007 of 16 March 2007, Concerning the Transfer of Cases to the Republic of Rwanda from the International Criminal Tribunal for Rwanda and From Other States.

7 For a review of Rwandan law and case law on genocide, see Avocats Sans Frontières, Vade-Mecum: *Le Crime de Genocide et les Crimes Contre L'Humanite devant les Juridictions Ordinaires du Rwanda* (The Crime of Genocide and Crimes Against Humanity in Rwanda's Courts) (2004), available at <www.asf.be/fr/publications> (visited 13 January 2011).

8 The *gacaca* courts are a state implemented but locally administrated transitional justice process that draws its name and some of its procedural aspects from a traditional Rwandan process of dispute resolution. Organic Law No. 40/2000 of 26/01/2001, *Gacaca* Jurisdictions and Organizing Prosecutions for Offences Constituting the Crime of Genocide or Crimes against Humanity Committed Between 1 October 1990 and 31 December 1994 (Official Gazette of the Republic of Rwanda, October 2001) (*Gacaca* Law 2001). For preliminary discussions see P. Clark, Hybridity, holism, and 'traditional' justice: The case of the *gacaca* courts in post-genocide Rwanda, 39 The George Washington International Law Review 765 (2007) and B. Ingelaere, The Gacaca Courts in Rwanda, in: L. Huyse and M. Salter (eds), Traditional Justice and Reconciliation after Violent Conflict: Learning from African Experiences (Stockholm: International Institute for Democracy and Electoral Assistance, 2008).

capacity as the central strength of their current practice. The courts' appraisal of the work of the ICTR and the role of international law are shaped by this primary internal concern. It is argued that acknowledging what the domestic courts themselves purport to achieve during a transitional period can usefully strengthen the domestic impact of international law. This argument is detailed in the following three sections.

The first section supports the position that during transitions, such as that following the Rwandan genocide, law has the potential to transform the prevailing meaning of legality in a particular country.[9] However, the role of law during a period of rapid change is contingent on the historical, political, and cultural context in which it operates. The impact of international law on domestic courts can be constructively examined through situating the work of these courts in their correct political and historical context. Rather than a doctrinal analysis of domestic case law, qualitative empirical research is used to examine how Rwandan judges and lawyers have interpreted the work of the domestic courts, illuminating the legal culture in which they have used and understood international law.

As will be discussed in the second section of this chapter, it is clear that international law has shaped the practice of the Rwandan domestic courts. In addition to the establishment of the ICTR, in a first domestic 'constitutional moment' Rwanda chose to pass legislation allowing for the prosecution of the international crimes of genocide and crimes against humanity.[10] This signalled a clear intention by the Rwandan state to hold accountable those involved in the extreme abuses perpetrated during the genocide while also supporting the domestic security agenda of the newly incumbent leaders. By 2003 there was a second 'constitutional moment' that was shaped once again, at least in part, by international law. The new Rwandan Constitution established that the international treaties ratified by Rwanda were 'more binding than organic and ordinary law.'[11] Following this legal change, in 2004 broad judicial reforms improved pre-trial detention laws and in 2007 the death penalty was abolished in order to meet the standards required by the ICTR to transfer cases to Rwanda under Rule 11 *bis*.[12]

Through these major legislative changes and with the concurrent operation of an international criminal tribunal, international law has shaped Rwanda's approach to post-genocide justice. However, the third section of this chapter argues that understandings of international law have also been shaped by the domestic courts' practice. Detailed empirical work inside the Rwandan national

---

9 R.G. Teitel, Transitional Justice 19 (New York: Oxford University Press, 2000).

10 Organic Law No. 08/96 of 30 August 1996, on the Organization of Prosecutions for Offences Constituting the Crime of Genocide or Crimes Against Humanity Committed since October 1, 1990.

11 Constitution of the Republic of Rwanda, Law No. Special of 2/05/2003, Article 190.

12 Organic Law No. 31/2007 of 25 July 2007, Relating to the Abolition of the Death Penalty.

courts shows that how the courts understood their own work impacted on how they engaged with and understood international law and the role of international institutions. As will be argued in this chapter, a contextual examination of Rwanda shows that for international law to be most beneficial to domestic rule of law requires a clear appreciation of what the national courts themselves are aiming to achieve, and why.

2. THE ROLE OF LAW DURING TRANSITIONS: A CONTEXTUAL PERSPECTIVE

Adopting a contextual perspective on the domestic impact of international law requires an initial methodological justification. The nature of a transitional period means that the social structures being studied are undergoing substantial change due to a shifting political, social, and legal landscape. The focus of academic debate around transitions has been on the two end points: autocracy to democracy,[13] and violence to peace.[14] A contextual perspective draws attention to the movement associated with transition, detailing how the processes of the national courts have operated during a period of rapid change.

Ruti Teitel argues that due to the extraordinary nature of a transitional period, from a normative perspective the role of law is to transform the prevailing meaning of legality. Rather than being perfectly prescriptive, the 'transitional perspective' of the rule of law is highly contingent on its social context and the 'popular understanding of legality in the ambient culture.'[15] While Teitel notes the importance of examining the legal culture of a particular country, the focus of her seminal publication is on the political and historical contexts of the countries in question. However, if we are to take seriously her call for contextualization, there is a need to examine the role of international law in the 'ambient culture' of the particular transitional society and the specific legal culture of the domestic courts where the law is developed and applied. This chapter is concerned with the latter.

The next two sections examine the political, historical, and cultural context in which international law has been applied in Rwanda. Clifford Geertz argues

13 S.P. Huntington, The third wave: Democratization in the late twentieth century, in: N.J. Kritz (ed.) Transitional Justice: How Emerging Democracies Reckon with Former Regimes (Washington: United States Institute of Peace, 1991). A nuanced critique of the third wave of democracy highlights the need to look at the existing political and social dimensions of the specific country concerned, as provided in T. Carothers, The End of the Transition Paradigm, 13(1) Journal of Democracy 5 (2002).

14 F. Ní Aoláin and C. Campbell, The Paradox of Transition in Conflicted Democracies, 27 Human Rights Quarterly 172 (2005).

15 Teitel, *supra* note 9, p. 19.

that it is through culture that a particular action is ascribed meaning.[16] To examine the legal culture of the domestic courts, this chapter investigates how Rwandan judges and lawyers have understood international law within the social practices of the national courts. This allows the researcher to explain the role of international law in the cultural context of these domestic courts, illuminating how the courts have interacted with the concurrent operations of the ICTR.[17]

A contextual analysis of the Rwandan national courts was carried out through the span of two periods of research in Rwanda and Tanzania. Data was collected through semi-structured interviews, participant observations, informal discussions, and the analysis of grey material and case law.[18] In total, 146 interviews were conducted with decision makers, lawyers, judges, and general participants within the ICTR, the criminal justice sector in Rwanda, and the National Service for *Gacaca* Courts.[19] Twenty-one of the participants were current Rwandan judges and lawyers in the national courts. Glaser and Strauss' grounded theory, in which the aim of qualitative research is not to obtain a randomized sample but rather to build a theory to explain the courts' relevant behaviour, guided this empirical work.[20] In line with this approach, the analysis emerged from the social data and the selection of participants developed through the research process.[21] The personnel interviewed inside the national courts included the Rwandan Minister of Justice Tharcisse Karugarama, the Prosecutor General Martin Ngoga, and the Deputy Chief Justice of the Supreme Court Justice Sam Rugege. In addition, interviews were conducted with High Court and District Tribunal judges along with prosecutors and criminal lawyers in two districts outside of the capital Kigali.[22]

16 C. Geertz, Thick Description: Toward an Interpretive Theory of Culture, in: C. Geertz (ed.), The Interpretation of Cultures: Selected Essays (London: Fontana Press, 1993).

17 Article 8 of the ICTR's Statute establishes primacy of the Tribunal, while acknowledging the concurrent jurisdiction of domestic prosecution. For a detailed and recent discussion of this concurrent operation see I. Onsea, The Legacy of the ICTR in Rwanda in the Context of the Completion Strategy: The Impact of Rule 11*bis*, in: C. Ryngaert (ed.), The Effectiveness of International Criminal Justice (Intersentia, 2009).

18 This empirical research has been further supplemented by addition interviews conducted by Phil Clark in Rwanda in April 2010, in which participants were asked a consistent set of semi-structured questions.

19 Officially termed the National Service for Gacaca Jurisdictions – the direct translation from the French name *Service National des Jurisdictions Gacaca* (SNJG) – personnel currently working inside the institution prefer the term 'National Service for Gacaca Courts'.

20 B.G. Glaser and A.L. Strauss, The Discovery of Grounded Theory: Strategies for Qualitative Research 35 (Chicago: Aldine Pub, 1967).

21 Glaser and Strauss, *supra* note 20, p. 47.

22 All interviews were conducted with the express consent of the participants, following either a verbal or written explanation of the aims and structure of the research as approved by the University of Oxford's Central University Research Ethics Committee (CUREC). The interviews were semi-structured and all began with the general question, 'What do you see as the central contribution of this court?' Quotes included in this chapter are not attributed to individuals, although not all respondents requested anonymity. In each instance they are

In adopting this contextual perspective, it is first important to note that the judges interviewed within the domestic courts explicitly identified the transformative role that law has played in Rwanda following the 1994 genocide. As one judge noted, 'Like everywhere else, here in Rwanda social development is moved through laws'[23] and as another judge more stridently articulated, 'this judiciary brought the country out of the doldrums, our new laws have changed the country.'[24] When examining which laws were understood to have had the greatest influence, the majority of Rwandan judges, prosecutors, and private lawyers focused on the 2004 judicial reform rather than the broad constitutional changes that had occurred the year before or the early use and application of international criminal law. As one judge succinctly articulated,

> There has been a large amount of positive evolution in judicial capacity and this needs to be recognized. 2004 was a turning point, a whole lot of new judges where employed and they had received better training.[25]

In the interviews the primary focus of the participants' discussions of the 2004 judicial reform was on the improved judicial training of the current Rwandan legal fraternity. In the words of another judge,

> The most important aspect of judicial reform has been hiring competent judges because before 1994, and actually before the reforms, the majority of judges were not qualified in law. I don't know what criterion was used to hire them but it wasn't a law degree. From 2004 to become a judge you must have a law degree. All except the lowest magistrates now have law degrees so that at least the people who are dealing with cases know the law and apply it,[26]

This focus on the use of legal regulation to improve judicial capacity is notable and was articulated in response to the open-ended interview question, 'What would you see as the major contribution of the national courts to the Rwandan transition?' As another prosecutor articulated,

---

always representative of a broader category of how participants were ascribing meaning to the courts' work.

23 Interview with Participant 3 (Kigali, Rwanda, 7 August 2008), interview conducted with P. Clark (notes and recording on file with author).

24 Interview with Participant 20 (Kigali, Rwanda, 14 April 2010), interview conducted by P. Clark (notes on file with author).

25 Interview with Participant 12 (Regional, Rwanda, 27 August 2008) (notes on file with author).

26 Interview with Participant 3 (Kigali, Rwanda, 7 August 2008), interview conducted with P. Clark (notes and recording on file with author).

> Rwanda has undertaken serious legal reforms since 2004, recruiting lawyers. We now have one hundred percent lawyers apart from the lower courts. From the High Court to the Supreme Court they are legally qualified persons with experience ...[27]

These statements encapsulate what the majority of Rwandan judges and lawyers saw as the most important development in Rwanda's domestic rule of law. The focus on such reforms was articulated during interviews in Kigali and in the research sites outside of the capital.

Although the participants in the qualitative study repeatedly focused on the post-2004 period, drawing particular attention to the new educational criteria for the judges and prosecutors, in practice there has been extensive judicial reform throughout Rwanda's transitional period. The most notable of these reforms is the promulgation of the new Constitution in May 2003.[28] As noted earlier, the Constitution formed the basis for many of the reforms introduced the following year and further incorporated international law into Rwandan domestic law. From 2003 all the international and regional human rights treaties that had been ratified by Rwanda, including the International Covenant on Civil and Political Rights (ICCPR),[29] were directly included in the country's domestic legislative framework.[30] In addition, from as early as 1996, Rwanda had enacted domestic legislation allowing for the prosecution of genocide and crimes against humanity.[31] It is therefore analytically important to explore why the current Rwandan judges and lawyers focused on their improved judicial training as the principal reform.

Proponents of international law might not expect this focus on legal education standards rather than on Rwanda's domestic legislative adoption of both international criminal law and international human right standards. As the introduction to this collection articulates, implementing international law in domestic criminal codes is expected to play a central role in the rule of law at the domestic level. It is thought to stabilize the legal order, contribute to the protection of fundamental rights, and help protect the separation of powers. Why then, when the Rwandan judges and lawyers reflected on which laws had most transformed their domestic practices, did they not make more direct

27 Interview with Participant 4 (Kigali, Rwanda, 13 August 2008) (notes and recording on file with author).

28 Constitution of the Republic of Rwanda, Law No. Special of 2/05/2003.

29 Rwanda ratified the ICCPR on 16 April 1975.

30 International law is referred to as a source of law in relation to the statute of limitations (Article 20), the right to asylum (Article 25), and the rights of the child (Article 28). In addition, as noted under Article 190, ratified international treaties are binding on Organic laws and ordinary laws, although the incorporation of these laws is subject to compatibility with the Constitution or amendment of the Constitution in line with Article 193.

31 Organic Law No. 08/96 of 30 August 1996 on the Organization of Prosecutions for Offences Constituting the Crime of Genocide or Crimes Against Humanity Committed since October 1, 1990 is passed into Rwanda law.

reference to the new Constitution, the use and value of international criminal law, or the compliance of Rwandan law with international legal standards?

To answer this question requires a broader examination of the role of international law in the Rwandan transitional period. International law has shaped the work of the Rwandan domestic courts but equally, the courts' understanding of international law has been shaped by the reality of their legal practice. How international law is currently understood inside the national courts must take account of the immediate post-genocide context, a transitional period characterized by continued insecurity and mass arrests carried out by domestic law enforcement agencies.

3. INTERNATIONAL LAW IN POST-GENOCIDE RWANDA

The role of international law in the Rwandan transition takes us into the heart of post-genocide politics. From July 1994 until 1999, the work of the national courts was heavily shaped by the Rwandan government's prioritization of on-going security concerns and the consolidation of political power. This resulted in wide-scale arrests, allegations of 'disappearances', and extensive detention without charge. Arrests were justified by the international legal requirement to prosecute the crime of genocide, an objective lauded and encouraged outside of the country,[32] but the resultant trials were criticized for their failure to adhere to due process standards and the inadequacy of available defence.[33] This tension between the use of international law both as the grounds for action and a basis of critique goes part of the way in explaining the reluctance of current Rwandan judges and lawyers to draw their legitimacy from international norms or best practices. A focus in 2008 and 2009 on legal reform and judicial training allows the present-day judges and lawyers a means of distancing their current work from the initial arrests and trials of the 1990s – during which time there was a deep tension between the use of international criminal law and international human rights standards, as described below.

---

32 International Crisis Group, Five years after the genocide in Rwanda: Justice in question 13 (7 April 1999); Amnesty International, Rwanda – Unfair trials: Justice denied 1 (AI-Index AFR 47/08/197) (8 April 1997); M.P. Scharf, Responding to Rwanda: Accountability Mechanisms in the Aftermath of Genocide, 2 Journal of International Affairs 621 (1999).

33 Amnesty International, Rwanda – Unfair trials: Justice denied, *supra* note 32 and Amnesty International, Rwanda – The troubled course of justice (AI-Index AFR 47/10/00) (April 2000).

3.1. INTERNATIONAL CRIMINAL LAW AND THE SECURITY OF THE RWANDAN STATE

The 1994 Rwandan genocide occurred in an environment of fear and uncertainty.[34] Amidst a civil war that had begun in 1990 through insurgencies from the Rwandan Patriotic Front (RPF)[35] and the insecurity following the introduction of multi-party politics, political power was consolidated along ethnic lines. Inside Rwanda, government and military leaders used racist propaganda to collapse civilian and combatant identities into the collective ethnic categorization of Tutsi. Youth militia were trained and arms flowed into the country. On 6 April 1994, President Juvénal Habyarimana's plane was shot down. Within hours of the president's death, moderate politicians were executed, roadblocks were set up, and 100 days of genocidal killing ensued.[36]

Predominantly targeting Tutsi civilians, at a local level the violence was characterized by brutal and intimate methods, taking the conflict inside the homes and lives of most Rwandans. On 17 July 1994, the RPF, having defeated the incumbent government forces, gained effective control of a body-strewn Rwanda. In that same month, 2 million people fled the country, travelling to Zaire through the 'humanitarian zone' created by the French-led *Opération Turquoise*. This mass movement of people was made up predominantly of Hutu civilians but also included the full retreating army and militia who had participated in the hundred day massacres.[37] The action of the newly constituted Rwandan government was shaped by both the perceived and real security threat posed by this refugee population. International criminal law provided a crucial legal basis for much of this state action.

On 28 September 1994, in a letter to the President of the United Nations Security Council, the Permanent Representative of Rwanda to the UN identified an international criminal tribunal as one means to respond to the security concern raised by the remaining ex-government fighters and *génocidaires* on the borders of the Rwandan territory.[38] As discussed below, in November 1994, as a non-permanent member of the Security Council, Rwanda would eventually vote

---

34 S. Straus, The Order of Genocide 87 (New York: Cornell University Press, 2006).

35 The Rwandan Patriotic Front was an armed force based in Uganda and made up predominantly of Rwandan refugees of Tutsi ethnicity who had fled earlier outbreaks of ethnic violence.

36 A. Des Forges, Leave None to Tell the Story: Genocide in Rwanda (New York: Human Rights Watch, 1999); L. Melvern, Conspiracy to Murder: The Rwandan Genocide (New York: Verso, 2004); G. Prunier, The Rwanda Crisis 1959–1994: History of the Genocide (London: Hurst, 1995).

37 G. Prunier, Opération Turquoise: A Humanitarian Escape from a Political Dead End, in: H. Adelman and A. Suhrke (eds), The Path of a Genocide: The Rwanda Crisis from Uganda to Zaire (New Brunswick: Transaction Publishers, 1999).

38 Letter from the Permanent Representative of Rwanda Addressed to the President of the Security Council (S/1994/1115) (28 September 1994).

against the ICTR's founding resolution.[39] However, the security concerns that led to the initial request continued to frame Rwanda's justice sector for the next ten years. Criminal justice was chosen by the RPF as the preferred means of securing effective control of Rwanda. This culminated in the forced closure of refugee camps and widespread arrests. Certainly many of the accused were worthy of arrest, and creating stability was rightly prioritized. However, the use of force was almost certainly excessive[40] and the actions had very severe practical and legal implications.

It was clear that from July 1994 the Rwandan government intended to pursue broad prosecutions. The proposal for a South African-style truth commission was repeatedly rejected on the basis that it would allow for a conditional amnesty, particularly for lower-level perpetrators.[41] The arrest of all suspected *génocidaires*, regardless of their level of responsibility, was intended to be used to help prevent any further military resistance to RPF control, making any type of amnesty militarily unpopular. In addition, inside Rwanda there was a very strong call for immediate accountability for the horrendous crimes of the genocide. The decision to arrest and prosecute these suspects aligned the objectives of the Rwandan government with a growing argument in international law that there was a legal obligation to pursue prosecutions for international crimes. Articulating a position taken by many advocates of international criminal law, Michael Scharf argued that amnesty in Rwanda was not an option as it would have been a violation of the Genocide Convention, to which Rwanda was a party,[42] and 'served as a virtual license to repeat the crimes'.[43]

---

39 M.H. Morris, The Trials of Concurrent Jurisdiction: The case of Rwanda, 7 Duke Journal of Comparative and International Law 349 (1996).

40 As discussed in the next section, in Polman's account of the closure of one of the refugee camps in Kibeho in south-western Rwanda, she estimates that as many as 4,000 people were killed. L. Polman, We Did Nothing: Why the Truth Doesn't Always Come Out When the UN Goes In (London: Viking, 2003).

41 This occurred at a conference in Kigali in October/November 1995 and was reiterated following a Rwandan delegation's trip to South Africa in 1997. W. Schabas, Justice, Democracy, and Impunity in Post-genocide Rwanda: Searching for Solutions to Impossible Problems, 7(3) Criminal Law Forum 528 (1996); International Crisis Group, Five years after the genocide in Rwanda, *supra* note 32, p. 5 and Clark, *supra* note 8, p. 781.

42 Rwanda had ratified the following treaties but had not specifically incorporated them into their penal code: Convention for the Prevention and Punishment of the Crime of Genocide, adopted 9 December 1948, 78 UNTS 277 (entered into force 12 January 1951); Geneva Convention Relative to the Protection of Civilian Persons in Time of War, adopted 12 August 1949, 75 UNTS 287 (entered into force 21 October 1950) (Geneva Convention IV); Protocol Additional to the Geneva Conventions of 12 August 1949, and Relating to the Protection of Victims of International Armed Conflicts, adopted 8 June 1977, 1125 UNTS 3 (entered into force 7 December 1978); Convention on the Non-applicability of Statutory Limitations to War Crimes and Crimes against Humanity, adopted 26 November 1968, 754 UNTS 73 (entered into force 11 November 1970).

43 Scharf, *supra* note 32, p. 25.

Despite this alignment, there was contestation over the role of both international criminal law and foreign legal involvement in the genocide-related prosecutions. This was first apparent in the Rwandan government's decision to vote against the establishment of the ICTR. In her account of the reasons for the break-down in the negotiations between the Rwandan state and the UN Security Council, Madeline Morris focuses on three central concerns: 1) the Tribunal had jurisdiction only from 1 January 1994 through to 31 December 1994, while Rwanda felt it should extend back to 1990 to include crimes committed by the previous regime during the civil war period; 2) the number of judicial personnel designated to staff the Tribunal was seen by the Rwandan government as insufficient to deal with the number of suspects, and showed the Tribunal's intention only to try the most senior accused; and 3) the Tribunal prohibited the use of capital punishment, which was still in force in Rwanda at the time. The government's objections, particularly regarding the size and staffing of the Tribunal, supports the position that wide-scale arrest of suspected lower-level perpetrators played a crucial role in the Rwandan security agenda as they were unwilling to agree on the exclusive use of a 'Nuremberg paradigm' in which only the very high-level accused would be prosecuted.

In response to these concerns about the ICTR, inside Rwanda the 1996 Organic Law established a Special Chamber of the Supreme Court to try both genocide and crimes against humanity, with a temporal jurisdiction from October 1990 until December 1994. The ICTR had been mandated to contribute to international peace and security and establish national reconciliation. The mandate established under the national courts was more simply articulated: 'to organize criminal proceeding against those accused of genocide and crimes against humanity.'[44] Theogene Rudasingwa, the Rwandan Ambassador to the United States in 1998, writes, 'this law simply proceeds from the premise that everyone who committed genocide would be made individually accountable for the crime that he or she committed.'[45] Importantly, and substantiating the argument presented above, this statement was framed by his opening remarks that in 1998 Rwanda continued to face serious security concerns from refugee populations on the borders of its territory.

Reflecting a keen awareness of the international debates at the time on the retroactive application of international criminal law, the 1996 Organic Law carefully addressed the problem. The preamble of the law states that prosecutions

44 Organic Law No. 08/96 of 30 August 1996.

45 T. Rudasingwa, The Rwanda Tribunal and Its Relationship to National Trials in Rwanda, 13 American University International Law Review 1486 (1998). In a deeply concerning turn of events on 14 January 2011, a Rwandan military court sentenced Theogene Rudasingwa to a prison term of between 20 to 24 years. Rudasingwa is currently in exile in the United States. See S. Kinzer, Kagame's authoritarian turns risk Rwanda's future, Guardian (London, 27 January 2011), available at www.guardian.co.uk/commentisfree/cifamerica/2011/jan/27/rwanda-freedom-of-speech (visited 28 January 2011).

must be based on the existing Penal Code.[46] Under Article 1 the international crimes of genocide and crimes against humanity are prohibited only to the extent that the underlying criminal offences of intentional homicide, accomplice of intentional homicide, serious assault against the person, sexual torture, and offences against property are provided for in the Penal Code. Schabas suggests that this was unnecessary as genocide and crimes against humanity have been recognized under both national and international law, and following the precedent of Nuremberg, severe punishment for perpetrating such crimes would have been both accessible and foreseeable.[47] However, this careful inclusion of international criminal law into the existing national law shows the importance of its domestic use in structuring Rwanda's legal framework.

International criminal law would provide the basis for much of the action of the Rwandan criminal justice sector over the next ten years. However, just as international criminal law was being carefully incorporated into Rwandan law, international human rights law was being drawn on to criticize its implementation as the forced repatriation of the refugees began, the conditions of incarceration for those arrested rapidly deteriorated, and the justice system was put under increasing strain.

3.2. INTERNATIONAL HUMAN RIGHTS LAW IN RWANDA

Closure of the refugee camps began on 22 April 1995 with the forced repatriation of over 150,000 internally displaced persons in Kibeho camp, the largest refugee camp on Rwandan soil, located in the south-western part of the country. The United Nations' voluntary repatriation programme had floundered amid rumours that inside Rwanda there were revenge killings and arbitrary arrests. In contrast, the newly constituted Rwandan Defence Force (RDF) acted far more quickly, unwilling to accept the potential for the consolidation of fighting forces in the refugee camps. It was estimated that over 4,000 people died during the actual closing of the Kibeho camp. The official figure, accepted by the then precarious government of national unity, was 348 lives lost; the deaths were largely attributed to 'criminal elements' operating in the camp.[48] This large-scale forced repatriation was coupled with the arrest of genocide suspects and a rapidly escalating prison population.

The exact figures of the prison population in Rwanda throughout the 1990s are difficult to verify. Quoting Human Rights Watch, Prunier estimates that 'from 1000 prisoners in August 1994, the numbers had risen to 6 000 at the end

46 Organic Law No. 08/96 of 30 August 1996.

47 Schabas, *supra* note 41, p. 536–537.

48 G. Prunier, From Genocide to Continental War: The 'Congolese' Conflict and the Crisis of Contemporary Africa (London: Hurst Publishers, 2009).

of the year and kept growing exponentially to reach 23 000 by March 1995.'[49] Later he suggests that the prison population was at 9,000 in February 1995 and jumped to 44,000 inmates by June 1995.[50] What is clear is that while some arrests were happening across the country, the closure of the camps such as Kibeho in April 1995 and those in Zaire from September 1996 caused the numbers to spike dramatically. As the numbers of genocide inmates grew, so the conditions of detention rapidly deteriorated. By 1998 there were officially two categories of civilian prisons in Rwanda: those under the authority of the Ministry of Justice and those run by the Ministry of the Interior.[51] Conditions in the prisons, with an estimated capacity of only 15,000 inmates, were 'harsh and life-threatening',[52] with minimal sanitation and over-crowding so pronounced that in some cases prisoners had to take turns to sit down.

The 'prisons' under the Ministry of the Interior – called *cachots communaux* – were at the end of this spectrum. Organized at the local level, these holding areas were initially under the exclusive control of the local mayors or *bourgmestres*[53] and took many forms, from warehouses and private homes to shipping containers and latrines.[54] Of the 183 places of detention listed by the International Committee of the Red Cross (ICRC) during this period, only 16 were actual prisons. International human rights law formed the basis for the argument made by international and domestic human rights NGOs against such incarceration, repeatedly arguing that they constituted cruel, inhuman, and degrading treatment.[55]

As the Rwandan prisons and *cachots* filled up, so the Constitution was amended[56] to allow for continued detention without charge as the burgeoning criminal justice system struggled to regularize prisoner arrest records. In June 1995, the Transitional National Assembly passed an act 'suspending the fundamental safeguards guaranteeing the pre-trial rights of individuals contained in the Code of Criminal Procedure (CCP).'[57] In a decision of 26 July 1995, the Rwandan Constitutional Court declared this legislation invalid.[58] The

49 Prunier, *supra* note 48, p. 9.

50 Prunier, *supra* note 48, p. 45.

51 M. Drumbl, Rule of Law Amid Lawlessness: Counseling the Accused in Rwanda's Domestic Genocide Trials, 29 Columbia Human Rights Law Review 572 (1998).

52 U.S. Department of State, Rwanda Country Report on Human Rights Practices for 1998 4 (26 February 1999).

53 International Crisis Group, Five years after the genocide in Rwanda, *supra* note 32, p. 12.

54 Drumbl, *supra* note 51, p. 571–547.

55 Amnesty International, Rwanda – Unfair trials: Justice denied, *supra* note 32, p. 1.

56 Article 6 of The Constitutional Amendment I, January 18, 1996, authorized derogation from Article 12(2) of the 1991 Constitution in cases of 'exceptional danger threatening the existence of the nation'.

57 Amnesty International, Gacaca: A Question of Justice 6 (AI-Index AFR 47/007/2002) (December 2002).

58 Schabas, *supra* note 41, p. 526. At the time, the Constitution in force was made up of four founding documents; the Declaration of the RPF made on 17 July 1994; the Protocol of

court ruled that the new detention procedural rules were incompatible with the presumption of innocence and the right to a fair hearing within a reasonable period of time. Following this reasoning, they held that these legislative changes were unconstitutional and invalid.[59]

However, despite this stance the reality of incarceration without charge remained, and on 18 January 1996 the Constitution was amended to prevent any future constitutional challenges to legislative derogations of prisoner rights. This opened the way for the promulgation of legislation on 8 September 1996 suspending several provisions of the CCP and authorizing the detention of genocide suspects, despite the irregularity of their files. Unlike the 1996 Organic Law, which carefully addressed issues of retroactivity, this law was immediately applied retroactively to 6 April 1994 and gave the *Parquet Général* (Public Prosecutors Office) 18 months to regularize the arrest reports and warrants and issue pre-trial detention orders where appropriate.[60] These derogations were extended on two further occasions through to 16 July 2001. In the first seven years following the horrors of the genocide, it is clear that the principles of international law were not as readily addressed in relation to prisoners' rights as they had been regarding the inclusion of genocide and crimes against humanity on the Rwandan statute books.

International human rights law provided the basis against which the changes to Rwanda's criminal procedures were assessed. While Amnesty International (AI) was hugely critical of these amendments, the International Crisis Group (ICG) suggested that they were necessary as a means of dealing with the rate of arrests, arguing that similar legislation was allowed in very exceptional circumstances under the ICCPR. However, ICG went on to state that the subsequent extensions of these derogations were badly drawn up, resulting in ambiguities that provided judicial authorities with 'an excuse for relaxing their efforts to ensure procedures are correctly implemented.'[61]

By May 1997, AI estimated that more than 100,000 people were held in prisons and detention centres across Rwanda. As discussed, the arrests were crucial to the RPF establishing effective control of the Rwandan territory and were complemented by a very clear decision by the government to pursue prosecutions. International criminal law was used as the legal justification for the arrests, but international human rights law provided the basis against which the procedures and conditions of these arrests were measured. The result was an

---

Agreement from the 24 November 1994 providing minor amendments; the Arusha Accords drawn up as part of the initial civil war Peace Agreement; and the 1991 Constitution. The former two had supremacy over the latter two. See F. Reyntjens, Constitution-making in Situations of Extreme Crisis: The Case of Rwanda and Burundi, 40(2) Journal of African Law 235 (1996).

59 Amnesty International, Gacaca: A Question of Justice, *supra* note 57, p. 6.

60 Amnesty International, Gacaca: A Question of Justice, *supra* note 57, p. 6.

61 International Crisis Group, Five years after the genocide in Rwanda, *supra* note 32, p. 7.

increasing tension in the use of international law in the country. The inability of the Rwandan judicial actors to reconcile these two bodies of international law grew out of the political prioritization of immediate security concerns and the impossibility that the domestic justice system could manage the resultant caseload.

3.3. MITIGATING THE TENSIONS IN INTERNATIONAL LAW AND DEALING WITH AN IMPOSSIBLE CASELOAD

When the Special Chambers began their work, they were faced with the overwhelming task of trying over 100,000 suspects, the majority of them charged with genocide. In an effort to respond to this unmanageable caseload, the 1996 legislation relied heavily on a plea-bargaining system that was intended to meet international procedural standards while processing the enormous number of cases. The system was based on categorizing the accused in four groups according to the severity of their offence.[62] This categorization formed the backbone of a confession and guilty plea procedure.

Under Articles 15 and 16 of the 1996 Organic Law, in return for a full confession and an apology, offenders in the second, third, and fourth categories benefit from substantial reduction in penalties. This reduction was increased if perpetrators confessed before the start of prosecution proceedings against them. Offenders in the first category, those accused of acting in local leadership positions during the massacres, could participate in the guilty plea procedure and benefit from the mitigated penalties, provided their names had not previously been published in the Official Gazette.[63] As Morris notes, this specialized plea-agreement system, while common in adversarial common law systems, was 'an unprecedented feature in Rwandan law.'[64] Plea-bargaining was introduced to try to mitigate against the growing tensions between the application of international criminal law and the accompanying human rights standards.

---

62 Category 1 was reserved for those suspected of being in positions of responsibility at the national, *prefectoral*, *sector*, or *cell*. A *prefecture* corresponds with a provincial structure and is made up of several *sector*s which in turn contain several *cells*. A *cell* is comparable to a neighbourhood in an urban setting. Category 2 consisted of those accused of being perpetrators and accomplices of intentional homicide or of serious assault against the person causing death. Category 3 applied to persons whose criminal acts or whose acts of criminal participation make them guilty of other serious assaults against the person and Category 4 related to those accused solely of committing property offences. In 2004 Category 2 and 3 were amalgamated, however by this stage the *gacaca* courts were in operation and had jurisdiction over Categories 2 and 3 leaving only Category 1 in the remit of the national courts.

63 Article 9 of Organic Law No. 08/96 of 30 August 1996.

64 Morris, *supra* note 39, p. 360.

Despite these initial efforts, in practice the domestic genocide cases, just like the initial arrests and conditions of incarceration, were heavily criticized by international and domestic human rights NGOs for failing to meet international procedural standards. The criticisms focused on three principal issues: the paucity of judicial personnel, particularly the limited number of defence counsel;[65] Rwanda's continued use of capital punishment;[66] and the restricted appeal procedure.[67] Plea-bargaining did not resolve the tension in Rwanda's use and application of international law. In addition to continued international criticism, the efforts to streamline the process through plea-bargaining failed to address the unmanageable caseload. By 1999 the national courts had heard only 1,274 cases, one percent of the total number of detainees then held in custody.[68] By early 2000 this number had nearly doubled, but progress remained slow. International criminal law had been incorporated into domestic law but, in practice, its application to all lower-level suspects impacted how international law was both applied and understood within the national courts.

The judges and lawyers who are currently working in the national courts acknowledged the immediate problems with charging international crimes and the requirements for a fair application of international law. As one participant in the empirical study stated,

> The 1990s were a crisis in the justice sector. There was much effort but limited outcomes due to limited personnel, legal information, logistical ability and infrastructure. We were also dealing with prison congestion and needed to work on an appropriate legal framework.[69]

As discussed, initially the 'appropriate legal framework' to try genocide suspects drew very heavily on international law. However, by 2003 it moved quite clearly away from it, as the initial domestic trials had been broadly discredited. The *gacaca* courts, a state-implemented but locally-administrated set of transitional justice processes, were introduced as a solution to Rwanda's 'problem of justice'.[70] Procedurally, these courts operated in an entirely different manner to the national courts or the ICTR. Crucially, there were no lawyers at the hearings and

---

65 Drumbl, *supra* note 51, p. 550.

66 N. Pillay, The Rwanda Tribunal and its Relationship to National Trials in Rwanda, 13 American University International Law Review 1477 (1998).

67 International Crisis Group, Five years after the genocide in Rwanda, *supra* note 32, p. 15.

68 Drumbl, *supra* note 51, p. 291.

69 Interview with Participant 9 (Kigali, Rwanda, 12 April 2010), interview conducted by P. Clark (notes on file with author).

70 Republic of Rwanda Office of the President, Report on the Reflection Meetings held in the Office of the President of the Republic from May 1998 to March 1999 3 (August 1999) (on file with author). It was at these reflection meetings that the decision was finally reached to introduce the *gacaca* courts. However, it must be noted that this report was not initially available to researchers, although requested from 2003. The current document was found in the archives of the National Unity and Reconciliation Commission in July 2008.

the trials were presided over by members of the local community, known as the *inyangamugayo*.[71] The majority of the genocide-related cases were transferred to these localized courts and this relieved some of the previous case-load strain on the national courts.

By mid-2002, the national courts in Rwanda had judged 7,181 persons accused of genocide. After 2002, there was a re-orientation of judicial activities towards the *gacaca* courts. These judicial developments allowed for a second 'constitutional moment' inside the national courts. Despite the clear statement made by the *gacaca* courts that the country would find domestic solutions to Rwanda's legal problems,[72] at this next 'constitutional moment' international law was once again drawn upon and further incorporated into Rwanda's domestic legislation. The new Rwandan Constitution refers directly to international law in relation to, among others, the right to asylum (Article 25) and the rights of the child (Article 28). In addition, as noted, under Article 190, ratified international treaties have primacy over domestic laws provided these treaties are compatible with the Constitution or amendments of the Constitution that are in line with Article 193. It was only after this extensive legal change that the national courts in 2004 halted work for a number of months and introduced the new legislated requirements on the educational standards of Rwandan judges and lawyers.[73]

This historical and political description of the work of the Rwandan courts illustrates how there has been both a use of and resistance to international law in the country. International law has certainly impacted Rwanda's domestic legal framework; however, the earlier tension between the use of international criminal law and the procedural standards of its implementation changed the understanding of international law in the Rwandan domestic courts. Inside the national courts it was understood that changes in legislation were insufficient to satisfy international critics. Within the national courts, there was a need to differentiate between the first set of trials, which had been widely discredited following the immediate transition, and the capacity of the national courts to receive current genocide-related cases from the ICTR. This differentiation had to happen without a change in the political dispensation. A focus on judicial capacity provided the Rwandan judges and lawyers with one means to do just that. But what has been the impact of this use of international law on current domestic practice? The endeavour by Rwanda to receive cases from the ICTR and the second 'constitutional moment' that occurred in 2003 both suggest that, despite the early tensions in its use and application, international law remains an important influence on Rwanda's domestic courts.

---

71 *Inyangamugayo* is a Kinyarwanda term translating to 'persons of integrity' and referring to the laypersons that preside as judges over the *gacaca* hearings.

72 A. Meyerstein, Between law and culture: Rwanda's gacaca and postcolonial legality, 32 Law and Social lnquiry 481(2007).

73 Human Rights Watch Report, Law and Reality: Progress on Judicial Reform in Rwanda (July 2008).

4. INTERNATIONAL LAW AND THE LEGAL CULTURE OF THE NATIONAL COURTS

The question that opened this chapter was: how have participants inside Rwanda's national courts understood the legal changes that have occurred in Rwanda since the 1994 genocide? Adopting an interpretive view on cultural analysis allows the researcher to examine the 'socially established structures of meaning'[74] that render the practice of law in Rwanda's transition intelligible.

As stated, what emerged as the dominant view from the Rwandan judges and lawyers who were interviewed was that judicial reform was the crucial legal change during the transitional period. The primary focus of the research participants was on improved judicial training, seen in the words of one of the prosecutors interviewed,

> We wanted to bring into the Rwanda judiciary competent and skilled personnel because for so many years from the 1960s, 70s, 80s the Rwandan judiciary was manned by poorly educated magistrates. Some of them had other qualifications but very few of them were lawyers so we insisted to have qualified staff, who had the legal training from the university and build their experience through their qualifications and practice.[75]

It has been argued that Rwanda's use of and resistance to international law in the 1990s in part explains the participants' focus in 2008 and 2009 on legal training and capacity-building rather than on the extensive incorporation of international law into Rwandan law. As the ICTR made explicit in the *Hategikimana* Rule 11 *bis* decision, outside Rwanda the inclusion of international law on the domestic statute books has been viewed to be insufficient to guarantee fair trial rights or ensure that international human rights standards are met.[76] In 2008 and 2009, the judges and lawyers inside the Rwandan national courts wanted to establish their capacity and competence to administer justice through other means.

However, this final section of this chapter will argue that this interpretation of the courts' work also suggests that international law has not been fully adopted within the Rwandan legal culture. In a dialectic process, international law has shaped the practice of the courts, but understandings of international law have also been shaped by the courts' practice. This requires a full discussion not only of how the work of the national courts has been understood, but also how the national court participants have assessed the concurrent work of the ICTR and

---

74 Geertz, *supra* note 16, p. 12–13.

75 Interview with Participant 4 (Kigali, Rwanda, 13 August 2008) (notes and recording on file with author).

76 ICTR Trial Chamber 19 June 2008, *Prosecutor v. Ildephonse Hategekimana*, Decision on the Prosecutor's Request for Referral to the Republic of Rwanda, No. ICTR-00-55B-R11*bis*, para. 35.

international law in general. What is argued in this section is that how the courts understand their own practice is consistent with how they assess international law in Rwanda.

For the national court judges and lawyers, the ICTR was generally evaluated against what they perceived as the major contribution of their own work, namely the development of judicial capacity. This interpretation starts to shed light on the legal culture of the Rwandan courts. Within the empirical study, the work of the ICTR was ascribed a meaning that was consistent with how the actions of the domestic courts were being assessed. As a senior prosecutor stated,

> The ICTR has attempted to play a supervisory role. If you can go on the record to say that Rwanda cannot be trusted, it is your biggest failure. It was their role to build the system. If they did not meaningfully engage with Rwanda and help our system to grow then their legacy is meaningless ...We have done a lot to accommodate the practice of the ICTR, they also need to adapt to the national system. It is a matter of law and legal tradition.[77]

When participants acknowledged the value of the ICTR, reference was made to its role in the judicial capacity building of Rwandan judges and lawyers. As one judge stated, 'some judges from Rwanda have gone to Arusha and here we have a library and they have given us some of the judgments and tapings.'[78] Another prosecutor was more forthright,

> The ICTR has contributed. First, I would say especially to the training, the Rwandan judges and prosecutors have been going to Arusha for training sessions and capacity building, especially in the last year and a half in preparation for the transfer of cases.[79]

Similarly, his colleague evaluated the ICTR in terms of its assistance in training the judges of the High Court and the Supreme Court.[80] Participants routinely iterated that their analysis of the ICTR came from the perspective of being a trained lawyer, 'As a lawyer I know it was necessary, Rwandans could not get their hands on the "big fish"',[81] and as another private lawyer stated, 'As a lawyer I am not sure that the ICTR has worked on the ground.'[82] It was important to participants that they established their technical expertise and examined the work of the ICTR on this basis.

77 Interview with Participant 9 (Kigali, Rwanda, 5 September 2008) (notes on file with author).
78 Interview with Participant 16 (Regional, Rwanda, 23 April 2009) (notes on file with author).
79 Interview with Participant 4 (Kigali, Rwanda, 13 August 2008) (notes and recording on file with author).
80 Interview with Participant 5 (Kigali, Rwanda, 13 August 2008) (notes on file with author).
81 Interview with Participant 5, *supra* note 80.
82 Interview with Participant 13 (Regional, Rwanda, 28 August 2008) (notes on file with author).

The value of international law more broadly was also described in a way that was consistent with this cultural interpretation. Participants specifically referred to international law and international legal standards as useful for improving the overall capacity of Rwandan lawyers and judges. As one judge said,

> The High Court will continue improving, especially given the emphasis on judicial training since 2004 … We've also conducted trainings on legal procedures and the UN will soon send personnel here to train us in human rights conventions.[83]

The work of the national courts and the ICTR has been understood in a single cultural context and the courts' actions are ascribed consistent meanings. The work of the national courts is asserted through a focus on the raised educational requirements of the judicial and legal personnel and the work of the ICTR and the value of international law have been assessed on this same basis. Understandings of international law have been shaped by what the national courts themselves are purporting to have achieved. How the actions of domestic courts are assessed affects how the concurrent work of the international criminal tribunal and international law more broadly is viewed and understood. This contextual approach suggests that the impact of international law on domestic courts is influenced by the use of such law in a particular post-conflict context. It shows that there is a need to acknowledge what the domestic courts themselves purport to achieve during a transitional period, as this will influence the role and impact of international law on these courts.

5. CONCLUSION

International law has undoubtedly influenced Rwanda's legislative framework following the genocide and the civil war. The decision to prosecute the crimes of genocide and crimes against humanity coincided with the growing support for an international obligation to ensure accountability for such crimes. However, the initial work of the courts was heavily influenced by continued insecurity in the country as the government's military objectives supported the mass arrest of genocide suspects. While international crimes were incorporated into domestic legislation, international procedural standards and human rights law provided the basis against which the resultant arrests, trials, and incarcerations were criticized, leading to tensions in the use and application of international law.

This chapter has shown that the incorporation of international law into the statute books is important. However, such an external examination fails to take account of the impact of this law on the national courts within their political,

83 Interview with Participant 3 (Kigali, Rwanda, 12 April 2010), interview conducted by P. Clark (notes on file with author).

historical, and cultural environment. When examined 'in context', international law has been both used and resisted in Rwanda. The Rwandan judges and lawyers who were interviewed in the empirical study consistently focused on their improved levels of legal education. This chapter has argued that this focus on internal judicial capacity rather than on Rwanda's adoption of a new constitution or the country's extensive use of international criminal law allows the judges and lawyers a means of circumventing the earlier criticisms raised against the domestic genocide trials. However, this particular understanding of the work of the national courts has far-reaching implications for how international law is understood in Rwanda.

The actions of the domestic courts and the ICTR are understood within a single cultural context, as is their use of international law. The national courts' assessment of the concurrent work of the ICTR and the national courts' position on what international law should achieve in a post-conflict country is consistent with how they have valued their own work. This contextual examination of Rwanda suggests that international law may be most beneficial to domestic rule of law when there is a clear appreciation of what the national courts themselves are aiming to achieve, and why. A failure to take account of the national courts' domestic agendas and needs may undermine the ultimate endeavour of strengthening domestic legal institutions.

VIRTUOUS FLEXIBILITY

The Application of International Human Rights Norms by the Bosnian Human Rights Chamber

Antoine BUYSE*

1. INTRODUCTION

When the long and brutal war in Bosnia and Herzegovina finally ended in 1995 with the conclusion of the Dayton Peace Agreement (DPA),[1] the country was in tatters. One of the many challenges facing post-war Bosnia was the establishment of a legal system based on the rule of law. This (re)building, from a human rights perspective, was characterised by three particular features. First, the key normative framework was the European Convention on Human Rights (ECHR), with which the Bosnian legal system was not familiar at all. Secondly, that treaty was not particularly geared towards the specific conflict-related problems Bosnia was facing, such as large-scale displacement and expropriation. Thirdly, the judiciary itself had, just as most of the power structures within the country, become divided along ethnic lines as a result of the war. Many citizens did not think of the country's courts as being impartial or independent.

In order to tackle these problems a *sui generis* court was created as part of the DPA: the Bosnian Human Rights Chamber. The Chamber was, in the first place, meant to cement effective supervision of the warring parties' new human rights obligations into the Bosnian state structure. In practice, however, it also served a second function: the Chamber became a judicial translator of norms in applying

* Dr. Antoine Buyse is associate professor and senior researcher at the Netherlands Institute of Human Rights (SIM), Utrecht University, the Netherlands. This research has been undertaken under the aegis of the focus area 'Conflicts and Human Rights' of Utrecht University and is partly based on the author's PhD research, 'Post-Conflict Housing Restitution. The European Human Rights Perspective, with a Case Study on Bosnia and Herzegovina' (Antwerp: Intersentia, 2008). The author can be contacted at: A.C.Buyse@uu.nl.

1 The General Framework Agreement for Peace in Bosnia and Herzegovina (Dayton Peace Agreement), entry into force on 14 December 1995. The Human Rights Chamber was established within Annex 6 of the DPA.

general international human rights law, preponderantly the ECHR, in a tailor-made fashion to the particular Bosnian post-conflict context. Its case law and practice in many ways incrementally embedded those external, international norms in the domestic legal order. The very existence of a new human rights institution and the direct applicability of international norms could, moreover, serve as points of connection for domestic judges and officials who were willing to strengthen the rule of law.

As a mixed institution, with both domestic and international elements, the Bosnian Human Rights Chamber provides a revealing case study on the ways in which international law can be applied nationally in post-conflict states. In order to assess how the Chamber inserted the legal *Fremdkörper* of international human rights in Bosnian practice, this chapter will look at how the Chamber interpreted and applied several substantive ECHR rights: the protection of property and housing rights. All of these rights reflected salient problems which the conflict had yielded, namely large-scale displacement and continuing ethnic tensions.

2. THE GENESIS OF A NEW INSTITUTION

The Bosnian Human Rights Chamber was part of a larger constellation of new and existing national and international institutions and organisations under the aegis of the DPA. In order to understand the Chamber's specific place and function in this constellation, it is important to contextualise. The armed conflict yielded a double legacy with which every relevant actor in Bosnia had to cope. First, the war itself involved massive human rights violations. Not only had hundreds of thousands died, among them many civilians, but at the end of the conflict tens of thousands of people were missing, about a million had fled abroad, and another million had become internally displaced within the country.[2] These human catastrophes were accompanied by a second reality on the ground: the territory of Bosnia was scarred by large-scale campaigns of ethnic cleansing. No longer, if it ever had been the case at all, was the state built around a national centre of power. Approximately half of the lands were in the hands of the Bosnian Serbs. The other half was a patchwork of loosely organised 'cantons' which were either dominated by Bosniaks[3] or by Croats. The DPA formalised these *de facto* statelets[4] into a highly decentralised federative structure. Two main units, or so-called 'Entities', were recognised: the relatively

2 P. Neussl, Bosnia and Herzegovina Still Far from the Rule of Law. Basic Facts and Landmark Decisions of the Human Rights Chamber, 20 Human Rights Law Journal 290, 291 (1999).

3 The name commonly used since the conflict for Bosnian Muslims.

4 V. Masenkó-Mavi, The Dayton Peace Agreement and Human Rights in Bosnia and Herzegovina, 42 *Acta Juridica Hungarica* 53, 57 (2001).

centralised Republika Srpska and the barely coherent Federation of Bosnia and Herzegovina, a vehicle of power for both Croat and Bosniak local leaders. Most governmental responsibilities were, in accordance with the situation on the ground, allotted to these sub-state administrative units.[5] The main reason for this was that it seemed to be the only way to successfully finalise the peace negotiations.[6]

The double legacy of human rights problems and ethnic divisions was a source of such concern to the external facilitators of the peace negotiations, such as the United States and various European countries, that they forced the warring factions to accept a legal and political antidote. The DPA was infused both substantively and organisationally with human rights protection, including non-discrimination clauses. In many ways, these two sides of the same coin were in open tension with each other. To mention just one example, the electoral system excluded people not identifying themselves as belonging to the three main ethnicities from certain top political functions. Fourteen years later, in 2009, the European Court of Human Rights would rule that this was contrary to the non-discrimination provisions of the ECHR.[7]

In any event, the two Entities were bound by the new Constitution, which was itself part of the DPA, to ensure what was in Article 2(II) of the Constitution specifically dubbed 'the highest level' of international human rights. The same provision also provided that the European Convention on Human Rights and the additional protocols were directly applicable in Bosnia – even before that state had signed or ratified the Convention.[8] In addition, the ECHR took priority over all other laws in Bosnia.

In order to ensure that these provisions would develop into more than lofty assertions about human rights, but would truly result in accountable national institutions, a Human Rights Commission was created. Its main role was, as the Peace Agreement stipulated, to 'assist' the parties – the state of Bosnia and its two Entities – in honouring their obligations.[9] Assistance was in a way a misnomer, for the Commission had no explicit training or advisory tasks. Rather, its task was confined to assessing allegations by citizens that one of the parties was not abiding by human rights. Wider and more general monitoring was left to other institutions, such as the [then] 'United Nations Commission on Human Rights, the OSCE, the United Nations High Commissioner for Human Rights,

5 This was formalised in Article III of the Dayton Peace Agreement and in Annex 2. On the legal systems of the Entities, see S. Popovic, Prosecution of War Crimes in Bosnian Cantonal and District Courts; the Role of the Rule of Law, in this volume at p. 221.
6 G. Nystuen, Achieving Peace or Protecting Human Rights? Conflicts between Norms Regarding Ethnic Discrimination in the Dayton Peace Agreement 252 (Leiden: Martinus Nijhoff Publishers, 2005).
7 Ect.HR, *Sejdic and Finci v. Bosnia and Herzegovina*, Appl. nos. 27996/06 and 34836/06.
8 Bosnia ratified almost seven years after the DPA, on 12 July 2002.
9 Article II(1) of Annex 6 DPA.

and other intergovernmental or regional human rights missions or organizations.' The parties were obliged to give all of these full access and assistance.[10]

The Commission itself was an umbrella name for two separate institutions. On the one hand there was an Ombudsman institution, whose function was that of a fact-finder and of an investigator. It could, however, only issue non-binding recommendations. On the other hand, a Human Rights Chamber was established, whose role was most akin to a court in matters of human rights. Individuals could directly apply to it, or through a referral of the Ombudsman institution. Its mandate was limited in time: only human rights violations which had been committed by any state authority – at whatever level – after the entry into force of the DPA (14 December 1995) would be considered. The only exceptions were older violations of a continuing nature.[11] In that sense the work of the Chamber was focused on the present and the future rather than on the past. In practice, many new violations were still closely connected to the war. One may think, for example, of formal expropriations of property taken during the conflict from certain ethnic groups.

In order to ensure that the new Chamber would be both impartial and independent, and perceived as such, a variety of safeguards were included. First, a number of immunities were set in place, providing a shield against undue interference. As Article II(4) of Annex 6 of the DPA stipulated:

> The Ombudsman and all members of the Chamber shall not be held criminally or civilly liable for any acts carried out within the scope of their duties. When the Ombudsman and members of the Chamber are not citizens of Bosnia and Herzegovina, they and their families shall be accorded the same privileges and immunities as are enjoyed by diplomatic agents and their families under the Vienna Convention on Diplomatic Relations.

A second key safeguard was the composition of the Chamber. Of the total of fourteen members, the majority – including the Chamber's president – was to be appointed by the Committee of Ministers of the Council of Europe. These eight 'international' members could not be citizens of either Bosnia itself or any neighbouring state. The remaining six members were appointed by the parties themselves: two members by the Serb Entity and four by the Bosniak-Croat Federation.[12]

The Chamber's decisions were binding upon all parties. Citizens could in principle only turn to the Chamber after exhausting local remedies. The introduction of this latter rule, known from international law, indicates that the Chamber was created as a quasi-international body. On the one hand it was more

10 Article XIII(2) of Annex 6 DPA.

11 Human Rights Chamber for Bosnia and Herzegovina (HRC BiH) 13 September 1996, *Josip, Bozana & Tomislav Matanović* (admissibility), (CH/96/1).

12 Article VII of Annex 6 DPA.

closely connected to the national legal order due to its mixed composition and its location in Sarajevo. On the other hand, it was detached from it by being placed at the top of the fundamental rights litigation hierarchy in Bosnia. It was quasi-international in yet another sense: the law it applied was mainly the European Convention of Human Rights, but through the DPA, the norms contained in that international treaty had become an integral part of domestic norms.

The Chamber was conceived as a temporary institution. Awaiting Bosnia's eventual ratification of the European Convention of Human Rights, the Chamber would function as a substitute for the European Court of Human Rights in Strasbourg.[13] It was meant to pave the legal road ahead and to avoid a vacuum in supervision. In effect, the Chamber was in operation from 1996 until the end of 2003. It certainly filled a gap, since the first decision regarding Bosnia by the European Court would be issued only in October 2005 and the first judgment a year later, in 2006.[14]

The Chamber faced a difficult task: it was applying general human rights norms to specific post-conflict problems. The mixed composition of the Chamber did help in that sense: international members could bring in human rights expertise, whereas Bosnian members were legal experts in domestic law. More than most international human rights mechanisms, the Chamber was closely connected to Bosnian reality, both in terms of time and space. Its decisions reverberated directly into the national politico-legal context. How it went about interpreting the European Convention on Human Rights is the subject-matter of the following sections. The emphasis will be on substantive law rather than procedural issues.[15]

3. THE SCOPE OF HUMAN RIGHTS – FLEXIBILITY IN PRACTICE

The Chamber extensively interpreted European human rights norms.[16] Since these norms were directly applicable throughout Bosnia and Herzegovina, the Chamber was able to consider acts and omissions of domestic authorities with

13 Masenkó-Mavi, *supra* note 4, p. 61.

14 Ect.HR, *Hadzić v. Bosnia and Herzegovina*, Appl. no. 11123/04 and Ect.HR, *Jelicić v. Bosnia and Herzegovina*, Appl. no. 41183/02, respectively.

15 For an elaborate analysis of the Chamber's work on procedural issues such as jurisdiction and admissibility, see my chapter entitled Hybrid Human Rights Mechanisms in Post-Conflict Transitions: The Experience of the Bosnian Human Rights Chamber, in: N. Palmer, D. Granville and P. Clark (eds), Critical Perspectives in Transitional Justice 147 (Antwerp: Intersentia, 2012).

16 To give an impression of the amount of cases with which the Chamber dealt: it registered 15,169 cases in the period 1996–2003. 6,243 of these were resolved in a total of 2,619 decisions, either in the form of friendly settlements, by declaring them inadmissible, or by issuing a decision on the merits (239 decisions). See M. Nowak, Reparation by the Human Rights

that yardstick at hand. Formally, the Chamber assessed whether the parties – the state and the Entities – had acted in accordance with Annex 6 (the human rights provisions) of the DPA. The Annex, in turn, made reference mainly to the ECHR and, in addition, to non-discrimination provisions in other human rights treaties.[17] To summarize, the Chamber interpreted the ECHR *in the context* of (Annex 6 of) the DPA. The case law of the Strasbourg institutions was the main source of reference for the Chamber in this respect.[18] European norms and national application were in this way closely connected, bringing Bosnia into the European legal order or, put the other way around, bringing the ECHR to Bosnia and giving it meaning in that context.[19] This was done with due regard to the practical shortcomings of the rule of law in Bosnia, as we shall see. Let us now turn to a few specific examples of substantive interpretation by the Human Rights Chamber of norms contained in the ECHR. These examples come from the field of housing and property rights, since this was the subject-matter of the vast majority of the Chamber's cases and thus is representative of the Chamber's work. The practice reflected in these examples is revelatory about how the Chamber interpreted European human rights law, and thus about how international norms were given meaning in a domestic context through judicial interpretation. This section will address the scope of key human rights notions – what falls within the ambit of a specific protected notion such as the home or possessions? The next section will be concerned with the extent of substantive obligations, both duties of non-interference and positive obligations.

The first illustration of the Chamber's case law concerns the notion of possessions. The right to peaceful enjoyment of one's possessions is stipulated in Article 1 of the first additional Protocol to the ECHR (P1–1). The Chamber interpreted the notion of 'possessions' very broadly, going beyond the protection of real property. It also included contractual rights under contracts for the purchase of property, even if these contracts did not of themselves give rise to real rights of property,[20] and the right under a lease to use business premises and the results of efforts to improve the space.[21] More specifically, in the context of housing the Chamber had to rule, crucially, on whether occupancy rights fell within the scope of P1–1. These rights were *sui generis* rights which were stronger than purely a contract to rent – rent was indeed due – but weaker than full

Chamber for Bosnia and Herzegovina, in: K. De Feyter a.o. (eds), Out of the Ashes. Reparation for Victims of Gross and Systematic Violations 245–288, 247 (Antwerp: Intersentia, 2005).

17 Article XIII(1) juncto Article II(2) of Annex 6 DPA.

18 M. Semih Gemalmaz, Constitution, Ombudsperson and Human Rights Chamber in Bosnia and Herzegovina, 17 Netherlands Quarterly of Human Rights 277, 326 (1999).

19 T. Cornell and L. Salisbury, The Importance of Civil Law in the Transition to Peace: Lessons from the Human Rights Chamber for Bosnia and Herzegovina, 35 Cornell International Law Journal 389, 421 (2002).

20 HRC BiH 7 November 1997, *Branko Medan, Stjepan Bastijanović & Radosav Marković v. BiH & Federation of BiH* (CH/96/3 a.o.), para. 32.

21 HRC BiH 11 June 1999, *Stanivuk v. Federation of BiH* (CH/97/51), para. 59.

property. Occupancy rights or, as they were often called, specially protected tenancies, were rather common in the former Yugoslavia for tenants of social housing apartments. No precedent existed in the case law of the European Court of Human Rights at the time.[22] This meant that the Chamber had to tread new ground here. In the case of *M.J.*, the Chamber held for the first time that 'an occupancy right is a valuable asset giving to the holder of the right, subject to the conditions prescribed by law, to occupy the property in question indefinitely. In certain circumstances at least it can be transferred.'[23] Therefore, the Chamber was of the opinion that the occupancy right was an asset constituting a 'possession'.[24] As a justification for this conclusion, the Chamber referred to the fact that the European Court had given a wide interpretation to the notion of possessions and had held that it covered a wide variety of rights.[25] At first sight, the Chamber's reasoning appears debatable. Occupancy rights could not be sold, and in that sense did not represent a substantive interest *directly* representing a pecuniary value. But there were three strong contextual arguments in favour of the inclusion of occupancy rights under the protective umbrella of P1–1. In the first place, Central and Eastern Europe under communist rule had developed a legal tradition of alternatives to private property rights, the remains of which still lingered in the legislation of successor states to the former Yugoslavia. Occupancy rights were a prime example of this. By contrast, the ECHR was drafted by countries in which the notion of private property was firmly entrenched. To exclude occupancy rights from the notion of 'possessions' would therefore deprive considerable groups of the protection of P1–1. Secondly, in the specific post-war context of Bosnia, such a conclusion was necessary to provide for pecuniary damages. This was crucial for example, whenever people had to rent alternative accommodation for the time they had no access to their original apartment. Finally, an inclusion in the scope enabled an assessment of a case on the merits, something which should always be endeavoured. Especially, one might add, in the context of biased post-civil war domestic institutions.

Going even one step further, the Chamber in *Darko Prodanović* held that a rental agreement was equally covered by the notion of possessions.[26] The applicant had concluded a rental agreement during the war with the legal representative of the owner. The agreement would be valid until the return of the owner to the house. He and his family had occupied the house ever since, until they received an eviction order in 1998. The Chamber considered the case under P1–1 *proprio motu* and held that 'the applicant's contractual right is of great

22 Even in *later* European case law, such as *Teteriny v. Russia*, of 30 June 2005 (Appl. no. 11931/03), the protected tenancy rights were different. They included, inter alia, the right to privatize the apartment one occupied.

23 HRC BiH 3 December 1997, *M.J. v. RS*, para. 32.

24 *M.J. v. RS*, *supra* note 23.

25 *M.J. v. RS*, *supra* note 23.

26 HRC BiH 11 June 1999, *Darko Prodanović v. RS* (CH/98/114).

value to him, granting as it does the right for he [sic[27]] and his family to occupy the house. This right therefore constitutes the applicant's "possession" within the meaning of Article 1 of Protocol No. 1.'[28] It seems as if the Chamber used a purely subjective notion of possessions – something excluded by the European Court. After all, a tenancy such as the one in this case never included the legitimate expectation of acquiring property.

The wide notion of possessions developed in Strasbourg was stretched almost beyond credible limits in Sarajevo. There is no clear legal ground for this in the ECHR, and nor did the Chamber itself provide this in any reasoned way. The only explanation seems to be the specific context of a post-communist, post-war society with national institutions which had lost most of their credibility. In that context the Chamber apparently wanted to offer as much human rights protection as possible. Since its jurisdiction was limited by existing human rights treaties, it had to interpret the substantive provisions of those treaties as broadly as possible. Whereas this may have justified political and moral rationales, the legal basis seems more tenuous.

A second example of the interpretation of the scope of human rights by the Bosnian Human Rights Chamber is the notion of home in the Bosnian context. The first decision in which it had to rule on the scope of this notion was the case of *Saša Galić*. In its decision, the Chamber took the first tentative and not very systematic steps on the path of interpretation of what the notion of the home entailed. Galić had left an apartment he owned a few months before the outbreak of hostilities to study abroad. After years of legal proceedings he regained possession of the apartment at the beginning of October 1997. Within one day after his return, however, local authorities evicted him by force. The Chamber assessed that since he had lived in the apartment before the war, it had been his home at the time. Since he regained possession on 3 October, the Chamber concluded that, therefore, 'in accordance with Article 8 of the Convention, the apartment should be considered his home as and from that date.'[29] The subsequent rapid eviction apparently did not put the situation outside the scope of 'home' again. Can it be inferred from this that voluntarily leaving one's house for studies does break the tie with the house, but that forced eviction does not? The *Galić* decision does not give a clear answer to that issue.

Soon after that decision, the Chamber started to link its jurisprudence on this point explicitly to that of the European Court in Strasbourg. In the case of *Ivica Kevešević*, the applicant had occupancy rights over an apartment from 1982 to 1993 when he fled, forced by the wartime circumstances. Later on, in 1996, Kevešević went back to his apartment and started paying all the bills, a fact which he himself stated confirmed that he wanted to continue living in the

27 Official English version of the decision.
28 *Darko Prodanović v. RS, supra* note 26, para. 56.
29 HRC BiH 12 June 1998, *Saša Galić v. Federation of BiH* (CH/97/40), para. 48.

house. As in *Galić*, the applicant and his family were soon evicted by the local authorities. The Chamber held that the situation fell within the notion of the home, since the applicant had continuously lived in the apartment until the war forced him to leave and had returned as soon as it was safe to do so. Consequently, the Chamber concluded that the links the applicant had 'retained with the apartment are sufficient for it to be considered "his home" at the time of the eviction.'[30] The Chamber explicitly referred to the Strasbourg case of *Gillow*.[31] It did not explicitly copy the 'sufficient and continuing link' criterion developed by the European Court in *Gillow* in its entirety. The Chamber rather mentioned the sufficiency of the link in this case, which had not been broken by the hostilities. Eviction caused by war apparently does not break the continuity of the link as long as there is no real chance to return.

The principle of the continuing link used in *Kevešević* was confirmed in subsequent case law. A clear example is *Dušanka Onić*, in which the applicant was prevented from returning, first due to the hostilities themselves and later on by the refusal of local authorities to allow actual return. Onić had litigated in vain to reclaim her house. In the Chamber's view, in this situation the links between the applicant and the house were sufficient.[32] In *Onić* and later decisions, the Chamber clarified that the *Kevešević* decision – and underlying it, *Gillow* – was the leading case on this issue. In *Neđeljko Ubović*, the principle was formulated as follows: sufficient links under Article 8 exist when 'the applicant had to leave his house or apartment due to the hostilities and wanted to return when it was safe.'[33] Two elements were thus crucial: involuntarily leaving one's house due to the war (or a forced eviction), and a proven intention to return. The intention could be proven either by actual return or by having instituted a restitution claim. The relevance of intention for the Chamber goes to show that the 'continuing link' element from *Gillow* was implicitly used after all. Although the Chamber's case law is faithful to its European peer institution, it has in this way also specified and applied the sufficient and continuing link criterion to the particular situation of Bosnia.

The Chamber's jurisprudence offers more clues on how, both implicitly and explicitly, Strasbourg case law served as an inspiration. The Chamber recognised that even a part of a house could be considered as a home[34] and equally, that business premises fell under that notion, with an explicit reference to the

---

30 HRC BiH 10 September 1998, *Ivica Kevešević v. Federation of BiH* (CH/97/46), para. 42.

31 Ect.HR, *Gillow v. United Kingdom*, Appl. no. 9063/80. This was the first case in which the European Court of Human Rights elaborated on the scope of the notion of 'home'.

32 HRC BiH 12 February 1999, *Dušanka Onić v. Federation of BiH* (CH/97/58), para. 48. See similarly, HRC BiH 7 September 2001, *Fatima Ramić v. Federation of BiH* (CH/97/114), paras 77–78.

33 HRC BiH 7 September 2000, *Neđeljko Ubović a.o. v. Federation of BiH* (CH/99/2425 a.o.), para. 153.

34 HRC BiH 6 July 2000, *Jasmin Odobašić v. RS* (CH/98/575), para. 53.

Strasbourg judgment in *Niemietz*, a case about a lawyer who held office in his own home.[35] It also indicated – in a specific and explicit reference to the leading Strasbourg case of *Loizidou*[36] – the limits of the notion of the home by specifying that mere intentions or emotional bonds do not constitute a sufficient link:

> It is not enough to maintain close ties to a previous home. The fact that one was born at a place or that one's ancestors had lived and were buried at a place is not sufficient for the place to be considered a 'home' for the purposes of Article 8 of the Convention. Also (…) the mere intention to establish permanent residence does not make this place his home.[37]

In wartime situations of displacement, houses abandoned by one family are often, due to the scarcity of housing, occupied by other people – often illegally, one may add. The Chamber also addressed the situation of these so-called secondary occupants. In the case of *D.K.*, the applicant had rented an apartment from a tenancy right holder, who had not officially registered as such herself. This was confirmed by a contract between the parties. Within a few months the authorities issued an eviction order, since the applicant was living in the apartment illegally. The Chamber held that the apartment in question could be considered as the applicant's home, since 'Article 8 of the Convention does not require the existence of a legal basis under national law for the place where a person lives to be considered his or her home.'[38] This may be stretching the concept too far though. Some form of legal interest in the house at stake is necessary, according to ECHR case law.[39] It is not surprising therefore that the Chamber did not provide a reference to specific Strasbourg cases to prove its point. The Chamber thus went beyond European jurisprudence. Again, this could be explained by the specific Bosnian context, in which the whole conception of legality was a grey area due to discriminatory wartime laws and the simultaneous existence of a multitude of old and new national and semi-international laws. However, it might have been more legally sound had the Chamber given the applicant the benefit of the doubt in assuming that he had a legal interest – especially considering the unclear legal situation in Bosnia – than to merely state that no legal interest was required whatsoever. This would have allowed for a similar substantive assessment of the applicant's case without legal overstretch of concepts.

---

35 HRC BiH 11 June 1999, *Ljiljana Gogić v. RS* (CH/98/800), para. 50. Ect.HR, *Niemietz v. Germany*, Appl. no. 13710/88.

36 The case related to a Greek-Cypriot woman who wanted to return to her lands in Turkish-occupied Northern Cyprus: Ect.HR, *Loizidou v. Turkey*, Merits, Appl. no. 15318/89.

37 *Ubović*, *supra* note 33, para. 149.

38 HRC BiH 10 December 1999, *D.K. v. RS* (CH/98/710), para. 31.

39 I. Loveland, When is a house not a home under Article 8 ECHR?, in: Public Law 221, 223 (2002).

The extent of the scope of a protected right is crucial for applicants: it determines the size of the protective umbrella of human rights. The Bosnian Human Rights Chamber, as has been argued here, was willing to stretch the umbrella in a flexible way to accommodate as many victims as possible, in order to assess their cases of alleged violations on the merits. The jurisprudence of the Chamber reflects to a large extent the judgments of the European Court of Human Rights. But on several occasions the Chamber went beyond that, truly applying a general human rights treaty to a local post-conflict context. From a legal perspective this may not always have been fully defensible, but from a practical, political, and moral point of view, there may have been virtues in this approach.

4. INTERPRETING SUBSTANTIVE OBLIGATIONS

Once the scope of the protected notion of a certain human right is ascertained, the extent of the connected substantive state obligations, both positive and negative, is crucial. In this section an example of such obligations from the jurisprudence of the Bosnian Human Rights Chamber will be assessed. Article 8 of the ECHR, specifically the right to respect for the home, will be the focus of the analysis. In general, the Chamber applied the test as developed by the European Court on the basis of Article 8: interferences with the right to respect for the home are only allowed when they are in accordance with the law, pursue a legitimate aim, and are necessary in a democratic society.[40] Laws and other regulations should be foreseeable and accessible. What kinds of interferences are relevant during and immediately after armed conflict? I would argue there are three: destruction, eviction, and denial of access. Of these three, destruction as such did not play a role in the Human Rights Chamber's case law.[41] This may be explained by the fact that most, though not all, of the destruction took place during the war in Bosnia, whereas the Chamber's temporal jurisdiction started on the day of the entry into force of the DPA.[42] As destruction is an instantaneous act, it could not be interpreted as a continuing violation either.

The other two interferences, evictions and the related denial of access, did lead to a deluge of applications. Only in some cases an eviction as such was complained about and led to a violation of Article 8. This happened when an applicant was evicted in spite of a Chamber order for a provisional measure not

40 W. Englbrecht, Property Rights in Bosnia and Herzegovina: The Contributions of the Human Rights Ombudsperson and the Human Rights Chamber, in: S. Leckie (ed.), Returning Home: Housing and Property Restitution Rights of Refugees and Displaced Persons 83–142, 101 (Ardsley: Transnational Publishers, 2003).

41 Result obtained by searching for 'destruction' in the Chamber's jurisprudential database.

42 This was decided in the Chamber's first case: HRC BiH 6 August 1997, *Josip, Bozana & Tomislav Matanović v. RS* (CH/96/1).

to evict. The Chamber held that a violation of such an order could not be 'in accordance with the law' under Article 8.[43] The European Court of Human Rights would perceive such a failure to comply with interim measures differently, namely as amounting to a violation of the effective exercise of Article 34 of the ECHR, the right of individual application.[44] Most of the complaints addressed the *consequences* of evictions and are therefore equally concerned with a *de facto* denial of access.

There is a striking difference between Strasbourg and Bosnian case law which points to a difference as to where the crux of human rights problems could be found. In the majority of the European Court of Human Rights' judgments concerning Article 8, the focus is on the question whether an interference was 'necessary in a democratic society'. By contrast, before the Bosnian Human Rights Chamber, most applications were decided under the legality test. Moreover, in all the cases in which the Chamber addressed the legality, a violation of Article 8 was found on that point[45] and therefore it was not necessary to assess whether a legitimate aim or necessity were present. The Chamber's case law on this point related both to the (lack of) quality and accessibility of the laws on the one hand and to the (non-)adherence of the Entities to those laws on the other hand. In the most severe instances an eviction had no legal basis at all. In *Cecilija Turcinović*, a decision to evict was based on references to articles 30 and 47 of a law that counted only 14 articles.[46] The jurisprudence of the Chamber focused on the laws of the Entities and their compatibility with the ECHR. The housing laws of the Croat-Bosniak Federation were the first to be judicially scrutinised. In the *Ivica Kevešević* decision of September 1998, a 1995 amendment of the Law on Abandoned Apartments, an old Yugoslav law regulating when apartments could be given to new inhabitants when the former ones had left it, was judged to be in violation of Article 8 of the ECHR in two respects: it was of insufficient accessibility and quality. Both related to the automatic and permanent cancellation of original, pre-war occupancy rights, unless people lodged a claim within 7 or 15 days from the date of publication of the law. Initially, however, the law was only posted on a single bulletin board in Sarajevo. The law was, tellingly,

43 *D.K.*, *supra* note 38, para. 36.

44 ECt.HR, *Mamatkulov & Askarov v. Turkey*, Grand Chamber, Appl. nos. 46827/99 & 46951/99, para. 128. The difference might be explained by the fact that Annex 6 of the DPA gives the Chamber jurisdiction over alleged violations of the rights contained in the ECHR, but does not enumerate these rights as such. However, in the ECHR itself, the right to individual application is to be found in Section II (the institutional part) of the Convention and not in Section I (rights and freedoms). The Chamber therefore may have considered this to be part of the organizational part of the ECHR. Since the Chamber functioned within its own institutional context, it did not need that part.

45 Englbrecht, *supra* note 40, p. 101.

46 HRC BiH 11 March 1998, *Cecilija Turcinović v. the Federation of BiH* (CH/96/31), para. 21. There was apparently a mix-up with another law, but the Federation never responded to the Chamber's request to clarify the legal basis. Therefore the Chamber concluded that there was no legal basis for the decision.

published in the Official Gazette exactly 15 days later. The Chamber concluded that it had to have regard to the large group of people:

> with a personal interest in the legal provisions in question as well as to the fact that these persons were to be found throughout the country and even abroad. In the Chamber's opinion, it would be wholly unrealistic to expect the contents of a notice posted on a single bulletin board in the capital to come to the notice of such a public. In the circumstances, therefore, publication of the Decision on the bulletin Board of the Presidency building could not suffice to render the law in question 'accessible'.[47]

For the other aspect, the quality of the law, the Chamber explicitly referred to Strasbourg by stipulating that a domestic law should meet the criteria of the rule of law.[48] These included safeguards against abuse. The Chamber held that the time limits themselves were in practice impossible to abide by. It found it intolerable that 'a law should deprive persons permanently of their rights if they do not fulfil a wholly unreasonable condition, such as the time-limit referred to, which could not possibly be fulfilled by the majority of those affected.'[49] In holding the Federation's amendment of the old Yugoslav law to be contrary to human rights, the Chamber showed its predilection for a strong model of the rule of law, which looks beyond mere technicalities and into the practical content of rules and laws.[50]

The Chamber's scrutiny was not one-sided, however. The legal framework of the Republika Srpska equally came under judicial attack. The immediate post-war Bosnian-Serb Law on the Use of Abandoned Property did not meet the standards of the European Convention on Human Rights either. In the case of *Esfak Pletilić a.o.*, a group of applicants tried to recover real property in the Republika Srpska which they had lost during the armed conflict. The Chamber held that the law did not meet the criterion of foreseeability. The effects of the procedure in a law on regaining possession were unclear. For example, that law allowed for return of property in the context of a settlement between the Republika Srpska, the Federation, and Croatia,[51] based on reciprocity, but did not spell out what the conditions of such a settlement should be. Nor did the law provide any elaboration on how the principle of reciprocity of restitution was to be applied in practice. The Chamber concluded that the law 'did not provide any

---

47 *Ivica Kevešević*, *supra* note 30, para. 56.

48 *Ivica Kevešević*, *supra* note 30, para. 57. The Chamber had earlier used this principle in a decision relating to the death penalty: HRC BiH 8 October 1997, *Stretko Damjanović v. Federation of BiH* (CH/96/30), para. 31. The Chamber, inter alia, made reference to Ect.HR, *Malone v. United Kingdom*, Appl. no. 8691/79, para. 67.

49 *Ivica Kevešević*, *supra* note 30, para. 57.

50 A similar preference can be seen in the Chamber's case law which relates to the question whether local remedies are truly effective. In that jurisprudence, the Chamber looked beyond appearances and into realities on the ground. See Buyse, *supra* note 15.

51 Article 39 of the RS Law on the Use of Abandoned Property.

safeguards against abuse, but was itself a source of arbitrariness and abuse.'[52] Various parts of the law therefore did not meet the criterion of legality inherent in Article 8 ECHR.

Apart from shortcomings in regulation, flaws and violations could also be found in the lack of adherence of the Entities' authorities to those laws. In the case of *Kovačević*, the Chamber held that the Bosniak-Croat Federation had violated the right to respect for the home in failing to decide upon an enforcement request concerning repossession in a timely manner. Although the legal requirement was to hand out a decision within thirty days, the authorities made the applicant wait for several years.[53]

The mere threat of a forcible eviction by the authorities could also be qualified as an interference with Article 8. The Chamber held, in the case of *Turcinović*, that the threatened and attempted eviction of the applicant was an interference of and by itself.[54] Subsequent jurisprudence followed through on this approach, in another echo of Strasbourg case law.[55] A decision by the authorities to evict was even considered to be a continuing violation as long as it was not revoked.[56] The majority of interferences of this kind did not pass the first limb of the paragraph 2 test of Article 8. In *Dragan Topić*, the Chamber held that the apartment in question was not entered into the records of abandoned property, as was required by the law of the Republika Srpska. Consequently, the threatened eviction did not pass the legality test of Article 8.[57] In the case of *Nenad Miljković*, an eviction order to vacate an apartment within three days – with an appeal option having no suspensive effect – equally amounted to a violation of Article 8. The applicant had not been given the opportunity to give his opinion *before* the decision was made, although again local law so required.[58]

Summarising on the issue of interferences with the right to respect for the home, even in the few cases in which the assessment by the Chamber went beyond the legality test, it was almost more of an *obiter dictum* than a true necessity. In *Cecilija Turcinović*, the decision on the mixed-up references to the law, the Chamber held that even if there was a legal basis, the interference was still in violation of Article 8 of the ECHR. The applicant lived in an apartment with her son-in-law's permission. He had entered into a purchase contract for the apartment. Nevertheless, the authorities refused to recognise the purchase contract, in violation of P1–1. The ensuing order to evict the applicant was, in the Chamber's view, 'designed to make effective the violation of the son-in-law's rights'. This could not be considered as a legitimate aim and for the same reason

52 HRC BiH 10 September 1999, *Esfak Pletilić a.o. v. RS* (CH/98/659 a.o.), paras 173–174.

53 HRC BiH 11 May 2001, *Savka Kovačević v. Federation of BiH* (CH/98/1066), paras 62–76.

54 *Turcinović*, *supra* note 46, para. 20.

55 Ect.HR, *Larkos v. Cyprus*, Appl. no. 29515/95.

56 See eg HRC BiH 11 June 1999, *Nada Blagojević v. RS* (CH/98/645), para. 49.

57 HRC BiH 5 November 1999, *Dragan Topić v. RS* (CH/98/894), paras 44–45.

58 HRC BiH 11 June 1999, *Nenad Miljković v. RS* (CH/98/636), para. 53.

could not be seen as 'necessary in a democratic society.'[59] The Chamber thus denied the authorities to do under one Convention provision (Article 8) what was unlawful under another (P1–1).

Aside from the legality of interferences, the Chamber also addressed the issue of positive obligations under Article 8 of the ECHR. This was particularly salient in Bosnia, since most people had been evicted in the period before the Chamber had jurisdiction and thus very often only the subsequent action or inaction of the authorities to help people regain their housing could be assessed. The leading case here is *Mehmed Blentić*.[60] The applicant (a Bosniak) and his wife in that case had been forcibly evicted by a Serbian refugee at the very end of the armed conflict. His house was located in Banja Luka in the Republika Srpska. The applicant instituted proceedings before the local court which ordered the eviction of the refugee. Nevertheless, several attempts to execute the court's decision failed due to the lack of police assistance for the court's officials and because dozens of citizens were obstructing the eviction. The applicant complained that the authorities' inaction violated Article 8. The Chamber explicitly assessed the case in the light of European case law. It held that Article 8 could give rise to positive obligations; that the 'fair balance' test[61] had to be applied; and that in such an assessment the aims mentioned in paragraph two of Article 8 were relevant.[62] These general European principles were then 'translated' into the Bosnian context. The Chamber was of the opinion that:

> The obligation to effectively secure respect for a person's home implies that there must be effective machinery for protecting it against unlawful interference of the kind which the applicant has suffered. In particular there must be effective machinery for restoring possession in accordance with the orders of a court.[63]

The Chamber continued by specifying that the authorities were bound by the positive obligation to take 'effective, reasonable and appropriate measures to deal with the difficulties posed by the assembly of people obstructing the applicant's return to his home.'[64] Put differently, an obligation of due diligence applied. Although the Chamber recognised that an eviction carried out in the face of

---

59 *Turcinović*, *supra* note 46, para. 24.

60 HRC BiH 3 December 1997, *Mehmed Blentić v. RS* (CH/96/17).

61 Balancing the interests of the individual and the general interest.

62 *Mehmed Blentić*, *supra* note 60, para. 26. The case refers to a number of Strasbourg judgments: Ect.HR, *Marckx v. Belgium*, Series A No 31 (1979) 2 EHRR 330, Appl. no. 6833/74; Ect.HR, *Airey v. Ireland*, Appl. no. 6289/73; Ect.HR, *X & Y v. The Netherlands*, Appl. no. 8978/80; Ect. HR, *Velosa Barreto v. Portugal*, Appl. no. 18072/91; and Ect.HR, *Lopez Ostra v. Spain*, Appl. no. 16798/90. The aims mentioned are 'national security, public safety or the economic well-being of the country, for the prevention of disorder or crime, for the protection of health or morals, or for the protection of the rights and freedoms of others.'

63 *Mehmed Blentić*, *supra* note 60, para. 27.

64 *Mehmed Blentić*, *supra* note 60, para. 28. The Chamber adopted this from the following Strasbourg case, in which the state was obliged to protect demonstrators against violent

public opposition may be legitimately delayed for reasons of public order, the authorities are bound to take action to deal with such a situation. In the present case the police had undertaken no action at all, in spite of an Entity law that obliged them to support the judicial authorities in such matters. Moreover, none of the persons responsible for obstructing the court order had been prosecuted. In conclusion, the Chamber held – in particularly strong wording – that 'such a situation is incompatible with the *rule of law* and involves a breach of Article 8'.[65] In the similar case of *Marija Bojkovski*, the Chamber again stressed that Entities were not only obliged to pass laws to protect individuals in accordance with Article 8, but also that they had to implement such laws. 'Otherwise the legislation is not effective', as the Chamber put it.[66] *A fortiori*, more extreme forms of Entity inaction also violated the ECHR. In *Đ.M.*, the applicant tried to reclaim her home under the Federation's *Law on Temporarily Abandoned Real Property Owned by Citizens*. None of the petitions that she sent and none of the proceedings she instituted led to any reaction by the authorities.[67] The Chamber concluded that this passivity of the authorities amounted to lack of respect for the applicant's home, for which no justification had been put forward, and was therefore a violation of Article 8 of the ECHR.[68] These cases show that the Chamber was of the opinion that the mere existence of legislation which in theory enabled persons to repossess their apartments was not sufficient. Implementation was deemed to be crucial.

It should be noted that the European Court of Human Rights adopted a similar approach, by reading a positive obligation into Article 8 to enforce a national court's eviction orders, in the later case of *Cvijetić v. Croatia*.[69] And like the Chamber in *Đ.M.*, the European Court held in *Cvijetić* that the particularly slow actions of the authorities did not only violate Article 6 for transgression of the trial within a reasonable time requirement,[70] but also of Article 8 separately. In all cases the fact that institutions may be weakened due to a recent civil war is apparently immaterial. The Strasbourg case was decided in 2004, several years after the Bosnian ones. Without suggesting a causal connection or direct influence between the two, this at least shows that (semi-inter)national

counter-demonstrators, as far as was reasonable and appropriate: Ect.HR, *Plattform Ärzte für das Leben v. Austria*, Appl. no. 10126/82.

65 *Mehmed Blentić*, *supra* note 60, with emphasis added.

66 HRC BiH 6 April 2001, *Marijha Bojkovski v. Bosnia and Herzegovina & Federation of BiH* (CH/97/73), para. 51. Confirmed in HRC BiH 11 May 2001, *Savka Kovačević v. Federation of BiH*, para. 67.

67 HRC BiH 14 May 1999, *Đ.M. v. Federation of BiH* (CH/98/756), para. 91.

68 *Đ.M. v. Federation of BiH*, *supra* note 67.

69 Ect.HR, *Cvijetić v. Croatia*, Appl. no. 71549/01.

70 The European Court had held in earlier case law, in the context of Article 6 ECHR, that there was a link between the timely execution of national court judgments and the rule of law (eg Ect.HR, *Hornsby v. Greece*, Appl. no. 18357/91, para. 41). The *Cvijetić* judgment in Strasbourg, *supra* note 69, was the first time in which non-execution led to a violation of Article 8 ECHR.

adjudicatory bodies can use and interpret the European Convention in the light of the specific needs of a society emerging from armed conflict.

As argued here, the jurisprudence of the Bosnian Human Rights Chamber on Article 8 more or less followed in Strasbourg's footsteps. There are some notable differences, however. The system of assessing the legality of interferences and the extent of positive obligations was similar between Sarajevo and Strasbourg, but the emphasis was different. The European Court of Human Rights either succinctly dealt with issues of eviction and denial of access as so grave that a justification was not possible, or assessed such matters more in depth, under the third limb of Article 8, paragraph 2 of the ECHR – the test of 'necessary in a democratic society'. Most of the Chamber's case-law, by contrast, focused on the first prong of that test, the requirement 'in accordance with the law'. This assessment centered on two issues. In the first place, in some cases the focus was on the domestic law itself. The Chamber assessed whether the laws of the Entities were in line with the European Convention's requirements, both in accessibility and quality. The latter related to safeguards against abuse and to laws realistically offering what they were formally developed for – a certain minimum degree of effectiveness. Instead of just repeating formulae from European Court case law, the Chamber gave Strasbourg jurisprudence renewed content. The requirement of accessibility was not just a standard formula, but a practical benchmark to evaluate whether a single bulletin board to proclaim a law with tight deadlines sufficed. Secondly, the Chamber scrutinized to what extent the domestic authorities themselves complied with the laws they had promulgated.

The third test of paragraph 2 of Article 8 of the ECHR, the necessity and proportionality test, was applied in very few cases. Like its Strasbourg counterpart, the Chamber did not apply the second and third tests, when an interference did not even pass the first test of legality.[71] The Chamber's jurisprudence reflects that interferences with the right to respect for the home are more difficult to justify against those who legally acquired housing and those acting in good faith than against illegal occupants or against those who have only temporary accommodation rights.

5. CONCLUSIONS

The Chamber's substantive interpretation of human rights attempted to do justice to their meaning in international law. At the same time, it transpires from the jurisprudence reviewed here that the Chamber tried to apply such international rights as much as possible to specific domestic phenomena, such as

71 An example of European Court of Human Rights case law in this respect is Ect.HR, *M.M. v. The Netherlands*, Appl. no. 39339/98, paras 45–46.

post-conflict evictions and the particular concept of occupancy rights. From a 'thin' rule of law perspective, in which only the precise application and strict interpretation of rules – irrespective of their legitimacy – counts, the Chamber's practice may sometimes have stretched the limits of reasonable interpretation. But from a 'thick' rule of law perspective, of which the protective umbrella of human rights is part and parcel, the increased protection for individuals facing injustice in post-conflict Bosnia was a positive spin-off of the flexible approach of the Chamber. One could call this a virtuous form of flexibility.

The overwhelming emphasis on legality in the Chamber's case law bears testimony to the specific Bosnian post-conflict context: a society in which the institutions of the state had been destroyed, were divided, and were continuing to work to achieve wartime goals of ethnic separation. Against that background, the delicate balance of interests developed in Strasbourg under the third limb of the paragraph 2 test of Article 8 of the ECHR, for example, was not the Chamber's main concern. Quite differently, the Chamber's case law can rather be seen as an exercise in reconstructing the rule of law. This explains the emphasis on the legality test. It also shows, once again, that the Chamber upheld a robust notion of the rule of law, in which it not only held up the Entities to their own standards (the procedural part of the rule of law), but also looked at these standards through a European looking glass (the content part of the rule of law, in this case focusing on human rights as laid down in the European Convention). This was not merely a negative exercise, since the Chamber also in some cases approved of laws in its decisions. The overall picture emerging from the Chamber's use of the Convention is thus that it was applied in such a way as to pinpoint the specific and most urgent legal problems in Bosnia.

As has been shown, the case law reflects an intriguing and flexible mix of Bosnian and international legal ingredients. Existing international standards were given renewed saliency for post-conflict situations through the Chamber's jurisprudence. In numerous cases local authorities were held to account. The Chamber's independent stance, both legally and politically, was no doubt greatly facilitated by its mixed composition. The Chamber's mandate ended on 31 December 2003, more than a year after Bosnia ratified the ECHR itself, bringing the state more firmly under European human rights supervision. An agreement signed by both Entities and the state of Bosnia provided that the Chamber's pending cases would be transferred to a new and specific Human Rights Commission within the Constitutional Court of Bosnia.[72] This new Chamber would have three Bosnian members and two international members – a symbolic shift of majorities.[73] No matter how much merit one may find in the former Chamber's approach, flexible interpretations have their boundaries. The

---

72 Agreement pursuant to Article XIV of Annex 6 to the General Framework Agreement for Peace in Bosnia and Herzegovina, 22 & 25 September 2003, available at www.hrc.ba.

73 For a more elaborate analysis of the Chamber's dissolution, see Buyse, *supra* note 15.

legacy of the Human Rights Chamber and its jurisprudence now lies in the hand of the Bosnian Constitutional Court, which faces continuing challenges in upholding the rule of law in a marred political context. The ongoing stalemate in negotiating reforms of the Bosnian Constitution means that the strong position of international law has not been changed. The Bosnian Constitutional Court continues to apply European human rights in its decisions to this day, pointing to an enduring entrenchment, at least at the top judicial level, of international norms.[74] However, the same stalemate also means that establishing a stronger basis for the rule of law remains tenuous and that every national institution in Bosnia, including the courts, remains under recurring verbal attack of separatist politicians. From that perspective, the way in which international law is interpreted by courts could even be said to be a relatively minor issue. A small excerpt from the Council of Europe's Commissioner of Human Rights report on Bosnia and Herzegovina of 2011 shows that there are continuing and severe threats to both judicial independence and the enforcement of judgments as such:

> The Commissioner has been informed that in May 2010 judges of the Constitutional Court of Bosnia and Herzegovina unanimously decided to remove Mr Krstan Simić (appointed by Republika Srpska) from his post as a Judge. A procedure for his removal was initiated following the publication in local media of a letter in which he had addressed the Prime Minister of Republika Srpska as his 'boss'. The grounds for his dismissal were that he had intentionally damaged the image and the dignity of the Court, as well as the image and the dignity of a judge. On 7 September 2010, the Republika Srpska National Assembly failed to appoint a successor to Mr Simić. There are currently five national and three international judges in the Constitutional Court. The Constitutional Court has a backlog of about 8,500 cases, mostly applications related to human rights violations.
>
> The Commissioner has noted that non-enforcement of domestic court judgments continues to be a systematic problem that seriously hinders the efficiency of the judicial system, thus threatening the rule of law in Bosnia and Herzegovina. In seven (out of a total of fourteen) judgments delivered from October 2006 to May 2010 against Bosnia and Herzegovina, the European Court of Human Rights found a violation of Article 6 of the European Convention on Human Rights due to non-enforcement of domestic court judgments. Around 100 decisions of the Constitutional Court of Bosnia and Herzegovina and the Human Rights Chamber have not been enforced since 2003.[75]

---

74 See eg Constitutional Court of Bosnia and Herzegovina, decision AP-1080/08 of May 2011. I have not done research into the extent to which lower Bosnian courts apply international human rights norms.

75 Report by T. Hammarberg, Commissioner for Human Rights of the Council of Europe, following his visit to Bosnia and Herzegovina on 27–30 November 2010, CommDH(2011)11, 29 March 2011, paras 174–175.

None of the gains made are thus secured. The virtues, and limits, of legal flexibility will continue to be tested time and again in the daily practice of Bosnian courts. But eventually, for the human rights situation in the country, the political context remains decisive.

WAR CRIMES CHAMBER OF THE COURT OF BOSNIA AND HERZEGOVINA: SEEDING "INTERNATIONAL STANDARDS OF JUSTICE"?

Katerina UHLÍŘOVÁ*

1. INTRODUCTION

Bosnia and Herzegovina (BiH), as one of the countries in the former Yugoslavia, went through the worst conflict in Europe since the Second World War.[1] BiH therefore ended on 'the long list'[2] of countries in post-conflict situations that need to rebuild the rule of law.[3] While it is true that the responsibility for (re) establishment of the rule of law rests primarily with the local population and should ideally be initiated or led by domestic actors in order to secure a 'local ownership' of the process,[4] this option is not always available, and external assistance may be needed.[5]

---

* Department of International and European Law, Faculty of Law, Masaryk University, Brno, Czech Republic.

1 For a detailed description of the conflict in the former Yugoslavia, see L. Silber and A. Little, Yugoslavia: Death of a Nation (1996).

2 See the list of the current UN peacekeeping operations, available at www.un.org/en/peacekeeping/currentops.shtml (visited 10 September 2010).

3 For purposes of my chapter, I will be referring to the rule of law as encompassing (1) 'the institutional attributes believed necessary to actuate the rule of law (such as comprehensive laws, well-functioning courts, and trained law enforcement agencies)' as well as (2) 'the ends that the rule of law is intended to serve within society (such as upholding law and order, or providing predictable and efficient judgments).' In R.K. Belton, Competing Definitions of the Rule of Law: Implications for Practitioners 3 (Carnegie Papers, Rule of Law Series, 2005), available at http://carnegieendowment.org/files/CP55.Belton.FINAL.pdf (visited 20 August 2010).

4 In this context, one can refer to a successful statebuilding process in South Africa. See L. Brahimi, State Building in Crisis and Post-Conflict Countries (2007). See also E. Schmid, Thickening the Rule of Law in Transition: The Constitutional Entrenchment of Economic and Social Rights in South Africa, in this volume at p. 59.

5 Cahin suggests three decreasing models of international involvement in post-conflict situations: (1) substitution to state authority (eg East Timor, Kosovo); (2) supervision over state authority (eg BiH); and (3) assistance to state authority (eg Afghanistan, Iraq). The Hague Academy of International Law Lectures (August 2009).

In the circumstances of BiH, the international community played a significant role by, inter alia, introducing various international components (including institutions, personnel, and new legislation incorporating international law) in order to actuate the rule of law.[6] This chapter examines how successful were such rule of law efforts that were not rooted in the local context, but rather imposed from outside.

The rule of law is a complex system which strives to achieve various goals.[7] The focus of this chapter is on two such goals: providing efficient and impartial justice, and upholding human rights. Due to the importance of the role of international law in achieving these goals, the chapter includes analysis of both the *process* of empowering domestic institutions to apply international law as well as on the actual *application* of international law.[8]

The chapter starts by looking at the involvement of the international community in what could be described as a first constitutional moment, ie the conclusion of the Dayton Peace Agreement (DPA), of which the new Constitution is an inherent part. The first part examines the complicated state structure of BiH established by the DPA, the special legal nature of the Constitution, and the position of international law in the Constitution and some of the challenges on the road towards a full-fledged democracy, including problems with the discriminatory nature of some of the constitutional provisions. Finally, effects of the current constitutional framework on harmonization of criminal legislation in BiH and implications for prosecution of international crimes are assessed. The first part serves also as an explanation of the complex environment in which the War Crimes Chamber of the Court of BiH has to operate.

The second part focuses on the War Crimes Chamber (WCC), which deals with atrocities committed during the 1992–1995 war. The establishment of the WCC can be viewed as another important and specific moment in the

6 In BiH, 'international community' is represented mainly by the key Western European states, the United States, Canada, Japan, and Turkey. In addition, various international intergovernmental (mainly the Office of the High Representative (OHR), the United Nations, the North Atlantic Treaty Organization (NATO), and the European Union (EU)) as well as nongovernmental organizations played an important role during the peacebuilding in BiH.

7 There is no homogenous content of the 'rule of law' notion. It is not unsual to find different definitions even within one international organization. For different views as to the definition and promotion of the rule of law and various goals it seeks to achieve, see K. Pistor, Advancing the Rule of Law: Report on the International Rule of Law Symposium Convened by the American Bar Association November 9–10 2005, 25(1) Berkeley Journal of International Law, available at www.boalt.org/bjil/docs/BJIL25.1_Pistor.pdf (visited 5 October 2010). For a suggestion to shift our attention from strict division between domestic and international rule of law to 'internationalized' rule of law see A. Nollkaemper, The Internationalized Rule of Law, 1 Hague Journal on the Rule of Law p. 74–78 (2009).

8 The post-conflict situation in BiH fits well into the discussion about the internationalized rule of law. If '[t]he internationalized rule of law is characterized by the fact that international law and international institutions can fill rule of law gaps at the domestic law...', then a strong involvement of international community in the whole legal sector of BiH provides a quite telling example. Nollkaemper, *supra* note 7, p. 76.

international community's rule of law efforts in BiH. The second part thus introduces the WCC, its applicable law, and its special relationship with the International Criminal Tribunal for the former Yugoslavia (ICTY). The actual application of international criminal law by the WCC is examined through the concept of Joint Criminal Enterprise (JCE), which has been widely used by the ICTY to prosecute international crimes.

While it is true that the JCE is applied mainly by the ICTY and other international criminal tribunals and this practice has already been described elsewhere,[9] its application is not limited to the international legal system. JCE is increasingly being applied also by hybrid or domestic courts in post-conflict countries, precisely due to the involvement of the international community in those countries.[10] The second part therefore provides a brief analysis of two selected cases which represent some of the first attempts of the BiH judiciary to justify and clarify the application of this 'legal transplant' of JCE domestically.

The concluding part summarizes how successful the international community was in achieving the ends which the rule of law is intended to serve, ie in our case, how effective the application of international law was as a means to improving and delivering justice to the victims of the war in BiH. The concluding remarks are influenced by the fact that international personnel will eventually leave the WCC (and BiH), leaving it in the hands of the local population only.

2. RULE OF LAW VERSUS 'RULE OF ETHNICITY'

2.1. FIRST CONSTITUTIONAL MOMENT: DAYTON PEACE AGREEMENT AND THE NATURE OF THE NEW CONSTITUTION

> Peace is not merely the absence of war but the presence of justice, of law, of order – in short, of government.[11]

The DPA was signed on 14 December 1995 in order to end the war in BiH.[12] The DPA entirely re-shaped BiH by separating warring parties into two Entities: the

---

9 See eg G. Boas, J.L. Bischoff and N.L. Reid, Forms of Responsibility in International Criminal Law (Cambridge University Press, 2007). See also C. Damgaard, Individual Criminal Responsibility for Core International Crimes (Selected Pertinent Issues) (Springer, 2008).

10 Examples of national courts or models referred to as 'hybrid', 'mixed', or 'internationalized' courts where JCE was or is considered to be used include, for example, the Extraordinary Chambers in the Courts of Cambodia, the Iraqi Special Tribunal, the Special Tribunal for Lebanon, the Special Panel for Serious Crimes in East Timor, or, in a rather different context, the US Military Commissions.

11 A. Einstein, in: O. Nathan and H. Norden (eds), Einstein on Peace 371 (New York: Schocken, 1968).

12 Known also as General Framework Agreement for Peace (GFAP), available at www.ohr.int/dpa/default.asp?content_id380 (visited 21 April 2010).

Muslim-Croat Federation (FBiH) and the Republika Srpska (RS). However, this stabilisation by separation into Entities set up a very complex, decentralized, and inefficient constitutional structure.[13] The DPA has been described by one commentator as a 'masterful diplomatic creation precisely because of its imprecision – allowing all sides to claim some kind of victory'.[14] Each Entity was granted a high level of autonomy in exercising its constitutionally defined powers.[15] FBiH was further divided into ten separate cantons, each with its own Assembly and Constitution. In addition, there is a third separate administrative and territorial unit: Brcko District.[16] As one Bosnian Croat observed, 'in no State do you have two entities, three nations, four constitutions, cantonal constitutions. How can you realize the rights? It is a forest of rules that no expert can go around in.'[17]

While the Preamble of the Constitution declares three constituent peoples (Bosniaks, Croats, and Serbs), Bosniaks and Croats have the status of constituent peoples only in the FBiH, and Serbs are constituent peoples just in RS. Thus, Bosniaks, Croats, and Serbs are constituent peoples, but not of the State of BiH, only of their 'ethnically clean' territory. Moreover, the constitutional requirements of equal representation of constituent peoples at state institutions paralyze the effective functioning of a state.[18] It is argued that such constitutional arrangements continue to support and feed the ethnic differences, which have a serious impact on the post-conflict rule of law efforts in BiH.[19] Instead of focusing on building the fragile statehood, the society in BiH is ethnically more divided than ever.

---

13 A. Maljevic, Legal and Actual Treatment of Juveniles within the Criminal Justice System of Bosnia and Hercegovina, in: J. Junger-Tas and S.H. Decker (eds), International Handbook of Juvenile Justice 415–436 (2006).

14 Z. Pajic, A Critical Appraisal of Human Rights Provisions of the Dayton Constitution of Bosnia and Herzegovina, 20(1) Human Rights Quarterly 136 (1998).

15 *See* Art. III of the Constitution of BiH (1995) ('Constitution').

16 Pajic, *supra* note 14.

17 Justice, Accountability and Social Reconstruction: An Interview Study of Bosnian Judges and Prosecutors, University of California, Berkeley and University of Sarajevo (2000), available at www.law.berkeley.edu/files/IHRLC/Justice_Accountability_and_Social_Reconstruction.pdf (visited 5 May 2010).

18 Requirement of equal representation affects a composition of the Parliamentary Assembly (Art. IV), the Presidency (Art. V), as well as that of the Constitutional Court (Art. VI).

19 For arguments for or against federalism as a tool for peacebuilding, see M. Böckenförde, 'Constitutional Engineering' and Decentralization: Federal Structures as Means for Peace-Building in Sudan, in: H. Eberhard, K. Lachmayer and G. Thallinger (eds), Transitional Constitutionalism 25–48 (Nomos, 2007). It is acknowledged that in certain situations federalism can contribute to stabilization during transitional periods by striking 'a balance between the separatist and unitary movements of a country'. Böckenförde, p.19. Accordingly, the DPA was supposed to stabilize and avoid disintegration of BiH. It is nonetheless argued that from a longer term perspective, such arrangement in the context of BiH did not prove to be effective.

As regards the nature of the Constitution, it forms an integral part of an international agreement – it was adopted as Annex 4 of the DPA. The Venice Commission in its Report stated that the Constitution is 'in its origin more a public international law than a constitutional law text. Its character seems more contractual than normative.'[20] As a result of this unique nature, the Constitutional Court of BiH stated in its landmark decision on *Constituency of Peoples*[21] that the Constitution could be interpreted according to the Vienna Convention on the Law of Treaties of 1969.[22]

2.2. ROLE OF INTERNATIONAL LAW IN THE NEW CONSTITUTION

> The constitution is a new suit of provisions in which the old, decrepit body of laws must be regenerated.[23]

Constitutions usually determine the position of international law within the domestic legal system of the country, and new constitutions adopted after conflicts or change of undemocratic regimes usually place a strong emphasis on international law.[24] Conversely, international law often re-conceptualizes the constitution and affects the domestic legal system as a whole.[25] Post-conflict legal arrangements in BiH are a clear example of this interdependence between international and domestic law.

Most of the new constitutions of the states from the post-communist block generously incorporated international law into their domestic legal systems. BiH faces a double legal challenge in this respect: in addition to coping with a legal legacy inherited from its communist past, it has to address a legacy of the war.[26] While the Constitution of the former Socialist Federal Republic of Yugoslavia (SFRY) (1974) provided for direct application of international treaties in general (not only human rights treaties),[27] the new BiH Constitution empowers the

20 Venice Commission Report, CDL-RA (96)001, available at www.venice.coe.int/docs/1996/CDL-RA(1996)001-e.asp#_Toc80416064 (visited 26 March 2010).

21 Constitutional Court of BiH 1 July 2000, *Constituency of Peoples*, Partial Decision, part 1, U-5/98.

22 'Therefore, Article 31 of the Vienna Convention of the Law on Treaties must be applied in the interpretation of all its provisions, including the Constitution of BiH'. *Constituency of Peoples*, *supra* note 21, para. 19.

23 Brahimi, *supra* note 4, p. 9.

24 See eg Constitutions of Germany, Hungary, Italy, Kosovo, or South Africa.

25 For a general overview of the role of international law during the constitution-making processes in transition periods see H. Eberhard, K. Lachmayer and G. Thallinger (eds), Transitional Constitutionalism (Nomos, 2007).

26 J.R. Locher III and M. Donley, Military Matters: Reforming Bosnia and Herzegovina's Defence Institutions, NATO Review (2004).

27 See Article 210 of the SFRY Constitution (1974).

domestic courts to apply only certain (ie human rights) international treaties, thereby partly limiting the practice of domestic courts with regard to the application of international law. It may well be argued that provisions on international law in the Constitution of the former SFRY were to a large extent dead letter provisions, as was the case in many other communist countries. However, it is suggested that the legal discontinuity caused an unnecessary departure from general provisions on international law, which, if effective, would be more appropriate than a mere incorporation of human rights treaties by the new Constitution of BiH.[28]

As regards the position of international law in the new Constitution, the relevant provisions for our purposes, except the Preamble,[29] are provisions on human rights copied from the European Convention on Human Rights (ECHR). Enumeration of human rights which are directly applicable in BiH and have priority over all other laws was inserted into the Constitution at the time when BiH was not yet a member of the Council of Europe and therefore not a party to the ECHR.[30] The Constitution also incorporates international agreements which are listed in Annex I to the Constitution.[31] In addition, the Constitution includes the term 'general principles of international law' and these principles are considered to be an integral part of the law of BiH and the Entities.[32] This provision aims to incorporate customary international law. Most constitutions do not use the term 'customary international law' explicitly. Instead, they use euphemistic wording such as 'generally accepted rules of international law',[33] 'obligations resulting from international law',[34] or 'legally binding norms of international law'.[35]

The first step of injecting international rules into domestic legislation in order to re-shape the domestic legal system has therefore been accomplished. The

---

28 This problem became obvious for example in the Czech Republic after the change of the regime when (similarly to the BiH Constitution) 'only' human rights treaties were incorporated into the domestic legal system. Because of the violations of human rights by the previous communist regimes, at the time of the adoption of new constitutions, the emphasis both in the Czech Republic and in BiH was on incorporation of human rights treaties without giving any consideration to other international treaties. The Czech Republic later had to change the relevant constitutional provision in order to incorporate international treaties other than human rights ones (providing certain constitutional requirements are met).

29 For the legal nature and character of the Preamble (which includes provisions on international law) as intrepreted by the Constitutional Court of BiH see the case of *Constituency of Peoples*, *supra* note 21.

30 Art. II(2).

31 Art. II(7).

32 See Art. III/3 (b).

33 The Preamble of the Constitution of the Socialist Federal Republic of Yugoslavia (1974), Art. 16(2) of the Constitution of Serbia (2006), Art. 25 of the Constitution of Germany (amended as of 1993).

34 Art. 1(2) of the Constitution of the Czech Republic.

35 Art. 19(2) of the Constitution of Kosovo.

second, more important step is the effective application of such rules, because constitutional proclamations of adherence to international obligations are meaningless if state institutions are not willing 'to give a life' to such constitutional commitments.[36] As regards effective protection of human rights, the Constitution on the one hand strongly promotes 'the highest level of internationally recognized human rights and fundamental freedoms'[37] for *all* on the territory of BiH. On the other hand, it restricts the eligibility of political participation only to 'constituent peoples', thus excluding the others on the basis of ethnicity. Such a restriction sharply contradicts the constitutional provisions on non-discrimination.[38] The case of *Sedjic and Finci v. Bosnia and Herzegovina*, described below, well illustrates this tension and the need to connect constitutional provisions providing a wide protection of human rights with the reality on the ground.

As for the international agreements listed in Annex I to the Constitution, the Constitutional Court in *Maktouf*[39] held that many international treaties, including the Convention on the Prevention and Punishment of the Crime of Genocide (1948), the Geneva Conventions I-IV Relative to the Protection of Civilian Persons in Time of War (1949), and its Additional Protocols I-II (1977) 'have a status equal to that of constitutional principles and are directly applied in Bosnia and Herzegovina'.[40] However, Annex I lists only treaties relating to human rights or humanitarian law. It is unclear what will be the general position of other international treaties within the domestic legal system of BiH. The new Constitution omits provisions indicating the position of international agreements other than those listed in Annex I. The Constitutional Court's decision in *Constituency of Peoples*[41] reveals this shortcoming. A majority of the judges referred to Article 31 of the Vienna Convention when interpreting the legal nature of the Preamble of the Constitution. Judge Popović, in his dissenting opinion, nevertheless stated that for the Vienna Convention to be applicable, it would be necessary to incorporate it in the legal system of BiH either by ratification or in some other way. Since he found that none of the ways for consent to be bound by the Vienna Convention existed in this particular case and 'the Vienna Convention, in terms of Article III/3 (b), cannot be deemed a "general principle of international law or an integral part of BiH and Entity

36 See also the Constitution of Kosovo (2008), which is regarded as one of the best constitutions in Europe as regards international law obligations, but in practise fails to provide sufficient (human rights) protection.

37 Constitution of BiH, Art. II(1).

38 Constitution of BiH, Art. II(4), (5).

39 Constitutional Court of BiH 30 March 2007, *Abduladhim Maktouf*, Decision on Admissibility and Merits, AP-1785/06.

40 *Maktouf*, *supra* note 39, para. 71.

41 *Constituency of Peoples*, *supra* note 21.

legislation"',[42] the Court had, in his view, wrongly referred to the Vienna Convention.

In sum, it is clear from the above that the legal discontinuity between the old and new legal system to a certain extent influenced the scope of application of international law,[43] and it is argued that some constitutional changes should be made in the near future in order for BiH to more adequately comply with various international obligations (other than human rights ones).

2.3. NEW CONSTITUTION FOUND TO BE IN BREACH OF THE EUROPEAN CONVENTION ON HUMAN RIGHTS: HOW ETHNICITY IN BIH STILL MATTERS

> Law and legislation may play a rather ambiguous role in the breakdown of law and order. One group in society may use law to entrench its own position while denying equal rights to opponents. *This abuse of law may have even triggered the original outbreak of violence.*[44]

Some constitutional provisions not only support ethnic differences, but in so doing are also discriminatory towards certain groups of people that are excluded from active political participation in BiH. This is illustrated by the 2008 decision of the European Court on Human Rights (ECtHR) in *Sedjic and Finci v. Bosnia and Herzegovina.*[45] The case was brought before the ECtHR by two politicians, one of Jewish and the other of Roma descent. Both are ineligible to become either members of the House of Peoples or to be considered for the Presidency on the grounds of their ethnicity. Article V of the BiH Constitution states unequivocally: 'The Presidency of Bosnia and Herzegovina shall consist of three Members: one Bosniac and one Croat, each directly elected from the territory of the Federation, and one Serb directly elected from the territory of the Republika Srpska'. As a result, only 'constituent peoples' would qualify for these positions. These constitutional provisions were 'included at the insistence of the parties to the conflict, notwithstanding the expression of human rights concerns by the international mediators involved'.[46] As the co-counsel for Finci noted, 'such rigid

42 *Constituency of Peoples, supra* note 21, Partial Decision, part 3, Dissenting Opinion of Judge Vitomir Popović, p. 78.

43 Pajic argues that departure from the former constitutional tradition may be caused, inter alia, by the strong influence of the United States in drafting the DPA. Pajic, *supra* note 14.

44 Pistor, *supra* note 7, p. 23 (quoting J. Fanton) (emphasis added).

45 Ect.HR, *Sedjic & Finci v. Bosnia and Herzegovina*, 483/2008 ECHR.

46 F. L. Morrison, The Constitution of Bosnia-Herzegovina, 13 Constitutional Commentary 145 (1996).

"power-sharing" was tried, with disastrous results, in Lebanon and Cyprus in the last century'.[47]

The ECtHR confirmed that the contested constitutional provision indeed violated both the right for free elections (ie Article 3 of Protocol No. 1) in conjunction with the prohibition of discrimination of Article 14 with regard to the candidacy for the House of Peoples and the general prohibition of discrimination (ie Article 1 of Protocol No. 12) in regard to the possibility to stand for election for the Presidency. Yet, the case was politically very sensitive, since the ECtHR had to subject to its scrutiny a part of the DPA which had been primarily concluded as a measure to stop the war, not so much as a legal basis for creating a functioning state.[48] While assessing whether the ethnicity requirement in the Constitution amounted to a human rights violation and/or supported the promotion of peace, the ECtHR acknowledged the difficulty of writing a proper constitution in an immediate post-conflict context, when a society is inevitably deeply divided.[49] When seen through the prism of historical events, the ECtHR noted:

> [T]his exclusion rule pursued at least one aim which is broadly compatible with the general objectives of the Convention, as reflected in the Preamble to the Convention, namely *the restoration of peace*. When the impugned constitutional provisions were put in place a very fragile cease-fire was in effect on the ground. The provisions were designed to end a brutal conflict marked by genocide and 'ethnic cleansing'. The nature of the conflict was such that the approval of the 'constituent peoples' (namely, the Bosniacs, Croats and Serbs) was necessary to ensure peace. This could explain, without necessarily justifying, the absence of representatives of the other communities (such as local Roma and Jewish communities) at the peace negotiations and the participants' preoccupation with effective equality between the 'constituent peoples' in the post-conflict society.[50]

It is acknowledged that certain shortcomings are unavoidable when (re) establishing the rule of law in a post-conflict society. Moreover, the needs and priorities of the affected society whilst in a midst of building the rule of law might be rather different from countries with a long rule of law tradition.[51] However, precisely due to the different motivations and needs of post-conflict societies, it may not be always the best idea to conclude (or even impose) the new constitution immediately after the conflict *and* without the proper engagement

---

47 C. Baldwin, A Belated Victory, in: Haaretz (28 February 2010).

48 J. Marko, Post-conflict Reconstruction through State- and Nation-building: The Case of Bosnia and Herzegovina, in: European Diversity and Autonomy Papers (April 2005).

49 See the discussion at http://echrblog.blogspot.com/2010/01/part-of-bosnian-constitution.html.

50 *Sedjic & Finci v. Bosnia and Herzegovina*, *supra* note 45, para. 45 (emphasis addded).

51 Belton, *supra* note 3.

of civil society. The constitution should be the product of a participatory process of local actors, rather than part of a rushed-through peace agreement.[52] Reconstruction efforts (including the legal sector) are not only an issue of principles, but also of means and timing. The current problematic situation in BiH proves this point and offers a lesson to be learned by the international community in other post-conflict situations. Furthermore, if it is agreed that differences of ethnicity were among the main causes of the war in BiH, then it is difficult to approve of the DPA (and some constitutional provisions) which again introduce the ethnicity requirements and therefore keep undermining the fragile rule of law. In other words, ethnicity came back full circle.

The reaction of the state authorities relating to the decision of the ECtHR remains to be seen. It is certain that 'Bosnia's ruling parties really have nothing against allowing Jews, Roma, or other ethnic representatives to run for office. The problem lies elsewhere: Provisions of the constitution also discriminate against Bosnian Serbs in the Bosniak and Bosnian Croat-dominated federation Entity, and against Bosniaks and Bosnian Croats in the Bosnian Serb-dominated Republika Srpska Entity. And the powers that be would prefer to maintain that status quo.'[53] One of the steps towards a deeper democratic consolidation would be to depart from the current status quo and replace the 'Dayton phase'. However, debates on the constitutional reform have so far been unsuccessful.[54] As a result, the ability of the ECtHR's decision to initiate any real change on the ground is rather limited.[55] BiH finds itself in quite a peculiar situation: the Constitution, which is a part of the international treaty (DPA), is in some of its provisions discriminatory, ie the application of an international treaty in this particular context is not improving, but rather worsening the situation of the persons international law purports to protect.

52 Cahin also argues that too early elections in a post-conflict country transfer ethnical division into political division. In BiH, he adds, most extremist parties benefited in elections held only some months after the war. The Hague Academy of International Law Lectures (August 2009).

53 A. Alic, Ethnic Hysteria and Status Quo Discrimination in Bosnia, in: Radio Free Europe (5 May 2010).

54 For a thorough analysis of the proposed and failed reform see J. Marko, Constitutional Reform in Bosnia and Herzegovina 2005–06, 5 European Yearbook of Minority Issues (2006/07).

55 See eg the comment by the co-counsel for Finci Baldwin that 'the US, EU and the other states who still play a major role in Bosnia, should ensure the ruling is put into immediate effect by backing a change in the constitution'. However, elections in October 2010 were again held on the basis of the (discriminatory) constitutional framework established by DPA. Quote from www.hrw.org/en/news/2009/12/22/european-court-landmark-ruling-racial-and-religious-exclusion (visited 14 September 2010).

2.4. EFFECTS OF THE CONSTITUTIONAL FRAMEWORK ON HARMONIZATION OF CRIMINAL LEGISLATION IN BIH: IMPLICATIONS FOR PROSECUTION OF INTERNATIONAL CRIMES

In addition to human rights issues, a constitutional framework creating a complicated state structure has also had a significant impact on the uniform prosecution of international crimes in BiH. According to Article III of the Constitution, BiH is in charge of the international and inter-Entity criminal law enforcement, including relations with Interpol; all other issues related to criminal law fall within the jurisdiction of the Entities.

The criminal law reform in BiH took place during 1992–2003. Even though all three Assemblies were influenced by and took their inspiration from the criminal law of the former Yugoslavia, they all took different paths toward harmonization of the criminal law with international standards. Nowadays, each of the Entities and the Brcko District have their own criminal codes. In addition, a new criminal code was adopted in 2003 at the state level (CC BiH). As a result of this process, the different criminal codes often adhere to different legal standards. This includes also an application of the principle of legality, according to which the applicable criminal law must be the one in force at the time the crime was committed unless the recent law is more lenient for the accused. In the context of the prosecution of international crimes committed between 1992 and 1995, the cantonal and district courts[56] often use the Criminal Code of the former Socialist Federal Republic of Yugoslavia (CC SFRY) as opposed to the WCC, which applies the current CC BiH.

Despite the fact that the Constitutional Court in *Maktouf* 'urged' the Entity courts to apply CC BiH,[57] different criminal codes still continue to be applied at the state and Entity levels.[58] A recent amendment to the CC BiH promises certain improvements, stating that 'the relevant bodies of the Federation of Bosnia and Herzegovina, Republika Srpska and the Brčko District of Bosnia and Herzegovina *shall harmonise* their respective criminal legislation *with this Law* within 90 days as of the day when the Law comes into effect'.[59] This is the first time since its adoption in 2003 that such a provision has been inserted into the CC BiH. If applied appropriately, such a change could support uniform harmonization of the criminal law of BiH with the criminal legislation standards existing in international law. Such a step would help to ensure legal certainty and protection

56 For an overview of prosecution of international crimes by cantonal and district courts see S. Popović, Prosecution of War Crimes in Bosnian Cantonal and District Courts; the Role of the Rule of Law, in this volume at p. 221.

57 OSCE, Moving towards a Harmonized Application of the Law Applicable in War Crimes Cases before Courts in Bosnia and Herzegovina 5–6 (August 2008). See also Popović, *supra* note 56, p. 19.

58 OSCE, Moving towards a Harmonized Application, *supra* note 57, p.6.

59 See Art. 111 of the CC BiH.

of human rights throughout BiH. However, it is too early to assess the effectiveness of this provision, as the amendment came into effect only at the end of April 2010.[60]

The following part will assess the establishment of the WCC, which fully applies the CC BiH and represents one of the most significant efforts in BiH to prosecute international crimes committed during the 1992–1995 war.

3. THE ESTABLISHMENT OF THE WAR CRIMES CHAMBER OF THE COURT OF BOSNIA AND HERZEGOVINA AS A CONTRIBUTION TO THE RULE OF LAW EFFORTS IN BIH

3.1. ESTABLISHMENT OF THE WCC

The above sections illustrated the complex legal environment in which the WCC must operate, ie a complicated state structure set up by the DPA, fragmented criminal legislation with different legal standards, and the prevailing 'rule of ethnicity' rather than rule of law, which also affects the performance of local judges and prosecutors, as discussed below.

As is often the case in post-conflict situations, many local institutions in BiH remained paralyzed several years after the conflict, which was also reflected by the passivity of these institutions and local decision-makers. In the beginning, therefore, international involvement was considered necessary in order to overcome that stagnation.[61] In addition to the reluctance of the local institutions to initiate any reforms or trigger prosecution of committed atrocities, other typical post-conflict factors indicating a need of external assistance were present in BiH, such as serious shortcomings in the whole justice system, including a lack of personnel in general, and lack of personnel trained in handling complex criminal cases in particular. There were also concerns about the independence and impartiality of local prosecutors and judges.[62] Last but not least, there was, as a remnant of the past communist regime, an already weak rule of law tradition.[63]

---

60 See Art. 112: 'The Law shall come into effect on the ninetieth day as of the day of its publication in the Official Gazette of BiH', PABiH, No. 474/10 (21 January 2010).

61 'The adaptation of the Bosnian jurisdiction to international rule of law standards and human rights was an innovation that would not have been made without the participation of international jurists': A. Schröder, Strengthening the Rule of Law in Kosovo and Bosnia and Herzegovina: The Contribution of International Judges and Prosecutors 19 (Berlin: Center for International Peace Operations, 2005).

62 R. Dicker, Letter to the High Representative for Bosnia and Herzegovina, Human Rights Watch International Justice Program (7 December 2009).

63 See eg comments made by Schröder relating to the role of the judiciary during the communist regime: 'Independence and impartiality of the judiciary were a dead letter. "Telephone justice"

It is important to note that broad international involvement was not only considered necessary but also possible as a result of the legal status of BiH. A strong role of the Office of the High Representative (OHR)[64] made it possible to integrate various international components into the domestic legal system of BiH regardless of any resistance by local political representatives.[65] In 2003, the United Nations Security Council passed Resolution 1503 endorsing the completion strategy of the ICTY.[66] As part of its completion strategy and in order to reduce its workload, the ICTY decided to refer certain cases to national authorities. However, as was noted by the former President of the ICTY, the completion strategy should not be understood simply as the need to get rid of cases, but it was planned as 'a strategy for the continuation by domestic actors of those activities that were initiated by the ICTY', with the aim of 'upholding the *international rule of law*, preventing impunity and widely sharing the Tribunal's institutional knowledge and jurisprudence... the "Completion Strategy" is an unprecedented attempt to contribute to the development of the *rule of law*, both in the region of the former Yugoslavia and beyond'.[67]

Accordingly, on the basis of a 'continued legacy building',[68] assistance in strengthening of the capacity of local jurisdictions was provided to national authorities in BiH. It follows that the establishment of the WCC was a joint initiative of the ICTY and the OHR and was therefore a result of a top-down, rather than bottom-up, approach. The two judicial institutions cooperate

---

was the name of the favored mechanism by which the ruling political party controlled judicial and prosecutorial actions.' Schröder, *supra* note 61, p. 17.

64 Competences of the OHR were well summarized by Ivanisevic: 'In the face of continued political obstruction by nationalist parties, in 1997 the OHR was endowed with special powers, commonly referred to as the Bonn powers, including the capacity to dismiss local officials at any level or to impose laws. The role of the OHR made BiH a de facto protectorate where international authorities carried out nation-building and thousands of foreign soldiers guaranteed security. The high representative has also been the EU's special representative (EUSR) since 2002. The EUSR's mandate is based on the EU's policy objective in BiH, a "stable, viable, peaceful and multiethnic BiH, cooperating peacefully with its neighbors and irreversibly on track towards EU membership.' Ivanisevic, *supra* note 64. For further information about the role of the OHR see Article V of Annex 10 – Agreement on Civilian Implementation of the DPA.

65 This scenario can be clearly distinguished from Croatia and Serbia, where, as Josipović argues, such an intervention into the domestic legal system would not be possible. Therefore, different approaches to application of international (criminal) law by domestic courts in the former Yugoslavia can be traced. See I. Josipović, Responsibility for War Crimes: Historical Roots and Recent Developments in: I. Josipović (ed.), Responsibility for War Crimes, Croatian Perspective-Selected Issues (2005). See also S. Weill and I. Jovanović, War Crimes Prosecution in a Post-Conflict Era and a Pluralism of Jurisdictions: The Experience of the Belgrade War Crimes Chamber, in this volume at p. 241.

66 See also Annex IV of the DPA in which Article II(8) states: 'All competent authorities in Bosnia and Herzegovina shall cooperate and provide unrestricted access to [...] the International Tribunal for the Former Yugoslavia[...].'

67 J. Pocar, Completion or Continuation Strategy? Appraising Problems and Possible Developments, 6 International Criminal Justice 655–665 (2008) (emphasis added).

68 Pocar, *supra* note 67.

extensively, as can be seen by the fact that the WCC basically accepted the 'legal concept' of the ICTY.[69] In addition, many former ICTY employees have joined the WCC and brought to it their expertise.

This brings us to the question of legal personnel serving at the WCC. It was agreed that mixed panels of both international and national judges would be created. The OHR appointed the international judges (and prosecutors), and the High Judicial and Prosecution Council of BiH appointed the domestic ones. The WCC began its work in 2005 with a majority of international judges, and their gradual phasing out was envisaged over five years.

3.2. CONTRIBUTION OF INTERNATIONAL PERSONNEL AT THE WCC TO RULE OF LAW EFFORTS IN BIH

The contribution of international personnel to the rule of law efforts in this area is at least twofold. First, international personnel, if properly chosen and trained, can bring expertise in the application of international law and modern approaches to legal interpretation.[70] Second, international crimes are characterized by a collective and large-scale character, often with a political dimension. Accordingly, their investigation, prosecution, and punishment are politically very sensitive. Possible interference by local politicians or decisions of judges appointed on political grounds could seriously hamper the application of (international) law. The appointment of international personnel should therefore also be seen as an important safeguard to secure independent and impartial prosecutions and punishment of crimes committed.[71] In other words, not only new domestic legislation incorporating international law (ie the Constitution and CC BiH), but also implementation of such law by judges who are independent *and* perceived as such, is crucial to judicial decisions being accepted by the local population, and to the success of the rule of law efforts on the ground.

Without international personnel at the WCC, political and ethnic considerations could prevail during proceedings before it, thereby influencing its role and limiting effective application of international law. This argument can be supported by the previous negative experience with other judicial institutions in BiH that were also empowered to apply international law:

---

69 Such as use of adjudicated facts established by the ICTY or reliance on the ICTY's case-law with regards to substantive law issues.

70 On this point, see Schröder, *supra* note 61, p. 5–6: 'Judges in the Yugoslav legal system had very little competence in interpreting the law. This exclusion of judges from the interpretation of laws is a clear violation of the principle of the separation of powers. Under the socialist legal system judges were in effect not much more than executive organs of the ruling party.'

71 For, on the other hand, some problems encountered in participation of international personnel in BiH see Schröder, *supra* note 61, p. 19–30.

> local judges at the Human Rights Chamber as well as at the Constitutional Court often took political aspects of a case into consideration or decided depending on the parties' ethnicity. As soon as a case was relevant for *the balance of power between the State of BiH and one of the three ethnic groups*, Bosnian judges would always vote in favor of their own ethnicity. This imbalance was particularly obvious in the case of the Serb judges who served at the Constitutional Court until 2002 and who argued as a matter of principle in favor of the constitution and laws of the Republica Srpska. Their arguments were political, not legal ones.[72]

It is also clear that international personnel cannot (and should not) stay at the WCC (or in BiH in general) indefinitely. It was originally expected that there should be purely national panels by December 2009.[73] However, representatives of BiH's judiciary repeatedly stressed that it was necessary to extend the mandates of international judges and prosecutors. For example, the President of the Court, Meddžida Kreso, stated: 'The unstable political situation in Bosnia and complaints of biased treatment of one ethnic group or another suggest the mandate of international judges and prosecutors needs extending. Local judges are able and ready to tackle these complex cases, but the international judges bring credibility and trust.'[74] The proposed extension of the mandates of international judges and prosecutors was not, however, adopted by the House of Representatives of the Parliament of BiH, where delegates from Republika Srpska blocked suggested amendments to the *Law on Court of Bosnia and Herzegovina*,[75] arguing, that 'Bosnia and Herzegovina cannot be a fully sovereign state if foreign personnel work with its judicial institutions'.[76] Following this failure to extend the mandate, strong pressure emerged from various (mainly international) actors. A Steering Board of the Peace Implementation Council (PIC)[77] was concerned with this situation and expressed that the departure of internationals at this stage 'would have a negative effect on the entire judicial system of Bosnia, contradict [Bosnia's] international obligations, and inhibit the UN Security Council's completion strategy for ICTY.'[78] As a result of this pressure, the OHR finally decided to intervene and to 'impose' an extension of the mandate of

72 Schröder, *supra* note 61, p. 24 (emphasis added).

73 See Judges Leave War Crimes Chamber Project, Project Implementation Plan Registry Progress Report, Balkan Investigative Reporting Network (BIRN) (October 2004), available at www.ohr.int//ohr-dept/rule-oflaw-pillar/pdf/wcc-project-plan-201004-eng.pdf (visited 10 February 2009).

74 N. Ahmetašević, International Judges Must Stay in Bosnia, BIRN's Balkan Insight (24 April 2008), available at www.balkaninsight.com/en/main/interviews/9661/ (visited 16 April 2009).

75 'Law on the Court of Bosnia and Herzegovina' regulates operation of the WCC, including its structure, procedural rules, and jurisdiction: Official Gazette of Bosnia and Herzegovina No. 29/00.

76 See Justice Report: No Mandate Extension for International Judges and Prosecutors, BIRN (4 September 2009), available at www.bim.ba/en/182/10/21995/ (visited 12 June 2010).

77 PIC is an international body which is charged with implementing the DPA. The Steering Board of the PIC provides the High Representative with political guidance.

78 Communique of the Steering Board of the PIC (19 November 2009).

international personnel until 31 December 2012,[79] warning of the negative consequences that would follow if the mandate were not extended, such as the need for witnesses to testify again.[80] The OHR's decision was positively received by international and many local actors.[81]

3.3. LEGAL BASIS OF THE WCC AND THE APPLICABLE LAW

The WCC operates within the Criminal Division of the Court of BiH at the state level.[82] Despite the international involvement in its establishment and the presence of international personnel, it is a domestic institution[83] which will continue its work even after the phasing out of international personnel.[84] The WCC has jurisdiction over cases transferred from the Referral Bench of the ICTY to national judicial authorities under Rule 11*bis*, which provides that a referral may be made to a state: (a) in which the crimes were committed; (b) the accused was arrested; (c) or which has jurisdiction and is willing and adequately prepared to accept the case. In addition to cases referred by the ICTY under Rule 11*bis*, the WCC can also initiate prosecution of its own cases. Under the strategy of the WCC regarding the selection of cases, 'highly sensitive' cases will fall under the jurisdiction of the WCC and 'sensitive' cases will be dealt with by the cantonal and district courts.[85]

---

79 In contrast to powers of international administration (in some countries) to impose laws, occupational law (in some other countries) limits powers to modify local laws. See on occupational law E. Benvenisti and M. Saliternik, The Treatment of Occupation Legislation by Courts in Liberated Territories, in this volume at p. 269.

80 See OHR Extends International Judges' Mandate, *BIRN* (16 December 2009), available at www.balkaninsight.com/en/main/news/24402/?tpl=299&ST1=Text&ST_T1=Article&ST_AS1=1&ST_max=1 (visited 22 January 2010).

81 Catherine Ashton, EU High Representative for Foreign Affairs and Security Policy and Olli Rehn, EU Enlargement Commissioner, issued a statement welcoming the decision and underlining that 'the continued presence of international judges and prosecutors is essential to pursuit of justice for the victims and to the work of the ICTY'. However, not everyone shares the enthuasiasm for extension of mandates. The Prime Minister of Republika Srpska, Milorad Dodik, even called for the abolition of the Court of BiH, including the WCC, as a condition for the above mentioned constitutional reform. Justice Report, *supra* note 76.

82 Another specialized chamber with international personnel operating within the Court of BiH is the 'Organized Crime, Economic Crime and Corruption Chamber'.

83 'The Law on the Court of BiH' was promulgated on 12 November 2000 by the High Representative and was subsequently adopted by the Parliament of BiH on 3 July 2002. For further information on the Court of BiH see its official website, www.sudbih.gov.ba.

84 Looking for Justice: The War Crimes Chamber in Bosnia and Herzegovina, 18(1)(D) Human Rights Watch (7 February 2006).

85 B. Ivanišević, The War Crimes Chamber in Bosnia and Herzegovina: From Hybrid to Domestic Court (International Center for Transitional Justice, 2008).

The first case transferred from the ICTY to the WCC was *Stankovic*.[86] Opposing the transfer to BiH,[87] the defence in *Stankovic* submitted to the ICTY that the WCC should not be considered as a 'national court' in the light of Article 9(1)[88] of the ICTY Statute, because it would as such have to be composed of judges who are nationals of the state. The ICTY nevertheless confirmed the domestic legal basis of the WCC.[89]

As was already noted, the WCC applies the new CC BiH. Due to the international involvement in its preparation, some important changes and departures from the former legal system were made in the CC BiH as well as in the Criminal Procedure Code of BiH (CPC BiH), both in terms of international law and international origins of law.[90] A question of legality immediately arises with regard to the application of the CC BiH to past crimes.[91] The issue of the retroactive application of the CC BiH, mainly in the context of the length of punishment, appears in almost all cases before the WCC. The WCC takes a firm position that the retroactive application of the CC BiH is not in violation of the ECHR.[92] The underlying justification for this stance, however, differs among judges.[93] In terms of substantive law, qualifications of certain crimes were

86 ICTY 17 May 2005, *Prosecutor v. Stankovic*, Decision on Referral of Case under Rule 11*bis*, Partly Confidential and Ex Parte, IT-96-23/2-PT.

87 Many accussed (including Stankovic) oppose referrals of their cases to domestic courts in the former Yugoslavia because sentencing practices of the ICTY are believed to be more lenient. One of the reasons may be, as one of the ICTY's officials noted, that the ICTY focuses on providing *restorative* rather than *retributive* justice. See also M.A. Drumbl, Atrocity, Punishment, and International Law 158 (Cambridge University Press, 2007).

88 Art. 9(1) of the ICTY Statute reads as follows: 'The International Tribunal and national courts shall have concurrent jurisdiction to prosecute persons for serious violations of international humanitarian law committed in the territory of the former Yugoslavia since 1 January 1991.'

89 The ICTY held that there is no justification for giving to the phrase 'national court' any other meaning than the normal connotation, which is 'a court of or pertaining to a nation'. The ICTY stated that the Court of BiH, of which the WCC is a component, is a court which has been established pursuant to the statutory law of BiH and it is therefore a 'national court'. *Prosecutor v. Stankovic*, *supra* note 86, para. 26.

90 As for the international origins of some laws, it could be noted that BiH historically belonged to a civil legal tradition. With the influence of an international community over new legislation, some changes based on the common law tradition were introduced. See Ivanisevic's argument that 'through this CPC key aspects of an adversarial procedure were imported into a country that had used a form of accusatorial procedure for many decades. This major change in the legal system includes a new and unique set of rules, hybrid in nature and similar to those of the ICTY.' Ivanišević, *supra* note 64, p. 13.

91 For more on the principle of legality in international criminal law see W.N. Ferdinandusse, Direct Application of International Criminal Law in National Courts 222 (2006).

92 Compare with the practice before the WCC in Serbia. See Weill and Jovanovic, *supra* note 65, n 38 and accompanying text.

93 See eg the reasoning in *Radmilo Vuković*, Case No. X-KRŽ-06/217, where the WCC cited with approval the decision of the ECtHR in *Karmo v. Bulgaria* Appl. no. 76965/01, Judgment of 6 December 2007. Compare with the reasoning of the Constitutional Court of BiH in *Maktouf*, *supra* note 39, which was repeated in the *Kravica* case, WCC, *Petar Mitrović and Others*, Case No. X-KR-05/24 ('*Kravica*' case), in front of the WCC. It is suggested that the reasoning in *Radmilo Vukovic* (and therefore in *Karmo v. Bulgaria*) should be preferred in order to secure

harmonized with definitions of international crimes as defined in the ICTY Statute by basically 'copying' relevant provisions of the ICTY Statute into the CC BiH. Hence, the WCC applies all three categories of international crimes – war crimes, crimes against humanity, and genocide[94] – and in so doing it frequently relies on ICTY case law.

Changes in the CC BiH affected not only the qualifications of crimes, but also modes of commission and forms of liability. The newly adopted Article 180 CC BiH[95] provides for individual criminal responsibility for international crimes in accordance with Article 7 of the ICTY Statute,[96] which (and thus arguably also Article 180 CC BiH) is said to *implicitly* include the concept of Joint Criminal Enterprise (JCE) – JCE being in turn considered to be part of customary international law.

The Commentary to the CC BiH is quite instructive in explaining the relationship between the CC BiH and the ICTY Statute in this context:

> The provisions of paragraph 1 [of Art.180] are worded exactly the same way as Art. 7 paragraph 1 of the ICTY Statute... It is obvious that the legislator followed the basic rules of criminal liability deriving from International Criminal Law and from the provisions in the ICTY Statute, as well as by the provisions in Art. 25(3)(a) through (e) of the Rome Statute, as he [the legislator] significantly broadened the possible acts of *perpetration and of accessory in the perpetration of criminal acts*.[97]

In short, JCE establishes a different mode of commission of international crimes. It can be described as a plurality of persons acting according to a common plan, which amounts to or involves the commission of a crime, and the accused must participate with the intent to pursue the common plan.[98] Three distinct

the unity in interpretation and application of the CC BiH in line with the ECtHR and its case-law, especially in the light of the fact that the ECHR is directly applicable in BiH and has priority over other laws.

94 *Kravica* case, *supra* note 93.

95 Art. 180(1) reads in relevant part: 'A person who planned, instigated, ordered, perpetrated or otherwise aided and abetted in the planning, preparation or execution of a criminal offence referred to in Article 171 (Genocide), 172 (Crimes against Humanity), 173 (War Crimes against Civilians), 174 (War Crimes against the Wounded and Sick), 175 (War Crimes against Prisoners of War), 177 (Unlawful Killing or Wounding of the Enemy), 178 (Marauding the Killed and Wounded at the Battlefield) and 179 (Violating the Laws and Practices of Warfare) of this Code, shall be personally responsible for the criminal offence.'

96 Art. 7 (1) reads in relevant part: 'A person who planned, instigated, ordered, committed or otherwise aided and abetted in the planning, preparation or execution of a crime referred to in articles 2 to 5 of the present Statute, shall be individually responsible for the crime.'

97 M. Babić, L. Filipović, I. Marković and Z. Rajić, Commentary on the Criminal Codes in BiH 593–594 (2005).

98 For a deeper analysis of this concept, see N. Piacente, Importance of the Joint Criminal Enterprise Doctrine for the ICTY Prosecutorial Policy, 2 Journal of International Criminal Justice (2004); K. Uhlířová, Joint Criminal Enterprise – Amorphous Concept or Viable Model for Prosecution of Crimes under International Law?, in: Global Governance, Human Rights and Development (2008).

categories of JCE were recognized in the case law of the ICTY: 'basic', 'systemic', and 'extended' JCE.[99]

3.4. APPLICATION OF JOINT CRIMINAL ENTERPRISE BY INTERNATIONAL (ICTY) AND NATIONAL COURT (WCC): WILL JCE SURVIVE THE TRANSPLANTATION INTO DOMESTIC LAW?

The issue of ethnicity unfolds as a common denominator throughout this chapter: it was said to be a main cause of the 1992–1995 war; it subsequently played a role during the drafting of the DPA and establishment of the current state structure and institutions; some constitutional provisions support ethnic differences; and concerns about 'ethnic bias' impacting prosecution of crimes were among the reasons for international involvement in establishing the WCC. Last but not least, ethnic cleansing, which was carried out in BiH during the war, can be also qualified as an international crime.[100] Ethnic cleansing is often planned by high-ranking state officials at the top levels. JCE, as one of the tools developed to prosecute cases of collective criminality (including ethnic cleansing), can become particularly useful in addressing such situations.

In several cases, ethnic cleansing was identified by the ICTY as having been one of the main purposes of the accused's participation in JCE.[101] Given the similarity of the legal provisions of the ICTY Statute and the CC BiH, the sharing of evidence, the assessment of similar or the same events, and the fact that some cases transferred from the ICTY to the WCC already included JCE in the indictment, the argument could be made that it would be legally consistent to apply the same tool for prosecuting the same pattern of atrocities. However, the situation is not that straightforward. The WCC made a two-pronged inquiry: first, whether JCE was part of customary international law, and second, whether (and to what extent) customary international law was part of the national law *at the time* the crimes were committed – all this in light of controversies surrounding the application of JCE at the international level.[102]

---

99 For a critique of the 'extended' category of JCE see eg M.E. Badar, 'Just Convict Everyone!' Joint Perpetration: From *Tadic* to *Stakic* and Back Again (2007).

100 Ethnic cleansing is not a legal term. However, depending on the circumstances, it can amount to war crimes, crimes against humanity, or genocide. See also an argument made by James Crawford before the International Court of Justice that ethnic cleansing presents an extreme form of racial discrimination: ICJ 8 September 2008, *Georgia v. Russian Federation*, Application of the Convention on the Elimination of All Forms of Racial Discrimination, Verbatim Record, p. 20, para. 2.

101 Those charged with participating in JCE in the context of ethnic cleansing include, for example, Slobodan Milosevic, Vojislav Seselj, Nebojsa Pavkovic, Milan Babic, or Ante Gotovina and Ivan Cermak.

102 Thorough examination of all concerns surrounding JCE would go beyond the scope of this chapter. See eg W. Schabas, Mens Rea and the International Criminal Tribunal for the Former Yugoslavia, 37 New England Law Review 1015–1036 (2002–2003).

Many arguments for or against JCE have been raised elsewhere.[103] Still, the application of JCE at the national level becomes an even more challenging 'enterprise'. There are two central issues which may be subsumed under the rule of law concerns: (1) application of JCE in the light of the principle of legality;[104] and (2) its alleged vagueness and expansiveness, which, according to some scholars, 'dilutes standard of proof, undermines the principle of individual criminal responsibility in favour of collective responsibility, infringes the nullum crimen sine lege principle and infringes the right of the accused to a fair trial (including the right to be informed promptly and in detail of the nature and case of the charges against him).'[105] In this light, the question may be raised whether *some* international concepts or categories are to be *automatically* considered as 'better' standards of justice, especially if there is no general agreement even at the international level as regards the scope of their application. Moreover, their 'transplantation' into the domestic legal system may lead to their mutually difficult coexistence with some domestic legal provisions, as will be shown below.

The following part will briefly examine the application and interpretation of JCE by the WCC because it presents a rare and unique opportunity to witness how a domestic court can rely on customary international law in criminal proceedings by applying a commonly used,[106] albeit contested, concept of international criminal law. It is fair to note from the outset that since there is no uniformity in the application of JCE at the international level, it can hardly be expected that a national court in a post-conflict situation will be perfectly familiar with all its nuances and would welcome the 'arrival' of JCE on the domestic legal scene.

3.4.1. Rasević and Todović Case (JCE Applied)

Rasević and Todović[107] were accused of participation in setting up and maintaining a system of mistreatment of Bosniak detainees (JCE), including a system of forced labour in the detention facility in Foča during the war. In 2008, both the accused were found guilty of crimes against humanity, including persecution in connection with acts of murder, enslavement, deportation or

---

103 See eg A.M. Danner and J.S. Martinez, Guilty Associations: Joint Criminal Enterprise, Command Responsibility and the Development of International Criminal Law, 93 California Law Review 75, 108 (2005); H. van der Wilt, Joint Criminal Enterprise: Possibilities and Limitations, 5 Journal of International Criminal Justice 91–108 (2007).

104 Discussed briefly above, 2.4. and 3.3.

105 Damgaard, *supra* note 9, p. 129.

106 It is estimated that 64% of the Indictments at the ICTY during 2001–2004 included JCE. See Danner and Martinez, *supra* note 103, p. 107–108.

107 WCC 28 February 2008, *Mitar Rašević and Savo Todović*, Case No. X-KR/06/275. This was the fifth case transferred from the ICTY to the WCC pursuant to Rule 11*bis* of the ICTY Rules of Procedure and Evidence.

forcible transfer, imprisonment, torture, enforced disappearance, and other inhumane acts.

The WCC held, first, that the ICTY Statute is part of international law;[108] second, that international law is incorporated into the domestic law of BiH; and third, as a consequence, that 'domestic Courts must consider the parent norms of international law and their interpretation by international courts'.[109] The WCC concluded that when Article 7 of the ICTY Statute was 'copied' into the law of BiH, 'it came with its international origins, definitions and its international judicial interpretation'.[110] The WCC confirmed that JCE was part of customary international law already at the time when crimes were committed (ie 1992–1994). Review of the 'concentration camp' cases after World War II led the WCC to conclude that, by 1992, systemic JCE had already 'crystallized into a theory of liability recognized by customary international law'.[111] It further pointed to the practice before the ICTY, where the form of systemic JCE was recognized as part of customary international law by the Appeals Chamber of the ICTY in *Tadic* and in many subsequent cases.[112]

Since JCE was found to have been part of customary international law, the next step consisted of finding that customary international law, in turn, was part of the law of BiH. On this point, the WCC added that, as a general principle, 'it seems that all national legal systems accept customary international law as an integral part of national law'.[113] An analysis of both Constitutions (SFRY and BiH), and of the CC SFRY[114] and CC BiH, followed in order to confirm that 'the provisions of customary international law, including the ones that pertained to JCE, were binding on Bosnia and Herzegovina (and before that on the SFRY)'.[115]

---

108 See also the decision in *Maktouf, supra* note 39, in which the Constitutional Court held that the ICTY Statute is an 'integral part of the legal system of Bosnia and Herzegovina.' The ICTY Statute is, according to the Constitutional Court, one of the documents that regulates the application of international law to which BiH is subject under Article III(3)(b) of the Constitution of BiH. *Maktouf, supra* note 39, para. 70.

109 *Mitar Rašević and Savo Todović, supra* note 107, p. 103 (quoting G. Werle, Principles of International Criminal Law 80 (2005)).

110 *Mitar Rašević and Savo Todović, supra* note 107, p. 103.

111 *Mitar Rašević and Savo Todović, supra* note 107, p. 109.

112 ICTY 15 July 1999, *Prosecutor v. Tadic*, Case No. IT-94-1, paras. 195, 220.

113 The Panel quoted E. Denza, The Relationship Between International Law and National Law, in: M. Evans (ed.), International Law 415, 428 (2003).

114 In this context, the WCC also refered to Article 26 of the CC SFRY, which resembles JCE. Article 26 reads: 'Anybody creating or making use of an organization, gang, cabal, group or any other association for the purpose of committing criminal acts is criminally responsible *for all criminal acts* resulting from the *criminal design* of these associations and shall be punished *as if he himself committed* them, *irrespective of whether and in what manner* he himself directly participated in the commission of ay of these acts' (emphasis added).

115 WCC 6 November 2008, *Mitar Rašević and Savo Todović*, Appellate Division, Case No. X-KRŽ -06/275, p. 26.

The WCC then turned from the ICTY case law to the ECtHR in order to examine the principle of legality in the light of the ECtHR's jurisprudence.[116] When interpreting Article 7 of the ECHR, the ECtHR had repeatedly held that in order to be found guilty under a principle of liability, this principle of liability must have been, first, a part of the law to which the accused were subject at the time of the commission of the crime and second, that it must have been reasonably *foreseeable* that the accused would be prosecuted for the commission of crimes under this principle of liability.[117]

For purposes of foreseeability, the WCC relied on the prosecution of the 'concentration camp' cases after World War II and observed that these were 'publicly tried and reported cases occurring in internationally overseen trials held in Germany in locations reasonably close to the former Yugoslavia, and the case law and conclusions of those tribunals were both public and accessible'.[118] According to the WCC, the requirement of foreseeability was thus also fulfilled.

3.4.2. Vuković Case[119] *(JCE Not Applied)*

Ranko and Rajko Vuković were accused of killing two Bosniak civilians and Ranko Vuković was additionally charged with raping a Bosniak woman in Foča. The WCC (Appellate Panel) rejected the application of JCE, which had been confirmed by the first instance. The WCC argued that JCE was not stipulated or defined in domestic legislation, although it admitted, albeit only in a footnote, that JCE was derived from Article 180(1). The WCC emphasized that JCE was not explained conceptually and it was therefore unclear whether 'this is a case of particular criminal offence or a form of criminal responsibility and if we accept the latter, the concept is hardly in accordance with classical concept of co-perpetration recognised by our CC'.[120]

The *Vukovic* case shows a diametrically different approach to JCE than that described in *Rasevic and Todovic*. It seems that some (mainly national) judges and prosecutors at the WCC perceived JCE as a foreign transplant alien to their

116 For example, it referred to Ect.HR 22 March 2001, *Streletz, Kessler and Krenz v. Germany*, Apps. Nos. 34044/96, 35532/97 and 44801/98, para. 105.

117 Compare with Cassese: 'when only international criminal rules are at stake, or when those rules conflict with national criminal law, the requirements of accessibility and foreseeability may legitimately diminish to the point of fading away. Thus, the need to make international values upholding human dignity (and the legal rules enshrining those values) prevail over diverging national legislation, tips the balance in favour of international law, to *the detriment of the accessibility and foreseeability of criminal law*' (emphasis added). A. Cassese, Balancing the Prosecution of Crimes against Humanity and Non-Retroactivity of Criminal Law: The *Kolk and Kislyiy v. Estonia* Case before the ECHR, 4(2) Journal of International Criminal Justice 417 (2006).

118 *Mitar Rašević and Savo Todović, supra* note 107, p. 107.

119 *Ranko Vuković and Another*, Case No. X-KRŽ-07/405.

120 *Ranko Vuković and Another, supra* note 119, p. 5.

classical concepts of national law (eg co-perpetration under Article 29).[121]Accordingly, the WCC in *Vukovic* did not seem to be prepared to automatically subscribe to the opinion expressed both in *Maktouf* and *Rasevic and Todovic*, ie that the ICTY Statute was an integral part of national law and that it arrived at the domestic legal system also with its international definitions and judicial interpretation, including JCE.[122]

4. CONCLUSION: THE RULE OF LAW STILL IN THE MAKING

The legal, political, and social environment in BiH is still unstable. The ECtHR in *Sejdic and Finci v. BiH* observed that there have been many significant positive developments in BiH since the conclusion of the DPA.[123] Many challenges remain, too, including those brought about by the DPA itself, such as the division of BiH along ethnic lines. As a result, there is an inherent tension between ethnic separation of BiH and declared human rights guarantees which should protect individuals regardless of their ethnicity.[124] In other words, we can still witness a prevailing 'rule of ethnicity' rather than a rule of law in many areas of Bosnian society.

Due to the passivity of local actors after the conflict and the ethnicity issues which keep undermining the fragile rule of law, international involvement was needed. One of the outcomes of the international intervention in the legal sector was the establishment of the WCC.[125] As regards the application of international law by the WCC in general, it frequently relies on international law by referencing international agreements, case law of the ICTY and other courts, and academic writings. There is a generous trend towards international law, including customary international law, which the WCC has held to be an integral part of

---

121 In many cases before the WCC, JCE is being charged in conjunction with the domestic concept of co-perpetration. In the *Vukovic* case, the WCC found it however unacceptable to use JCE in parallel with co-perptration under Article 29 'as these two are mutually exclusive and their co-existence is not possible.' *Ranko Vuković and Another, supra* note 119, p. 6. Due to the different focus of this book and limited scope of this chapter, discussion of these two concepts does not form part of this chapter. For an analysis of the uneasy relationship between JCE as a concept of international law and co-perpetration as a concept of national law of BiH see A. Strippoli, National Prosecution of International Crimes: Cases and Legislation National Courts and Genocide The Kravica Case at the Court of Bosnia and Herzegovina, 7(3) Journal of International Criminal Justice 577–595 (2009).

122 *Mitar Rašević and Savo Todović, supra* note 107, p. 103.

123 *Sedjic & Finci v. Bosnia and Herzegovina, supra* note 45.

124 Pajic, *supra* note 14.

125 See also A. Buyse, Virtuous Flexibility – The Application of International Human Rights Norms by the Bosnian Human Rights Chamber, in this volume at p. 175, on the establishment of the Human Rights Chamber.

BiH national law. In this respect, it is worth noting that the practice of the WCC 'differs from practice of all other courts prosecuting international crimes in the territory of the former Yugoslavia'.[126]

The international law-friendly approach at the WCC is the result of its accepting (or having to accept) the 'legal concept' of the ICTY, the presence of international personnel, and training seminars organized for the domestic personnel. It should be emphasized that the ICTY's influence over the application of international criminal law holds true only for the WCC, and does not affect the cantonal and district courts, which operate independently of the WCC.

As regards the application of JCE in particular, the two cases discussed above illustrate two main approaches before the WCC in relation to JCE. Similar reasoning resonates in other cases where the application of JCE has been considered.[127] The brief review of the two selected cases demonstrates that the WCC uses the case law of the ICTY as 'persuasive authority without engaging in any innovative interpretation.'[128] The WCC is confident in areas where the case law at the ICTY is well developed, as shown by the analysis of the systemic form of JCE in *Rasevic and Todovic*. However, the WCC is less persuaded when JCE is confronted with certain national provisions, such as co-perpetration as in *Vukovic*.[129] In addition, as *Vukovic* revealed, even if it is legally possible for the WCC to apply the full spectrum of international criminal law, national law may often be simply more accessible for domestic actors.

As for the legacy of the WCC, it remains to be seen whether its frequent reliance on international law will disappear with the departure of the internationals. As for JCE, the domestic actors will have to decide whether JCE should continue to play a role in cases before the WCC. In the opinion of one BiH defence lawyer, 'judging from the current jurisprudence, this option is highly unlikely'.[130] Part of the reason is that domestic actors did not participate in these changes to their legal system and they identify international law with international origins of law, as something that came from without, not within the state.[131]

Some of the WCC's shortcomings, such as confusion or uncertainty in the application of international law, are inevitable for a new court tasked with complex legal issues. On the positive side, as compared to other legal settings in post-conflict situations,[132] the WCC has been extremely active during its five

126 Ivanišević, *supra* note 85.

127 For a chart of cases where JCE was charged in front of the WCC see Ivanišević, *supra* note 85, p. 51–56.

128 Strippoli, *supra* note 121.

129 Strippoli, *supra* note 121.

130 J. Pjanic, Joint Criminal Enteprise, p. 7, available at www.okobih.ba/files/docs/Jasmina_Pjanic_ENG_i_BHS.pdf (visited 5 December 2009).

131 Compare with South Africa: Schmid, *supra* note 4, note, Introduction.

132 *Supra* note 10.

years of existence and has shown the capability to conduct trials professionally, efficiently, and in a speedy manner. Despite the fact that the WCC is the result of a top-down approach, the cooperation of international and local judges and prosecutors has also shown positive results on local capacity-building[133] which can be further supported by the fact that 'judgments passed with international participation are often quoted by lower local Bosnian courts'.[134]

So far, the WCC has proved that it is not 'only a bad substitute of the ICTY',[135] and although it is 'another measure imposed on BiH',[136] this does not automatically preclude positive results. The WCC has a potential for seeding 'international standards of justice' into the domestic legal system of BiH. It is nevertheless highly desirable to form a wider strategy (which depends on political will) by focusing also on Entity courts in order to secure uniform application of international standards. The newly amended CC BiH requires the Entities and the Brcko District to harmonize their criminal legislation with the CC BiH. If complied with, such a step could help to ensure fair and effective prosecutions of international crimes and increase the legal certainty on the whole territory of BiH.

Finally, the legal outcomes and practice of the WCC have important theoretical and policy implications as they can inform and inspire domestic prosecutions in other post-conflict societies. The WCC is offering its 'transfer of knowledge' to the Extraordinary Chambers in Cambodia,[137] and a similar institutional model was suggested for Burundi[138] or for the Democratic Republic of Congo.[139] International law in general is playing an increasingly important role in restoring 'constitutional democracy' elsewhere, which illustrates a further

---

133 Mixed panels at the WCC contribute to higher penetration of norms of international law if compared with previous UNMIK arrangements in Kosovo: see Schröder, *supra* note 61, p. 5.

134 Schröder, *supra* note 61, p. 18.

135 Shelving justice-war crimes prosecutions in paralysis, Report of Amnesty International, available at http://archive.amnesty.org/library/index/engeur630182003 (visited 23 February 2010).

136 Shelving justice-war crimes prosecutions, *supra* note 135.

137 See eg the visit and presentations by officials from the Court of BiH at the Extraordinary Chambers in Cambodia, The Court Report (August 2008), available at www.eccc.gov.kh/english/cabinet/fileUpload/67/2008_August-Court_Report_FD.pdf (visited 10 December 2009).

138 See Letter from the Secretary-General to the President of the Security Council (S/2005/158) (11 March 2005), available at http://daccess-dds-ny.un.org/doc/UNDOC/GEN/N05/264/71/PDF/N0526471.pdf?OpenElement (visited 10 October 2009). See also SC Resolution 1606 (20 June 2005).

139 'The addition of a mixed chamber in the Congolese justice system with support from international judicial experts – *based primarily on the model of the War Crimes Chamber of Bosnia and Herzegovina* (WCC) – could provide the national justice system with the boost it needs to tackle rampant impunity for the worst crimes' (emphasis added) in: A 'mixed' chamber for Congo?' available at www.hrw.org/en/news/2009/11/19/mixed-chamber-congo (visited 10 October 2009).

step in the internationalization of rule of law efforts.[140] The findings of this chapter may be therefore used in a broader discussion about the effectiveness of rule of law efforts in other post-conflict countries.

140 See eg SC Resolution 10054 (14 October 2010) on Haiti, which emphasized the efforts of both Haitian actors and the international community 'to ensure the holding of credible and legitimate presidential and legislative elections [...] which will further consolidate democracy, allow for the completion of constitutional reform and contribute to the reconstruction process.' See also various SC Resolutions on Ivory Coast, which can be viewed as an intervention in the constitutional set up of the country (as opposed to military intervention).

PROSECUTION OF WAR CRIMES IN BOSNIAN CANTONAL AND DISTRICT COURTS: THE ROLE OF THE RULE OF LAW

Sanja Popovic*

1. INTRODUCTION

Memories of the conflict in Bosnia are still fresh for those studying post-conflict nations and their rehabilitation efforts. With these efforts to restore peace and order, the common *lingua franca* of rule of law is actively engaged, including a multitude of actors, goals, and perceived operational successes.[1] In the context of Bosnia, one of the clearest examples of formalizing and establishing the rule of law or, perhaps more accurately, the International Rule of Law (IRL), was facilitated with the creation of the International Criminal Tribunal for the

* B.A. (Hon.), LL.B., LL.M (NYU).
Thanks are due to Davinia Abdul Aziz whose comments greatly improved the draft; Anna Abbott, Articling Student at Gowling Lafleur Henderson LLP for her research assistance; and The Hon. Patrick J. LeSage, C.M., O.Ont., Q.C. for sharing his experiences and insightful guidance.
The author was inspired to write this paper following her internship experience with Human Rights Watch (HRW) from January 2008 to January 2009. She was responsible for analysing the domestic war crimes cases and for drafting small parts of the report under the guidance of Joshua Franco. This research was later incorporated into the Human Rights Watch report, Still Waiting: Bringing Justice for War Crimes, Crimes against Humanity, and Genocide in Bosnia and Herzegovina's Cantonal and District Courts, 9 July 2008.
Any similarities between the analysis of the cases in the HRW report and in this paper can be attributed to the fact that the author drafted parts of both documents. However, the views expressed herein are solely the author's.

1 'Rule of law reform is a term that covers a range of initiatives and projects, means different things to different organizations, and has ranged in content and focus over time ... should be distinguished from the Law and Development phase that preceded it in the 1960s and early 1970s, although there are clearly overlaps. The current rule of law reform programming is a more global phenomenon, supported by a far greater number of agencies and countries, and is rationalized on the basis of economic development, democracy, and peace. Its approach to the issues of reform and rebuilding of a legal system is on the whole more nuanced.' K. Samuels, Rule of Law Reform in Post-Conflict Countries- Operational Initiatives and Lessons Learnt, in: Social Development Papers 1 (World Bank, October 2006).

Former Yugoslavia (ICTY).[2] The ICTY was mandated to 'bring to justice those responsible for serious violations of international humanitarian law committed in the former Yugoslavia since 1991 and thus contribute to the restoration and maintenance of peace in the region.'[3] Concurrent with this international initiative, the local courts in Bosnia were tasked with trying 'less serious' war crimes cases.[4]

With the closure of the ICTY, the ability of Bosnian courts to prosecute war crimes cases will become a major manifestation of this IRL implementation because they will be the only ones engaged in these prosecutions. Thus, the ability of local courts to prosecute war crimes and their compliance with international law and general standards of fairness represents a tangible way of assessing the impact of IRL in a post-conflict society and highlights potential problems in its implementation. The work of local courts is also illustrative of the process of re-strengthening the domestic rule of law by the introduction of international legal oversight and international legal institutions. For example, the Office of the High Representative (OHR) was appointed to help focus the number of courts, their locations, jurisdiction, and ethnic balance.

Post-conflict adjudication systems must account for factors outside of structural and rule of law implementation mechanisms, and acknowledge that the post-conflict restructuring efforts must be comprehensive and account for economic, sociological, historical, cultural, and anthropological aspects of the society in question. For the implementation of the rule of law is hindered not only by legal procedural and substantive issues, but by larger political and social limitations. Neither *thin* nor *thick* concepts of the rule of law can exist without a desire by the individuals and the society as a whole to be *bound* by these laws. Institutions without the support of the people are nothing more than hollow, abstract structures.

With these considerations in mind, this chapter will examine some of the decisions taken by the local courts in Bosnia. The domestic cases were compiled by the Organization for Security and Cooperation in Europe (OSCE) and Human Rights Watch.[5] Although Bosnian law provides for access to information, it is difficult in practice, for an individual researcher to obtain these decisions. There were no online research resources for local courts at the time this research was completed.[6] This research therefore primarily rests upon domestic cases gathered by the OSCE.

---

2 UNSC Resolution 827 (25 May 1993).

3 ICTY Mandate, available at www.icty.org/sid/320 (visited 5 December 2010).

4 I will elaborate on this concept of 'less serious' later in the chapter.

5 Current until 2008.

6 When contact with the courts was established, they at times demanded that 'all the cases' that were desired be listed. Therefore, it was difficult to establish if there were additional cases of interest that ought to have been reviewed.

Specifically, this chapter will examine the capacity and ability of the local BiH courts to comply with and uphold international criminal law norms and standards, and the receptiveness of the judicial branch in this post-conflict situation to the international rule of law. This analysis will highlight the local Bosnian courts' failure, in some instances, to follow international precedent. While acknowledging that appropriate international precedent may in some instances be debatable, and standards may be applied differently by the various international tribunals and institutions, this chapter will establish that local domestic court decisions in Bosnia are at times irreconcilable with basic principles of war crimes prosecution. For example, the Mostar Cantonal Court held that the existence of 'war-time circumstances' during the commission of a war crime constituted a mitigating factor in sentencing[7] – a result antithetical to any international criminal legal standard applied or adopted in international law. In other instances, reference was made to the passage of time between the actual commission of the crime and the trial as a mitigating factor in sentencing.[8] The acceptance of these circumstances as mitigating factors undermines the basic understanding and purpose of international criminal law.

The chapter concludes by proposing potential ways to rectify these and other judicial inadequacies.

2. BACKGROUND: FROM THE TRENCHES TO THE HAGUE AND THEN BACK AGAIN ...

The Socialist Federal Republic of Yugoslavia (SFRY) was created after the Second World War.[9] It was composed of six republics: Bosnia, Croatia, Macedonia,

---

7 Mostar Cantonal Court 28 June 2004, *Case of Zvonko Trlin*, Verdict Number K-41/02, p. 15; Mostar Cantonal Court 26 April 2004, *Case of Romeo Blazevic*, Verdict Number K-43/02, p. 18; Mostar Cantonal Court 6 July 2004, *Case of Mario Matic*, Verdict Number K-28/03, p. 14; see Still Waiting: Bringing Justice for War Crimes, Crimes against Humanity, and Genocide in Bosnia and Herzegovina's Cantonal and District Courts (Human Rights Watch, 9 July 2008), available at www.hrw.org/en/reports/2008/07/09/still-waiting-0 ('HRW Report').

8 Mostar Cantonal Court 28 June 2004, *Case of Zvonko Trlin*, Verdict Number K-41/02, p. 15; Mostar Cantonal Court 26 April 2004, *Case of Romeo Blazevic*, Verdict Number K-43/02, p. 18; Mostar Cantonal Court 6 July 2004, *Case of Mario Matic*, Verdict Number K-28/03, p. 14. See HRW Report, *supra* note 7.

9 For further information about the history of SFRY and of her peoples, see eg M. Cherif Basssiouni and P. Manikas, The Law of the International Criminal Tribunal for the Former Yugoslavia 1–63 (New York: Transnational Publishers, 1996); J. Archer, Red Rebel – Tito of Yugoslavia (New York: Simon & Schuster); T. Judah, The Serbs: History, Myth and the Destruction of Yugoslavia (Yale University Press, 1997); J. Kalvoda, Tioism and the Masters of Imposture (New York: Vantage Press); J. Lampe, Yugoslavia as History – Twice there was a Country (Cambridge: Cambridge University Press, 1996); P. Lendvai and L. Parcell, Yugoslavia without Yugoslavs: the roots of the crisis, 67(2) International Affairs 251–261 (1991); H. Poulton, The Balkans – Minorities and States in Conflict (United Kingdom:

Montenegro, Serbia,[10] and Slovenia, and united under the common identity of Yugoslavs. In the early 1990s, the SFRY began its eventually violent demise. Slovenia first sought independence and attained that objective in relative peace. However, the independence movements in Croatia,[11] Bosnia, and later in Serbia[12] were anything but peaceful.

The international community eventually reacted to the conflict in the Balkans. On 25 May 1993, the UN Security Council established the International Criminal Tribunal for the Former Yugoslavia (ICTY),[13] which was granted primary jurisdiction over international crimes committed in the former Yugoslavia. It was therefore able to assume jurisdiction over cases from the domestic courts throughout the former Yugoslavia.

Two years after the creation of the ICTY, peace was established in Bosnia. A general peace agreement, the Dayton Agreement,[14] was signed in December 1995, in Dayton, Ohio. The Dayton Agreement provided for a new Constitution in Bosnia and Herzegovina along with a territorial settlement between the Muslim-Croat Federation and the Serb Republic. The Dayton-mandated Constitution established two separate Entities in Bosnia and Herzegovina: the Federation of Bosnia & Herzegovina (FBiH) and the Republika Srpska (RS). Although some powers were reserved for the Federal Authority, the majority of power was delegated to two primary Entities within the government.[15]

Minority Rights Group, 1991); C. Rogel, The Breakup of Yugoslavia and the War in Bosnia (Wesport: Greenwood Press); D. Stremac, War of Words: Washington tackles the Yugoslav Conflict (US: Praeger Publishers, 1999); S. Stankovic, The end of the Tito era-Yugoslavia's Dillemmas (Stanford: Hoover Press Publications); M. Tanner, Croatia – A Nation Forged in War (US: Yale Nota Bene, 2001).

10 Within Serbia there were also two autonomous regions of Kosovo in the South and Vojvodina, in the North.

11 Croatia desired independence, which was met with resistance from its minority of Serbs in the region of Krajina. The war lasted until August 1995 when between 150,000–200,000 Serbs were expelled from the region.

12 Within Serbia, conflict arose when the Kosovo-Albanian majority in the autonomous province of Kosovo (its autonomy was revoked in 1989) made claims for independence from Serbia.

13 SC Resolution 827 (S/Res/827) (25 May 1993).

14 The General Framework Agreement for Peace in Bosnia and Herzegovina, signed 14 December 1995 ('Dayton Accords').

15 See W. Burke-White, Domestic Influence of International Criminal Tribunals: The International Criminal Tribunal for the Former Yugoslavia and the Creation of the State Court of Bosnia-Herzegovina, 46 Columbia Journal of Transnational Law 286 (2007–2008); in general for this section see Burke-White and the Dayton Accords, *supra* note 14. On the Bosnian Human Rights Chamber created pursuant to Dayton, see A. Buyse, Virtuous Flexibility – The Application of International Human Rights Norms by the Bosnian Human Rights Chamber, in this volume at p. 175. For detailed discussion of the War Crimes Chamber of BiH, see K. Uhlířová, War Crimes Chamber of the Court of Bosnia and Herzegovina: Seeding "International Standards of Justice"?, in this volume at p. 195. The Constitution also largely delegated the judicial authority in the state to the two Entities, RS and FBiH.

2.1. ENTITY JUDICIARIES

In addition to the state Ministry of Justice, FBiH and RS each have their own independent justice ministry and court system. Both Entities are divided into judicial districts; FBiH into ten cantons, and RS into five administrative units.[16] Initially, the primary responsibility for enforcement of war crimes fell under the judicial systems created within the two Entities.

The judiciary in the two Entities attempted to prosecute war crimes, with little success. Because of the loss of members of the legal profession combined with the destruction and lack of proper facilities and equipment, the courts were unable to function properly. The courts in both Entities were dominated by members of the majority ethnicity in the respective region, the judges were inexperienced and they were appointed on ethnic or political grounds.[17] Cases were politicized and allegations of arbitrary arrests and unfair trials were widespread. Many convictions were made *in absentia* with sentences that included the death penalty or life imprisonment.[18]

In response to many of these concerns, the 'Rules of the Road' procedure, established under the Rome Agreement of 18 February 1996, was put in place, forcing Bosnian officials to submit potential cases to the ICTY for review before arrest and indictment.[19] The ICTY would review the case and indicate whether it was suitable for further investigation and trial by it or by the local courts. Notably, the ICTY described the engagement of the Rules of Road procedure as a way of re-establishing the rule of law.[20]

Since 2002, judicial reform efforts in Bosnia have helped to streamline the process of case prosecution allocation.[21] Between 2002 and 2004, a federal State Court was established to deal with organized crime, war crimes, and crimes in the federal penal code, removing some of the responsibility for such matters from the constituent Entities. With the increased confidence in domestic courts

---

16 *Supra*, note 14.

17 OSCE Mission to Bosnia and Herzegovina – Human Rights Department, War Crimes Trials before the Domestic Courts of Bosnia and Herzegovina: Progress and Obstacles (March 2005).

18 Progress and Obstacles, *supra* note 17.

19 Book of Rules on the Review of War Crimes Cases, Art. 2(1); Rome Agreement, signed 18 February 1996; Progress and Obstacles, *supra* note 17; HRW Report, *supra* note 7.

20 Throughout its existence, the ICTY Office of the Prosecutor (OTP) has worked closely with the new states and territories that emerged from the former Yugoslavia on their domestic prosecutions. A number of key programmes have helped re-establish the rule of law in criminal matters in this war-torn region; ICTY Document, Working with the region, available at www.icty.org/sid/96.

21 The Office of the High Commissioner Representative was appointed to help focus the number of courts, their location, jurisdiction, and ethnic balance. Additionally, judges were evaluated, and where bias or corruption was found, they were replaced. Moreover, the court moved from a civil law system to an adversarial system.

due to judicial reform, the ICTY finally began to refer cases back to the State Court of Bosnia and Herzegovina.

The Rules of the Road program ended on 1 October 2004. Shortly thereafter, the ICTY Prosecutor stated that the ICTY would 'no longer be in a position to review war crimes cases and that the Court of Bosnia and Herzegovina Prosecutor should take over responsibility.'[22] The Completion Strategy 'required the ICTY to reduce its caseload and to encourage domestic trials as a cost-effective alternative to international prosecutions.'[23] As a result, the ICTY shifted its role from being the primary, and in part supervisory, adjudicator, to that of being a complementary judicial body. Under this model, the ICTY can send cases to national courts, monitor domestic proceedings, and remit cases to the ICTY if it sees fit.[24]

Although war crimes prosecution was slow after the war, after 2005, and in part in accordance with the completion of the Rules of the Road program and the Completion Strategy adopted by the Security Council,[25] the number of prosecuted cases increased. Also, in 2005, a specialized War Crimes Chamber of Bosnia and Herzegovina was established as one of the divisions of the State Court.[26] It was in part established due to a belief that the Entities in Bosnia could not prosecute crimes 'credibly and impartially in accordance with international standards of due process.'[27] This did not mean that the State Court was given full jurisdiction over war crimes; state prosecutors determine whether cases are 'highly sensitive' or 'sensitive',[28] and the State Court is responsible for adjudicating cases that are 'highly sensitive', whereas the cantonal courts (RS) and district courts (FBiH) are responsible for adjudicating 'sensitive' cases.[29]

22 Working with the region, *supra* note 20, p. 321.

23 Burke-White, *supra* note 15, p. 320.

24 Burke-White, *supra* note 15, p. 320.

25 The 'Rules of the Road' Program ended on 1 October 2004.

26 I will reference this as the 'State Court' throughout the paper. On the War Crimes Chamber, see Uhlířová, *supra* note 15.

27 L. Johnson, Late-Breaking Issues and the International Criminal Tribunals, 99 American Society of International Law Procedure 285 (2005).

28 Progress and Obstacles, *supra* note 17, p. 18: 'The sensitivity criteria, intended to serve as guidance for BiH Prosecutor's office in the determination of the appropriate venue for trial, has been elaborated upon by the BiH Prosecutors Office in the document "Orientation Criteria for Sensitive Rules of the Road Cases", adopted by the Collegium of Prosecutors on 12 October 2004 as an Annex to the BoR. "Highly Sensitive" cases must be tried by the BiH Court while "sensitive cases may, contingent upon the discretion of the Chief Prosecutor, be remitted for trial to the cantonal and strict courts." It is anticipated that "highly sensitive" cases will form only a small proportion of the total number of outstanding domestic cases.' However, these guidelines are sometimes still confusing. See eg *Matic and Kresic* from the Mostar Cantonal Court; Orientation Criteria for Sensitive Rules of the Road Cases (Annex to the Book of Rules on the Review of War Crimes Cases) (A-441/04) (12 October 2004) ('Orientation Criteria').

29 This determination is set out in the Orientation Criteria, *supra* note 28. The purpose of this chapter is not to examine this classification and whether it is appropriate. Due to limitations

While the ICTY has jurisdiction over the most serious cases, the State Court thus has responsibility over 'highly sensitive cases' and the local courts over 'sensitive cases'. This classification does not, however, devalue the importance of the work relegated to the Entities. Despite the terminology and classification, the local courts are confronted with cases that are quite serious in nature and of immense importance to the local communities. The perpetrators are not abstracted politicians or high-ranking officials, but more often than not, they are the victim's neighbours and former colleagues, who at times continue to reside in the same small communities as the victims.

The case of *Dominik Ilijasevic* highlights the potential seriousness of the cases examined by the local courts.[30] In that case, the accused was convicted for a number of killings, burning of homes, and torture. In one incident, the accused, along with Miroslav Antic, placed a bleeding decapitated arm on the back of an automobile. The accused drove the car with the arm on display around the village. Once the vehicle stopped, the accused exited the vehicle and pointed to dead Muslim soldiers' bodies in a derogatory gesture. Antic then took a decapitated head of one of the soldiers and placed it on the front marker of the vehicle.[31] In another case, involving Mario Matic, the accused approached a column of prisoners, including civilians, and after calling out to one of them in a derogatory manner, proceeded to beat another civilian. He then ordered a civilian, Ismet Kovacevic, to step out of the column, whereupon he fatally shot him.[32] In the *Fikret Smajlovic* case, the accused was a prisoner who befriended the camp guards, and then, in this newfound position of authority, beat a number of prisoners to death.[33]

In some sense, and for many victims, these cases could be more significant than those of higher courts because they concern people who were the direct perpetrators of crimes rather than persons in a position of authority who were responsible for ordering or allowing the crimes.[34] These cases are personal, sensitive, and worthy of careful analysis. Most importantly, the ability to historically integrate the story of the conflict, the relevant actors, and to allocate punishment where it is due, and the eventual successful legitimization of this process will assist in the reconciliation process of the Bosnian nation. It is difficult to fathom how a country can move past such a monumental conflict

of space, I omit any further discussion on the appropriateness of these classifications and the impact of the same upon the prosecution of crimes.

30 Supreme Court 22 January 2008, *Case of Dominik Ilijasevic*, Verdict Number 070-0-Kz-07-000387.

31 *Case of Dominik Ilijasevic*, *supra* note 30, p. 3–4.

32 Mostar Cantonal Court 6 July 2004, *Case of Mario Matic*, Verdict Number K-28/03, affirmed, Supreme Court of FBIH 1 December 2005, Verdict Number Kz-382/04.

33 Tuzla Cantonal Court 13 February 2002 *Case of Fikret Smajlovic* (a.k.a. Piklic), Verdict Number K-25/01, affirmed, Supreme Court of FBiH 16 February 2005, Verdict Number Kz-208/05.

34 HRW Report, *supra* note 7, in general.

without effectively addressing crimes which still cause pain and unease within the local communities.

Any effective restructuring of the legal system and establishment of the rule of law requires examination of factors such as the structuring and functioning of government institutions, the impact of the media, and law enforcement mechanisms and training. For example, if the government does not support prosecution, if the media demonizes the process, or if the police fail to enforce decisions, international attention focused solely on local courts as IRL implementers seems too thin. In the case of Bosnia, a post-conflict state, a thicker version is preferable.

For there to be any fruitful discussion about the role of the rule of law in a post-conflict society, factors such as societal cohesion, institutions and their democratic accountability must be kept in mind, along with legal reform. Although detailed analysis of such extra-legal factors is beyond the scope of the present chapter, it should be read with these considerations in mind. Thus, any critique of the failure of local courts to properly apply international law must be considered in the context of discord within domestic civil society and antagonism towards international influences, including international assistance and various other capacity-building measures.[35]

The chapter will now turn to examining and evaluating the application of international law in the domestic context.

3. TO PROSECUTE A WAR CRIME: DETERMINING THE APPROPRIATE LEGAL STANDARD

Bosnia's War Crimes Processing Strategy was adopted by the Council of Ministers of Bosnia and Herzegovina in December 2008.[36] Its adoption meant that less complicated cases would be transferred to local courts, which would then address these cases using the standards established by the State Court. Under this model, the Criminal Code of Bosnia would be the applicable law. However, the local courts continue to apply the old Yugoslav laws to war crimes prosecution, and the implementation of the Completion Strategy is slow. In order to assist the transfer to lower courts, the Bosnian Parliament adopted amendments to the Law on Criminal Proceedings of Bosnia in September 2009.[37]

---

35 Rowen, Social Reality and Philosophical Ideals in Transitional Justice, 7 Cardozo Public Law Policy and Ethics Journal 93 (2008–9). See the issue of 'corrupt judicial practices', at p. 114.

36 High Judicial and Prosecutorial Council of Bosnia and Herzegovina, Annual Report 2009, p. 139.

37 D. Dzidic, Slow Transfer of Cases Undermines War Crimes Strategy, BIRN BIH (5 January 2010), available at www.bim.ba/en/200/10/24791/.

But as the referrals to Bosnian local courts are occurring at a slow pace, this may mean that the target completion goals for war crimes cases may not be met.[38]

A few sub-issues are highlighted in this section. The first is the application of the appropriate criminal law and relevant articles in the adjudication of war crimes. The second is the local courts' ability to interpret international criminal standards, including the interpretation of key concepts like command responsibility. The third sub-issue, which is related to the second, is the courts' approach to sentencing.

3.1. DETERMINING THE DOMESTIC LEGAL STANDARD

There have at times been as many as four different criminal codes in use simultaneously by various Bosnian courts.[39] In 2003, Bosnia and Herzegovina instituted a new Criminal Code (BiHCC). This code is used by the State Court,[40] but the local courts tend to prosecute under the former Socialist Federal Republic of Yugoslavia Criminal Code (SFRY CC), the code in force during the armed conflict. In addition, a small number of courts have also applied the interim 1998 Federation of Bosnia and Herzegovina Criminal Code (FBiH CC).[41]

According to interviews by Human Rights Watch with staff of the State Court of Bosnia, the application of the appropriate criminal code 'has been the source of some confusion and disagreement.'[42] The application of the SFRY CC resulted primarily from the rationale that the application of a new criminal code would be an act of retroactive application of law for the war crimes committed. However, these crimes were included in the SFRY CC, so it would not have been an application of *new* law, per se. The OSCE has reported that the difference in the application of criminal codes can be explained by the inconsistent understanding of the 'principle of leniency' that prescribes application of a more lenient law to the accused if the law has been changed.[43]

This overlap of criminal codes has resulted in varied sentences and interpretations of the same factual scenarios. For example, a sentence in the State Court can include sentences of up to forty-five years, whereas for the same offense, the application of SFRY CC would mean a sentence of up to fifteen

38 Dzidic, *supra* note 37.

39 N. Jelacic, BIRN Submission (1 September 2006), available at www2.ohchr.org/English/bodies/hrc/docs88/BIRN_submission_Sep_2006.doc.

40 In a few cases courts had even used the interim 1998 Federation of Bosnia and Herzegovina Criminal Code. OSCE Report, Moving towards a Harmonized Application of the Law, Applicable in War Crimes Cases before Courts in Bosnia and Herzegovina 5 (August 2008) ('OSCE Harmonization').

41 OSCE Harmonization, *supra* note 40, p. 5.

42 HRW Report, *supra* note 7.

43 OSCE Harmonization, *supra* note 40, p. 10.

years.[44] State Court sentences are twice as long as sentences delivered by the Entity courts.[45] The actual definitions of crimes are also impacted by the lack of uniformity. The BiH CC has a more comprehensive definition of war crimes, and it has provisions for crimes against humanity; it defines command responsibility, and does not account for the defense of 'superior orders'.[46] Enacting a uniform standard of criminal law for both the local courts and the State Court can rectify this problem.

In March 2007, the Constitutional Court of BiH ruled that this lack of uniformity in the Criminal Codes 'undermined the rule of law and the equal treatment of citizens before the law.'[47] It 'urged' the local courts to use the BiH CC.[48] These concerns were echoed by the High Representative, the Parliamentary Assembly of the Council of Europe, and the OSCE,[49] which recommended the use of the BiH CC because it would 'likely result in the more effective administration of justice', assist with greater consistency in sentencing, and more appropriately address serious violations as it is consistent with the jurisprudence established by the ICTY.[50] Following this decision, the National War Crimes Strategy elaborated that 'harmonization of the court practice will also be facilitated by decisions of the Court of BiH on the transfer of cases', meaning that the transferred cases by the lower courts 'may be obliged to apply the substantive law of Bosnia and Herzegovina. By applying the existing provision contained in Article 13 of the Law on Court of BiH, the Court of BiH shall issue binding directions containing the Court's interpretation in relation to the applicable law.'[51] As of 2011, the criminal codes have not been unified.

---

44 Dzidic, *supra* note 37.

45 See OSCE Harmonization, *supra* note 40, p. 8, citing n 11: 'Since the adoption of the Criminal Code of Bosnia and Herzegovina, the Court of Bosnia and Herzegovina has found 12 individuals guilty of war crimes and crimes against humanity and imposed upon them an average sentence of 17 years of imprisonment. In the same period, courts in the two entities and in the Brcko District have 47 individuals guilty of war crimes with an average sentence of nine years.' Compare also the cases of *Mato Derek* of 21 June 2005 from the Novi Travnik Cantonal Court with that of *Goran and Zoran Damjanovic* from the State Court. In the *Derek* decision the court sentenced the accused to one year and eight months for cruel treatment of prisoners, whereas the court in *Damjanovic*, for a similar crime, gave a sentence of ten and half years.

46 See OSCE Harmonization, *supra* note 40, p. 5.

47 *Abduladhim Maktouf* argued that the retroactive application of the BiHCC violated Article 7 of the EIDHR. The Constitutional Court rejected this argument. It ruled that BiHCC was applicable because the criminal activities were already in accordance with the general principles of law recognized by civilized nations.' Constitutional Court of Bosnia and Herzegovina, *Case of Abduladhim Maktouf*, Decision on Admissibility and Merits, AP-1785/06; OSCE Harmonization, *supra* note 40, p. 5.

48 OSCE Harmonization, *supra* note 40, p. 6.

49 OSCE Harmonization, *supra* note 40, p. 6, citing BIRN, Justice Report Interview, Miroslav lajcak: Bosnia Needs Justice (6 August 2007), available at www.bim.ba/en/75/10/3795; Parliamentary Assembly of the Council of Europe's Resolution 1564 (2007).

50 OSCE Harmonization, *supra* note 40, p. 6.

51 National War Crimes Strategy (December 2008), p. 16, available at www.adh-geneva.ch/RULAC/pdf_state/War-Crimes-Strategy-f-18-12-08.pdf.

3.2. APPLICABLE LAW: INTERNATIONAL OR DOMESTIC?

The ability to prosecute war crimes domestically by applying international criminal law (ICL) is frustrated in at least two aspects: it is at times difficult to determine the applicable ICL,[52] and even when the law is relatively clear, courts frequently fail to apply it.

ICL exists as a combination of criminal law and international law. Although criminal law is generally firmly entrenched in domestic law, international law 'include[s] unwritten, fluid rules of customary international law.'[53] In other words, international law can be vague and subject to a tension between different principles of international law.[54] Academics have offered that 'international criminal law is [a] relatively new discipline and it does not pretend to be a complete system of criminal law … it has inconsistencies and incoherencies that are the result of its formation in political negotiations.'[55] In other words, ICL itself may require 'harmonization'.[56]

Some ICL standards have a longer standing history, such as the concept of command responsibility which derives its origins from the Nuremberg and Tokyo Tribunals. Originally, it was understood as a positive legal norm by virtue of its application in the 1977 Additional Protocol I to the 1949 Geneva Conventions. However, the international criminal tribunals have expanded its scope and 'since then, command responsibility as a mode of liability has become firmly anchored in customary international law.'[57] As such, it includes the responsibility for 'failure to act'.[58]

The *Cupina* case demonstrates the failure of the court to take into account the law regarding command responsibility and, specifically, accountability for a superior's 'failure to act'.[59] In a 2001 decision, the Mostar Cantonal Court held that there was a responsibility to treat prisoners humanely and that the legislation should be interpreted to include a failure to prevent the offense from occurring.[60]

---

52 E. Kristjánsdóttir, A. Nollkaemper and C. Ryngaert, Introduction, in this volume at p. 6–7.

53 S. Joseph and A. McBeth (eds), Research Handbook on International Human Rights Law 242 (Edward Elgar Publishing, 2010).

54 Kristjánsdóttir, Nollkaemper and Ryngaert, *supra* note 52, p. 6–7.

55 R. Cryer, H. Friman, D. Robinson and E. Wilmshurst, International Criminal Law and Procedure 452 (Cambridge University Press, 2008).

56 Cryer, citing L. Green, Grave Breaches are Crimes Against Humanity? 8 US Air Force Academy Journal of Legal Studies 19 (1997–1998).

57 Joseph and McBeth, *supra* note 53, p. 263–4.

58 Joseph and McBeth, *supra* note 53, p. 263–4. Note also the Introduction, *supra* note 52, and S. Weill and I. Jovanović, War Crimes Prosecution in a Post-Conflict Era and a Pluralism of Jurisdictions: The Experience of the Belgrade War Crimes Chamber, in this volume at p. 257 *et seq.*, discussing the difficulty of the level of 'control' that is applicable for command responsibility.

59 Mostar Cantonal Court 6 July 2001, *Case of Mirsad Cupina*, Verdict Number K-24/99.

60 *Case of Mirsad Cupina*, *supra* note 59. The court held that the legislature did not intend to omit 'failure to act' from Article 144 SFRYCC. 'Failure to act' or a 'failure to do' are included

However, the Federation Supreme Court ordered a re-trial. In the re-trial, the Mostar Court held that a failure to act could not be punished under the SFRY CC.[61] It was accepted that the application of international criminal law is broad[62] but that ultimately, for it to be applicable, it had to be considered in light of the Indictment.[63]

In order to achieve a sustained, fair, and equitable implementation of IRL, domestic decisions need to be well reasoned, clear, and in compliance with ICL, to the extent possible. Otherwise, decisions that are convoluted applications of ICL, or worse still, those that stray from established ICL norms, set dangerous precedents and stifle the progression towards a coherent conception of international law. The next part focuses on specific problems of implementation.

4. SPECIFIC PROBLEMS IN THE CANTONAL AND DISTRICT COURTS IN APPLYING INTERNATIONAL CRIMINAL LAW

Prosecution of war crimes in general is difficult. In a post-conflict society, and especially in rural areas with limited infrastructures, inadequately trained judiciaries, and a distrustful civil society, successful prosecution may not be a realistic aspiration. This is further complicated by other factors, such as availability and treatment of witnesses' evidence.

Rules of international law cannot exist as mere abstract principles of law without being grounded in procedural and structural confines of a domestic legal system. In other words, principles of international law, without actual practical implementation mechanisms, have little force in the domestic context. Evidentiary issues are therefore fundamental for the legitimization of international law principles within a domestic context.

---

in the commission of a crime. Although Article 144 makes a distinction between 'commanding' and an 'act', implicit within this legislative act is also the notion of a 'failure to act'.

61 See for example, Mostar Cantonal Court 24 January 2007, *Case of Mirsad Cupina*, Verdict Number K-24/99, and Supreme Court of Federation BiH 11 September 2003, *Case of Mirsad Cupina*, Verdict Number K-455/01; see also HRW Report, *supra* note 7, p. 60. The court interpreted the Indictment to hold the accused responsible for behaviour during that specific time period, but that it does not hold him responsible for participating in particular events. This personal participation was a necessary requirement of Article 144 of SFRY. HRW Report, *supra* note 7, p. 43.
Further, the court interpreted that Article 144 does not account for the act of failing to act and for the failure to punish people. It requires the action of commanding.

62 For example, the court reference about the existence of international law, including the Geneva Conventions.

63 Mostar Cantonal Court 24 January 2007, *Case of Mirsad Cupina*, Verdict Number K-24/99.

4.1. CAN INTERNATIONAL LAW MAKE CONCESSION FOR INADEQUATE EVIDENCE AT LOCAL LEVEL?

Evidence gathering represents a unique challenge in war crimes prosecutions at both the international and domestic levels. In the context of prosecuting international crimes on a mass scale, involving numerous offenders, the problem of evidence amplifies the difficulties. Serious evidentiary challenges may give rise to the perception that the local courts are incompetent.[64]

The difficulty of gathering evidence in domestic war crimes prosecutions was demonstrated by the case against Edin Semic before the Cantonal Court in Zenica,[65] affirmed by the Supreme Court of Bosnia and Herzegovina.[66] The accused had participated in an operation to confiscate illegal weapons as a member of the army of BiH. During this activity, he entered the home of the victim, Dragan Radivojevic. Shots were fired at the victim. The dispute at the trial was whether the accused was responsible for the fatal shots. The court concluded that the initial shots were fired by the accused, but that later shots (the fatal shots) were or may have been fired by another individual, Ibrahim Bosno, who was dead at the time of the trial.[67]

In its decision, the court articulated a number of problems it faced in this case: 'In a normal situation, the post-mortem of the victim would have been completed by a qualified individual, not by a general practitioner. The scene of the crime would have been marked, rather than cleaned; the access to the crime scene would be restricted; and the weapons confiscated …'[68] In this instance, none of these general methods of obtaining and evaluating evidence were available. The case was based on inconclusive evidence and witness testimony. No evidence conclusively pointed to the accused. In other words, the court was being asked to issue a criminal verdict on the basis of evidence that would not hold up in a 'normal' (peace-time) prosecution. The international fight against impunity for war crimes through local criminal procedures thus starkly juxtaposed domestic and international rule of law concerns. Did the prosecution of war crimes require the court to relax the standards of due process?

During the war, evidence was often politicized and compiled in a manner such that it could assist the cause of the particular majority or those in power in

64 Also, at times, evidence was actually destroyed by the local police: see HRW Report, *supra* note 7, p. 28.

65 Zenica Cantonal Court 26 March 2007, *Case Against Edin Semic*, Number 004–04-K6–000 019.

66 J. Mrkic-Bjelovic, Zenica: Fear Puts War Crimes Trials in Danger. Local Justice Puts War Crimes Trials in Danger (14 November 2007), available at www.bim.ba/en/89/10/5808/.

67 This assessment was made in part due to the testimony of the soldiers that were present at the scene.

68 Zenica Cantonal Court 26 March 2007, *Case Against Edin Semic*, Number 004–04-K6–000 019, p. 11.

the given region. As such, even if evidence were available, its value or validity might be questionable.

In addition to these problems, there is not enough coordination and information-sharing between the various judicial bodies in BiH. In order to guide this process, there should be greater collaboration between the State Court and the local courts, between the ICTY and the local courts, and between the local courts and the former republics of the SFRY. The State Court is already tasked with cases similar to those of the local courts, yet there are no formal mechanisms in place for accessing relevant information. Although access to the ICTY database may not have been fully possible, the prosecutors in various courts have been reluctant to access the resources that are available, including those available from the ICTY liaison office in Bosnia.[69] Establishing cooperation between the former republics is imperative for the strengthening of the quantity and quality of available evidence. There is an agreement on cooperation between FBiH and Croatia,[70] but the prosecutors need to actually use this mechanism, and this mechanism needs to be practicable.[71]

4.2. WITNESS ISSUES

There is a significant problem with the reliance on witnesses as the primary source of evidence in local war crimes prosecutions. The most obvious problem is the 'battle of witnesses'. War, unlike singular acts of civil disobedience, involves a multitude of individuals. Crimes may be committed by groups or by members of groups against a single person or against a group of individuals. Presumably, in regions where the accused's ethnicity is favoured, it should be relatively easy for the defence to gather individuals sympathetic to the accused to discredit and discourage the witnesses from testifying, especially considering that the witness may already be fearful of testifying. This is generally a problem for the application of international law in a domestic context, because – in this case – ICL has to account for the unique problems presented with its application that do not arise in other domestic contexts.

At times, testimony provided by witnesses has been reformulated by the judges, and asserted in a way that was not intended by the witnesses. Intimidated

---

69 Applicability of ICTY evidence may be disputed by the courts: HRW Report, *supra* note 7, p. 29–30.

70 Agreement Between the Government of Bosnia and Herzegovina, the Government of the Federation Bosnia and Herzegovina, and the Government of the Republic of Croatia, on Legal Assistance in Civil and Criminal Matters, Official Gazette of the Republic of Bosnia and Herzegovina – Special Edition, International Agreements (27 May 1996).

71 In the past, cooperation was lacking. For example, with regards to the *Mirolav Antic* decision, Croatia refused to extradite Antic, and in 2001, a court in Split released Antic on the grounds that the Sarajevo Cantonal Court did not submit the evidence required to proceed.

by the process, or perhaps indifferent to it, many witnesses do not raise this reformulation as an issue. In the *Ilijasevic* trial, a few of the witnesses made admissions about the difference between their knowledge of the events and the recorded statements.[72] Ultimately, this serves to undermine the credibility of the witness even when the witness is truthful.

In the trial of Edin Hakanovic,[73] the court specified how the only witness, Milica Kegelj, refused to testify, stating that she did not have faith in the court system. The other witnesses' testimonies, according to the court, were found to constitute hearsay evidence. Interestingly, a year prior to this trial, Ivica Kegelj testified at an ICTY hearing and directly placed the accused at the scene of the crime. However, when questioned, the ICTY witness had no knowledge about the *Hakanovic* trial which was in process concurrently with the ICTY proceedings.[74]

In addition to problems that arise during trial, there are special infrastructural and political issues that must be accounted for with regard to witnesses. Bosnia's War Crimes Processing Strategy includes measures regarding witness protection. The witness and victims support system was not established as of January 2010.[75] One such example includes witnesses in Bosnia often reporting death threats and harassment after participating in the judicial process. In turn, this decreases the number of witnesses willing to testify, impacting both the prosecution and the defence teams.

Although such issues are largely financial and infrastructural, there is also a culture of insensitivity when it comes to witness protection. Specifically,

---

72 Balkans Justice Bulletin, The Trial of Dominik Ilijasevic (Human Rights Watch, January 2004), available at www.hrw.org/legacy/backgrounder/eca/balkans0104.htm#_ftnref10. In note 12, HRW states 'Himzo Likic, testifying in the trial of Dominik Ilijasevic on March 25, 2003, denied that during the interrogation in Vares, in October 1993, Ilijasevic had put a gun into his mouth, although the statement recorded by the investigating judge contained that claim; Rusid Avdic said on April 22, 2003, that the investigation minutes distorted the content of a conversation between the witness and the accused in mid-1993. In the trial of Tomo Mihajlovic, the number of witnesses who complained about the adequacy of their recorded statements from investigation was particularly high.'

73 21 July 2005, *Case of Edin Hakanovic*, Verdict Number K-6/03; Anonymous, Zenica: Hankavic one year of prison for crimes against Croats, *Slobodna Dalmacija* (27 January 2009), available at [in BCS]: http://urednik.slobodnadalmacija.hr/BiH/tabid/68/articleType/ArticleView/articleId/39724/Default.aspx. In the case of *Edin Hakanovic* the court examined and acquitted the accused with regard to his responsibility in the formation of human shields. An appeal was made and the case was re-tried by the local courts. In January 2009, the court found the accused guilty and sentenced him to one year in prison.

74 ICTY 9 March 2004, *Prosecutor v. Enver Hadzihasanovic and Amir Kubura*, Transcript Excerpts, Case number IT-01-47-T.

75 E. Mackic, War Crimes Strategy Misses One Deadline After Another, BIRN BIH (8 January 2010), available at www.bim.ba/en/200/10/24864/; Roundtable discussions regarding witness protections include entity and district court level members. See for example, S. Ucanbarlic, OSCE: Safe Environment for Witnesses, BIRN Report (December 2009), available at http://birn.eu.com/en/1/200/24394/?tpl=30.

measures such as separating the witnesses from the defendant's family could be undertaken at minimal cost. Non-governmental organizations in the region have reported that witnesses were sometimes transported in buses alongside the accused's friends and family.[76] Also, in cases where the witnesses are to testify anonymously, behind a screen, his or her name may be read out in court and later published.[77] Such incidents could be avoided given greater awareness. Prosecutors, courts, and other relevant personnel need to be aware and sensitive to the needs of the victims.

Victims and witnesses protection issues at the local level may be even more sensitive than at the ICTY in The Hague, where their comings and goings at the courthouse are not as obvious to the community. As with evidence, the special circumstances of war and its underlying tensions raise serious due process and rule of law challenges at the local level as domestic courts grapple with the requirements of international law and the international fight against impunity. More technical support and awareness-raising should accompany the international community's demand for international justice at home.

4.3. SENTENCING

One of the most glaring issues in the cantonal and district courts' imposition of sentences is their interpretation and application of mitigating and aggravating circumstances. The mitigating circumstances at times make reference to the state of war, or the lowered mental capacity of the accused due to the state of war, which seems incongruent to the idea of a 'war crime'. In fact, it hardly seems appropriate to apply 'state of war' as a mitigating circumstance to a crime of 'war' when war itself is a necessary precondition for a war crime.

For example, in the *Ivica Mlakic* case, the accused was sentenced to six years' imprisonment for committing a war crime against a civilian population. The court considered as one of the mitigating circumstances the fact that the crime took place 'in specific circumstances, during time of war in BiH, in circumstances [at a time] in which most of the offenders of crimes believed that the acts that they did, which were clearly against the law, in that particular setting, were permissible.'[78] There are also numerous examples from the Mostar Cantonal

76 Also, due to limited infrastructure, witnesses at times must sit in the same rooms with the accused or may in fact see the accused while they wait for the hearing in court. See E. Ponder, Bosnian Courts face Witness Problem, IWPR (16 April 2010), available at www.iwpr.net/report-news/bosnian-courts-face-witness-problem.

77 Ponder, *supra* note 76.

78 The court also took into account that the crime was committed over 14 years ago. However, the prosecutor appealed to the Supreme Court and recalled that the fact that the crime took place 14 years ago cannot be taken into consideration, and that the severity of the crime must

Court where the court cites the stressful conditions of war as a mitigating circumstance.[79] Invocation by the court of these mitigating circumstances of war, during war, deprives the domestic laws of oftheir very protections and meaning, since these laws exist to protect civilians and prisoners of war during times of war.[80]

In other instances, the passage of time between the commission of the crime and the trial was considered to be a mitigating factor. For example, in the *Mato Miletic* case, although the courts relied upon the accused's apparent compliance with the law over a period of time, 'from the time the acts were committed to now, a significant period of time has passed where the accused did not have trouble with the law.'[81] The Mostar Cantonal Court cited 'normalization'[82] of life in Bosnia as a reason for the reduction in sentence, contrary to the ICTY's decision[83] that does not permit the passage of time to be used as a mitigating factor.

This approach to sentencing is problematic, because its application deprives some laws of their very purpose, and therefore, of their substance. If war can be used as a mitigating factor in the commission of a war crime, and if delays in bringing the perpetrators to justice can mitigate their overall sentences, the very idea of 'war crime' and the fight against impunity is undermined.

5. LESSONS FROM BOSNIA

This section briefly outlines some potential and limited lessons that might be extrapolated from the Bosnian experience. Any post-conflict society attempting to institute a formalized judicial system to prosecute war crimes is likely to encounter similar problems. Thus, while a post-conflict society may not

be given greater value. The prosecutor, however, did not mention the fact that one of the mitigating circumstances was the 'circumstance of war'. The Supreme Court held that the fact the crime occurred 14 years ago was a correctly determined mitigating circumstance, merely objected to the fact that not enough proper consideration was given to the seriousness of the crime, and so the Supreme Court increased the sentence from six to seven years.

79 Mostar Cantonal Court 28 June 2004, *Case of Zvonko Trlin*, Verdict Number K-41/02, p. 15; Mostar Cantonal Court 26 April 2004, *Case of Romeo Blazevic*, Verdict Number K-43/02, p. 18; Mostar Cantonal Court 6 July 2004, *Case of Mario Matic*, Verdict Number K-28/03, p. 14. See HRW Report, *supra* note 7.

80 ICTY 29 July 2004, *Prosecutor v. Blaskic*, Sentencing Judgment (Appeals Chamber), Case No. IT-95-14-A, para 711. HRW Report, *supra* note 7.

81 Travnik Cantonal Court 29 March 2005, *Case of Mato Miletic*, Verdict Number K-19/04-Rz, affirmed, Supreme Court 26 April 2006, Verdict Number 070-0-Kz-06-000037.

82 Mostar Cantonal Court 6 July 2004, *Case of Mario Matic*, K.28/03, p. 13; Mostar Cantonal Court 26 April 2004, *Case of Romeo Blazevic*, Verdict Number K-43/02. HRW Report, supra note 7, p. 18.

83 HRW Report, *supra* note 7. ICTY 18 December 2003, *Prosecutor v. Dragan Nikolic*, Sentencing Judgment, Case No. IT-94-2-S, paras 272–73.

necessarily have the problem of a two-tiered criminal justice system (one applicable to the State Courts and the other to the local courts), it will most certainly have to address the issues of the interpretation of international criminal law.

In an effort to aid the Bosnian domestic courts in terms of applicable ICL, the ICTY appears the natural choice for providing guidance and precedent for adjudicating violations of international criminal law, or as a tool for strengthening rule of law efforts. Some have argued that the aims of the ICTY are 'in inherent tension' and at other times 'lack consensus regarding the priority' of each goal.[84] Nevertheless, it is undeniable that the ICTY provides a breadth of case law and direction for ICL. In fact, even if there is confusion with ICTY decisions, surely, after closure of the ICTY, a system could be established of consultation with former ICTY judges. The limitation to that suggestion would of course be primarily funding and a willingness of the local courts to seek assistance with judicial interpretation of ICL. However, should this initiative be undertaken, it would symbolize an important effort towards strengthening of the rule of law in Bosnia.

Secondly, assuming courts can establish the applicable legal standard,[85] effective implementation is required on the part of domestic courts: that is, taking the abstract rule of law concepts and implementing them in practice. Training of judges is expensive.[86] Finding qualified lawyers in the field of ICL is difficult, even in the international sphere, if only because this is an emerging area of law. However, some incremental steps or procedural safeguards can be put in place. Cooperation between domestic and international courts must be one of

---

84 Some of the goals listed include: 'to bring a sense of justice to war-torn places; to re-establish the rule of law; to provide a sound foundation for lasting peace; to enforce international law, and end impunity for violations, especially for senior political and military leaders; to bring repose to victims and provide an outlet to end cycles of violence and revenge; to demonstrate that culpability is individual, and not the responsibility of entire groups; to provide a safe forum for victims to tell their stories; to demonstrate fairness and the highest standards of due process; to provide exemplary procedures to serve as a model for rebuilding a legal system devastated by war crimes and human rights violations; to create an accurate historical record, to forestall those who might later try to deny that wide-scale violations of international law occurred; public education in general; in a didactic mode, to illuminate explanations about what caused the violations, and illustrate particular patterns of violations; to develop and expand the application and interpretation of international law and norms; to function with maximum transparency and public scrutiny; and to provide a forum for considering restitution and reparations.' M. Schrag, Lessons Learned from ICTY Experience, 2(2) Journal of International Criminal Justice 428 (Oxford University Press, 2004); Report of the Secretary-General (S/25704), para. 26; T. Taylor, The Anatomy of the Nuremburg Trials 634–641 (New York: Knopf, 1992).

85 Of course, in some instances, this standard will be easier to determine and to apply. For example, the idea that 'war' is not a justification for mitigating a sentence is relatively uncontroversial.

86 Rowen, *supra* note 35, p. 109.

the priorities when establishing post-conflict domestic courts, and those domestic courts need to view the international courts as complementary actors, offering guidance and resources where appropriate.

Lastly, and perhaps most importantly, existing structures should be further utilized. For example, unification of the Criminal Codes is relatively inexpensive, but the implementation of this unified code would be of significant benefit to the prosecution of war crimes in the local context. It would at least increase the potential for procedural fairness and a more progressive standard of international criminal law. Furthermore, it would pave the way for creating further jurisprudential consistency amongst the local courts, furthering the establishment of the basic principles of the rule of law.

For those familiar with the conflict and with Bosnia, it is clear that the progress made in the adjudication of war crimes is no small victory. However, the local courts must be closely monitored and their decisions scrutinized by the international community or by civil society within the state to ensure that the process is fair, impartial, and legitimate. After all, these are the grounding principles underlying any successful rule of law initiative. This chapter has highlighted only some of the problems that arose in this process, and has offered some potential solutions. Specifically, in looking at issues of evidence and witnesses, the chapter suggests that the inclusion of international legal norms, and the ability of local courts to base their system on international criminal legal standards, faces serious but not insurmountable obstacles. Working with local communities and effectively bridging the gap between the international order and the domestic court system is essential, and the intrinsic problems must be made clear in order to be effectively addressed. This process of close analysis must be maintained until confidence is attained in the local courts' ability to prosecute war crimes.[87]

Although this chapter cannot possibly address the multitude of factors that are necessary for the establishment of a society that is *bound* by the laws, it does highlight some elementary and basic gaps and it offers potential solutions. Ultimately, the entrenchment and respect for the rule of law must come from within the state through a comprehensive effort that includes strengthening the legal system, but also undertakes an examination of aligning sociological, cultural, and anthropological aspects of the society with the desire to be governed and bound by the rule of law system of governance. Without such a comprehensive effort, laws will not be implemented, and even if they were to be procedurally administered, they may lack the internal legitimacy. Whilst this

---

87 A national court system that is unstable may upset the delicate balance that is established following a conflict. In Rwanda, between 1994 and 1997, over 300 survivors scheduled to testify as witnessed were murdered. See J. Widner, Courts and Democracy in Post Conflict Transitions: A Social Scientist's Perspective on the African Case, 95 American Journal of International Law 64, 67–68 (2001).

chapter cannot provide a complete framework for the rule of law efforts in Bosnia, it is hoped that by providing insight into aspects that can be improved, it may assist Bosnia in bringing it a few steps closer to the comprehensive concept of the rule of law.

WAR CRIMES PROSECUTION IN A POST-CONFLICT ERA AND A PLURALISM OF JURISDICTIONS: THE EXPERIENCE OF THE BELGRADE WAR CRIMES CHAMBER

Sharon WEILL and Ivan JOVANOVIĆ*

1. INTRODUCTION

The international rule of law subjects the international order to the principles of the rule of law – a concept that originates in domestic frameworks – and externalises its rationales to the relations between states and other subjects of international law.[1] One of the main principles of the rule of law requests the law to be equally enforced by an independent judiciary.[2] For this purpose, the international legal framework has shouldered national courts with a major responsibility to enforce international humanitarian and criminal law.[3] In accordance with this structure, domestic courts, which constitute an important pillar of the international judicial enforcement mechanism, have two judicial functions: they operate as agents of the international legal systems, and as conventional domestic institutions.[4] While the international judicial system, composed of national and international courts, has been established,

* PhD candidates at the University of Geneva. Sharon Weill is a visiting lecturer at Tel Aviv University and Université Paris II; Ivan Jovanovic is the head of the War Crimes Unit, Rule of Law Department, OSCE Mission to Serbia. The views expressed in this article are those of the authors and do not necessarily reflect the official position of the OSCE.

1 S. Beaulac, The Rule of Law in International Law Today, in: G. Palombella and N. Walker (eds), Relocating the Rule of Law 204 (Oxford: Hart Publishing, 2009). See also A. Watts, The International Rule of Law, 36 German Yearbook of International Law 15 (1993).

2 A.V. Dicey, Introduction to the Study of the Law of the Constitution (London: Macmillan, 1959, 10th ed.); J. Raz, The Rule of Law and Its Virtue, 93 The Law Quarterly Review 195 (1977).

3 See eg the grave breaches regime established in the Geneva Conventions (Arts. 146–147 of the Fourth Geneva Convention) and the complementarity principle of the Rome Statute of the International Criminal Court.

4 R. Falk, The Role of Domestic Courts and World Legal Order 14, 22–23 (1964).

international law has also continuously been enforced by political actors, which have been traditionally confined to that role through the exercise of diplomacy. From a rule of law perspective, it has been hoped that the growing practice of courts would gradually replace the political enforcement of international law, and that the proper function of national courts in their application of international law, along with the work of international courts, will dictate the extent to which the international order is governed by the international rule of law. This chapter examines the function, in a post-conflict context, of one of these national judicial actors: the Serbian War Crimes Chamber.

In 1993, as a reaction to atrocities in the wars in the former Yugoslavia,[5] unprecedented in Europe since World War II, the international community established the ad hoc International Criminal Tribunal for the former Yugoslavia (ICTY), mandated under Chapter VII of the UN Charter to try those responsible for such crimes.[6] Although the Statute of the ICTY (Article 9) establishes its jurisdiction with primacy over the national courts, it has never been implied that it limits their responsibility in prosecuting war criminals. Each state of the former Yugoslavia has retained its own jurisdiction over the crimes falling under the ICTY Statute and its own obligation, both under international and national laws, not to leave such crimes unpunished.[7]

Consequently, ten years after the ICTY was created, the Serbian War Crimes Chamber (WCC) was established within the District Court of Belgrade. The WCC is one of the few domestic courts in the world to prosecute systematically its own nationals for war crimes committed in a conflict that ended just a few years before its creation. With the creation of the Belgrade WCC, a unique legal situation was created in which two different jurisdictions – international and national – deal with similar events, and sometimes with the same facts.

Within this context the present chapter examines the role of the WCC in Serbia's post-conflict era. This is done in two parts. The first is a background of the WCC's creation and the legal framework in which it operates, along with an introduction of its organizational and jurisdictional features, indicating to what extent domestic legislation endorsed international law and provided the possibility for the national court to apply it. The second part, a critical analysis of the WCC's first final decisions, examines how this court applies international law

---

5 The armed conflicts were taking place in Croatia (1991–1995), Bosnia and Herzegovina (1992–1995), and in Kosovo (1998–1999, including the NATO bombing of the Federal Republic of Yugoslavia from March to June 1999).

6 See the Statute of the International Tribunal for the Prosecution of Persons Responsible for Serious Violations of International Humanitarian Law Committed in the Territory of the Former Yugoslavia since 1991 established pursuant to UN Security Council Resolution 827, 25 May 1993 (S/Res/827) (1993) (ICTY Statute).

7 'It was not the intention of the Security Council to preclude or prevent the exercise of jurisdiction by national courts'. Report of the UN Secretary-General pursuant to paragraph 2 of Security Council Resolution 808 (1993), (S/25704) (3 May 1993), para 64.

in practice and attempts to evaluate its role as an active actor in the broader context of the international rule of law.

2. THE ESTABLISHMENT OF THE BELGRADE WAR CRIMES CHAMBER

2.1. BETWEEN INTERNAL DEMOCRATIC CHANGES AND EXTERNAL PRESSURE: A BACKGROUND

On 1 July 2003 the Serbian Parliament, in a regular legislative procedure, adopted the Law on Organisation and Competence of Government Authorities in War Crimes Proceedings ('War Crimes Law').[8] This law set up the War Crimes Chamber and the War Crimes Prosecutor's Office, and established their jurisdiction and competences. This was a key constitutional moment in giving effect to accountability for war crimes as an international obligation and opening a new area in relations between international and domestic law in Serbia. The decision to design these institutions and to adopt the War Crimes Law came as a result of political changes within Serbia, along with external pressures and changes in the Serbian approach to foreign affairs. It represents a combination of domestic commitments and international influence.

During the conflicts in the 1990s and the Milošević regime, trials for war crimes in Serbia were rare exceptions and impunity was almost a political and social norm. Even in the first years after the overthrowing of Milošević in October 2000, only a handful of individuals belonging to the Serbian side were tried for crimes committed against other ethnic groups. The very scarce trials in Serbia were to a large extent assessed as being below the acceptable standards, with poor indictments and almost disinterested prosecution, acquittals because of lack of evidence, or inappropriately low sentences.[9] As the state and law enforcement agencies were behind many of the crimes, they were more involved in covering up such crimes than in investigating them. The political and social environment in Serbia, deeply involved in conflicts in the neighbouring countries and on its own territory, was filled both with denial and ignorance, as a result of admiration for and fear of the war lords, self-perceived victimization, and justifications that the wars had been necessary for the defence of the Serbs.

---

8 Law on Organisation and Competence of Government Authorities in War Crimes Proceedings [*Zakon o organizaciji i nadležnosti državnih organa u postupku za ratne zločine*], Official Gazette of the Republic of Serbia [*Službeni glasnik Republike Srbije*] no. 67/2003, with subsequent amendments in Official Gazette 135/2004, 61/2005, 101/2007, available at www.osce.org/documents/fry/2005/11/18508_en.pdf ('War Crimes Law').

9 See especially report by the OSCE Mission to Serbia and Montenegro, War Crimes before Domestic Courts (Belgrade, October 2003), available at www.osce.org/documents/fry/2003/11/1156_en.pdf.

A number of factors made the Serbian government decide, at the end of 2002, to initiate domestic prosecution of war crimes:

- After the fall of Milošević it was no longer as much of a taboo or as dangerous to openly discuss war crimes, and the public in Serbia became less hostile towards accountability for war crimes of their co-nationals. An active civil society in Serbia played an important role in galvanizing the officials and the public to support accountability for war crimes.
- Serbia needed to improve its image and respect abroad. Over the preceding years, it had achieved the status of a rogue state in world affairs and become almost a synonym for war crimes and ethnic cleansing. It was important to prove the break-up with the previous Serbian regime and to send signals of commitment to the rule of law and shared values to the world. This, along with important economic and diplomatic pressure from the European Union and the United States, also prompted the post-Milošević pro-European Serbian government to start cooperating with the ICTY.
- In supporting domestic trials, the Serbian authorities were also hoping that these could substitute, to a certain extent, for the surrender of Serbs to the ICTY. The reason was the ever-present concern of the authorities that surrenders to the ICTY might jeopardise the stability of the country.[10] The ground for such hopes for deferral of some of the war crimes cases to Serbia was the ICTY completion strategy, which includes transfer of indictments against low-level accused and incomplete investigations to the national courts in the former Yugoslavia.[11] The ICTY conditioned the transfer of cases on the functioning of credible domestic courts with well-trained staff and proper legislation.[12]
- The diplomatic pressure relating to the potential accession to the EU and economic assistance, and especially the US conditioning of financial and

10 Although the arrests of ICTY indictees have been followed, on a few occasions, only by short-lasting protests and minor sporadic riots, the potential of such arrests in mobilizing still strong remnants of the Milosevic regime and his security forces against the fragile government in the early 2000s should not be underestimated. For example, the top members of the notorious Special Operations Unit of the Serbian state security agency, deeply involved in the wars in the FRY, were those who directly carried out assassination of the Serbian Prime Minister Djindjić, in March 2003, acting together with the organized crime clans. They justified their motivation for the plot by fear from being surrendered to the ICTY by Djindjic's government. On interplay between attempts by the ICTY and the diplomatic community to obtain Serbia's cooperation with the ICTY and Serbian internal political frictions, see generally V. Peskin, International Justice in Rwanda and the Balkans 61–91 (Cambridge: Cambridge University Press, 2008).

11 Ninth annual report of the International Criminal Tribunal for the former Yugoslavia submitted to the UN General Assembly, Fifty-seventh session, UNSC Resolution 1503 (28 August 2003) (S/RES/1503) (2003), para 6.

12 See Address by Ms. Carla del Ponte, ICTY Chief Prosecutor, to the OSCE Permanent Council, Vienna (PC.DEL/1278/03) (4 November 2003).

international political support to Serbia, played an important role in setting up a war crimes court in Belgrade.[13] Another politically less influential, but very operative and standard-measuring international actor, was the Organization for Security and Co-operation in Europe (OSCE), which had rule of law and regional stability among its focuses and operated active field missions in the former Yugoslavia.

- A systematic suppression of growing and threatening organised crime that the state was preparing in 2002 also triggered the ideas of extending competence of a future organised crime court to cover war crimes. Prosecuting war criminals together with mobsters was a discrete way to slip war crimes trials into the criminal justice system without attracting too many negative reactions from the still strong nationalistic circles, political parties, and significant parts of the public.

2.2. SERBIAN WAR CRIMES CHAMBER AND WAR CRIMES PROSECUTION OFFICE

The model that was chosen for prosecuting war crimes in Serbia was the establishment of a specialised, but still national, judicial chamber and prosecutor's office.[14] The international community, mainly the OSCE Mission to Serbia, the US Embassy in Belgrade, and independent international experts, exerted a decisive influence on the final outcome of the creation of these specialised judicial agencies in Serbia.[15] It was a compromise made in order to strengthen the independence and competence of such institutions, while preserving them within the parameters of the existing structure of the national judiciary and criminal legislation. The participation of international judges and prosecutors in trials, as suggested by international experts, was rejected by the

---

13 For example, the US, which financed a new building for organized crime trials, conditioned its support by requesting that this new infrastructure had to be used for war crimes trials as well. Interview with Mr. Predrag Dejanovic, Assistant-Minister of Justice of the Republic of Serbia 2001–2003 (Belgrade, 20 September 2009).

14 Other courts that have been dealing more or less systematically with war crimes are either hybrid (Sierra Leone, Cambodia, Kosovo, or, previously, East Timor), or domestic courts with international presence (Bosnia and Herzegovina, and as allowed by its statute, the Iraqi Special Tribunal), or they are regular national courts without exclusive jurisdiction (such as in Croatia, Montenegro, Macedonia). Some authors classify the WCC, together with the Iraqi High Tribunal, in the group of 'courts established by a state with international support'. R. Cryer, H.Friman, D. Robinson and E. Wilmshurst, An Introduction to International Criminal Law and Procedure 161–162 (Cambridge: Cambridge University Press, 2007).

15 OSCE Mission to Serbia and Montenegro, Strategy on Support to the National Judiciary in Conducting War Crimes Trials (Belgrade, 11 April 2003) (on file with the authors) ('OSCE Strategy'). A detailed account of the drafting process is provided by the then Executive Director of the International Bar Association. M.S. Ellis, Coming to Terms with Its Past – Serbia's New Court for the Prosecution of War Crimes, 22 Berkeley Journal of International Law 165, 165–194 (2004).

Serbian authorities. The United States, for example, supported such a position of the Serbian government.[16] The government wanted to demonstrate that the Serbian judiciary was capable of handling such cases in line with international standards with its own human resources. One of the arguments against inclusion of international staff in the court or in the prosecution office was that such internationalised structure could be perceived as another ICTY-like court and be seen as imposed justice, prompting animosity among the public in Serbia.[17]

2.2.1. Structure

The War Crimes Chamber is a specialised department established within the District Court in Belgrade in 2003.[18] On 1 January 2010, as a part of an overall reorganization and reform of the Serbian judiciary, the Belgrade District Court was renamed the 'High Court in Belgrade', but the WCC, now renamed the 'War Crimes Department', continues to exist in that new court.[19] The judicial reform had not aimed at changing the specialised war crimes bodies and they have remained mostly unaffected by it.

The WCC judges have been selected among the regular criminal law judges of the Belgrade District Court or other district courts in Serbia, and they have been assigned, by the decision of the president of the Belgrade District Court and with their consent, to the WCC for a renewable term of four years.[20] There are eight judges on the WCC. The Chamber sits in trial panels of three professional judges, which is different from the courts of ordinary jurisdiction, where panels also include lay judges. The court of appeal is, after 2010, the Appellate Court in Belgrade, which also has specialised five-member War Crimes Department (before 2010 the appellate function was with the Supreme Court of Serbia).

The War Crimes Prosecutor's Office (WCPO) of the Republic of Serbia is a specialised prosecutorial office. The WCPO is headed by the War Crimes Prosecutor, elected in 2003 directly by the Serbian Parliament, unlike other prosecutors in the country who were, at the time, appointed by the government.[21] The War Crimes Prosecutor's mandate is limited to a renewable term of six years

---

16 Ellis, *supra* note 15, p. 189.

17 In Croatia, Montenegro, and Macedonia, courts of ordinary jurisdiction deal with war crimes and they have no international staff either. In Bosnia and Herzegovina an internationalized model of a war crimes chamber at the state level was pushed for by the international community, and was accepted by some while opposed by other ethnic constituencies in that state: see K. Uhlířová, War Crimes Chamber of the Court of Bosnia and Herzigovina: Seeding "International Standards of Justice"?, in this volume, at p. 227.

18 War Crimes Law, Arts. 9(1) and 10(1).

19 In this chapter, the term High Court may be used alternatively with District Court, except for references to decisions and actions taken before 1 January 2010, while the WCC, as a now well-established name, will be used throughout the entire article and its meaning will also be used to refer to the post-2010 War Crimes Department.

20 War Crimes Law, Art. 10(2) and (3).

21 War Crimes Law, Arts 4(4) and 5(1).

as for other public prosecutors.[22] The WCPO acts both in first instance trials and on appeal, which is another difference from the regular prosecution offices. There is a general obligation for citizens and public or private entities to cooperate with any public prosecution office, but the War Crimes Law nevertheless includes specific provisions obliging all state bodies and institutions to provide information and documents or render any other assistance to the War Crimes Prosecutor at his request.[23] This special status of the WCPO is a result of the consultation process in drafting the War Crimes Law, in which one of the key benchmarks, especially prompted by the participating international experts, was to provide for a prosecutor with wide competencies and a strong position and independence.[24]

2.2.2. Jurisdiction

The War Crimes Chamber/Department and the War Crimes Prosecutor's Office have the exclusive jurisdiction in Serbia over genocide and war crimes, whenever they have been committed.[25] Therefore, any court or prosecutor in Serbia has to defer to their competence in these cases. The WCC can try persons for any crime within its *ratione materiae* jurisdiction committed in the wars in the former Yugoslavia, regardless of nationality of the victim or the perpetrator.[26] This means that the WCC can assert universal jurisdiction, but the scope is limited by the requirement that the crime has to have been committed somewhere on the territory of the former Yugoslavia.

2.2.3. Relationship with the ICTY

The War Crimes Law acknowledges the primacy of the ICTY and reflects the influence of the Tribunal and the determination of Serbia to maintain a partnership with the ICTY in on-going and new cases before the WCC.[27] Some of the procedural norms in the Law that reveal the acknowledgment of the ICTY's primacy are, for example, the requirement that protective measures for the Tribunal's witnesses ordered by the ICTY chambers remain in force when such witnesses testify before the WCC, or authorization to representatives of the

---

22 Law on Public Prosecution, Official Gazette of Serbia No 116, Art. 16.

23 War Crimes Law, Art. 7.

24 See Ellis, *supra* note 15, p. 180.

25 War Crimes Law, Arts 2(1), 4(1) and 9(1).
The proceedings for war crimes in which the indictment became effective prior to the Law's entry into force, in 2003, had to be concluded before the courts which initially had jurisdiction. War Crimes Law, Art. 21.

26 War Crimes Law, Art. 3.

27 The other aspect of cooperation with the ICTY, which includes fulfilment of the Tribunal's request for access to documents and witnesses and surrender of the accused, is not within the scope of this article.

ICTY to be informed of and to attend all phases of domestic proceedings, including closed sessions.[28] A direct link to the ICTY is also made in a provision concerning transfer of the ICTY cases to Serbia. Such transfers, in which the ICTY refers its own indictments to national judiciaries, are among key elements of the Tribunal's completion strategy and, as they are carried out pursuant to Rule 11*bis* of the ICTY Rules of Procedures and Evidence, they are known as '11 *bis* referrals'.[29] In the instance of an 11 *bis* referral, the Law obliges the War Crimes Prosecutor to base charges in the 'domesticated' indictment on the same facts as those contained in the referred ICTY indictment.[30] The rationale behind this provision was also to bind the War Crimes Prosecutor not to depart from the factual basis of the ICTY indictment, to preserve its integrity, and to avert any possible pressure on the Prosecutor to change facts in cases dealing with events deemed politically sensitive in Serbia. The Law also allows the War Crimes Prosecutor to rely on the evidentiary material and information from the ICTY, irrespective of 11 *bis* referrals, in its own investigations and as a basis for its indictments, and authorises the WCC to admit evidence from the ICTY in its own trials.[31] Application of a few other procedural novelties introduced by the War Crimes Law itself, such as video-link hearings, or assignment of protective measures to witnesses, which later became embraced also by the general criminal procedure law in Serbia, was inspired by and borrowed extensively from ICTY procedure and practice.[32]

The influence of the ICTY is reflected in procedural matters, not in substantive law. Any reference to the jurisprudence of the ICTY was omitted

---

28 War Crimes Law, Art. 14a(5) and (7).

29 Out of 8 indictments, with 13 accused referred to the local judiciaries in the former Yugoslavia, one indictment was referred from the ICTY to the Belgrade WCC, in which the accused was a national of Serbia. ICTY 17 November 2006, *Prosecutor v. Vladimir Kovačević*, Decision on referral of case pursuant to rule 11 *bis*, ICTY-IT-01–42/2. The referral of the *Kovačević* case has not resulted in a trial in Serbia because the defendant was found, both by the ICTY and by the WCC, unfit to stand trial due to his mental illness. Other cases were referred to Bosnia and Herzegovina (ten accused) and Croatia (two accused) as the crimes were committed on the territory and by nationals of these states.
For status of cases referred by the ICTY, see www.icty.org/sid/8934.

30 War Crimes Law, Art. 14a(1). This provision mirrors the Croatian Law on Application of the ICC Statute from 2003 which governs cooperation with the ICC, but applies to some aspects of cooperation with the ICTY.

31 War Crimes Law, Art. 14a(2 and 4). In practice, the WCC accepts evidence from the ICTY, including those collected by the Tribunal's Office of the Prosecutor, under a condition that such type of evidence would be admissible before the ICTY too; for example, War Crimes Department of the District Court in Belgrade 12 June 2008, *Dragan Slavković et al*, Judgment, KV 5/2005, p. 47–48 ('*Zvornik I* case'). The Croatian 2003 Law on Application of the ICC Statute law also has a very similar provision allowing for admissibility of ICTY evidence if collected in line with the ICTY Statute and Rules of Procedure and Evidence.

32 War Crimes Law, Art. 15. Such procedural in-court witness protection measures are closed sessions, voice distortion or use of pseudonyms. Such provisions have proven instrumental in obtaining acceptance of witnesses from Croatia, Bosnia, or Kosovo, as well as insider witnesses, to testify before the WCC.

from the Law, and it was left to the discretion of WCC judges to decide whether or not to follow it. The Law also intentionally does not require the Prosecutor to adhere to the same legal accusations as set forth in the ICTY indictment. This is because names and definitions of crimes and forms of criminal responsibility in Serbian criminal legislation are not completely equivalent to the list of international crimes in the ICTY Statute. This is particularly the case with crimes against humanity and command responsibility, which did not exist as crimes, or a form of responsibility, in Serbian law at the time the crimes were committed in the 1990s.

2.3. LEGAL FRAMEWORK FOR THE WAR CRIMES TRIALS

2.3.1. Relationship between International and Municipal Law

Serbia is a party to the 1949 Geneva Conventions and its Additional Protocols and to the Genocide Convention.[33] The applicability of international law and the hierarchy of norms are determined by the Serbian Constitution from 2006. International treaties and generally accepted rules of international law (the domestic legislative synonym for customary international law) are defined by the Constitution as being part of the internal legal order and superior to national laws.[34] Treaty and customary law are equally superior to national laws. The same provision existed in the former Constitution of the Federal Republic of Yugoslavia (in force from 1992 to 2003) and the Constitutional Charter of Serbia and Montenegro (from 2003 to 2006). Treaties, however, according to the Serbian Constitution of 2006, cannot overrule any constitutional provision.[35]

The Constitution furthermore confirms the direct applicability of international law by setting forth in an article on the principles of the judiciary that the courts shall adjudicate 'on the basis of the Constitution, law, ratified international treaties and generally accepted rules of international law'.[36] The Law on Judges, applicable as of January 2010, also authorises judges to render decisions by applying 'ratified treaties and generally accepted rules of international law'.[37] As a result, treaties do not necessarily need to be

33 Although the status of the Federal Republic of Yugoslavia and Serbia as a party to these conventions, especially between 1992 and 2001, was not without legal perplexities, it suffices to say for the purpose of this analysis that the former Yugoslavia was a party to all these conventions and they were continuously in force during the conflicts in the 1990s. This has never been contested by domestic courts.

34 Constitution of the Republic of Serbia, adopted on 8 November 2006, Official Gazette of the Republic of Serbia no. 98, Art. 16(2). For the primacy of international law over domestic legislation, see Art. 194(4) and (5) of the Constitution.

35 Constitution of Serbia, Art. 194(4).

36 Constitution of Serbia, Art. 142(2).

37 Law on Judges [*Zakon o sudijama*], Official Gazette of the Republic of Serbia no. 116, 22 December 2008, Art. 1(2).

transformed into implementing legislation in order to have a legal effect in Serbia.

Thus, international treaties and customary international law make an integral part of the body of municipal law, and they can be directly applied by the courts. Prosecutors, or parties to a case, do not have to bring up international law in a proceeding in order for the courts to apply it; courts are free to invoke international law *proprio motu*. It is within the competence of the court to find a legal basis, including international law, for its own decisions. The practice of the WCC shows that if the parties to a case – and particularly the prosecutor in the indictment – are more expansive in referring to international law provisions in support of their case, especially when presenting elements of crimes, the court appears more likely to respond in its judgment by more thorough deliberations on international law.

The impact of such a dominantly monist framework that enables application of international law in its domestic system is, however, limited by the constitutional principle of legality in criminal law (*nullum crimen, nulla poena sine lege*). As the Serbian Constitution establishes that both a crime and a penalty must be defined at the time of the commission by a domestic law,[38] it excludes the possibility of directly construing a criminal offence from an international source if such offence was not previously incorporated into domestic penal legislation. Nevertheless, as will be further demonstrated below, treaty or customary law norms can and must serve as a basis for the interpretation of provisions of the Serbian penal law when establishing whether a war crime has been committed.

2.3.2. Substantive Criminal Law

The applicable criminal code in trials before the Serbian Court for war crimes committed in the Balkan wars in the 1990s is the Criminal Code of the Federal Republic of Yugoslavia (FRY CC) from 1992, which was in force at the time the crimes were committed, as required by the principle of legality.[39] The FRY CC

38 'No person may be held guilty for any act which did not constitute a criminal offence under *law* or any other regulation based on the *law* at the time when it was committed': Constitution of Serbia, Art. 32(1). 'Criminal offences and penalties shall be laid down by law': Constitution of Serbia, Art. 32(1). The original Serbian word that the Constitution uses in this provision – '*zakon*' – has been translated as law, and it regularly means an act of legislation adopted by the Parliament, a statute, as opposed to '*pravo*', which also often translates in English as law, but has a broader meaning that encompasses all legal instruments, including international law.

39 Criminal Code of the Federal Republic of Yugoslavia [*Krivični zakon Savezne Republike Jugoslavije*], Official Gazette of the FRY, no. 35/92, 37/93, 24/94, 61/01. Upon the creation of the State Union of Serbia and Montenegro, in 2003, this code is transformed into the Basic Criminal Code of the Republic of Serbia (Official Gazette of the Republic of Serbia, no. 39/03), but the content of the provisions relevant for this analysis remained the same. On the principle of legality, see, for example, C.M. Bassiouni, The Sources and Content of International Criminal Law: A Theoretical Framework, Principles of Legality; the *Ratione Materiae* of

applies also to international crimes committed in the first year of the conflict, in 1991, according to the *lex mitior* principle (mandatory application of more lenient law): namely, it set forth twenty years as the maximum penalty, whereas the 1976 SFRY CC, which was still in force in 1991, provided for the death penalty for the gravest crimes. There are fourteen international crimes from the FRY CC falling under the jurisdiction of the WCC, but the most frequently applied is the offence of War Crimes against Civilians (Article 142 FRY CC).[40]

The definition of the crime in Article 142 – with a structure unchanged since 1976 – begins with a chapeau and continues with an exhaustive list of underlying acts of commission.[41] The chapeau reads: 'Whoever, in violation of the rules of international law in time of war, armed conflict or occupation... orders... or commits' any of the enumerated underlying acts.[42] It contains the key condition that, in order to convict a person, it has to be proved that a criminal act listed in the provision was committed in violation of the rules of international law applicable during armed conflict. The prosecution and the Court have to examine and find a violation of an international humanitarian law rule in order to apply Article 142. Since the chapeau speaks about 'international law', that includes both treaties and customary international law. Here, the jurisprudence of international courts becomes particularly relevant. The new Serbian Criminal Code of 2006 (not applicable to crimes committed during the 1990s) retains the same provision referencing international law. The chapeau requirement of Article 142 brings the FRY CC into a category of domestic regulations of international crimes that has been described as a 'dynamic reference to international law by national criminal law provisions'.[43] Such regulation does not only allow for the use of international law as a source of norms; it actually requires courts to rely on international law and to introduce it into the case. It is a part of the elements of the crime.

International Criminal Law, in: International Criminal Law – Crimes 33 (New York: 1999, 2nd ed.).

40 Other crimes in Chapter XVI of the FRY CC include genocide (Art. 141), war crimes against the sick and wounded, war crimes against prisoners of war, and different violations of international humanitarian law such as marauding, use of prohibited means of warfare, destruction of cultural and historical monuments, misuse of international emblems, and others.

41 Such underlying acts include, inter alia, subjecting civilian population to killings, torture, inhuman treatment, biological experiments, immense suffering or violation of bodily integrity or health, forcible prostitution or rape, intimidation and terror, taking of hostages, unlawful deportation or displacement, unlawful arrests and confinement, forced labour, attacks on objects protected by international law, indiscriminate attacks upon civilian objects, etc.

42 In the current 2006 Criminal Code, war crimes against civilians are promulgated in Art. 372, Criminal Code of the Republic of Serbia [*Krivični zakonik Republike Srbie*], Official Gazette of the Republic of Serbia, no. 85 (available in English at www.osce.org/documents/fry/2006/02/18196_en.pdf).

43 H. Kreicker, National Prosecution of Genocide from a Comparative Perspective, 5 International Criminal Law Review 312 (2005).

2.4. STRENGTHENING THE CAPACITY OF THE WAR CRIMES CHAMBER

The international community became very much involved in supporting and assisting the operations of the new institutions in Serbia in order to strengthen their capacity. The OSCE developed a multi-year program of assistance to the new Court, prosecutor's office, defence attorneys, and police investigation unit, which included a number of clusters of activities, such as training, public outreach, or facilitation of regional and international cooperation.[44] Similar and complementary assistance activities have also been run by the US Embassy, the United Nations Development Program (UNDP), and by the Humanitarian Law Center (HLC), a local NGO. ICTY staff also regularly engaged in delivering training.

Trainings on international law were mainly organised during the early days of the WCC/WCPO. Later knowledge transfer assistance has been much more focused on areas such as investigative techniques and analysis, prosecutorial strategy, building up cases and case management, use of evidence from the ICTY and from other national jurisdictions, and witness protection and support. Consultations and experience exchange meetings between Serbian judges and prosecutors and their colleagues from Croatia and Bosnia, organised by the OSCE, have been particularly well accepted. This is due to the fact that each training or meeting was designed in agreement with the local judicial practitioners, who felt that they had been provided with enough training and literature on international law and that they needed more practical skills.[45] The position of the judiciary was that they are first to gather evidence and apply the domestic criminal code, while the role of international law is secondary.

The exclusivity of the jurisdiction of the WCC and WCPO has greatly facilitated capacity-building and knowledge-transfer in Serbia, since the training providers and donors have been able to concentrate their efforts on a relatively small, easily identifiable, and permanent target group. This functional concentration of human resources and jurisdiction may be one of the reasons why judicial practitioners from other jurisdictions in the ex-Yugoslav countries,

---

44 OSCE Strategy, *supra* note 15. The program has been continuously run since 2004 and the activities have been to a large degree financed from direct contributions of the Netherlands and Norway to the OSCE.

45 For an overview of the activities and methodologies applied in the capacity building in this field, see especially OSCE-ODIHR in conjunction with ICTY and UNICRI, Supporting the Transition Process: Lessons Learned and Best Practices in Knowledge Transfer – Final report (Warsaw, 2009), available at www.osce.org/documents/odihr/2009/09/39685_en.pdf (visited 10 October 2010). See also N. Palmer, Understandings of International Law in Rwanda: A Contextual Approach, in this volume at p. 153, on the primary importance assigned by Rwandan judges to improved judicial capacity.

where competence over war crimes cases is divided among different national courts, may have felt lack of capacity building.[46]

3. THE FIRST YEARS OF THE BELGRADE WAR CRIMES CHAMBER: AN ASSESSMENT

Within its first six years of operation, the War Crimes Chamber rendered judgments in 25 cases involving 64 defendants, out of which 12 judgments, concerning 41 defendants, are final.[47] By November 2010, the WCPO raised indictments against 114 persons. In addition, investigations have been opened against at least 110 individuals, most of them Serbs.[48]

The next part of this section analyses the first two decisions of the WCC that became final, as well as an additional recent one.[49] The analysis of these decisions offers an insight into the functioning of the WCC – how it applied international humanitarian law (IHL), referred to international jurisprudence, and established the facts in light of the post-conflict national narrative – in one case in which it was free from any political pressure, and, in another case, where it had to face considerable political constraints.

Through these case studies, which reflect the ability and willingness of the Court to apply international law in its particular post-conflict context, the authors' aim is to decipher the role played by the Belgrade WCC within the broader perspective of the international rule of law of which domestic courts constitute an important pillar, and to evaluate its commitment to the international rule of law. This is assessed in consideration of two aspects: (1) its objective ability to apply international law: whether the judges have the necessary expertise and knowledge of international law (including treaty law and international customary law as well as international and national court decisions and academic writings); and (2) its subjective willingness to enforce international law: whether the Court equally enforces the law without applying double

---

46 For capacity building in Bosnia see especially S. Popovic, Prosecution of War Crimes in Bosnian Cantonal and District Courts; the Role of the Rule of Law, in this volume at p. 221.

47 See generally www.tuzilastvorz.org.rs/html_trz/index_eng.htm (visited 18 November 2010). The figure of final verdicts also includes two trials that had started before the time the WCPO and WCC were established, but were later represented by the WCPO at the re-trial.

48 Of the total number of 114 accused, 91 of them (80 percent of the total number of accused) are ethnic Serbs. As of beginning of November 2010, there have been 9 first instance trials, with 50 defendants before the War Crimes Chamber. Interview with Trial Monitors of the OSCE Mission to Serbia (Belgrade, 17 November 2010).

49 At the time of writing this article other final judgments have been rendered. We discuss a third case, which is relevant for the analysis of the Court's application of international law. However, the other cases are not addressed here; most of these cases concern individual acts of killing and have been less challenging both on law and fact.

standards, and whether the judicial system is independent, ie to what extent local or international political interests influence the judicial decision-making.

3.1. CASE STUDIES

3.1.1. The Anton Lekaj Case

Anton Lekaj, a Kosovar Albanian and a member of the former Kosovo Liberation Army (KLA), was the first person tried by the WCC to be convicted in a final decision. He was found guilty of war crimes against a civilian population during the armed conflict in Kosovo and, on 18 September 2006, sentenced to thirteen years in prison.[50] This first case was a relatively easy one, not only because the WCC was judging 'the enemy' and not its own national for committing war crimes, and thus was not encumbered by domestic political inconvenience, but also because the factual and procedural issues were rather simple. The Belgrade-based Humanitarian Law Centre, which monitors the war crimes trials and represents the victims in most cases, at first criticized the fact that the case was held before a Serbian court and not before a court in Kosovo. At the same time, at the end of the trial it concluded that a fair trial had been conducted.[51]

Anton Lekaj was accused of committing unlawful confinement, rape, inhuman treatment, torture, and murder, between 12 and 15 June 1999, in the region of the city of Đakovica in Kosovo, during the armed conflict. According to the indictment, Lekaj, along with other KLA members, captured thirteen non-Albanian civilians (twelve Roma and a Serb) in the middle of a wedding parade and confined them for four days and nights in a basement of a hotel, where they were tortured and sexually assaulted. According to the 1992 FRY CC, which was in force at the time the alleged acts were committed, the prosecution had to prove that the alleged criminal acts were listed in Article 142 of the Code (War Crimes against Civilians), and that they were committed in violation of a rule of international law applicable during armed conflict. Thus, the accusations were based on both the national criminal code and on IHL.[52]

---

50 War Crimes Chamber of the Belgrade District Court 18 September 2006, *Anton Lekaj case*, Judgment, K.V. 4/05 ('*Lekaj* Judgment') (in Serbian, unofficial translation in English on file with authors). The ruling was confirmed by the Serbian Supreme Court on 5 April 2007.

51 The main problem encountered, according to this NGO, was a number of witnesses from Kosovo refusing to testify in Belgrade. Humanitarian Law Center, The Trial to Anton Lekaj was Fair Although Conducted Before a Non-Jurisdictional Court (press release, 23 September 2006), available at www.hlc-rdc.org/Saopstenja/1316.en.html (visited 20 September 2009).

52 International rules mentioned in the indictment included provisions from the Fourth Geneva Convention (GC IV) and both Additional Protocols (AP I and AP II): Art. 2(1) GC IV (definition of international armed conflict), Art. 3 GC IV (non-international armed conflict), and Art. 27(1) and (2) of GC IV; and Art. 51 (protection of the civilian population), Art. 75

The qualification of the conflict and the applicable treaty law

As a starting point, the WCC defined the nature of the conflict. An accurate qualification of the conflict is of major importance as the applicable IHL treaty law depends on this preliminary determination. The WCC found that in the period relevant to the facts, 12 to 16 June 1999, two armed conflicts existed – a non-international armed conflict between the KLA and the FRY and Serbian police forces, and an international armed conflict between NATO and the armed forces of the FRY.[53] This analysis of the facts, which fragments the conflict into its components, follows the doctrine of IHL, which recognises that two types of conflicts may exist simultaneously, or that a conflict may be of a mixed character. In such a situation, the law of international armed conflicts applies to the fighting between the armed forces of two states and the law of non-international armed conflicts to the fighting between the government and rebel forces.[54] Yet, while the WCC rightly assessed that the armed conflict in Kosovo was composed of two parallel conflicts, it failed to properly apply the relevant legal framework consequent to this finding. The WCC simultaneously applied to Lekaj's alleged crimes both sets of laws[55] – an impossible situation according to IHL. An act can be in nexus either to an international armed conflict or to a non-international armed conflict, but not to both at the same time. A more accurate ruling would have been to qualify the acts of Lekaj as being part of the non-international armed conflict and consequently to apply merely the law applicable to such type of conflict.

Protected persons status

As the acts of Lekaj were linked to a non-international armed conflict, the special protected persons regime, regulated in Article 4 of the Fourth Geneva Convention, was not applicable. However, the WCC's first finding was that the victims, FRY nationals from Kosovo, were protected persons:

> Such acts of the defendant constitute grave breaches of international humanitarian law as the defendant was a belligerent of the armed conflict (member of the KLA),

(fundamental guarantees), and Art. 76 (protection of women) of AP I, Art. 4(1) and (2) (a,e) and Art. 13 of AP II.

53 *Lekaj* Judgment, *supra* note 50, p. 8.

54 See eg M. Sassoli, The legal qualification of the conflicts in the former Yugoslavia: double standards or new horizons for international humanitarian law?, in: Wang Tieya and Sienho Yee (eds), International Law in the Post-Cold War World: Essays in Memory of Li Haopei 314 (London: Routledge, 2001).

55 The WCC applies simultaneously Art. 27 of GC IV, AP I, AP II and Art. 3 of GC IV. The Supreme Court of Serbia upheld such an approach when confirming Lekaj's conviction. Supreme Court of Serbia 26 February 2007, *Anton Lekaj case*, Appeals Judgment, Kž. I RZ 3/06, p.7 (in Serbian).

> while the victims were civilians who have not directly taken part in the hostilities, and who were under the status of protected persons pursuant to the Fourth Geneva Convention on protection of civilians during war of 12 August 1949.[56]

The legal status of protected persons grants enemy nationals special protection during international armed conflict. With the aim of adapting the law to the specific conflict in Bosnia, and to include as many civilians as possible under the special protection regime, the ICTY in the *Tadic* case, after qualifying the conflict as international, interpreted the definition of protected persons in a broad manner; it ruled that the nationality requirement should be interpreted as an allegiance test.[57] When the WCC ruled that civilians of Kosovo, who were FRY nationals, were protected persons, it seemed to apply the *Tadic* allegiance test without explicitly mentioning it. Indeed, the WCC stated on several occasions that the victims had been loyal to the adverse party of the armed conflict.[58] By using the term 'loyal', the WCC appeared to implicitly assert that the allegiance, and not the nationality test, is the legal test applicable to determine who is a protected person. As the allegiance test had been applied only by the ICTY, and not without criticism,[59] it would have been appropriate had the WCC elaborated on this issue and provided an explicit stance on this question.

Conviction

The WCC found that the acts of Lekaj that included rape, murder, torture, and illegal detention violated both the rules of international armed conflict and non-international armed conflict.[60] Although this finding is not accurate, and only the rules of non- international armed conflict apply, ie common Article 3 of the Geneva Conventions and Additional Protocol II, the final result remained the same, as Lekaj's acts were all illegal according to the law of non-international armed conflict, and therefore complied with the requirement of Article 142 of the FRY CC.

---

56 *Lekaj* Judgment, *supra* note 50, p.26.

57 ICTY 15 July 1999, *Prosecutor v. Tadic*, Appeals Judgment, IT-94-1-A, paras 166 and 168. Likewise, ICTY, *Celebici*, Appeals Judgment, paras. 73 and 98, *Blaskic*, Appeals Judgment, para. 634.

58 'The victims were civilians ... who did not represent any real threat to the safety of the defendant and other KLA members. The only reason for their treatment in such manner was their ethnicity... under the assumption that they collaborated with Serbs ... and hence KLA members considered them *disloyal* to them': *Lekaj* Judgment, *supra* note 50, p. 39.

59 See, eg M. Sassòli and L.M. Olson, The judgment of the ICTY Appeals Chamber on the merits in the *Tadic* case, 839 International Review of the Red Cross 741 (2000).

60 The WCC mentions Art. 3(1) and Art. 27(1) and (2) of GCIV, Arts 51, 75, and 76 of AP I, Article 4(1) and (2) and Article 13 of the AP I. *Lekaj* Judgment, *supra* note 50, p. 39.

Customary international law

In order to avoid the task of qualifying the conflict, the WCC could have referred solely to customary law rules that are applicable to both kinds of armed conflicts. Yet, although customary international law may be relied upon by Serbian courts in establishing the content of international norms that were violated, by virtue of the chapeau of Article 142 FRY CC, the WCC did not make any reference to this source of law – not in this case and not in any other. In this regard, the WCC differs from the approach taken by the ICTY, which had not made an explicit qualification of the conflict since the intervention of NATO. In the two first ICTY judgments rendered on Kosovo, the *Limaj* and *Haradinaj* cases, the ICTY dealt only with what it considered as a non-international armed conflict, as the facts were relating to events that took place in 1998, before NATO's bombing campaign.[61] It was only in 26 February 2009, in the *Milutinovic* case, that the ICTY rendered a judgment dealing with crimes committed after the beginning of the international armed conflict. In this case the Chamber established that there was an armed conflict starting in 1998, continuing into 1999, and ending with the cessation of the NATO bombing, but without qualifying it in further detail. As the ICTY indictment did not charge grave breaches of the Geneva Conventions, but only violations of customary law applicable to all conflicts, there was no need for the ICTY to determine whether the armed conflict was internal or international.[62]

3.1.2. 'The Scorpions' Case

Unlike *Lekaj*, the *Scorpions* case was a trial with significant political overtones, as it had the potential of bringing up the matter of Serbia's involvement in the Srebrenica genocide.[63] The WCC certainly did not ignore this fact. The case dealt with war crimes committed in July 1995 against civilian prisoners brought from Srebrenica to a place near the town of Trnovo in south-east Bosnia. The arrest of the accused in Serbia followed immediately upon the release of a video

61 The ICTY case *Prosecutor v. Haradinaj et al* (IT-04–84) concerns crimes allegedly committed in Kosovo between 1 March and 30 September 1998. On the basis of the evidence before it, the ICTY Trial Chamber found that a non-international armed conflict existed in Kosovo from and including 22 April 1998 onwards. The case of *Limaj* included crimes committed during May-July 1998. During this period the Trial Chamber found the existence of a non-international armed conflict. See ICTY 30 November 2005, *Prosecutor v. Limaj et al*, Trial Chamber Judgment, IT-03–66-T, para.173.

62 ICTY 26 February 2009, *Prosecutor v. Milutinovic et al*, Trial Chamber Judgment, IT-05–87, para 1217.

63 On 2 August 2001 Bosnian Serb Army General Radislav Krstic was the first person to be convicted of genocide by the ICTY. The Appeals Chamber ruled that Krstic should have been convicted only of aiding and abetting genocide, but it confirmed the finding that genocide had taken place in Srebrenica.

that documented the shooting of prisoners from Srebrenica by members of the paramilitary unit 'Scorpions' in a very brutal manner.[64] The video had been filmed by one of the members of the Scorpions, and ten years later, in 2005, it was screened for the first time before the ICTY. Reactions in Serbia to the screening of the video were immediate. The footage was aired on most of the television stations across the Balkans as well as around the world, and had a strong impact on Serbian public opinion. Serbian authorities arrested the paramilitary members shown in the video, including the Scorpions' commander, and their trial commenced on 20 December 2005.

The video became the key piece of evidence in the criminal trial of the Scorpions in Belgrade, but not only there. Between 2005 and 2007, this video evidence was at the centre of major international proceedings before two international jurisdictions – the ICTY and the International Court of Justice – in cases relating to the genocide committed in Srebrenica. These cases raised not only complex legal questions, but also significant political issues. Hence, the *Scorpions* case represents a particular legal situation in which different international and national jurisdictions dealt with similar facts, and provides us with a rare opportunity to examine their interplay. The next part presents the international courts' findings relating to the Scorpions unit that were rendered before the Belgrade Court's ruling, so the WCC's decision could be assessed in light of them.

The Scorpions video before the ICTY and the ICJ

The Scorpions video was screened for the first time on 1 June 2005 before the ICTY Trial Chamber in the *Milošević* trial, during the cross-examination of a defence witness.[65] By showing the video, the prosecution strategy aimed to prove that the Scorpions had taken an active part in the Srebrenica massacres, and to establish that they had acted as *de facto* agents of the Serbian Ministry of the Interior.[66] If the control of Serbia over the Scorpions was proven, Milošević could be held criminally responsible for committing the genocide in Srebrenica through the doctrine of command responsibility and/or his participation in a

64 The video footage shows six prisoners first brought by the truck, disembarked by the Scorpions members and then led up a hill and into a clearing where they are shot from behind, two by two, by the Scorpions. The entire version of the film is available at www.bosniafacts.info/web/trnovo_execution_video.php. (visited 12 September 2009).

65 C. Del Ponte and C. Sudetic, Madame Prosecutor: Confrontations With Humanity's Worst Criminals and the Culture of Impunity 322 (New York: Other Press, 2009). See also p. 32282 of the transcript of the hearing in the *Milosevic* case, 1 June 2005 ('*Milosevic* Transcript'), available at http://icr.icty.org/LegalRef/ CMSDocStore/Public/English/Transcript/NotIndexable/IT-02–54/TRS2375R0000127803.doc (visited 18 September 2009).

66 *Milosevic* Transcript, *supra* note 65, p. 40251, 40260, 40267.

joint criminal enterprise as a co-perpetrator.[67] The ICTY Chief Prosecutor affirmed that the prosecution had obtained the necessary evidence to establish, according to the overall control test,[68] the link between the Scorpions and the central command in Belgrade. She referred especially to the secret minutes of the FRY Supreme Defence Council.[69] The minutes and other secret files were provided to the ICTY by the Serbian authorities on condition that they would remain confidential and used only at the trial before the ICTY. Therefore, the ICTY had afforded this evidence protective measures for 'national security criteria', according to Article 54 *bis* of the ICTY Rules of Procedure, in a confidential decision of 5 June 2003.[70] As Milošević died on March 2006, a few months before the close of the hearings in his trial, a final ruling on this question was never rendered. Since then, the evidence has remained in the ICTY's files without having been made public.[71]

In parallel, the International Court of Justice (ICJ) had to determine whether Serbia bore state responsibility for genocide in Bosnia and Herzegovina. Bosnia presented the video of the Scorpions to the Court in January 2006.[72] The applicants aimed to prove the *de facto* link between the unit and the Serbian state to attribute the acts of the Scorpions, including the massacres at Srebrenica, to the FRY according to the principles of state responsibility. Unlike the ICTY, the ICJ applied the effective control test to define who was a *de facto* state agent, as it had already established in the *Nicaragua* case.[73] Bosnia requested the ICJ to call

67 ICTY 22 November 2002, *Prosecutor v. Slobodan Milosevic*, Amended indictment, IT-02–54-T, para. 32. For further analysis see E. van Sliedregt, Joint Criminal Enterprise as a Pathway to Convicting Individuals for Genocide, 1 Journal of International Criminal Justice 184–207 (2007).

68 The ICTY set the 'overall control' test to establish which organ constitutes a *de facto* state agent in *Tadic*, para. 160. This test differs from the test established by the International Court of Justice: see below, n 73.

69 Del Ponte and Sudetic, *supra* note 65, p. 173, 202, 357. This was also affirmed by Florence Hartmann, a former spokesperson of the ICTY Office of the Prosecutor, in F. Hartmann, *Paix et châtiment. Les guerres secrètes de la politique et de la justice internationales* p. 103–104, 114–122 (Paris: Flammarion, 2007).

70 Hartmann, *supra* note 69, p. 122. On 14 September 2009 Florence Hartmann was convicted of contempt of the Tribunal by the ICTY for revealing these facts. ICTY 14 September 2009, *The Case against Florence Hartmann*, Judgment on Allegations of Contempt, IT-02–54-R77.5.

71 Yet, the ICTY Chamber found that there was prima facie evidence to establish Milošević's responsibility in committing genocide. ICTY 16 June 2004, *Prosecutor v. Milosevic*, Decision on Motion for Judgment of Acquittal, IT-02–54-T.

72 ICJ 26 February 2007, *Case Concerning the Application of the Convention on the Prevention and Punishment of the Crime of Genocide (Bosnia and Herzegovina v. Serbia and Montenegro)*, Judgment, www.icj-cij.org/docket/files/91/13685.pdf (visited 10 September 2009) ('*ICJ Genocide Case*'), para. 289.

73 The ICJ in the *Genocide Case* tried to reconcile its previous *Nicaragua* judgment and the ICTY *Tadic* judgment, by stating that the test applicable to determine a state's responsibility (effective control) can differ from the one that determines individual criminal responsibility (overall control) (*ICJ Genocide Case, supra* note 72, paras. 402–5). This approach was previously rejected by the ICTY in *Tadic*, para. 104. See also A. Cassese, On the Use of

upon Serbia and Montenegro to produce 'the "redacted" sections of documents of the Supreme Defence Council of the Respondent, i.e. sections in which parts of the text had been blacked out so as to be illegible'.[74] The ICJ refrained from doing so, arguing that Bosnia 'has extensive documentation and other evidence available to it, especially from the readily accessible ICTY records'.[75] On 26 February 2007, the ICJ held in its judgment that the act of genocide at Srebrenica could not be attributed to the FRY as, among other things, it had not been proven that the Scorpions were acting under its effective control.[76]

It remains unknown whether the evidence held by the ICTY would have satisfied the ICJ's effective control test and established the status of the Scorpions as *de facto* agents of the FRY (and whether this finding would have resulted in establishing the responsibility of the FRY for the Srebrenica genocide). According to Carla Del Ponte and Florence Hartmann, the former spokesperson of the ICTY Prosecutor's Office, the protection provided to the FRY's Defence Council minutes on a national security basis by the ICTY was related also to the fact that at the same time the ICJ was dealing with the *Genocide* case. While the Serbian government accepted to provide the evidence related to the trial of Milosevic, one of Serbia's main concerns was that if it were found by the ICJ to be responsible for genocide, the compensation that it could be required to pay would destroy the country's economy. Therefore, the Serbian government wanted insurance that the evidence could not be used in the ICJ proceedings.[77] This revelation well illustrates that political pressures bring international courts to make compromises, and that fact-finding is not merely a neutral task of revealing the truth, but often involves political decisions.[78] Such pressures at the international level, which can be fairly expected to be even more influencing on the national jurisdiction, frame the limits of the rule of law within the international legal order, and demonstrate the deficiency of the potential impact of these international jurisdictions on the Belgrade Court. This deficiency occurred not only because of the factual background that remains blurred following the ICTY protective measures, but, more troublingly, because of the international jurisdictions' divergence on the doctrinal level. As remarkable as it may seem far

---

Criminal Law Notions in Determining State Responsibility for Genocide, 5(4) Journal of International Criminal Justice 875–887; Sassòli and Olson, *supra* note 59, p. 575 (2007).

74 *ICJ Genocide Case*, *supra* note 72, paras 44 and 205.

75 *ICJ Genocide Case*, *supra* note 72, para 206. Judge Al Khasawneh in his dissenting opinion labelled this reasoning of the Court as 'worse than its failure to act', and he added that 'it is a reasonable expectation that those documents would have shed light on the central questions of intent and attribution': *ICJ Genocide Case*, Dissenting Opinion of Vice-President of Al Khasawneh, para 35. See also *ICJ Genocide Case*, Dissenting opinion of Judge ad hoc Mahiou, para. 56.

76 *ICJ Genocide Case*, *supra* note 72, para 395.

77 See C. Del Ponte and C. Sudetic (n. 65), p. 356-357 and F. Hartmann (n. 69), p. 159-162.

78 M. Shapiro, Court – A Comparative and Political Analysis 42 (Chicago: The University of Chicago Press, 1981).

away from The Hague, the legal message sent from the international courts was that the legal test to determine a *de facto* state organ depends on the jurisdiction that is required to apply it. Which of these tests should the national court in Belgrade apply? As this answer was not provided by The Hague, Belgrade could simply choose the test that brought about the more convenient political result.

The Scorpions *case before the Belgrade WCC*

On 10 April 2007, less than two months after the ICJ rendered its judgment, the WCC convicted four members of the Scorpions, including their commander, but found no link between the Scorpions to the FRY.[79] In the indictment it was alleged that the crime had taken place on 16 or 17 July 1995; that the accused, Slobodan Medic, commander of the Scorpions unit, had received an order by his superior from the Army of Republika Srpska to execute the prisoners; and that the prisoners who were shot had been brought from Srebrenica. However, in its ruling, the WCC portrayed the acts documented in the video as an isolated incident, while the broader context of the war and the massacres in Srebrenica was totally lacking. The WCC ruled that it could not establish if the unit had received an order from a higher command from Republika Srpska, the exact date of the commission of the crime, and whether the victims arrived from Srebrenica, although the victims' family members who testified confirmed that all the victims had been from Srebrenica and that they had disappeared shortly after Serbian forces had entered the town on 11 July 1995. Unlike the ICTY, which qualified the conflict in Bosnia in some of its judgments as international, whereas in others did not qualify it at all, the WCC qualified the conflict in Bosnia in 1995 as a non-international armed conflict.[80] In its conclusion it also ruled that the Scorpions had been subordinated only to the army of the Bosnian Serb Entity

---

79 War Crimes Chamber of the District Court in Belgrade 10 April 2007, *Slobodan Medić et al. (Scorpions case)*, Judgment, K.V. 6/2005 ('*Scorpions* case'). Slobodan Medic, the commander of the Scorpions, and Branislav Medic, were sentenced to 20 years in prison. One of the accused who pleaded guilty was sentenced to 13 years, and the last one, convicted for aiding and abetting, was sentenced to five years imprisonment, the minimum sentence prescribed for war crimes. In 2008, the Supreme Court reduced the term of imprisonment of Branislav Medić from 20 to 15 years. For criticism on the level of punishments see B. Ivanišević, Against the Current – War Crimes Prosecutions in Serbia (2007) (International Center for Transitional Justice, 2008), p. 17, available at www.ictj.org/images/content/7/8/780.pdf ('ICTJ report').

80 See *Scorpions* case, *supra* note 79, para. 13.3. After establishing in *Tadic* that the FRY exercised overall control over the army of Republika Srpska, the ICTY qualified the conflict in Bosnia as an international armed conflict. In *Milošević*, the ICTY prosecution also qualified the conflict as an international armed conflict: see ICTY 22 November 2002, *Prosecutor v. Milosevic*, Second Amended Indictment, IT-02–54-T. Yet, the ICTY qualification of the conflict as international was not without contestation. See T. Meron, Classification of armed conflict in the Former Yugoslavia, Nicaragua's Fallout, 93 American Journal of International Law 237–39 (1998); see also M. Sassòli and L.M. Olson, *Prosecutor v. Tadic* (Judgment), Case No. IT-94-a-A, 38 International Legal Materials 1518 (1999), 94 American Journal of International Law 575 (2000).

Republika Srpska, and clearly established that the army of Republika Srpska had no connection with the FRY, without specifying what legal test it applied in reaching this conclusion. According to the Court, no proof was shown that pointed at the formation, organization, and function, as well as the status or belongings, of the Scorpions unit, on the basis of which it could have been determined that the Scorpions unit was formed as a special unit of the Ministry of the Interior of Serbia.[81]

3.1.3. *The Ovčara Case*

A final verdict in another war crimes case before the WCC has been issued during the writing of this article and may indicate a new trend in the application of international law by the WCC. The War Crimes Department (WCD) of the Appellate Court in Belgrade confirmed, in June 2010, the verdict in the *Ovčara* case, which commenced in March 2004 and had a long procedural history of quashing and retrial. The case concerns torture and murder, at the site Ovčara, of at least 200 members of the Croatian forces captured by the then Yugoslav regular armed forces – the Yugoslav National Army (JNA) and the local Serb forces under JNA control – after their takeover of the city of Vukovar, in Croatia, in November 1991. The accused were convicted for war crimes against prisoners of war (Article 144 of the FRY CC), while the conflict in which the crime took place was qualified a non-international one.[82] Although the facts established at the trial showed unambiguously that the Croatian captives were *de facto* treated as prisoners of war (PoWs) by the Serbian side, the prosecution did not attempt to explain in its submission how PoW status is legally possible in a non-international armed conflict; nor did the WCC and the previous Supreme Court of Serbia dwell at all in their decisions on this substantive law question.[83] The

81 *Scorpions* case, *supra* note 79, para 13.4. According to the Belgrade Humanitarian Law Center, 'in reaching its Decision the Trial Chamber was clearly influenced by political rather than judicial reasons'. This is reflected in its intention to adjust its position to that of Serbia's authorities with respect to the genocide in Srebrenica in the context of the International Court of Justice decision'. Humanitarian Law Center, War Crimes Trials in Serbia 7–8 (December 2007) ('HLC 2007 Report'), available at www.hlc-rdc.org/uploads/editor/War%20Crimes%20Trials%20in%20Serbia%20Report.pdf (visited 12 September 2009).

82 The WCPO, WCC, and then the WCD considered the conflict as non-international because Croatia was internationally recognized as an independent state only on 15 January 1992. In the judgment dealing with the same crime, the ICTY did not opt for a particular qualification of the armed conflict as it was deciding on charges applicable in both types of conflicts. The ICTY's holding of Yugoslav Army forces as 'government authorities' and Croatian as 'organised armed groups' suggests, however, that it considered events in Vukovar in 1991 a non-international armed conflict. ICTY 27 September 2007, *Prosecutor v. Mrksic et al*, Trial Judgment, IT-95-13/1-T, paras. 409–418.

83 See Amended *Ovčara* Indictment (*Miroljub Vujevic et al*), 16 September 2005, p. 14–15, available in English at www.tuzilastvorz.org.rs/html_trz/OPTUZNICE/O_2005_09_16_ENG.pdf (visited 10 November 2010).

Appellate Court's WCD was the first to have picked up and deliberated on this legal issue.

The Court confirmed the non-international character of the conflict, but it further held that the ground for the PoW status of the victims in such a conflict was to be found, based on documentary evidence from the trial, in unilateral declarations of the JNA, as a party to the conflict, as well as in the JNA agreement with the Croatian side that the Croat forces were to be considered PoWs and that Geneva Convention III was to apply.[84] The Court did not specify which article of the Geneva Conventions or international jurisprudence it had specifically in mind, but its conclusion nonetheless stayed in line with Article 3(2) – applicable in non-international armed conflict – of the Third Geneva Convention, which reads: 'The Parties to the conflict should further endeavour to bring into force, by means of special agreements, all or part of the other provisions of the present Convention.' Moreover, the ICTY Appeals Chamber, when judging on the same crime, but against different individuals, also reached the same conclusion.[85] The defence also raised some of the international law-related issued in their appeal, mostly focusing on PoW status. Given that the WCC and the Supreme Court in their previous decisions did not elaborate on the issue in response to similar submissions by the defence, leaving them as almost self-evident, it seems more likely that the appellate WCD this time considered as its *ex-officio* call to provide a deeper legal reasoning when making references to international law, rather than feeling compelled to do so by the argument of the defence. The President of the War Crimes Department also confirmed in an interview that judges in the Department felt obliged to shed more light and clarify *proprio motu* some of the legal issues that previous judicial panels usually leave unexplained; they wanted to establish a new legal culture of judgment drafting which would duly establish and deliberate on the legal basis for convictions in international law.[86]

---

84 War Crimes Department of the Appellate Court in Belgrade 23 June 2010, *Miroljub Vujević et al.* (*Ovčara case*), Appeals Judgment, Kž1, PO2-1/2010, paras.75–76 ('*Ovčara* Appeals Judgment').

85 The ICTY held that 'even in the context of an internal armed conflict, Geneva Convention III applies where the parties to the conflict have agreed that the Convention shall apply'. ICTY 5 May 2009, *Prosecutor v. Mrksic and Sljivancanin*, Appeals Judgment, IT-95-13/1-A, para. 69.

86 Interview with President of the War Crimes Department (WCD) of the Belgrade Appellate Court (Belgrade, 2 November 2010). In the *Ovčara* verdict, the WCD made a few other references to international law, and to ICTY jurisprudence, even on issues that are of procedural and not of international law nature. The references relate, inter alia, to the rule that in case of doubt, enemy captives should be treated as PoWs, until decided otherwise by a competent tribunal, which reflects Art. 5 of the GC III (*Ovčara* Appeals Judgment, *supra* note 84, para. 85). References were also made to the ICTY *Blaskic* Appeals Judgment, in relation to the acquisition of PoW status (see *Ovčara* Appeals Judgment, *supra* note 84, para. 83), or on a procedural issue such as credibility of witness, in reference to the ICTY *Kupreskic* Trial Judgment (see *Ovčara* Appeals Judgment, *supra* note 84, para. 68).

3.2. PATTERNS AND TRENDS

3.2.1 Legal Framework for Application of International Law

Serbia has a legal system conducive to the enforcement of international law by national courts. Courts are required to construe different forms of war crimes set forth in the national criminal code in line with both customary and treaty international law. The international law renvoi was not a novel creation in the legal framework of the Serbian transitional democracy, but it was simply inherited from the pre-war socialist Yugoslavia. What was a new constitutional moment, however, was the establishment of specialised judicial institutions and procedural norms expected to create conditions in a post-conflict society in which international law can be given effect through individual criminal accountability for serious violations of international law during the 1990s armed conflicts in the former Yugoslavia. The model was established and supported through mainly a top-down approach – the government's political decision to show the new face of the state, with some influence of civil society, and with support, but also close scrutiny of international actors which aimed to stabilise the rule of law in Serbia and in the whole region of the former Yugoslavia. Such a model is a backward-looking; it was created not to avert future human rights violations, but to provide redress for the past ones which were the result of collective and state campaigns. It faces challenges such as concurrent legal and factual interpretations of its international predecessors (the ICTY), the existing national narratives, and the legacy of state interests.

3.2.2. The Ability of the WCC to Enforce International Law

The *Lekaj* and *Scorpions* cases reveal two observations related to the capacity of the WCC to apply international law as required by rule of law doctrine. First, it can be noticed that the level of IHL expertise of the judges is falling short. In the Serbian legal framework, in which the WCC is explicitly required by the Serbian criminal code to apply international law in order to convict alleged war criminals, knowledge of international law is a fundamental requirement from a domestic perspective. Yet, as demonstrated in *Lekaj*, international treaty law is not accurately applied and references to international jurisprudence and customary law are lacking. At the same time, judges seriously engage in referring to international treaty law, although not always explicitly or accurately, and perceive it as an authoritative legal framework. Such application of international law is a matter of lack of skills and of a legal tradition that often sees international law merely as a required referencing formality, rather than a result of a negative stance towards international law or the ICTY, on whose experience and evidentiary material the WCC relies a lot. Therefore, this problem can be resolved by improving skills and knowledge of the legal practitioners and by developing a legal culture in which judgments address not only factual, but also legal questions. This is, as demonstrated in the *Ovcara* case appellate decision, an emerging tendency in Serbia, but it depends on individual judges' legal mindsets. Chances for making references to the ICTY jurisprudence, shown in the *Ovcara* case, are rising also because the Serbian war crimes judges have been more and more exposed to contacts with the ICTY and international judges – through mutual cooperation as well as training organised by the international community.

A second observation relates to the capacity of the Court to reconcile political goals with valid international legal arguments. National courts in post-conflict situations are supposed to combat impunity, and international law is supposed to provide them a neutral framework to effectuate this task. Yet, as the application of international law will always be a compromise between justice and politics,[87] political choices made by the judges while interpreting the law or establishing the facts are an integral part of the international rule of law as long as the positive law is not distorted and the legal framework is respected. In this regard, the Serbian Court is another example of a judicial institution that makes its own efforts to apply IHL while trying to find a proper balance between the application of the law and international and local political pressures. While both international and local courts may be influenced by political pressure and interests, as the *Scorpions* case may demonstrate, the striking difference between them is their material capacity to incorporate these political goals into the legal framework of international law. For example, it can be argued (although not affirmatively confirmed) that the ICTY and the ICJ relied on two distinct control doctrines in order to reach a desired conclusion in light of the evidence at their disposal. At the same time, each jurisdiction provided an extensive legal argument in support of their political choice. In contrast, the WCC relied almost exclusively on fact-finding and did not develop any legal justification on a doctrinal level. While the WCC's final conclusion is predictable as a matter of policy, the absence of doctrinal argumentation seems to be related to the judges' professional deficiency rather than a political choice, as the Court could have easily relied on the ICJ ruling to attain the result it opted for.

3.2.3. The Willingness of the WCC to Apply International Law

In a post-conflict society, rule of law reform needs to be capable of serving justice at all sides of the conflict – however unpalatable politically. It is fundamental that the law is enforced in an equal manner without having national interests prevail that could lead to a double standards application. Having said that, one

87 See, eg, M. Koskenniemi, From Apology to Utopia: The Structure of International Legal Argument 590–596 (Cambridge University Press, 2006).

should be conscious of the limits of the Court as a state institution. When the legislative framework promotes equal enforcement of international law – as it does in the case of Serbia – it is fundamental to observe whether international law is enforced in an equal manner irrespective of who is the victim and perpetrator, or whether the courts use double standards in their application of international law. In the case of the latter, does the double standard phenomenon result from institutional deficiency of the judiciary and lack of independency, or from a policy of restraint of the courts that is, to a certain extent, predictable and inevitable in order to safeguard their legitimacy at the domestic level?

The trial of Lekaj, in which the Court was judging the conduct of what the majority in Serbia perceived as the enemy side, was handled relatively fast, without encountering internal political obstacles. Having in mind that only a few cases were completed in several years – as a number of them being remanded for re-trial by decisions of the previous Supreme Court of Serbia, which were considered by many observers as dubious[88] – it may not be a mere coincidence that the first conviction of the WCC confirmed on appeal was an Albanian from Kosovo in a case in which the victims included a Serb. While this choice could be perceived as a double standards attitude exercised by the Court, its motivation could have related to legitimate institutional considerations: this first case could contribute to the perception of legitimacy of the Court within Serbian society – a legitimacy that needed to be acquired in order to secure its future institutional function, as war crimes convictions against Serbs are still politically and emotionally very sensitive.

The *Scorpions* case well portrays the limits of the Belgrade Court. Although the WCC convicted four Serbian members of the paramilitary unit Scorpions, the WCC ruling was in line with the political interest of the state, as it did not engage in connecting the defendants' acts with the broader context of genocide that was on-going at the time and place, nor establish any link with the command in Belgrade. The Scorpions' crimes were portrayed as an isolated act, lacking any reference to the on-going Srebrenica genocide.[89] Yet, the outcome of the ruling was predictable and it seems that such restrictions on the rule of law are still inevitable. In the Balkans' post-conflict political context, as it would have probably been in any other place, it is hardly imaginable that a national court would reach a ruling that would engage such a far-reaching outcome as a link to

88 There are reports suggesting that the decisions of the Supreme Court in quashing several first instance convictions against Serb defendants went against facts established at the trial in an attempt to avoid taking unpopular responsibility to confirm convictions of Serbs. ICTJ Report, *supra* note 79, p. 18–19, Human Rights Watch, Unfinished Business Serbia's War Crimes Chamber (28 June 2007), p. 30–31, available at www.hrw.org/en/reports/2007/06/28/unfinished-business (visited 24 October 2010).

89 As the NGOs observing the trial reported: 'the position of the Trial Chamber can only be explained by political motives whose objective is to separate the execution of the six Bosniak civilians from the killing of 8,000 Bosniaks from Srebrenica in the period from July 11 to July 19, 1995': HLC 2007 Report, *supra* note 81, p. 7; see also ICTJ report, *supra* note 79, p. 16.

the commission of genocide in opposition to the state's official narrative. National courts of democratic states with a long tradition of judicial independency have developed different self-restraint doctrines, such as the act of state doctrine or the political question doctrine, in order to avoid rendering rulings on issues with colossal political consequences. Emerging democratic states in a post-conflict era have to deal on a daily basis with sensitive issues of reconciliation and to surmount numerous economic obstacles and other difficulties. Their courts are supposed to take these fragilities into account, probably more and certainly not less than any other court in a stable and powerful state. Therefore, in post-conflict societies, the judiciary alone cannot provide the required justice reform unless it is supported by other mechanisms that reinforce its local position.

4. CONCLUSION

A national legal framework that empowers local courts to apply international law is a precondition for legal norms being adopted at international level to be enforced in national jurisdictions. The creation of specialised judicial institutions and particular procedural tools can also be of a significant help for such enforcement. The legal framework alone, however, does not guarantee the enforcement of international law in a manner that is always both legally correct and free of political considerations. This is particularly the case when a national court is addressing serious violations of international humanitarian law – a field of law which has been much shaped by international courts and tribunals – in a post-conflict society, which makes it, in such circumstances, subject to strong political and social influences.

The extent to which a domestic court functions in accordance with the principles of the international rule of law in a post-conflict society depends both on its objective material ability to apply international law, and its subjective political willingness to do so. Not all judges and lawyers are equipped with the necessary knowledge of international law, and, in some cases, it appears that the main problem with respect to the rule of law is a simple misapplication of the law. Naturally, obstacles related to the willingness of the court to apply international law are more difficult to resolve. At the same time, while it is essential that the law be enforced in an equal and independent manner, it must be recalled that courts dealing with transitional justice are subject to important institutional limitations. Their endorsement of political considerations, as well as the practice of double-standard application of the law, do not necessarily result from an institutional deficiency related to judicial independence or disregard for the principles of the rule of law, but most often rather from a predictable policy of self-restraint that aims at safeguarding courts' local legitimacy and meeting the expectations of their societal and state interests. Therefore, for a post-conflict reform to succeed, it cannot be expected that the judiciary alone will uphold the rule of law and provide redress for gross human rights violations. It has to be supported by other actors and mechanisms that reinforce its domestic position, such as other state institutions and political elites, public awareness raising through the media and education system, the strengthening of civil society, and construction of a national post-conflict narrative through truth commissions and other such means.

THE TREATMENT OF OCCUPATION LEGISLATION BY COURTS IN LIBERATED TERRITORIES

Eyal BENVENISTI and Michal SALITERNIK*

1. INTRODUCTION

This chapter focuses on the jurisprudence of courts in liberated territories concerning the laws and administrative acts promulgated and applied by the occupying power. These courts must balance the international legality test against the adverse effects that the enforcement of international law could have on the local population and the returning government. As we show, national courts in the aftermath of occupation tend to attach higher priority to the transitional needs of their societies, and this could lead them, in cases of conflict, to downplay questions of international legality.[1]

Our observations suggest that the need to respect legitimate expectations of individual parties has prompted some courts to validate transactions that were conducted in accordance with the occupant's orders even when such orders exceeded the limits that international law placed on the occupant's regulatory power. Moreover, there is some indication that the commitment of national courts to the processes of national reconciliation and the reshaping of national identity may also be stronger than their commitment to enforcing international law. Finally, considerations concerning the courts' own reputation may also lead them to downplay the international legality test.

---

* Eyal Benvenisti is Professor of Law, Tel Aviv University, Faculty of Law. Michal Saliternik is a PhD Candidate at the Zvi Meitar Center for Advanced Legal Studies at the Tel Aviv University Faculty of Law. Research for this article was supported by grant 121/08 from the Israel Science Foundation.

1 In fact, since its emergence, the international law of occupation has been influenced and shaped by the jurisprudence of national courts. The law of the occupant has been considered not only by national courts in liberated territories, but also by courts under occupation, by courts in the unoccupied part of a partially occupied country, by the occupants' own courts, and by courts in third countries. These courts have had other constraints that have influenced their approaches, but the study of those is beyond the scope of this chapter. For an overview of the phenomenon of occupation, see E. Benvenisti, The International Law of Occupation ch 1 (Princeton University Press, 1993).

The 'transitional bias' of post-occupation courts which prefer transitional considerations over enforcing international law usually benefits domestic constituencies and local institutions. Obviously, however, this bias also reduces the effectiveness of the strictures of the law of occupation: future occupants would realize that their illegal measures would nevertheless be respected by the returning sovereign's courts, whereas appropriate legal measures might be ignored. While the 'transitional bias' is perfectly understandable, we argue that courts should nevertheless explicitly invoke this bias in their reasoning, thereby doing justice in a particular case while at the same time refining and developing the *ex ante* obligations of the occupants. One such example of retaining a distinction between the *ex ante* legality of the occupant's measures and the *ex post* validity of their outcomes was demonstrated by the International Court of Justice (ICJ) 1971 *Advisory Opinion concerning the South African rule in Namibia*.[2] The so-called 'Namibia Exception' recognizes the need to respect legitimate expectations that are based on illegitimate legislation.

In order to appreciate the challenges faced by national courts in post-occupation periods, and to explore strategies they adopt in response to those challenges, this chapter examines several judicial decisions delivered in different post-occupation situations. These case studies include judgments in which national courts examined the validity of personal and commercial transactions conducted during World War II in accordance with occupation orders (part 1); a judgment of the Namibian Supreme Court concerning discriminatory allocation of public resources by the previous South African regime (part 2); the Iraqi High Criminal Tribunal's decision to impose capital punishment on Saddam Hussein, notwithstanding the suspension of this punishment by the occupation authorities (part 3); and, finally, cases from East Timor and Kosovo in which prescriptive measures of UN territorial administrations were scrutinized by national courts (part 4). These case studies represent all post World War II judgments related to our discussion that are available in English and that offer a fairly clear sense of the relevant factors considered by the courts. On the basis of these cases, part 5 suggests an integrated analysis of the treatment of occupation laws by national courts in post-occupation situations, and addresses the implications of this jurisprudence on the international law of occupation.

2. OCCUPATIONS DURING WORLD WAR II

Article 43 of the Hague Regulations requires occupants to restore and ensure public order and civil life in the occupied territory, 'while respecting, unless

2 ICJ, *Legal Consequences for States of the Continued Presence of South Africa in Namibia (South West Africa) Notwithstanding Security Council Resolution 276 (1970)*, Advisory Opinion, 1971 ICJ Reports 16 ('*Advisory Opinion concerning Namibia*').

absolutely prevented, the laws in force in the country'.[3] The phrase 'absolutely prevented' has received multiple interpretations by various commentators over the years. By the onset of World War II, the only consensus that had emerged was that the occupant may enact laws that are necessary for the security of its forces.[4] In practice, however, occupying powers during and immediately after World War II adopted a far more permissive interpretation of the phrase 'absolutely prevented', or simply disregarded the Hague Regulations altogether, and exercised wide regulatory authority in those territories occupied by them.[5] Subsequently, in the War's aftermath, national courts of returning sovereigns had to address the consequences of such regulatory measures. As we show below, it seems that these courts primarily sought to uphold expectations of inhabitants who legitimately relied upon the occupant's prescriptions, and to prevent the unjust enrichment of those who tried to take unfair advantage of such prescriptions. In some cases – as in the Italian case discussed below, and perhaps to a lesser degree in the Luxembourg case – these goals went hand in hand with delineating the appropriate contours of the occupant's law-making authority under the law of occupation. In other cases – as demonstrated by the Greek case – the 'transitional bias' of the court resulted in a problematic application of the international legality test.

2.1. BULGARIAN OCCUPATION OF GREECE: THE *KOMOTINI* CASE

In the *Komotini* case, a Greek national living in the Bulgarian occupation zone of northern Greece dictated his last will and testament to a Bulgarian judge according to provisions of Bulgarian law that was applicable in that area. After liberation, the heirs named in his will filed a claim in the court in Rhodpe, Greece, against individuals who were in possession of the deceased's property. The defendants argued that, since the Bulgarian occupant had exceeded its authority under international law, the will was void.[6] The court rejected that claim and asserted that the will was valid. It noted that:

> *It is an indisputable fact that the Bulgarians … endeavored to remove all trace of Greek sovereignty with a view to 'denationalization'.* The Bulgarians introduced their civil, commercial and penal legislation into this region; … they abolished the Greek courts

3 Article 43 of the Regulations Respecting the Laws and Customs of War on Land, Annex to the Convention Respecting the Laws and Customs of War on Land, signed at The Hague, 18 October 1907 'Hague Regulations'.

4 See Benvenisti, *supra* note 1, p. 13–14.

5 Benvenisti, *supra* note 1, p. 59.

6 *In re P* (*Komotini Case*) [1948] 15 Annual Digest and Reports of Public International Law Cases (AD) 566 ('*Case No. 187*').

> and replaced them by Bulgarian courts, composed of Bulgarian judges ... who applied Bulgarian legal procedure and substantive law.[7]

The court went on to explain that:

> It is true that after the Greek judges left, the occupation authorities should have organized provisional Greek justice (with magistrates of Greek nationality rendering justice according to Greek law). However, *this was not possible because of the persecution of all educated persons of Greek nationality. This* de facto *situation made it impossible to do otherwise than organize Bulgarian justice. Since the application of Greek law was not practicable, the application of Bulgarian justice became consistent with international law.* Accordingly it was proper for Bulgarian law to be formally applied to the document containing the will on which the case was based.[8]

This reasoning is hard to understand. Describing the legal vacuum faced by the Bulgarian occupant as a '*de facto* situation' that leads to the conclusion that 'the application of Bulgarian justice became consistent with international law' seems to endorse the intentional 'denationalization' by the occupant.[9] According to the court's interpretation of international law,[10] an occupant may, by its own wrongful acts, create a situation in which it is 'absolutely prevented' from respecting the local law. Hence, it seems to undermine the basic rationale of Article 43 of the Hague Regulations that aims to preserve the *status quo* in the occupied territory while providing for the occupied population.

The same line of reasoning as was adopted in the *Komotini* case is apparent in the jurisprudence of a higher Greek instance – the Court of Appeal of Thrace – which validated real estate contracts drawn up by Bulgarian judges in accordance with Bulgarian law.[11] The Court of Appeal explained that since 'Greek officials, judges and notaries had left the country in order to avoid serving under the Bulgarian yoke',[12] the Bulgarian occupant was compelled to nominate its own

---

7 *Case No. 187, supra* note 6, p. 566 (emphasis added).

8 *Case No. 187, supra* note 6, p. 566–567 (emphasis added).

9 As Raphael Lemkin notes, in the Bulgarian-occupied part of Greece, '[t]he Greek administrative agencies were abolished and Bulgarian institutions introduced instead ... The personnel of the administration was Bulgarized completely' (R. Lemkin, Axis Rule in Occupied Europe: Laws of Occupation – Analysis of Government – Proposals for Redress 187–188 (Washington DC: Carnegie Endowment for International Peace, 1944)).

10 Our discussion of World War II cases is based on their reports in the AD and International Law Reports (ILR). These reports sometimes refer in general to 'international law' or to 'the international law of occupation', without mentioning a specific source. We do not know whether the original judgment included such specific reference or not. In any event, it seems safe to assume that unless explicitly mentioned otherwise, the international law referred to in these cases is Article 43 of the Hague Regulations, which was at that time, the only treaty-based law that delineated the regulatory authority of the occupant.

11 See *L v. N (Bulgarian Occupation of Greece)* [1947] 14 AD 242 ('*Case No. 110*'), and *Thrace (Notarial Services)* [1949] 16 AD 466 (*Case No. 167*).

12 *Case No. 110, supra* note 11, p. 244.

judges and apply its own laws in order to fulfil the duty placed on it by Article 43 to restore and ensure public order and civil life. This skewed presentation of the circumstances – ie, the Greek officials having left voluntarily rather than being forced to leave – further demonstrates the Greek courts' willingness to de-emphasize the occupant's illegal measures.

A possible explanation for this line of cases is the courts' determination to uphold private transactions that took place during the occupation in reliance upon the prevailing law. But still the question remains whether in such cases other legal strategies could reach the same result without legitimizing illegal occupation practices. Several alternative approaches could be considered. First, courts could assert that, despite the breach of the law by the occupant, they are entitled to decide, *ex post*, that an act performed under unlawful occupation law is nevertheless valid. In order to minimize legal uncertainty, courts could even develop criteria – such as good faith or lack of alternatives for the affected individuals – for validating acts conducted under invalid laws. This alternative is costly, because it would require a separate examination of each act conducted under illegal occupation laws, and this might overburden the courts with numerous proceedings.[13]

A second strategy to which courts in such situations could turn would be to adopt a purposive interpretation of the domestic law that should have been applied by the occupant, and hold that its formal requirements that were not complied with during the occupation were insignificant under the circumstances and therefore could be waived. Such an interpretive strategy was actually endorsed by the Supreme Court of Poland. When addressing the validity of real estate contracts made between Polish nationals during the German occupation without the approval of a notary as required under Polish law, the Polish court determined that it had authority to regard such contracts as valid.[14] It reasoned that compliance with that formal requirement was impossible due to an unlawful order of the German occupant which replaced Polish notaries with German ones and instructed the latter to prevent any attempt by Polish nationals to dispose of immovable property.[15] In a subsequent case, the Supreme Court of Poland similarly held that a will executed during occupation without a notary approval was not necessarily invalid, and it ordered the district court to re-hear the case to decide whether the will expressed the actual intention of the deceased.[16]

13 The method of individual validation was adopted in France (by the political branches, not the courts). A French ordinance promulgated on 15 September 1944 provided that German judgments rendered in some areas that were annexed by Germany in 1940 must be declared enforceable by French authorities in order to become effective (see *Dame Reimann v. Procureur-General* [1960] 38 ILR 470).

14 *B v. T* [1949] 24 ILR 962.

15 This instruction was made in order to facilitate the implementation of yet another illegal German ordinance that permitted the confiscation of Polish nationals' property.

16 In re *Will of Josef K.* [1949] 24 ILR 966.

A third strategy available to courts wishing to uphold transactions that are based on illegal measures of the occupant is to apply the 'Namibia Exception', which was developed by the ICJ in its *Advisory Opinion concerning Namibia*[17] and was endorsed by the European Court of Human Rights (ECtHR).[18] According to the Namibia Exception, the invalidity of acts performed by an illegal regime 'cannot be extended to those acts, such as, for instance, the registration of births, deaths and marriages, the effects of which can be ignored only to the detriment of the inhabitants of the territory'.[19]

It is true that these three alternative strategies risk motivating future occupants who are aware that their illegal prescriptions might ultimately be effective to disrespect international constraints on their regulatory authority. However, unlike the Greek courts' approach, these three possible strategies retain a crucial distinction between asserting the illegality of the occupant's prescriptions *ex ante*, while recognizing the validity of transactions conducted in accordance with them *ex post*. This distinction leaves some uncertainty regarding which transactions would eventually be enforced, and it also affects the occupant's reputation as law breaker. It therefore potentially enhances the incentives of future occupants to comply with international law.

2.2. GERMAN OCCUPATION OF LUXEMBOURG: THE CASE OF *G V H*

With the occupation of Luxembourg, German military authorities promulgated a decree stating that all debts owed in Luxembourgian currency could be discharged by payment in the same or in German currency. In accordance with this decree, the defendant tendered part of her pre-war debt to the plaintiff in Reichsmark; however, the latter refused to accept the money. The defendant lodged a complaint with the German authorities, who fined the plaintiff for his refusal. After the end of occupation, the plaintiff filed a tort suit against the defendant claiming the amount of the fine that he had paid.[20]

The District Court of Luxembourg found for the plaintiff and held that under the Hague Regulations, the German authorities had not been entitled to introduce German currency into the occupied territory at par with the local currency or to permit the satisfaction of pre-war debts by payment in Reichsmark.

17 See note 2 above.

18 See Ect.HR (2001), *Cyprus v. Turkey*, App. No. 25781/94, paras 93–98, and Ect.HR (2010), *Demopoulos and Others v. Turkey*, App. Nos. 46113/99, 3843/02, 13751/02, 13466/03, 10200/04, 14163/04, 19993/04, 21819/04, paras 93–96. The Namibia Exception has also gained support in states' practice (see J. Crawford, The Creation of States in International Law 167 (Oxford University Press, 2006, 2nd ed.); *Cyprus v Turkey*, para. 97).

19 *Advisory Opinion concerning Namibia*, *supra* note 2, p. 56.

20 *G v H* [1951] 18 ILR 633 ('*Case No. 198*').

Moreover, the court held, if the defendant believed that her rights had been violated by the plaintiff's refusal to accept the payment, she should have applied to a local court and not to the German military authorities. The defendant's application to the German authorities was, according to the court, 'unjustified, and it could only have been intended to serve the purpose of causing these authorities to exert pressure on G. in order to procure an advantage to the defendant'.[21]

In contrast to the Greek courts, the Luxembourg court did not hesitate to declare the occupant's decree unlawful and to invalidate a transaction that was conducted in reliance upon it. The court's remarks about the defendant's inappropriate attempt to take an advantage of the devaluation of German currency implied that its judgment, just like the Greek decisions, reflected transitional considerations – only, in this case, they were more compatible with international law.[22]

2.3. ALLIED OCCUPATION OF ITALY: THE *DU BAN* CASE

Following an order from the Allied Military Government, the local authority of Gorizia, a town in the occupied area in Italy, entered into an agreement with the plaintiffs for the reconstruction of buildings destroyed in the war. After the occupation ended the local authority refused to pay the contractors the remainder of its debt under the contract, asserting that it was not bound by a contract that it had signed due to the occupant's order. The Italian Court of Cassation rejected the claim, reasoning that the military government's order was within the limits of its authority under international law and the armistice treaty between the Allies and Italy, and therefore the local authority was obliged to adhere to it.[23] International law, according to the court, entailed

> the acceptance by the occupied State of particular activities of the Occupant, especially activities of an administrative nature which, while the powers of the Occupied State are in abeyance, are shown to be necessary for the organization of society within the occupied territory and which answer the needs of that society.[24]

---

21 *Case No. 198*, *supra* note 20, p. 634.

22 The finding that the introduction of the occupant's currency at par with the local currency constituted a violation of the Hague Regulations was shared by other national courts. See *Taik v. Dooply* [1948] 18 ILR 576 (Case No. 191); *Dooply v. Taik* [1950] 18 ILR 641 (Case No. 202) (Burma), and *Tse Chung v. Lee Yau Chu* [1951] 18 ILR 636 (Case No. 200) (Hong Kong). Cf. *Haw Pia v. China Banking Corp* [1948] 18 ILR 642 (Case No. 203); *Gibbs v. Rodriguez* [1950] 18 ILR 661 (Case. No 204) (Philippines).

23 *Du Ban and Icoredit v. Public Works Administration* [1960] 40 ILR 467.

24 *Du Ban and Icoredit v. Public Works Administration*, *supra* note 23, p. 471.

In the short term, the Italian court decision protected the plaintiffs' legitimate expectations to be paid in accordance with the contract. In the long run, the enforcement of a commercial contract that was signed under complex legal and political circumstances conveyed a positive message to potential contractors and investors and therefore enhanced market stability. It also provided assurance for occupants wishing to promote the interests of the local population. Thus, the *Du Ban* case provides a remarkable example of a post-occupation judgment that promotes transitional policies while refining our understanding of the authority of occupants under international law.

3. SOUTH AFRICAN RULE IN NAMIBIA: THE *CULTURA 2000* CASE

The South African rule in Namibia was generally not regarded as occupation. However, the law of occupation can be considered applicable to this regime, or at least it could inform courts in the newly independent country. The judgment in the *Cultura 2000* case therefore provides another example for a court in a liberated area that deals with expectations of individuals acquired as a result of unlawful measures of a former regime.[25]

Shortly before transition to Namibian rule in March 1990, the South African Administration allocated valuable public assets to 'Cultura 2000', an association incorporated during South African rule for the preservation of the culture of the Afrikaans, German, Portuguese, English, and other communities of European descent. The newly founded Namibian Parliament asserted that the main purpose of the association, and of the allocation of funds, was to ensure the continued distribution of financial privileges on a racial basis, and thus it promulgated the State Repudiation (Cultura 2000) Act of 1991 (the Cultura 2000 Act). The Act repudiated the donation of any property to Cultura 2000 and ordered the return of property and monies already allocated to the association.

The Cultura 2000 Act was adopted pursuant to a provision of the Namibian Constitution which deemed all actions committed under South African law prior to the date of independence 'to have been done by the Government of the Republic of Namibia […] unless such action is subsequently repudiated by an Act of Parliament'.[26] Cultura 2000 claimed that the Act was unconstitutional, and the first instance court agreed. It held that the authority of the Parliament to repudiate actions could not be applied to the allocation of funds to Cultura 2000 because this act had already been completed by the South African

25 *Government of the Republic of Namibia v. Cultura 2000* (SA 2/92) [1993] NASC 1 ('*Cultura 2000* judgment'), available at www.saflii.org.

26 Article 140(3) of the Namibian Constitution.

administration, and there was no further obligation for the Namibian government to perform.[27]

The Supreme Court of Namibia rejected the conclusion of the first instance and held that the power of repudiation granted to the Parliament by the Constitution was not limited to uncompleted actions. Therefore, the provision of the Cultura 2000 Act that repudiated the allocation of funds to Cultura 2000 was constitutional and valid. In the regular course of events, the Supreme Court would have then gone on to examine the legality of the provisions of the Cultura 2000 Act that determined the consequences of the repudiation. But the Namibian government had confined its appeal only to the declaration of the first instance that the repudiating provision of the Cultura 2000 Act was unconstitutional, and it did not oppose the finding that the provisions demanding the return of allocated properties were void. Thus, Cultura 2000 was not required to return property or repay the government, and in fact the decision of the Supreme Court had no practical consequences.

Why, then, was it so important for the Supreme Court to uphold the legality of the repudiating clause that it was willing to adopt what was arguably a far-fetched interpretation of the Constitution? The court explained that its decision was informed by the most fundamental aims of the new Constitution – to condemn the racial policies of the South African regime, and, as its Preamble articulated, to cherish and protect the gains of the Namibian people in their long and bitter struggle against such policies. In the eyes of the court, the repudiation of the discriminatory act had expressed the wish of the Namibian Parliament to draw a line between the old regime and the new one, a line that must not be blurred by legal fictions that attribute acts of the former to the latter.

In denying the legitimacy of the occupant's measures while preserving the outcomes of these measures, the Namibian Supreme Court's decision seems to apply the rationale of the Namibia Exception (although this exception was not explicitly mentioned in its judgment, nor were other questions of international legality). As indicated above, the Namibia Exception as stipulated by the ICJ referred to 'neutral' acts such as the registration of births, deaths, and marriages. It is not clear whether the ICJ would have endorsed the extension of the Exception to the allocation of benefits to a white association on the basis of a discriminatory policy. Obviously, the expectations that are created by such an act cannot be compared to expectations of inhabitants depending on local registries and other official acts for conducting their day-to-day affairs.[28]

---

27 *Cultura 2000* judgment, *supra* note 25, p. 18.

28 It should be noted, however, that while the examples of valid acts mentioned in the ICJ Advisory Opinion clearly share a non-political nature, the opinion does not explicitly exclude acts of a different nature from the scope of the 'Namibia Exception'. Only Judge De Castro, in his separate opinion, asserted that

> A distinction must be made between the private and the public sector. It would seem that the acts of the *de facto* authorities relating to the acts and rights of private persons should

4. COALITION OCCUPATION OF IRAQ: THE TRIAL OF SADDAM HUSSEIN

On 5 November 2006, a five-judge panel of the Iraqi High Criminal Tribunal (IHCT) found former Iraqi President Saddam Hussein responsible for severe crimes committed in 1982 against the inhabitants of the Iraqi village of al-Dujail and sentenced him to death by hanging.[29] This verdict was criticized for imposing the death penalty despite the occupation laws that prohibited such punishment. Other critics challenged the jurisdiction of the IHCT on the basis that it had been established by the coalition that occupied Iraq. This section explores the manner in which these conflicting accusations – on the one hand of collaboration with the occupant, and on the other hand of not respecting its legitimate law-making power –played out in the Iraqi context.

The IHCT was established by the Coalition Provisional Authority (CPA) during its occupation of Iraq.[30] Hence, the main question that the IHCT addressed in response to Saddam Hussein's preliminary motion regarding its jurisdiction was whether the CPA was vested with the authority to set up the court. The IHCT held that the CPA's authority to establish a special tribunal to try the crimes of the former government stemmed from Security Council Resolution 1483.[31] The court also noted that the democratically elected Iraqi government had amended and in fact re-promulgated the original IHCT Statute, and by doing so further enhanced the court's legitimacy. Notably, the court did

---

> be regarded as valid (validity of entries in the civil registers and in the Land Registry, validity of marriages, validity of judgments of the civil courts, etc.). On the other hand, other States should not regard as valid any acts and transactions of the authorities in Namibia relating to public property, concessions, etc. States will thus not be able to exercise protection of their nationals with regard to any acquisitions of this kind. (*Advisory Opinion concerning Namibia*, *supra* note 2, p. 218–19.)

In a recent decision concerning the expropriation of Greek Cypriots' property by the Turkish Republic of Northern Cyprus (TRNC), the ECtHR confirmed that the Namibia Exception can be applied to situations and acts different from those mentioned in the ICJ Advisory Opinion. See *Demopoulos v. Turkey*, *supra* note 18, paras 93–96. See also *Cyprus v. Turkey*, *supra* note 18, paras 93–98.

29 Iraqi High Tribunal Trial Chamber, Case No. 1/9 First/2005 Al-Dujail Lawsuit, 5 November 2006. An unofficial English translation of the Trial Chamber's judgment, provided by the IHCT, is available at the Grotian Moment website, http://law.case.edu/saddamtrial/dujail/opinion.asp.

30 CPA Order No 48 (10 December 2003), Section 1(1), authorized the Governing Council (the provisional government of Iraq appointed by the CPA) 'to establish an Iraqi Special Tribunal … to try Iraqi nationals or residents of Iraq accused of genocide, crimes against humanity, war crimes or violations of certain Iraqi laws'. Available at www.iraqcoalition.org/regulations.

31 UN Doc. S/RES/1483 (2003). SC Resolution 1483 recognized the coalition in Iraq as an occupying power subject to the Hague Regulations of 1907 and to the Geneva Conventions of 1949. The resolution did not explicitly endow the CPA with the authority to establish a criminal tribunal.

not base its finding directly on the authority of the occupying powers, but on that of the Security Council and the Iraqi government.

The IHCT tried to steer the middle course between supporters and detractors of the former regime as well as the growing opposition to the occupation, not only with respect to explaining its jurisdiction but also with respect to its decision to impose the death penalty. Defying the CPA's authority to abolish capital punishment can be understood in this context as a way to assert the court's independence of the occupants. The Iraqi court's argument was actually not out of line with the law of occupation. The Iraqi Penal Code, 1969 permitted the use of capital punishment. The IHCT reasoned in its verdict that, since the CPA Order merely 'suspended' capital punishment,[32] and since the CPA had been dissolved prior to the initiation of the proceedings against Hussein, this provision no longer limited the court's ability to impose the death penalty. Addressing the principle of *lex mitior*, endorsed by the Iraqi Penal Code,[33] the court explained that it relates to a choice between the law in force at the time the crime was committed, and the law in force at the time of the verdict – both of which allowed the death penalty in the *Hussein* case – and leaves little room for applying the law that prevailed in between. This deliberation allowed the court to defy the CPA's legislation on the basis of what it believed to be sound legal reasoning, while not directly challenging the CPA's authority.

We can see, then, that both in relation to its jurisdiction and in the context of its authority to impose death penalty, the Iraqi court evaded a direct examination of the legality of the occupants' measures under international law. It sought neither to endorse the legality of the CPA rule nor to criticize it, all the while invoking its own indigenous authority to apply Iraqi law as an exercise of the Iraqi rule of law.

5. UN ADMINISTRATIONS

Historically, occupation was a phenomenon primarily associated with the use of force and a conflictual relationship with the local people and its government. Recent years have seen the practice of another type of foreign administration

---

32 CPA Order No. 7 (10 June 2003), Section 3(1), available at www.iraqcoalition.org/regulations.

33 Section 2 of the Iraqi Penal Code (Law No 111) 1969 reads:

> (1) The occurrence and consequences of an offence are determined in accordance with the law in force-at the time of its commission and the time of commission is determined by reference to the time at which the criminal act occurs and not by reference to the time when the consequence of the offence is realised.
>
> (2) However, if one or more laws are enacted after an offence has been committed and before final judgment is given, then *the law that is most favourable to the convicted person is applied.* (emphasis added).

The Iraqi Penal Code, 1969 is available at the Grotian Moment website: www.law.case.edu/saddamtrial/documents/Iraqi_Penal_Code_1969.pdf.

that has been exercised by the UN or other international organizations to facilitate peaceful transitions to self-government in post-conflict territories. The differences between these two types of foreign control have led many commentators to reject the conceptualization of UN territorial administrations as 'occupations'.[34] Other commentators, however, have questioned the distinction between 'classic' occupations and UN administrations.[35]

For the purpose of examining the views expressed by national courts in relation to legal measures adopted by occupants, we adopt the latter approach and consider the two regimes as slightly different manifestations of the same phenomenon of foreign domination. This approach is based on our definition of the term 'occupation' as the effective control of a power over a territory to which it has no sovereign title.[36] As we will show, the tactics and strategies that national courts adopt when reviewing laws enacted by state-occupants and those they adopt when reviewing the laws of UN administrators have much in common.[37] That said, it should be noted that UN administrations have not perceived themselves bound by the Hague Regulations or the Geneva Conventions, but rather by the specific agreement or Security Council resolution that created them. So far, the most comprehensive mandates of contemporary international administrations have been granted by Security Council Resolution 1244 relating to Kosovo,[38] and by Security Council Resolution 1272 relating to East Timor.[39] The case studies discussed below are illustrative of how these mandates were interpreted by the respective UN missions, on one hand, and by local courts, on the other hand.[40]

---

34 See eg D. Shraga, Military Occupation and UN Transitional Administrations – The Analogy and its Limitations, in: M.G. Kohen (ed.), Promoting Justice, Human Rights and Conflict Resolution through International Law 479, 493–96 (Leiden: Koninklijke Brill, 2007).

35 See eg R. Wilde, International Territorial Administration: How Trusteeship and the Civilizing Mission Never Went Away 346–56 (Oxford University Press, 2008); S. Ratner, Foreign Occupation and International Territorial Administration: The Challenges of Convergence, 16 European Journal of International Law 695 (2005).

36 Benvenisti, *supra* note 1, p. 4.

37 As Steven Ratner notes, 'both missions [administration by international organizations and occupations by states] can resemble each other in the eyes of those living in the occupied or administered territory' (Ratner, *supra* note 35, p. 696). Richard Caplan similarly observes that 'from the standpoint of the unwilling "host" – for instance, Serbia in the case of Kosovo – there may be little difference between a NATO-backed UN administration and a foreign military occupation' (R. Caplan, International Governance of War-Torn Territories: Rule and Reconstruction 3 (Oxford University Press, 2005).

38 UN Doc. S/RES/1244 (1999).

39 UN Doc. S/RES/1272 (1999).

40 Note that the courts whose decisions we discuss were formally domestic courts but included also foreign judges.

5.1. UN TRANSITIONAL ADMINISTRATION IN EAST TIMOR: THE *DOS SANTOS* CASE

After East Timor gained independence and the UN Transitional Administration in East Timor (UNTAET) was resolved, the Court of Appeals of East Timor was asked to determine the criminal responsibility of Armando Dos Santos, a member of a Pro-Indonesian militia group charged with crimes against humanity that he allegedly committed over the course of 1999.[41] As a preliminary matter, the court had to define which criminal law applied in East Timor at the time that the alleged crimes were committed, ie, prior to 25 October 1999, the time when the UNTAET was established. The first regulation promulgated by the UNTAET, Regulation 1/1999, provided in Section 3.1:[42]

> Until replaced by UNTAET regulations or subsequent legislation of democratically established institutions of East Timor, the laws applied in East Timor prior to 25 October 1999, shall apply in East Timor...

The court considered two possible interpretations of Section 3.1: the applicable law prior to 25 October was either Portuguese law – the law in effect prior to the occupation of East Timor by Indonesia – or Indonesian law, which was introduced into East Timor upon occupation.

During the period of UNTAET administration it was widely accepted by East Timorese courts that 'the laws applied in East Timor prior to 25 October 1999' meant Indonesian law. But after independence, the Court of Appeals decided otherwise, invoking the illegality of the Indonesian occupation. It found that since Indonesian law 'has never been validly in force in the territory of East Timor', the UNTAET Regulation must be interpreted as referring to the Portuguese law: 'UNTAET did not want to subject to the Indonesian law the territory and the people they had just liberated from the Indonesian yoke and were now under UN administration.'[43]

In fact, however, it is quite unlikely that the UNTAET had actually intended to turn Portuguese law into the applicable law in East Timor.[44] Moreover, even

---

41 Court of Appeals of East Timor 15 July 2003, *Public Prosecutor v. Armando Dos Santos*, case no. 16/2001 ('*Dos Santos* judgment'). An English translation is available at www.jsmp.minihub.org/judgmentspdf/courtofappeal/Ct_of_App-dos_Santos_English22703.pdf. See further Y. Ronen, The Use and Abuse of International Law: Choice of Applicable Criminal Law in Post-Conflict East Timor, part 4, in this volume at p. 298, for discussion and analysis of *Dos Santos*.

42 UNTAET regulations are available at www.unmit.org/legal/UNTAET-Law/Regulations%20English/regenglish.htm.

43 *Dos Santos* judgment, *supra* note 41, p. 4.

44 The intention of the UNTAET to apply Indonesian law can be learned from Sections 3.2 and 3.3 of UNTAET Regulation 1999/1. Section 3.2 lists several laws that 'shall no longer be applied in East Timor'. Section 3.3 states that '[c]apital punishment is abolished'. As Judge Jacinta Correia da Costa noted in her Dissenting Opinion regarding the applicable law in East

granting that the Indonesian occupation was illegal according to the international law of occupation,[45] the illegality of an occupation in itself does not entail that laws enacted by the occupant are invalid. Additionally, the court's decision ignored the fact that the East Timorese have lived under Indonesian rule for more than two decades. During that period they have relied on Indonesian law in virtually all areas of life, including marriages, divorces, commercial acts, bank loans, and perhaps even acts that were considered criminal under Portuguese law but not under Indonesian law. Invalidation of Indonesian law undermined the legitimate expectation of the East Timorese that the acts and transactions they had carried out in accordance with the prevailing law would be respected.

The court did not address these concerns in its judgment. Nor did it express concern about the possible division and confusion that it would cause within East Timor jurisprudence, even though it was aware of the fact that Section 3.1 had until then been understood as referring to Indonesian law.[46] It seems that the court was so eager to deny the authority of the Indonesian occupant that it was simply indifferent to these considerations. Another explanation that might account for the court's approach has to do with the fact that after the Indonesian invasion, about 150,000 Indonesian migrants – completely unfamiliar with Portuguese law and language – settled in East Timor, to the resentment of the local population.[47] Treating Portuguese law as the only applicable law in East Timor was particularly detrimental to the settlers who remained in East Timor after independence and who may have reflected a hidden desire for vengeance.

While the East Timorese court failed to follow in the footsteps of courts which recognized the validity of prior occupants' laws, in this case it was the legislature that intervened. The East Timorese Parliament hastened to react to the *Dos Santos* precedent and reverse it. In a law enacted a few months after the judgment, Parliament clarified that the term 'applicable law in East Timor' in

---

Timor, the laws listed in section 3.2 and the capital punishment abolished by section 3.3 existed only under Indonesian law. According to da Costa, one must read the provision of Section 3.1 in conjunction with these sections, and conclude that in Section 3.1 the UNTAET intended to apply Indonesian law. The dissenting opinion of Judge da Costa was expressed in the case of *Armando dos Santos*, but her supporting arguments were only presented later in the case of *Agustino da Costa v. the Prosecutor General,* criminal case No 3/2002 (18 July 2003), available at www.jsmp.minihub.org/judgmentspdf/courtofappeal/Dissenting_Opinion%20 ENGLISH23703.doc. Additional arguments that support the conclusion that UNTAET intended to apply Indonesian law are set out in the East Timor Judicial System Monitoring Program (JSMP) Report on the *Dos Santos* case (August 2003), 14–19, available at www.jsmp.minihub.org.

45 On the illegality of the annexation of East Timor by Indonesia *see* Benvenisti, supra note 1, p. 150–59.

46 *Dos Santos* judgment, *supra* note 41, p. 3.

47 M. Jardine, East Timor: Genocide in Paradise 66 (Monroe: Odonian Press, 1999). About half of the Indonesian settlers were evacuated from East Timor following the 1999 vote for independence. See G. Robinson, East Timor 1999: 'Crimes against Humanity 65' (Dili & Jakarta: HAK Association & ELSAM, 2006).

UNTAET Regulation 1999/1 meant 'all Indonesian laws applied and that were in force "de facto" in East Timor prior to 25 October 1999'.[48]

5.2. UN INTERIM ADMINISTRATION MISSION IN KOSOVO: THE *THERMOSYSTEM* CASE

Unlike the case studies discussed so far, the *Thermosystem* case related to the legality of an act of an incumbent administration rather than of a previous regime. But, together with the *Dos Santos* judgment, it raises an important aspect that relates to the role of national courts in resolving inter-ethnic tensions in the context of post-conflict administration. In both Kosovo and East Timor, the UN administration was preceded by an oppressive foreign regime (introduced by Serbia and Indonesia, respectively) that discriminated against the ethnic majority within the occupied territory. In our analysis of *Dos Santos* we noted that the court's decision to un-recognize all Indonesian laws could have had adverse consequences on the Indonesian minority group had it not been reversed by the Parliament. In contrast, in the *Thermosystem* case discussed here, the Kosovo court took the interests of the ethnic minority (in this case the Serbian minority) into account by holding that a regulation promulgated by the UN interim administration mission in Kosovo (UNMIK) did not provide sufficient protection for the Serbian minority and therefore should not be applied. In our view, a careful analysis of these two cases can highlight the extent to which national courts in post-occupation situations can contribute to the peaceful and just end of foreign occupation and to a transition to stability in the relations between rival ethnic communities.

The *Thermosystem case*[49] was issued by a Special Chamber of the Supreme Court of Kosovo on Kosovo Trust Agency Related Matters (the Special Chamber), which was established by the UNMIK for the purpose of resolving disputes arising from the privatization process in Kosovo. In its judgment, the Special Chamber invoked international human rights standards as grounds for avoiding the application of an UNMIK prescription,[50] which entitled employees of

---

48 Interpretation of Section 1 of Law No. 2/2002 of 7 August and Sources of Law, Law No. 10/2003 (20 November 2003), Section 1.

49 Special Chamber of the Supreme Court of Kosovo 9 June 2004, *Thermosystem v. KTA*, SCEL 04-0001. Unfortunately we were unable to get hold of the full text of the *Thermosystem* judgment. Our description of this decision is based on the judgment summary as it appeared on the Special Chamber website (judgment summary); on an UNMIK-OSCE report, Privatization in Kosovo: Judicial Review of Kosovo Trust Agency Matters by the Special Chamber of the Supreme Court of Kosovo (May 2008) (UNMIK-OSCE Report on Privatization); and on Rebecca Everly's analysis of the case (R. Everly, Reviewing Governmental Acts of the United Nations in Kosovo, 8 German Law Journal 21 (2007)).

50 Section 10 of UNMIK Regulation No 2003/13 (9 May 2003). UNMIK regulations are available at www.unmikonline.org/regulations/unmikgazette/index.htm.

Socially-Owned Enterprises to a share of the proceeds from the privatization. To be eligible for such a share, employees had to prove that they had been employed with the enterprise at the time of privatization and that they had been on its payroll for no less than three years. Employees who did not meet these conditions due to discrimination were still eligible to a share, but provided that they could offer sufficient documentation to that effect. In the *Thermosystem* case, a group of Kosovo Serbs claimed that, as a result of ethnic discrimination, they were excluded from the Thermosystem list of eligible employees. Despite the lack of proper documentation, the Special Chamber decided to accept the oral testimonies of the complainants as sufficient proof of discrimination. It found that the UNMIK requirement for documentary evidence of discrimination was 'in itself discriminatory, in light of the jurisprudence of the European Court of Human Rights regarding Article 14 of the European Convention on Human Rights'.[51] The court also invoked the Kosovo Law on Contested Procedure principle, according to which facts that are a matter of common knowledge need not be proved.[52] The court held that it was common knowledge that, under the circumstances that prevailed in Kosovo when privatization processes began, many employees, in particular members of the Serb minority group, who were persecuted and discriminated against due to their ethnic origin, were unable to show up for work for security reasons and therefore could not be considered employed at the time of the privatization or the initiation of liquidation.

The Special Chamber reiterated the *Thermosystem* precedent in subsequent judgments.[53] In its reasoning the court seemed to partially blame UNMIK for the inability of Serbs to arrive at work safely. While addressing the facts which it deemed to be common knowledge requiring no proof, the court stated that

> [b]efore 1999, employees were, to a great extent, able to attend work without interruption. However, after the divisive conflict and *the international intervention in 1999*, people were mostly unable to safely travel within Kosovo. The effect is that employees living in a different circumstance (belonging to minority groups, living in segregation from the Albanian majority) were deprived of the opportunity to attend work *without affirmative assistance of the governing body.*[54]

---

51 Judgment summary, *supra* note 49. Article 14 of the 1950 European Convention for the Protection of Human Rights and Fundamental Freedoms (ECHR) (adopted 4 November 1950, entered into force 3 September 1953) 213 UNTS 221, states: 'The enjoyment of the rights and freedoms as set forth in this Convention shall be secured without discrimination on any ground …'.

52 Article 221.4 of the Law on Contested Procedure (Official Gazette of Socialist Federal Republic of Yugoslavia No. 4/77–1478, 36/80–1182, and 69/82–1596).

53 See UNMIK-OSCE Report on Privatization, *supra* note 49, p. 20–21.

54 See for example Special Chamber of the Supreme Court of Kosovo 14 June 2006, *Coca Cola Employees v. KTA*, SCEL-05-0004 (Special Chamber website) (emphasis added).

In these cases, the court used two vehicles to avoid the unfair application of an UNMIK prescription, namely international human rights standards and domestic law. Referring to international human rights law as the basis for overcoming the evidentiary requirement of the UNMIK prescription was reconcilable with the UNMIK legislative corpus, because the first regulation promulgated by the UNMIK explicitly subjected its legislative power to internationally recognized human rights standards.[55] However, the court's resort to the domestic Law on Contested Procedure is harder to reconcile, because the same regulation explicitly gave precedence to UNMIK legislation over domestic law whenever a conflict existed.

6. LESSONS LEARNED

The study of the jurisprudence of national courts in the aftermath of occupations is significant both for refining our understanding of the law of occupation, and for understanding the dilemmas posed in its application by courts in the post-occupation phase. It also offers insight into post-occupation justice and the justice of transitional processes as perceived by domestic institutions. Finally, it reveals aspects of the post-occupation courts' own struggle for reputation and the strategies they pursue for maintaining it, and it thereby contributes to our understanding of the institutional aspects of post-conflict transitions. This part addresses each of these aspects.

In theory, the post-occupation jurisprudence of indigenous national courts could have shaped the contours of the law of occupation by interpreting and applying the relevant treaty provisions and thereby delineating the limitations on the exercise of authority by the occupant. Such jurisprudence could have been important for future occupants as well as for the occupied, and also relevant to third parties engaged in trade and other transactions with the occupied area. Greater clarity and predictability could have constrained future occupants interested in ensuring the long-term effects of their policies and stabilized other stakeholders' expectations. Assuming the occupant's compliance with the law, the reduced uncertainty as to the long-term effects of occupation measures could have contributed to improving the socio-economic conditions necessary for economic development.

However, the case studies discussed above indicate that the possibility of deriving conclusions concerning the legitimate powers of occupants from post-occupation national courts jurisprudence is limited. Some of these cases

---

55 Section 2 of UNMIK Regulation No. 1/1999 (25 July 1999). This provision was supplemented by Section 1.3 of UNMIK Regulation No. 1999/24 (12 December 1999), which mentioned several human rights conventions – including the ECHR – as reference for internationally recognized human rights standards.

demonstrate a 'transitional bias', namely an inclination of national courts to emphasize mainly *ex post* considerations out of concern for the transitional needs of their post-occupation societies rather than for the enforcement of the international law of occupation. In the aftermath of occupation, these courts act as a one-time actor in a non-reiterated game, since the recurrence of the occupation is deemed sufficiently remote. Thus, there seems to be no good reason for those courts to be aware of the implication that their rulings could have on the manner in which the authority of occupying powers is understood and implemented in general.

The most evident transitional policy of national courts in the aftermath of occupation has been the validation of transactions that were conducted in accordance with occupation laws, even if such laws were enacted in breach of international law. The tendency of national courts to uphold such transactions has depended, among other factors, on the behaviour of the party that relied upon occupation laws (expectations acquired in good faith were respected, whereas expectations acquired in bad faith were ignored); on the amount of damage that this party might suffer if the transaction were invalidated; and on the amount of damage that other parties might suffer if the same transaction is validated. The identity of the parties may also be an important consideration. For example, in the *Komotini* case, the testator and the heirs named in his will acted in good faith while the defendants could not prove their good faith reliance on changes in the law introduced by the occupant, and this may have been a factor in finding the will valid. Conversely, in the case of *G v. H*, the Supreme Court of Luxemburg was appalled by the behaviour of the defendant, who under the guise of compliance with the occupant's laws tried to evade payment of part of her debt and also informed the German authorities about the plaintiff's refusal to accept the payment. The court ruled against her. In both the *Du Ban* and the *Cultura 2000* cases, the fact that the decision to uphold transactions concluded during occupation placed a burden on public authorities with 'deep pockets' may have been an important factor – albeit not explicitly mentioned – in the courts' considerations. Finally, in the *Dos Santos* case, the Parliament had to reverse the court's wholesale rejection of Indonesian law because it ignored the needs of the East Timorese population that had lived under Indonesian law for more than 25 years.

Post-occupation justice entails not only substantive considerations of individual rights but also collective aspects. Incumbent institutions and transitional processes of national reconciliation require legitimization, often by differentiating them from former regimes. National courts in post-occupation litigation are in a position to do so, as evident in *Cultura 2000*, both in its reasoning and in its result. The Namibian Constitution, cited at length by the court, reflects the central role that differentiation from the discriminating South African administration played in the creation of the Namibian collective identity.

The court's elaboration of the importance of repudiation adhered to this legacy. In the Kosovo *Thermosystem* case, as well, the particularly strong protection granted to Serbian employees by the court can be understood as an attempt to distinguish the new regime from the one that preceded the UN administration. In *Dos Santos*, the interpretation of the term 'applicable law', though purportedly reflecting objective international law principles, was clearly influenced by a strong revulsion against the Indonesian occupation of East Timor.

The *Cultura 2000*, *Dos Santos*, and *Thermosystem* cases alert us to the important role of national courts in ensuring equal treatment of different ethnic groups both during and after occupation. Occupants might be tempted to discriminate among different ethnic groups for a variety of reasons, or might even create new minorities by moving settlers into the occupied area. When the occupant or the post-occupation administration affects minority rights, for example by rescinding privileges granted to them by the previous administration (*Cultura 2000*), or by insufficiently protecting their rights and expectations (*Dos Santos* and *Thermosystem*), courts can serve an important function to determine the validity of such measures and can reduce or expand the protection granted to minority groups. This insight suggests an important nuance to the international law of occupation. Literature on occupation law usually lumps the interests of the indigenous population together, suggesting that occupants should balance their interests against those of the local population and perhaps also the ousted sovereign. These cases show, however, that the occupant should also be alert to potential internal conflicts of interest among the occupied population, and should ensure that it balances the conflicting demands fairly and without discrimination.

Another 'transitional bias' characteristic of post occupation jurisprudence refers to the institutional considerations that courts might have in mind. As we suggested in our analysis of the *Komotini* case, post-occupation courts might tend to reduce the amount of litigation by asserting the general effectiveness of occupation acts. The *Saddam Hussein* judgment has taught us that these courts might also be concerned with distinguishing their own reputation from the unpopular occupant which established them.

Post-occupation judicial decisions that give decisive weight to transitional considerations and do not clarify the limits of the occupant authority under international law reduce both the ability and the inclination of occupants to respect this law. While the 'transitional bias' of domestic courts often reflects appropriate concerns, it would seem preferable that courts address in their judgments both *ex ante* and *ex post* considerations and explicitly invoke their bias in the reasoning. Doing so would offer courts greater possibilities for just decisions in the particular case, while at the same time refining and developing *ex ante* obligations of occupants, thereby increasing incentives of occupants to comply with the law of occupation.

As far as individual expectations are concerned, two different alternatives to the simplistic *ex post* preference of acquired expectations can be juxtaposed. The first examines both the *ex ante* validity of the occupants' acts under the law of occupation as well as their *ex post* consequences and gives more weight to individual expectations that relied on lawful occupation measures and less to expectations based on patently unlawful measures (for example, discriminatory acts). When expectations that relied on blatant violations of international law need to be respected, the court would still have an opportunity to uphold transactions without recognizing the former occupant's laws (for example, by asserting that these transactions were valid under the applicable domestic law). In such cases, however, it may be preferable to apply the alternative approach, which explicitly recognizes the *ex post* validity of measures despite their illegal origins because of the necessity of individuals who are subject to a foreign regime to rely on the only legal system available to them. This approach follows the 'Namibia Exception' first recognized by the ICJ in its Advisory Opinion concerning Namibia, and later developed by the ECtHR in cases relating to Northern Cyprus.[56]

The Namibia Exception informs an occupant who has decided not to establish an occupation regime according to international law that its acts – except for certain acts that will be recognized as having created legally valid expectations – will not be recognized. The Namibia Exception has been developed and applied in the context of illegal occupations in which the occupying powers attempted to annex the occupied territory or otherwise failed to establish an occupation regime. In addition, the Exception has referred to the obligation of third countries to recognize only certain acts of the occupant. This does not mean, however, that the Namibia Exception cannot be used by national courts of occupied territories in cases where the occupant has established an occupation regime and acknowledged its duties under the law of occupation. In these cases, the Namibia Exception may be applied only to those laws that deviate from the occupant's mandate, provided that they created legitimate expectations.

7. CONCLUSION

The international law of occupation, which regulates the conduct of occupying forces, has always suffered from a certain ambiguity. It might have been expected that review of occupants' acts by indigenous national courts would have contributed to the clarification of the legislative powers of the occupant. But as this survey of post-occupation case laws indicates, the post-occupation jurisprudence of national courts has, at best, left the law of occupation as vague

[56] See *supra* notes 17–19.

as it was previously, and in some cases, it has further obscured it. National courts' rulings in the aftermath of occupations have stood more for addressing the needs of post-occupation transitions than for the clarification of the legitimate powers of future occupants, and have seemed more concerned with the desire to protect legitimate expectations of individuals, promote the reconstruction of national identity, facilitate national reconciliation, address inter-ethnic tensions, and build their own reputation and stature. This was so not only because the immediate transitional concerns were complex enough and left no room for other considerations, but also because, after the end of occupation, the courts were no longer interested in the law of occupation. It can be expected that other national courts, such as the occupant's own courts or courts in third countries, will have other constraints that would lead them to deviate from a disinterested application of the law of occupation.

Given these countervailing concerns, we suggest that it is preferable that courts distinguish between *ex ante* and *ex post* considerations and do not invoke the law of occupation as the basis for their *ex post* findings, thereby contributing to distorting this law. Instead, courts could use doctrines that enable them to distinguish between the breach by the occupant and the valid outcomes of its measures, notwithstanding the initial violation, such as the Namibia Exception. Using such doctrines would allow courts to participate in shaping the evolution of the law of occupation while precluding the harsh consequences of its implementation. Such doctrines offer courts the ability to create justice *ex post* without undermining the authority of the law *ex ante*, or in other words, to settle hard cases without making bad law.

THE USE AND ABUSE OF INTERNATIONAL LAW: CHOICE OF APPLICABLE CRIMINAL LAW IN POST-CONFLICT EAST TIMOR

Yaël Ronen*

1. INTRODUCTION

In the process of empowering domestic institutions, particularly the judiciary, the use of international law is often perceived as a means of stabilizing the legal order, contributing to the protection of fundamental rights, and protecting the separation of powers. Legal scholarship which scrutinizes situations of post-conflict reconstruction of legal systems often assumes implicitly, or even expressly, that reliance on international law as the source of substantive norms and processes is beneficial to the domestic system because international law imposes a more stringent standard for protection of human rights than domestic law does. However, international law operates at various levels and in various contexts, and in some of them it may have a destabilizing effect on the domestic system. Moreover, courts are often perceived as the guarantors of the application of international law, shielding individuals from the excesses of government. Yet, in practice, courts no less than other institutions may abuse their power, and such abuse carries particular weight as it is carried out under the guise of law.

This article concerns an incident in which the Court of Appeal of East Timor invoked international legal principles relating to the consequences of illegal annexation when determining the domestic law of East Timor under UN administration and after independence, without giving due regard to their implications in the field of human rights. Rather than enhance the post-conflict reconstruction, this invocation risked destabilizing the emerging political and legal apparatus; it could have brought about a fundamental transformation of

* Yael Ronen, PhD (Cantabury), Senior Lecturer, Sha'arei Mishpat College, Israel. This article was first presented at the workshop held by the COST Working Group on the International Rule of Law in Domestic Courts in Amsterdam in October 2009. I am grateful to participants for their helpful comments. Usual caveats apply.

East Timor's legal system. While the Court of Appeal's attempt to bring about this change was thwarted by the objection of the legal community and the legislature, the incident demonstrates that the recourse to international law must be discriminative so that it does not subvert the very purpose for which this law is invoked.

Section 1 of this article provides a brief background to the post-conflict process in East Timor. Section 2 describes the dilemma concerning the choice of applicable law in post-conflict East Timor, and the role of international law in shaping that choice, while section 3 examines the role that the Court of Appeal attached to international law with regard to the same question. Section 4 analyses the ruling of the Court of Appeal and the implications for domestic law of unqualified reliance on certain branches of international law. It also places the East Timorese experience in a wider context of post-conflict determinations of applicable law in light of international legal principles.

2. BACKGROUND

Until the mid-1970s, East Timor was a colony of Portugal.[1] In 1974, Portugal began a process of decolonization which included the territory of East Timor. Neighbouring Indonesia opposed independence for East Timor. Disagreement among factions within East Timor on the territory's future spurred a civil war in 1975, which led to a rushed and disorganized Portuguese withdrawal from the island. Indonesian forces intervened in the internal conflict and, on 7 December 1975, occupied East Timor. In July 1976, Indonesia annexed East Timor as its 27th province and extended Indonesian law to the territory.[2] Indonesia attempted to justify its use of force on various grounds. It claimed to be acting in self defence, by invitation by the East Timorese, out of concern for the future stability of Indonesia and Southeast Asia, and also for humanitarian purposes. None of these claims were sustainable as a matter of fact or law.[3] Indonesia's actions were in violation of the prohibition on the use of force and of the obligation to respect the East Timorese people's right to self-determination.[4]

1 UNGA Resolution 1542 (XVI) (15 December 1961).

2 Indonesian Law 7/76 on the Legalisation of the Integration of East Timor into the Unitary State of the Republic of Indonesia and the Formation of the Province of East Timor (1976), Item 4 in the general part of the elucidation to the Law: 'With the unification of the Unitary State of the Republic of Indonesia, then the territory of East Timor thereby becomes the territory of the Unitary State of the Republic of Indonesia… and all legislation of the Republic of Indonesia applies in the territory of East Timor'.

3 See R.S. Clark, The 'Decolonization' of East Timor and the United Nations Norms on Self Determination and Aggression (1995), updated and corrected version (on file with the author) of article which appeared in 7 Yale Journal of World Public Order 19–43 (1980).

4 Statement of the representative of Portugal, UN Doc. S/PV.1864 (15 December 1975) para. 59; UNGA Resolution 31/53 (A/RES/31/53) (1 December 1976); eg UN Doc. A/52/152, Note

The prohibition on the use of force and the right to self-determination are both regarded as peremptory obligations.[5] Their violation gives rise to an obligation on states not to recognize the legal effect of the violating conduct,[6] irrespective of the effectiveness or apparent success of those responsible for the conduct in question.[7] The function of non-recognition is to prevent the validation of an act performed in violation of international law,[8] in order to incentivize the perpetrator to revert to a lawful situation.

Few concrete measures were taken to sanction Indonesia's delinquency.[9] No collective policy of non-recognition was ever expressly adopted. General Assembly Resolution 3485(XXX) of 12 December 1975 called upon Indonesia:

Verbale dated 19 May 1997 from the Permanent Mission of Portugal to the UN addressed to the Secretary-General (20 May 1997), para 1. A. Cassese, Self-Determination of Peoples, A Legal Reappraisal 226 (Cambridge: Cambridge University Press, 1995); M. Alkatiri, The Democratic Republic of East Timor (Statement in the Fourth Committee of the United Nations General Assembly), 7 Journal of Contemporary Asia 280 (1977); R.S. Clark, Obligations of Third States in the Face of Illegality – Ruminations Inspired by the Weeramantry Dissent in the Case Concerning East Timor, in: A. Anghie and G. Stugess (eds), Legal Visions of the 21st Century: Essays in Honour of Judge Christopher Weeramantry (The Hague: Martinus Nijhoff, 1998); C. Drew, The East Timor Story: International Law on Trial, 12 European Journal of International Law 651 (2001); J. Dunn, East Timor: A People Betrayed (Milton: Jacaranda, 1983); L. Hannikainen, The Case of East Timor from the Perspective of *Jus Cogens*, in: International Law and the Question of East Timor 103 (London: Catholic Institute for International Relations and International Platform of Jurists for East Timor, 1995); S.D. Korman, The Right of Conquest: The Acquisition of Territory by Force in International Law and Practice 281–292 (Oxford: Oxford University Press, 1996); I.G.M. Scobbie and C.J. Drew, Self-Determination Undetermined: The Case of East Timor, 9 Leiden Journal of International Law 185 (1996).

5 ICJ, *Military and Paramilitary Activities in and against Nicaragua (Nicaragua v. US)*, Merits, 1986 ICJ Reports 14, 100–101 [190]; International Law Commission (ILC), Draft Articles on State Responsibility for Internationally Wrongful Acts, Report of the International Law Commission on the work of its Fifty-third session (A/56/10) (23 April-1 June and 2 July-10 August 2001), Article 40 Commentary, para. 4 (ILC Draft Articles); ICJ, *Case Concerning East Timor (Portugal v. Australia)*, 1995 ICJ Rep 90 [29]; ICJ, *Legal Consequences of the Construction of a Wall in the Occupied Palestinian Territory*, Advisory Opinion, 2004 ICJ Rep 136 [155]-[156].

6 ICJ, *Legal Consequences for States of the Continued Presence of South Africa in Namibia (South West Africa) notwithstanding Security Council Resolution 276 (1970) (Advisory Opinion)*, 1971 ICJ Reports 16 [125]; ICJ 9 July 2004, *Legal Consequences of the Construction of a Wall in the Occupied Palestinian Territory (Advisory Opinion)*, 2004 ICJ Reports 136; ILC Draft Articles, *supra* note 5, Articles 40, 41; A. Orakhelashvili, Peremptory Norms in International Law 189–203 (Oxford: Oxford University Press, 2006). For pre-ILC Draft Articles law and practice see J. Dugard, Recognition and the United Nations (Cambridge: Grotius, 1987).

7 V. Gowlland-Debbas, Collective Responses to Illegal Acts in International Law: United Nations Action in the Question of Southern Rhodesia 276–277 (Dordrecht: Martinus Nijhoff, 1990).

8 Sir Hersch Lauterpacht, Recognition in International Law 413 (Cambridge: Cambridge University Press, 1947); R.Y. Jennings, Nullity and Effectiveness in International Law, in: Cambridge Essays in International Law (Essays in Honour of Lord McNair) 66 (1965); D. Raič, Statehood and the Law of Self-Determination 109 (The Hague: Kluwer Law International, 2002).

9 T.D. Grant, East Timor, the UN System, and Enforcing Non-Recognition in International Law, 33 Vanderbilt Journal of Transnational Law 273, 298–99 (2000).

> to desist from further violation of the territorial integrity of Portuguese Timor and to withdraw without delay its armed forces from the territory in order to enable the people of the Territory freely to exercise their right to self-determination and independence.

Subsequent resolutions were even less explicit with regard to the unlawfulness of the Indonesian intervention.[10] In 1989, after Australia and Indonesia entered into a treaty concerning exploitation of East Timor's natural resources,[11] Portugal submitted a claim to the International Court of Justice (ICJ) against Australia for violating, inter alia, the obligation to respect the right of the people of East Timor to self-determination. In the *Case Concerning East Timor*, the ICJ found the case inadmissible on the ground that it concerned Indonesia's rights and obligations while Indonesia was not party to the proceedings. The ICJ rejected Portugal's claim that the UN resolutions could be read as imposing an objective obligation not to recognize Indonesia's authority or to deal only with Portugal.[12]

In May 1999, following internal political changes, Indonesia agreed with Portugal to hold a referendum in East Timor under UN auspices in order to determine East Timor's political future.[13] In August 1999, a referendum presented the population with a choice between either independence or integration within Indonesia as an autonomous region. Over 78 percent of the half million voters chose independence.[14] Once the results of the vote were released, pro-integration militia groups went on a violent rampage, assisted by the Indonesian military.[15] An International Force for East Timor (INTERFET), led by Australian forces, moved into East Timor to restore order. In October

10 UNSC Resolution 384 (22 December 1975) (S/RES/384) (1975), UNSC Resolution 388 (6 April 1976) (S/RES/388) (1976), UNGA Resolution 31/53 (1 December 1976) (A/RES/31/53), UNGA Resolution 32/34 (28 November 1977) (A/RES/32/34), UNGA Resolution 33/39 (13 December 1978) (A/RES/33/39), UNGA Resolution 34/40 (21 November 1979) (A/RES/34/40), UNGA Resolution 35/27 (11 November 1980) (A/RES/35/27), UNGA Resolution 36/50 (24 November 1981) (A/RES/36/50), UNGA Resolution 37/30 (22 November 1982) (A/RES/37/30). In 1983 the Commission on Human Rights adopted a resolution on the right of the East Timorese to self-determination which reaffirmed the inalienable right of the people of East Timor to self-determination and independence. Commission of Human Rights Resolution 1983/8, UN Yearbook 833–834 (1983).

11 1989 Treaty between Australia and the Republic of Indonesia on the Zone of Cooperation in an Area between the Indonesian Province of East Timor and Northern Australia, 1654 UNTS 105.

12 ICJ, *Case Concerning East Timor (Portugal v. Australia)*, 1995 ICJ Rep 90 [31].

13 1999 Agreement between the Republic of Indonesia and the Portuguese Republic on the Question of East Timor 2062 UNTS 8, 1999 Agreement Regarding the Modalities for the Popular Consultation of the East Timorese through a Direct Ballot (Portugal-Indonesia), 2062 UNTS 40.

14 UN Secretary-General Press Release (SG/SM/7119 SC/6722) (3 September 1999).

15 By late September, hundreds of people were killed and an estimated 400,000 – over half the population – was forced to flee their homes. G Robinson, East Timor 1999: Crimes Against Humanity 42–44 (Geneva: Report commissioned by the UNOHCR, 2005).

1999, the UN Security Council established the United Nations Transitional Administration in East Timor (UNTAET), to administer East Timor before handing it over to an elected Timorese government. On 20 May 2002, East Timor became independent.

Upon gaining independence, East Timor took the position that it had previously been subject to an illegal regime. The preamble to its 2002 Constitution of East Timor provides:[16] 'Following the liberation of the Timorese People from colonisation and illegal occupation of the Maubere Motherland by foreign powers…'. The same perception was reflected in various legislative instruments.[17]

3. THE ROLE OF INTERNATIONAL LAW IN POST-TRANSITION DETERMINATIONS OF THE LAW OF EAST TIMOR

Upon taking control of East Timor, UNTAET was immediately confronted with the need to decide on the law of the territory. Security Council Resolution 1272(1999), which established UNTAET, conferred upon it legislative powers but did not obviate the need to identify a subsidiary legal system. The Resolution authorized a Special Representative of the UN Secretary-General 'to enact new laws and regulations and to amend, suspend or repeal existing ones'.[18] There is no reference in the Resolution or in the debate preceding its adoption[19] to the source or content of these 'existing' laws and regulations. For example, there is no reference to whether they are those actually enforced (Indonesian law), or those applied to the territory previously (Portuguese and customary East Timorese law). In the immediate term, East Timorese customary law was inadequate; customary international law was applicable in East Timor but it was clearly insufficient to regulate many spheres of life. The East Timorese political elite expressed a clear preference for the application of Portuguese law, with which it was familiar from its long exile in the former Portuguese colonies in Africa.

UNTAET soon decided to apply Indonesian law as the subsidiary law of East Timor. This decision was made solely for practical reasons: first, to avoid a legal

16 On illegality of occupation and the principle of non-recognition, see Y. Ronen, Illegal Occupation and its Consequences, 41 Israel Law Review 201, 232–241 (2008).

17 Eg the preamble to Law 1/2003 of 10 March (Law on the Juridical Regime of Real Estate Part 1 – Ownership over Real Estate) states that '[t]he occupation of Timor-Leste between 1975 and 1999 was an illegal act as recognized worldwide, namely by United Nations Security Council Resolutions 384 of 22 December 1975, and 389 of 22 April 1976. This is the reason why Indonesia was unable to succeed the Portuguese Administration in Timor-Leste'.

18 UNSC Resolution 1272 (25 October 1999) (S/RES/1272) (1999), para. 6.

19 UN Doc. S/PV.4057 (25 October 1999).

vacuum in the initial phase of the transitional administration; second, to avoid a situation in which local lawyers, virtually all of whom had obtained their law degrees at Indonesian universities, had to be introduced to an entirely foreign legal system.[20] UNTAET Regulation 1999/1, adopted in November 1999 and put into force as of 25 October 1999, provided, inter alia:

> Section 2: Observance of internationally recognized standards
> In exercising their functions, all persons undertaking public duties or holding public office in East Timor shall observe internationally recognized human rights standards, as reflected, in particular, in:
> The Universal Declaration on Human Rights of 10 December 1948;
> The International Covenant on Civil and Political Rights of 16 December 1966 and its Protocols;
> The International Covenant on Economic, Social and Cultural Rights of 16 December 1966;
> The Convention on the Elimination of All Forms of Racial Discrimination of 21 December 1965;
> The Convention on the Elimination of All Forms of Discrimination Against Women of 17 December 1979;
> The Convention Against Torture and other Cruel, Inhumane or Degrading Treatment or Punishment of 17 December 1984;
> The International Convention on the Rights of the Child of 20 November 1989.
> They shall not discriminate against any person on any ground such as sex, race, colour, language, religion, political or other opinion, national, ethnic or social origin, association with a national community, property, birth or all other status.
> Section 3: Applicable Law in East Timor
> 3.1 Until replaced by UNTAET regulations or subsequent legislation of democratically established institutions of East Timor, the laws applied in East Timor prior to 25 October 1999 shall apply in East Timor insofar as they do not conflict with the standards referred to in section 2, the fulfillment of the mandate given to UNTAET under United Nations Security Council resolution 1272 (1999), or the present or any other regulation and directive issued by the Transitional Administrator.

UNTAET avoided expressly identifying 'the laws applied in East Timor prior to 25 October 1999' that 'shall apply'[21] as Indonesian law. This was a lesson learnt

---

[20] H. Strohmeyer, Policing the Peace: Post-Conflict Judicial System Reconstruction in East Timor, 24 University of New South Wales Law Journal 171, 174 (2001); H. Strohmeyer, Collapse and Reconstruction of a Judicial System: The United Nations Missions in Kosovo and East Timor, 95 American Journal of International Law 46, 58 (2001). Strohmeyer was the Acting Principal Legal Adviser at the time when Regulation 1999/1 was promulgated; W. Hayde, Ideas and Realties of the Rule of Law and Administration of Justice in Post Conflict East Timor, 8 International Peacekeeping: The Yearbook of International Peace Operations 65, 81 (2004).

[21] The term 'shall apply' is ambiguous and can be interpreted as establishing *de jure* applicability or a *de facto* arrangement. The Portuguese text, which is also an official UNTAET language (UNTAET Regulation 1991/1 Section 5.2), uses the term '*manter-se-ão válidas*', ie 'shall

from the UN experience only a short time earlier, in Kosovo. The UN Mission in Kosovo (UNMIK), an international administration similar to UNTAET, had also been faced with the dilemma whether to adopt Serbian law, which had been enforced on the eve of international forces' entry into the territory in March 1999, or Kosovar law, which had been applied until March 1989, when Serbia annulled Kosovo's autonomous status. Like UNTAET, UNMIK was guided by pragmatic considerations. It chose to apply Serbian law, which it referred to as 'the laws in force in Kosovo prior to 24 March 1999'.[22] UNMIK's decision was met with resentment and outrage by Kosovar judges and prosecutors, who insisted on interpreting the UNMIK Regulation as including only pre-1989 Kosovar law.[23] Eventually, UNMIK amended the Regulation itself so as to give legal validity to the practice in the courts, and to apply Kosovar rather than Serbian law.[24] Conscious of the sensitivity of this issue, and weary of generating a new crisis, UNTAET drafted Regulation 1999/1 in a manner that would not make the application of Indonesian law entirely obvious. Nonetheless, UNTAET's intention was clear to all those involved.

UNTAET Regulation 1991/1 introduced international human rights law as a standard by which domestic law is to be assessed. This was in line with practice elsewhere and reflected the common perception that international law guarantees a higher standard of human rights protection than is available under domestic law.[25] Regulation 1999/1 also abrogated the application of various Indonesian laws with respect to East Timor, such as of capital punishment, because they 'do not comply with the standards referred to in section 2 and 3 of the present regulation'.[26] Despite proposals to conduct a systematic review of Indonesian legislation in East Timor, no such review was carried out.[27]

The arrangement under UNTAET Regulation 1999/1 was carried through into independent East Timor through a constitutional provision on continuity. Section 165 of East Timor's Constitution stipulates:

---

remain valid'. This formulation is also problematic, because it expressly identifies prospective law through previously-valid law, the scope of which may be controversial. Under Regulation 1999/1, the English version of the Regulation prevails over the Portuguese.

22 UNMIK Regulation 1999/1 (25 July 1999) on the Authority of the Interim Administration in Kosovo.

23 F.M. Lorenz, The Rule of Law in Kosovo: Problems and Prospects, 11 Criminal Law Forum 127, 128–130 (2000).

24 UNMIK Regulation 1999/24 (12 December 1999) on the Law Applicable in Kosovo.

25 Eg UNMIK Regulation 1999/1 (25 July 1999); Security Council, General Framework Agreement for Peace in Bosnia and Herzegovina, attached to Letter dated 29 November 1995 from the Permanent Representative of the United States of America to the United Nations addressed to the Secretary-General (30 November 1995) (S/1995/999), Annex 6, Article I.

26 UNTAET Regulation 1999/1 (25 October 1999), Sections 3.2, 3.3.

27 J. Morrow and R. White, The United Nations in Transitional East Timor: International Standards and the Reality of Governance, 22 Australian Yearbook of International Law 1, 9–11 (2002).

> Laws and regulations in force in East Timor shall be applicable to all matters except to the extent that they are inconsistent with the Constitution or the principles contained therein.

This provision was given effect by an interpretative law, which provided that 'legislation applicable in East Timor on 19 May 2002 shall remain in force...' subject to the Constitution and necessary modifications.[28] This extended the application of UNTAET's regulations into East Timor.

4. THE ROLE OF INTERNATIONAL LAW: PRE-OCTOBER 1999 LAW AND THE *DOS SANTOS* AFFAIR

While Regulation 1999/1 ostensibly imposed international human rights law as a benchmark for the application of East Timor's domestic law, it was unexpectedly utilized as a vehicle for introducing into domestic law other international legal standards, which address inter-state relations rather than human rights law. This occurred when the Court of Appeal read into Regulation 1999/1 the requirement to implement the principle *ex injuria jus non oritur* in determining the domestic law of the territory. The matter arose in the context of criminal trials relating to events that had occurred prior to October 1999, as will be discussed in the following sections.

Regulation 1999/1 was adopted on 27 November 1999 and was given retroactive effect from 25 October 1999.[29] Consequently, together with all subsequent legislation referring to it, it only regulates the *prospective* law of East Timor, from October 1999 onwards. UNTAET did not attempt to determine what the law of East Timor had been prior to October 1999. This was considered a political issue that would be determined in due course by the sovereign authorities of East Timor. Regulation 1999/1 took account of the fact that in practice Indonesian law had been enforced prior to October 1999 as a matter of *fact*, but it was silent on whether that practice was lawful or not under international law.

At the same time, UNTAET could not altogether ignore the question concerning the law governing criminal and civil cases relating to acts and omissions that occurred before 25 October 1999. Specifically, UNTAET established a court system, including Special Panels for Serious Crimes (SPSCs), to try criminal cases related to the 1999 riots which had all taken place before 25 October 1999. The SPSCs had exclusive jurisdiction over crimes of genocide,

---

28 Law No 2/2002, Interpretation of the Applicable Law on 19 May 2002, Section 1.

29 UNTAET Regulation 1999/1, Section 8.

crimes against humanity, war crimes, torture, sexual offenses, and murder.[30] The regulations establishing the jurisdictions of the courts of East Timor provide that 'the courts in East Timor shall apply the law of East Timor as promulgated by Section 3 of UNTAET Regulation No. 1999/1'.[31] Unlike Regulation 1999/1 and the Constitution, this formulation does not determine the *territorial* law of East Timor; rather, it provides that the law *governing specific cases* adjudicated by the courts of East Timor, relating to pre-October 1999 events, would be the law referred to in Regulation 1999/1. The question of pre-October 1999 territorial law remained unaddressed.

Within East Timor, until July 2003, judicial practice was to apply Indonesian law as the subsidiary law in all cases, regardless of the date on which the relevant acts were committed. In July 2003, the question of the applicable law arose for the first time in *Public Prosecutor v. Armando dos Santos*.[32] The attempt to resolve this issue by reference to international law revealed the potential harm in an unqualified application of international law without regard for the context in which it is invoked.

Dos Santos had been indicted of murder and other inhumane acts as crimes against humanity, with regard to acts committed in April 1999. He had been convicted in September 2002 by the SPSC, under Indonesian law, of murder, and was sentenced to twenty years' imprisonment.[33] The prosecution appealed the decision, submitting that dos Santos should have been convicted of crimes against humanity rather than murder.

Although the prosecution's appeal did not raise the question of the law governing the case, this was the first issue which the Court of Appeal addressed. The Court did not explain why that issue suddenly arose then and why it had not arisen before. As a point of departure for its analysis of this issue, the Court cited the Constitution, which maintains the applicability of 'laws and regulations in force in East Timor'. Since this referred to UNTAET Regulation 1999/1, the Court then proceeded to examine whether the common understanding of the phrase 'laws applied prior to 25 October 1999' in Regulation 1999/1 as referring to Indonesian law, was correct.

---

30 UNTAET Regulation 2000/11; UNTAET Regulation 2000/15, Sections 1, 4; UNTAET Regulation 2001/25, Section 9. Jurisdiction over the three last categories was limited to crimes allegedly committed between 1 January 1999 and 25 October 1999.

31 UNTAET Regulation 2000/11, Section 5.1; UNTAET Regulation 2000/15, Sections 3.1 and 4. These regulations were later replaced by Regulation 2001/25, which reproduces the jurisdiction provisions, Section 5.1.

32 *Public Prosecutor v. Armando dos Santos*, available at www.jsmp.minihub.org/judgmentspdf/courtofappeal/Court_of_Appeal_Decision_15-07-03_Case16-2001.pdf, English translation at www.jsmp.minihub.org/judgmentspdf/courtofappeal/Ct_of_App-dos_Santos_English22703.pdf.

33 On the *dos Santos* affairs see D. Cohen, Indifference and Accountability 83 (East-West Center, 2006).

The majority of the Court of Appeal noted that Indonesia's annexation of East Timor had been illegal under international law and therefore invalid *ab initio*. Thus, it said, under international law, Portuguese law remained the law of the territory throughout the period of Indonesian annexation. Emphasizing that the 'laws applied in East Timor prior to 25 October 1999' could only be those which had legitimately been in force in accordance with the principles of international law, the Court concluded that Regulation 1999/1 referred to Portuguese law. The Court considered that if UNTAET had intended to adopt Indonesian law despite its invalidity, it would have done so explicitly. The majority then proceeded to declare dos Santos guilty of crimes against humanity under Portuguese law. It subsequently repeated its ruling that the law of East Timor was Portuguese law in twenty-three other cases, most of them on criminal matters.[34]

In all these cases, Judge Jacinta Correia da Costa appended dissenting opinions.[35] She conceded that Section 3.1 of Regulation 1999/1 could be considered ambiguous if read in isolation; however, in her opinion, Section 3 as a whole referred more evidently to Indonesian law. This was because although Indonesia's presence was not recognized *de jure*, it was recognized *de facto*, and the application of its laws could not be denied. Furthermore, the legislation referred to in Sections 3.2 and 3.3 of the Regulation existed only under Indonesian law and not under Portuguese law, so these sections could only be meaningful if Section 3.1 were interpreted as adopting Indonesian law.[36]

The Court of Appeal's judgments caused confusion and division in the East Timorese legal community and the community at large. East Timor's Prime Minister Mari Alkatiri described the decision as 'incompetent and unconstitutional'.[37] The Prosecutor-General of East Timor filed an application with the Supreme Court of Justice requesting a declaration clarifying the issue of the applicable law in East Timor. He argued that the mistaken rulings of the Court of Appeal would render illegal the decisions of the courts in all the criminal cases heard in the preceding three years. Furthermore, they would have far-reaching implications and consequences for the system of justice in East Timor and for the governance of East Timor as a whole.[38] The majority of the

34 In *Foo Hau Kuin v. JJ McDonald*, Dili District Court Case No. 29/2001, an appeal was made to the Court of Appeal to apply Portuguese law in a civil case.

35 In *dos Santos* she only appended her opinion that the law governing the case was Indonesian law. On the circumstances of this statement see Cohen, *supra* note 33, p. 85. In the following case, *Agustinho da Costa v. The Prosecutor General*, she elaborated her position.

36 *Agustinho da Costa v. The Prosecutor General*, Case No. 3/2002, Judgment of 18 July 2003, available at www.jsmp.minihub.org/judgmentspdf/courtofappeal/Dissenting_Opinionby_Judge_Jacinta_in_Court_%20Appeal_DecisionRegardingApplicable_Law%20_nEastTimor.pdf, [5], [8].

37 J. Jolliffe, Old European tongue brings chaos to newest Asian nation, Sydney Morning Herald (26 July 2003), available at www.etan.org/et2003/july/18-21/26oldeur.htm.

38 Information Release from the Office of the Prosecutor-General (24 July 2003), available at www.etan.org/et2003/july/18-21/23prosec.htm. East Timor's Supreme Court still has not yet been established, and its functions are performed by the Appeals Court.

legal community operating in East Timor, both international and local, also rejected the *dos Santos* decision.[39] The SPSC and the Dili District Court continued to apply Indonesian law. The SPSC rejected the argument based on the unlawfulness of the Indonesian occupation as inconclusive with respect to the applicable law,[40] and it interpreted Regulation 1999/1 as referring to Indonesian law on the basis of arguments similar to those of Judge Correia da Costa.[41]

In order to clarify the situation, East Timorese parliamentarians tabled a bill in Parliament, stating expressly that Indonesian law was the subsidiary law under Regulation 1999/1, and accordingly under the East Timorese Constitution. The debate preceding the adoption of the law was charged with political tension, focusing on the ramifications of the legislation for relations with Portugal and with Indonesia, and on the message that the proposed legislation conveyed regarding the legacy left to East Timor by the Portuguese and Indonesian rulers. East Timorese judges, public prosecutors, and public defenders, most of whom had graduated from Indonesian universities and studied Indonesian law, threatened to resign from their positions unless the Parliament voted in favour of adopting Indonesian law as East Timor's subsidiary law.[42] They underlined the fact that few Timorese police or court officials were fluent in the Portuguese language or knew Portuguese law, making the application of Portuguese law unfeasible.[43] Opponents of the Indonesian option, including the President of the

---

39 JSMP, Dili District Court, Final Report 2003 (Dili, November 2003), available at http://jsmp.minihub.org/reports.htm.

40 It noted that 'the UN also branded the continued Portuguese occupation as illegal': *Public Prosecutor v. Joao Sarmento and Domingos Mendonça*, Decision on the Defense (Domingos Mendonça) Motion for the Court to Order the Public Prosecutor to amend the indictment, Case No. 18a/2001, decision of 24 July 2003, [40]. In fact, the UN has never called either the Portuguese or the Indonesian occupation illegal. It only deplored and condemned various aspects of the Portuguese administration (UNGA Resolution 1699(XVI) (19 December 1961), UNGA Resolution 1807(XVII) (14 December 1962), and deplored the Indonesian intervention (see resolutions in note 10). Nor did the Court of Appeal in *dos Santos* claim that the UN had declared the Indonesian occupation illegal, but said that 'the UN never recognized that military occupation'. *Public Prosecutor v. Armando dos Santos*, available at www.jsmp.minihub.org/judgmentspdf/courtofappeal/Court_of_Appeal_Decision_15-07-03_Case16-2001.pdf, English translation at www.jsmp.minihub.org/judgmentspdf/courtofappeal/Ct_of_App-dos_Santos_English22703.pdf, 4. In fact, The UN maintained East Timor on the list of non-self governing territories as a Portuguese territory on the one hand, but did not clearly reject the annexation by Indonesia on the other hand.

41 *Public Prosecutor v. Joao Sarmento and Domingos Mendonça*, Decision on the Defense (Domingos Mendonça) Motion for the Court to Order the Public Prosecutor to amend the indictment, Case No. 18a/2001, decision of 24 July 2003, [35]–[39].

42 KESTA, 'Parliament Passed Law on Applicable Law', Selected Postings from East Timor (Dili, 1 October 2002), available at www.etan.org/et2003/october/01-6/00parlmnt.htm.

43 Portuguese and Tetum are the official languages of East Timor. In 2009, only 37% of the East Timorese population spoke Portuguese, mainly people aged 10–24. Tetum is known at some level to some 86% of the population, since it is the language used in church services. However, Tetum is primarily an oral language and not a written one. M. Quinn, Letting go of Indonesian, 96 Inside Indonesia (April–June 2009), available at http://insideindonesia.org/content/view/1191/47/.

Court of Appeal, countered by pointing out the dangerous juridical dependence on Indonesia that would ensue if Indonesian law were adopted.

Proponents of applying Indonesian law prevailed, and in October 2003 the East Timorese Parliament adopted Law 10/2003 (Interpretation of Article 1 of Law 2/2002 of 7 August on the Sources of Law), expressly declaring Indonesian law to be the subsidiary law in East Timor. The Law provides:[44]

> Interpreting a law literally, outside its context and system, aloof from reality, and in violation of the most elementary rules of legal hermeneutics, leads to an absurdity, which may undermine the country's stability, as it tends to bring about a situation of institutional crisis that would otherwise not exist.
>
> ...
>
> Section 1: Authentic interpretation
> Under the terms of the provision of section 1 of Law No. 2/2002, of 7 August, applicable legislation in East Timor on 19 May 2002 means all Indonesian laws applied and that were in force 'de facto' in East Timor, prior to 25 October 1999, as provided by UNTAET Regulation No. 1/1999.

The Law was made applicable retroactively to East Timor's day of independence, 20 May 2002.[45]

5. LEGAL FACTORS IN THE DETERMINATION OF EAST TIMOR'S DOMESTIC LAW

The Court's ruling purported to be grounded on international law, specifically on a principle that protects the right to self-determination. As the latter is a *ius cogens* norm, *prima facie* such a principle enjoys priority over other norms of international law. The ruling was therefore a potential constitutional moment, which would have put domestic law in line with the international law regulating the international status of the territory. But this moment was based on a misconception, because it took the international norm out of context in a manner which distorted it. It was not clearly an innocent error in application, but possibly a deliberate attempt to employ international law to grant legitimacy to a controversial political goal.

The *dos Santos* affair was brought about by a series of errors on the part of the Court of Appeal's majority. Some of those errors were in the interpretation of

---

44 Translation from www.unmit.org/legal/RDTL-Law/index-e.htm.

45 Portugal's State Secretary for Foreign Affairs and Cooperation reacted, saying that the decision caused him 'some disappointment', but that it would not affect bilateral relations. Lusa (*Agência de Notícias de Portugal*, Portugal's news agency), Lisbon says adoption of Indonesian law no threat to relations (Dili, 2 October 2002), available at www.etan.org/et2003/october/01-6/02lisbon.htm.

Regulation 1999/1. The Court of Appeal's construction was based on a mistaken literal reading of Regulation 1999/1, which – contrary to the Court of Appeal majority's analysis of the non-authoritative Portuguese version of the Regulation – referred to 'laws applied', rather than to 'law applicable', prior to October 1999.[46] In other words, the Regulation did not make a normative statement on the law applicable prior to October 1999 but took into account merely the fact that Indonesian law had been enforced in practice. As the dissenting judge noted, the majority's interpretation is also inconsonant with the remaining part of the Regulation, and, one would add, with other UNTAET regulations.[47] UNTAET's intention to apply Indonesian law was also beyond doubt.

Most importantly, the Court of Appeal mistakenly gave paramount importance to the international legal principle that the acts of an illegal regime, including its laws, cannot have legal consequences, when it was actually deciding on the law applied by a lawful regime (UNTAET and subsequently independent East Timor). Regulation 1999/1 determined the content of post-October 1999 law; there was no imperative legal reason why East Timor (or UNTAET on its behalf) could not adopt Indonesian law as its own. The choice of domestic legal system of a state emerging out from under an illegal regime is grounded in the constitutional law of that state, not in international law. Likewise, a reversion to the *status quo ante* (ie application of Portuguese law) would also have been a constitutional choice and not an application of international law. Such reversion would have reflected a political stance and conveyed a political message as to the relationship between East Timor and the preceding, illegal Indonesian regime. But it would have been a policy choice rather than a legally-mandated consequence of Indonesia's previous illegal status in the territory. There was no *legal* flaw in UNTAET's choice to adopt Indonesian law as the subsidiary law of East Timor. The situation would have been different if UNTAET had purported to declare Indonesian law as the territorial law prior to October 1999. However, Regulation 1999/1 does not concern that period.

Another error of the Court of Appeal was that it considered the matter in abstract terms of the applicable pre-October 1999 territorial law of East Timor (the subject matter of Regulation 1999/1) rather than of the law to be applied in court. Ordinarily, the territorial law and the law applicable in individual cases are one and the same. But there may be exceptions,[48] and situations of transition

46 Cohen, *supra* note 33, p. 84–85.

47 Eg UNTAET Regulation 2000/30, Section 53.2 on Transitional Rules of Criminal Procedure, states that it 'takes precedence over Indonesian laws on criminal procedure'. Executive Orders 2000/2 and 2001/6 decriminalize certain offences in the Indonesian Criminal Code, and Executive Order 2001/6 mentions that the Indonesian Code is the applicable law in East Timor pursuant to Regulation 1999/1. In addition, the Regulation uses the term 'laws' rather than 'law', suggesting that at issue were specific instruments enforced in practice rather than a normative statement on the legal system.

48 In civil law it is a common phenomenon, regulated by the rules on conflicts of law.

from illegal regimes constitute such an exception. UNTAET regulations provided that the law to be applied in court was Indonesian law, *regardless* of whether that was also the territorial law, prior or subsequent to the transition. The only reason to reject these regulations would have been if they themselves led to a violation of international human rights law. Indeed, the majority in the Court of Appeal argued that since Portuguese law was the governing law, convicting dos Santos on the basis of any other law would amount to retroactive penalization, violating the principle *nullum crimen sine lege*.[49] However, contrary to the majority's assertion, it was actually the application of any criminal law other than *Indonesian* law that would have resulted in a violation of international human rights law and specifically of the *nullum crimen sine lege* principle. One of the fundamental principles of criminal law is that no one should be held guilty of a criminal offence on account of an act which did not constitute a criminal offence under national or international law at the time it was committed.[50] This gives rise to a general duty on states to define criminal offences precisely by law in the interest of legal certainty.[51] Avoidance of retroactive penalization required the Court to take account of the law that had been enforced in practice, in order to ensure that the law enforced was the law which the defendant could have known and acted upon, rather than to have recourse to law which had been only formally valid under international law. In the choice between convicting a person under Indonesian or Portuguese law, this principle has direct implications. After twenty-four years of Indonesian rule, exclusively under Indonesian law, there was no anticipation by individuals that Portuguese law would be enforced against them. The use of Portuguese law in these circumstances would have been

49 *Agustinho da Costa v. the Prosecutor General*, Case No. 3/2002, Judgment of 18 July 2003, available at www.jsmp.minihub.org/judgmentspdf/courtofappeal/Dissenting_Opinionby_Judge_Jacinta_in_Court_%20Appeal_DecisionRegardingApplicable_Law%20_nEastTimor.pdf. In the case of indictment under international criminal law, the question may seem immaterial, as the prohibiting norms are deemed to have existed whether or not incorporated into domestic law. *Public Prosecutor v. Joao Sarmento and Domingos Mendonça*, Decision on the Defense (Domingos Mendonça) Motion for the Court to Order the Public Prosecutor to amend the indictment, Case No. 18a/2001, decision of 24 July 2003, [11]-[34]. In fact, dos Santos was indicted for crimes against humanity, which formed part of customary international law at the time of their commission; there should therefore not have been any issue of retroactivity. Nonetheless, since the mandate of the domestic courts in East Timor is not limited to international crimes, the general question of the applicable law remains pertinent. The manner in which the domestic courts applied international criminal law by the domestic courts was also subject to severe criticism. Overview of the Jurisprudence of the Court of Appeal in its First Year of Operation since East Timor's Independence 9 (Dili, August 2004); Cohen, *supra* note 33, p. 86.

50 International Covenant on Civil and Political Rights (opened for signature 19 December 1966, entered into force 23 March 1976), Article 15; compare with the European Convention on Human Rights and Fundamental Freedoms (opened for signature 4 November 1950, entered into force 3 September 1953), Article 7.

51 N. Manfred, U.N. Covenant on Civil and Political Rights: CCPR Commentary 359–361 (Kehl: N.P. Engel, 2005, 2nd ed.).

contrary to the fundamental principle of legal certainty, which is given concrete expression, inter alia, in the prohibition on retroactive penalization. Instead, it is the internationally-invalid but internally-enforced Indonesian norms that were foreseeable and accessible.[52]

A separate question is whether it was the role of the Court, as the judicial arm of the sovereign state of East Timor, to determine the applicable law of the land. The Court of Appeal considered itself competent to do so.[53] The SPSC, proceeding on the basis that the law had already been definitively determined by UNTAET and the Timorese legislature, considered that the principle of separation of powers, entrenched in the East Timorese Constitution, precluded the Court of Appeal from departing from the legislated norm.[54] Commentators suggest that where there is an irreconcilable difference of opinion between the courts as to the correct interpretation of a law, and where the interpretation of that law also involves a political element, it is appropriate for the national parliament to resolve any confusion or uncertainty by new legislation.[55] This was done in the adoption of Law 10/2003.

The Court of Appeal's majority opinion brings to the fore the potential conflict between two sets of considerations regulated by international law. One is inter-state law and policy, where the principle *ex injuria jus non oritur* may play a role. The other is international human rights law, applicable between the state and the individual, which informs the law governing individual cases. International law itself gives human rights law superiority over inter-state policy. During the existence of the illegal regime, this superiority is embodied in the qualification to the obligation of non-recognition of illegal acts, that it should not be pursued where to do so would result in detriment to the population under

---

52 Compare with the ECtHR rulings in *Protopapa v. Turkey*, that for the purpose of the principle *nullum crimen sine lege*, the law of the Turkish Republic of Northern Cyprus may be regarded as valid: Ect.HR 24 February 2009, *Protopapa v. Turkey*, App. no. 16084/90, unreported, [93]; and in *SW v United Kindgdom*, that a defendant cannot claim that penalization was retroactive where the evolution of a criminal offense had reached a stage where the judicial interpretation of the offense had become a reasonably foreseeable development of the law: Ect.HR 22 November 1995, *SW v. United Kingdom*, App. no. 20166/92, Judgment (Merits), [43], Series A335-B.
This assumes that on the whole, the rule of law applied within the purported legal system of the illegal regime. Where it did not, as is arguably the case in East Timor, additional problems arise, unrelated to the international status of the regime.

53 *Public Prosecutor v. Armando dos Santos*, available at www.jsmp.minihub.org/judgmentspdf/courtofappeal/Court_of_Appeal_Decision_15-07-03_Case16-2001.pdf, English translation at www.jsmp.minihub.org/judgmentspdf/courtofappeal/Ct_of_App-dos_Santos_English22703.pdf, 7.

54 *Public Prosecutor v. Joao Sarmento and Domingos Mendonça*, Decision on the Defense (Domingos Mendonça) Motion for the Court to Order the Public Prosecutor to amend the indictment, Case No. 18a/2001, decision of 24 July 2003, [39].

55 JSMP, Report on the Court of Appeal Decision in the Case of Armando dos Santos 7 (Dili, August 2003).

the illegal regime.[56] Once the illegal regime comes to an end, the new, lawful regime is the source of authority. It is free to pursue the consequences of the previous illegality or abandon them, but it is still bound by international human rights law. The Court of Appeal chose to examine the general validity of Indonesian criminal law solely in terms of inter-state relations, namely on the basis of the regime's illegality. However, it is precisely in order to protect the individual from matters of politics that international human rights law takes priority over inter-state policy in these circumstances.

6. THE POLITICS OF DETERMINING DOMESTIC LAW – A COMPARATIVE ASSESSMENT

The choice of domestic law in post-conflict situations is a particularly pertinent issue in instances of transition from an illegal regime, although not unique to it. East Timor's experience can therefore be assessed against previous cases of transition from illegal regimes. Examples include Zimbabwe's independence in 1980 after fifteen years of the Ian Smith regime; Namibia's independence in 1990 after twenty-four years of South African administration; and the Baltic States' restoration of their independence in 1990–1991 after half a century of Soviet annexation. In all these cases, the law previously enforced by the illegal regime was adopted as the prospective law, either expressly or implicitly.[57] Moreover, in none of these cases was there an attempt to nullify the effect of the norms that had been applied under the illegal regime. A slightly different case is that of Kosovo, which in 1999 came under UN administration after a decade of non-autonomous status within Serbia. The annulment of Kosovar autonomy was not illegal under international law, but it was perceived by the Kosovar community as both illegitimate and illegal under domestic law. This led, as described earlier, to Kosovo's reversion in 1999 to its pre-1989 law.

Two models emerge, both of which concern the law applicable from the time of transition: one is the adoption of the illegal regime's law (in all except Kosovo); the other is the rejection of the illegal regime's law (in Kosovo). However, in none of these cases was there an attempt to revisit the law applied *prior to* the time of transition. The *dos Santos* ruling attempted to establish a third model, under which the previous regime's law is rejected not only prospectively, but also retroactively. The debate following the *dos Santos* ruling ultimately led to the adoption of the first model. But despite this humble conclusion of the affair, its

56 ICJ, *Legal Consequences for States of the Continued Presence of South Africa in Namibia (South West Africa) notwithstanding Security Council Resolution 276 (1970) (Advisory Opinion)*, 1971 ICJ Reports 16 [125].

57 Y. Ronen, Transition from Illegal Regimes in International Law ch. 5 (Cambridge University Press, 2011).

very occurrence suggests that East Timor is somehow different from the other cases. The present section considers some possible unique characteristics of East Timor that may explain this unique event.

First, it is a crucial factor that the the controversial rulings by the Court of Appeal were decided by the international members of the bench. The practice of introducing international judges into domestic courts is intended to fill a capacity vacuum that emerges when as a result of the conflict there is no qualified cadre of jurists, and where familiarity with international human rights standards is particularly poor. However, in East Timor the reliance on international judges proved a disappointment. The *dos Santos* ruling, like many others, can be put down simply to professional inadequacy of the judges.[58] The international judges opted for a political statement on the illegality of the previous regime by pursuing its consequences even within the domestic system, to the extent that they compromised the observance of international human rights standards to which their office was eminently committed. This raises the question why the international judges chose to attach so much weight to the international illegality of the Indonesian regime in the first place. The majority judges were correct when they reportedly said that the issue was 'a matter of politics'.[59] Although the judges were 'international', they were not disinterested parties. Their politics was the advancement of Portuguese culture in East Timor. Both majority judges had received their legal training in Portugal and were recruited there (although the President of the Court of Appeal, who led the move to apply Portuguese law, is ethnically East Timorese). They may have been more inclined toward a legal construction that would have enabled them to use Portuguese law because they were less familiar with Indonesian law.[60] The phenomenon of international judges in hybrid courts relying on their acquaintance with the law under their own domestic jurisdictions is neither surprising nor exceptional,[61] but rarely do they have an opportunity to openly impose their national law on the post-conflict state. The Portuguese-trained judges had this opportunity in East Timor, because of the legal history of the territory.

By the same token, the dissenting, East Timorese judge's advocacy of applying Indonesian law might be explained by her own familiarity with Indonesian rather than Portuguese law. But it is no less significant that her opinion was led by considerations of stability and pragmatism, which called for taking account of the fact that these norms were used in practice, rather than for a formal upholding of international law.

58 S. Katzenstein, Hybrid Tribunals: Searching for Justice in East Timor, 16 Harvard Human Rights Journal 245 (2003); Cohen, *supra* note 33, p. 83–87, Morrow and White, *supra* note 27, p. 1.

59 Cohen, *supra* note 33, p. 85.

60 Although they failed even in applying that law: Cohen, *supra* note 33.

61 D. Terris, C.P.R. Romano and L. Swigart, The International Judge 168–170 (Lebanon: Brandeis University Press, 2007).

Although the move proposed by the Court of Appeal was not anticipated and took the legal community by surprise, the matter had gone beyond the personal inclinations of the judges. When the matter came to debate in the East Timorese Parliament, opinions were divided. As noted above, the debate focused on the implications of the choice of applicable law on relations with Indonesia and with Portugal. But the choice between maintaining the law of the illegal regime and reversion to the law applicable earlier also had clear, tangible implications, with different effects on different segments of the population. There were strong political forces consisting of persons who were perceived as standing to gain a substantial economic advantage from the adoption of Portuguese rather than Indonesian law, particularly in the area of land holdings.[62] Accordingly they had an interest in a blanket adoption of Portuguese law. Conversely, other forces objected to the application of Portuguese law in order to advance their own policies. The conflict of personal and political interests was generated into a dispute over the adoption of one legal system or another. In this, East Timor differed from the other post-conflict instances, where the indigenous population was perceived as uniformly deprived under the previous regime,[63] and thus interests in choosing one legal system over another were uniform.

The eventual confirmation by the Timor-Leste legislature in 2003 of Indonesian law as the subsidiary law of East Timor put the country on par with other post-conflict states. All have faced the unavoidable tension between the symbolic value of the principled rejection of the illegal regime's law and the need to maintain that law as positive law in order to ensure legal and social stability. A number of factors may explain the prevalent choice of continuity from the previous regime's law, and explain why in Kosovo and East Timor there were attempts to depart from this choice, with more success in the former than in the latter.

One factor is the relative legitimacy of the illegal regime's law and the law preceding it, particularly in the eyes of the local population. Where the preceding law also suffered from illegitimacy, the incentive to cause upheaval in order to reinstate it would be smaller than in situations where that law enjoys legitimacy on the part of the local population in terms both of origin and content. For example, in Zimbabwe and Namibia, and similarly in East Timor, rejection of the illegal regime's law would have meant reversion to earlier colonial law. This hardly generated enthusiasm amongst the local population. The situation was

62 This refers primarily to members of the UDT party.

63 As a matter of fact, this perception was misplaced in other instances of transition. For the experience in Estonia see M. Feldman, Justice in Space? The Restitution of Property Rights in Tallinn, Estonia, 6 Cultural Geographies 165, 170–173 (1999). For the experience in South Africa see M. Ramutsindela, The Geographical Imprint of Land Restitution with Reference to Limpopo Province, South Africa, 98 Tijdschrift voor Economische en Sociale Geografie 455, 460–461 (2007); C. Walker, The Limits of Land Reform: Rethinking 'the Land Question', 31 Journal of Southern African Studies 805, 809 (2005).

different in Kosovo and in the Baltic States, where the law preceding that of the illegal regime law enjoyed strong formal and substantive legitimacy on the part of the local population.

A related factor is the period of time during which the illegal regime imposed its law. In the Baltic States, where reversion to pre-Soviet law enjoyed political legitimacy, half a century had passed since that law had last applied. Pre-Soviet law was ill-equipped to regulate modern life. This may have militated against reversion to it as a practical measure. Similarly in East Timor, Portuguese law had not been utilized for 24 years. In Kosovo, Kosovar law had not been utilized for only a single decade – and in some context applied voluntarily even during that period – so the reversion to pre-1989 law might have appeared feasible. In practice, it proved a harmful choice, which resulted in a morass of uncertainty and confusion.[64]

These factors led to a greater adherence to the international legal principle *ex injuria jus non oritur* in Kosovo than in East Timor.

7. CONCLUSION

The *dos Santos* affair demonstrates the conflict that can be created by the attempt to follow international legal principles at different levels, not all of which are geared towards the enhancement of a domestic legal system emerging from a conflict situation. The principle *ex injuria jus non oritur* vindicates some of the most important norms of international law, namely the prohibition on the use of force and the obligation to respect the right of people to self-determination, but it envisages the regulation of inter-state relations; applying it without reservation in post-conflict East Timor could have resulted in legal – and political – upheaval.

The preoccupation with the choice of domestic law in both East Timor and Kosovo suggests that a high level of post-conflict international involvement is a more receptive environment for formal arguments based on inter-state legal relations than ordinary domestic jurisdictions. Moreover, in East Timor, these formal arguments themselves came essentially from international actors. International involvement, on both a normative and capacity level, therefore had an unexpectedly negative effect on promoting the rule of law in the post-conflict situation. Fortunately for the development of East Timor, by the time the matter arose, experience had proven the perils of yielding to formalistic stances, and insistence on a pragmatic, human rights-based approach was adopted.

---

64 Lorenz, *supra* note 23, p. 127, 129–130.

CONCLUDING OBSERVATIONS

Edda Kristjánsdóttir, André Nollkaemper
and Cedric Ryngaert

Having presented the preceding thirteen case studies of how domestic courts apply, or do not apply, international law in various post-conflict and transitional settings (specifically, in Afghanistan, Bosnia and Herzegovina, East Timor, Iraq, Nepal, the Russian Federation, Rwanda, Serbia, and South Africa, as well as two cross-cutting studies), the time has come to take stock and draw some conclusions, while duly acknowledging the heterogeneity of the legal systems and post-conflict situations studied. We structure these Concluding Observations under the headings that we identified in the Introduction, and use these to integrate the lessons learned from the case studies.

In section 1, we provide an overview of the types of 'constitutional moments' that allowed for an increased role of national courts in the application of international law in the various situations studied. In section 2, we discuss the form and substance of domestic courts' empowerment to apply international law in the different settings. In section 3, we review the role of the various actors involved in receiving or importing international law. Any concerns of the reader that an overly optimistic picture is presented by this overview of empowerment techniques should be immediately assuaged in section 4, which addresses the various limitations of applying international law in domestic courts which may have grown more accustomed to a violent and authoritarian political order than to a robust rule of law. Finally, section 5 discusses the effects and legacy of international law implementation by domestic courts in post-conflict or transitional situations. It questions whether the application of international law really makes a difference for post-conflict societies, and whether international intervention produces any lasting effects in terms of rule of law entrenchment or broader societal stabilization.

It is to be stressed up front that the conclusions in section 5 concerning recent changes in the countries studied are by necessity tentative and can only be assessed conclusively over a longer time-horizon. Also, we do not suggest that the gap between official support for international law and the actual application of international law by domestic courts is a phenomenon peculiar to post-conflict societies. In many legal systems, also of developed countries, domestic courts use various avoidance techniques to prevent international law from playing a decisive role in disputes.[1] The crucial difference, however, lies in how the international community and external actors, in the name of the international rule of law, exert their influence in countries transitioning from conflict or oppression – hence the focus of this book on transition.

1. CONSTITUTIONAL MOMENTS

1.1. TYPES OF TRANSITION

The case studies in this volume provide examples of a variety of situations in which international law has been received or imported into a national legal order to empower national courts to apply it. Some of them took place in an immediate aftermath of armed conflict. In Serbia and in Bosnia and Herzegovina (BiH), this was put into effect right at the conclusion of the war in 1995. The Dayton Peace Agreement was the instrument which imported international law, in particular international human rights law, and it established the necessary institutional mechanisms for giving effect to these rights.[2] Likewise, in Rwanda, the changing role and use of international law, in particular in international criminal law, was directly tied to the end of the conflict in 1994, although the response was more delayed than in the Balkans.[3] It was only in 1996, in response to concerns about the International Criminal Tribunal for Rwanda (ICTR), that the Organic Law was adopted, establishing a Special Chamber of the Rwandan Supreme Court to try both genocide and crimes against humanity, with a temporal jurisdiction from October 1990 until December 1994. In East Timor, the importation of international law, primarily through the UN Transitional Administration in East Timor (UNTAET), followed as a direct result of the end of the armed conflict that erupted after the pro-independence vote on independence.[4]

---

1 See generally P.A. Nollkaemper and E. Kristjánsdóttir (eds), Casebook on International Law in Domestic Courts (forthcoming 2012).

2 See A. Buyse, Virtuous Flexibility – The Application of International Human Rights Norms by the Bosnian Human Rights Chamber, in this volume at p. 175; K. Uhlířová, War Crimes Chamber of the Court of Bosnia and Herzigovina: Seeding "International Standards of Justice"?, in this volume at p. 195; S. Weill and I. Jovanović, War Crimes Prosecution in a Post-Conflict Era and a Pluralism of Jurisdictions: The Experience of the Belgrade War Crimes Chamber, in this volume at p. 241; and S. Popovic, Prosecution of War Crimes in Bosnian Cantonal and District Courts; the Role of the Rule of Law, in this volume at p. 221.

3 See N. Palmer, Understandings of International Law in Rwanda: A Contextual Approach, in this volume at p. 153.

4 See Y. Ronen, The Use and Abuse of International Law: Choice of Applicable Criminal Law in Post-Conflict East Timor, in this volume at p. 291.

In addition to the termination of large-scale conflict and transition to a new legal regime, international law has been applied in other types of situations to bring about the (re)establishment of the rule of law. In Nepal, for instance, the momentous *Dhakal* case – in which the Nepalese Supreme Court directly applied the Convention Against Enforced Disappearances and ordered the executive to take investigate measures based on that convention – was the result of a variety of factors, including the collapse of the active monarchy in April 2006, the formal end of the armed conflict in November 2006, the promulgation of the Interim Constitution in January 2007, and the consensus-oriented political environment in which the election of the Constituent Assembly took place. In this enabling situation, the local judiciary appeared ready to take into account international norms for dealing with past human rights abuses where the executive had failed to do so.[5]

The situations of the Russian Federation and Iraq are examples of constitutional change that arose not so much from the end of a conflict as from a transition to a post-authoritarian regime (although in the case of Iraq the regime change and the armed conflict which began in 2003 were of course inextricably linked). In Russia, the strengthened role of international law followed from the disintegration of the Soviet Union and the establishment of Russia as a separate state in December 1991, and from the later confrontation between the Supreme Council (former Parliament) and the presidential power in October 1993, which led to the establishment of a new form of government and adoption of a new constitution in December 1993.[6] In Iraq, one can as yet hardly speak of effective importation of international law despite the considerable outside involvement in the country. Nonetheless, the events that followed the fall of Saddam Hussein's regime show the type of window that may open for importing international law. Under the Hussein regime, while Iraq was party to many treaties and the courts could formally apply international law, such practice was in fact very limited. The Coalition Provisional Authority (CPA) incorporated greater human rights protections guaranteed in international law into Iraqi judicial proceedings by enacting orders and memoranda amending Iraqi law in various ways and incorporating the substance of international legal protections into existing Iraqi law. As the chapter by Hamoudi suggests, the CPA trusted the secular judiciary more than it did the Islamist politicians who were evidently poised to win the first election held in post-Hussein Iraq. The subsequent drafting of the interim constitution, known as the Transitional Administrative Law, was a later moment

5 See R. Wagle, Judicial Activism and the Use of International Law as Gap-Filler in Domestic Law: the Case of Forced Disappearances Committed During the Armed Conflict in Nepal, in this volume at p. 83.

6 See S. Marochkin, International Law in the Russian Courts in Transitional Situations, in this volume at p. 35.

in which the possible importation of international law was considered – even though this ultimately did not amount to much change.[7]

A final example of a constitutional transition that was due more to a change in regime than an open armed conflict is that of South Africa.[8] After the end of apartheid, a deliberate effort was made in the 1996 Constitution to harmonise the new Bill of Rights with international law.

1.2. MOMENTS IN TIME

Although we speak in this book of constitutional 'moments' at which international law is received into national legal orders, it is important to note that these need not be, and perhaps are unlikely to be, a single event at one single point in time. In many cases, a 'constitutional moment' is in fact a series of connected events occurring over a period of time. This is illustrated for instance by the developments in Bosnia and Herzegovina and in Serbia. In both cases, the process set in motion with the Dayton Peace Agreement had later spin-offs. In the case of BiH, eight years after Dayton, the United Nations Security Council in 2003 passed Resolution 1503 endorsing the completion strategy of the International Criminal Tribunal for the Former Yugoslavia (ICTY).[9] As part of the completion strategy and in order to reduce its workload, the ICTY decided to refer certain cases to national authorities. This in turn led to the increased use of local Bosnian courts in the prosecution of war crimes,[10] and to the establishment of the Bosnian War Crimes Chamber (Bosnian WCC),[11] which provided for further importation of international law in Bosnia-Herzegovina both from a substantive and institutional perspective. The ICTY completion strategy likewise prompted the establishment of the War Crimes Chamber (Serbian WCC) and the War Crimes Law in Serbia.[12]

In Rwanda, the constitutional moments were also spread over time. After the initial response that was the 1996 Organic Law, the new Rwandan Constitution of 2003 established that international treaties ratified by Rwanda were 'more binding than organic and ordinary law'. As in the former Yugoslavia, this second wave of legal change was in part initiated in order to meet the standards required by the ICTR completion strategy for transferring cases to Rwanda's domestic

---

7 See H.A. Hamoudi, International Law and Iraqi Courts, in this volume at p. 107.

8 See, eg, *Azanian Peoples Organization and ors v. President of South Africa and ors*, Direct access to the Constitutional Court, CCT 17/96; 1996 (4) SA 671 (CC); ILDC 648 (ZA 1996), para. 29 (doubting that the Geneva Conventions would be applicable at all to the conflict in South Africa).

9 See also Annex IV of the DPA in which Article II(8) states: 'All competent authorities in Bosnia and Herzegovina shall cooperate and provide unrestricted access to [...] the International Tribunal for the Former Yugoslavia[...].'

10 See Popovic, *supra* note 2.

11 See Uhlířová, *supra* note 2.

12 See Weill & Jovanović, *supra* note 2.

jurisdiction under Rule 11*bis*.[13] Despite this formal empowerment of local judges to apply international law, however, the ICTR bench still has not considered the *11bis* standards to have been met, and it has refused to refer cases to Rwandan courts.[14]

Whether or not a single constitutional moment creates lasting international rule of law-entrenching effects depends on whether the relevant state institutions have a sustained respect for international norms. Not unusually, domestic courts might give effect to such norms were it not for a fear of embarrassing the executive. For instance, the status and effect of the constitutional entrenchment of international law in the Russian Federation cannot be understood apart from the practice of the courts, which have confirmed international law to be an integral part of the Russian legal system while at the same time stopping short of actively reviewing acts of the political branches in politically sensitive matters.[15] The same holds for South Africa, where the Constitutional Court has developed extensive jurisprudence on socio-economic rights and in so doing has relied upon international norms, while at the same time rejecting the minimum core standard of the Centre for Economic and Social Rights and relying instead on a 'reasonableness standard' deferential to the executive.[16]

2. FORM AND SUBSTANCE OF EMPOWERMENT

As has become clear throughout the book, international law reforms and the attendant empowerment of domestic courts in transitional situations take on many forms and manifestations. In some cases, the constitutional moments may involve the adoption of a new constitution allowing courts to apply international law, such as in the Russian Federation,[17] South Africa,[18] and Bosnia and Herzegovina.[19] In other cases, the constitutional moment involves the adoption of new laws, which empower national courts to apply international law in particular areas, or the creation of new institutions with a mandate to apply international law. Examples include the application of international criminal law in the Belgrade War Crimes Chamber,[20] the inclusion of international criminal

13 See Palmer, *supra* note 3.

14 See E. Schmid, Thickening the Rule of Law in Transition: The Constitutional Entrenchment of Economic and Social Rights in South Africa, in this volume at p. 59. For discussion, see also I. Onsea, The Legacy of the ICTR in Rwanda in the Context of the Completion Strategy: The Impact of Rule 11*bis*, in: C. Ryngaert (ed.), The Effectiveness of International Criminal Justice 173–194 (Antwerp: Intersentia, 2009).

15 See Marochkin, *supra* note 6.

16 See Schmid, *supra* note 14.

17 Constitution of the Russian Federation, 1993 (as amended), Art. 15(4).

18 Constitution of South Africa, 1996, Art. 39.

19 Constitution of Bosnia and Herzegovina, Dayton Peace Agreement, initialed in Dayton, Ohio 21 November 1995, signed in Paris 14 December 1995, Annex 4, Art. 3(b).

20 See Weill and Jovanović, *supra* note 2.

law in Rwandan domestic law by the Organic Law of 1996, and the more recent due process (human rights) modifications of Rwandan law at the urging of the ICTR.

In still other cases, the constitutional moment involves not the creation of new formal arrangements for the status of international law or the power of courts to give effect to it, but the creation of the political or judicial will to enable the use of such powers. Examples include the far-reaching invocation of international law in the 2007 *Dhakal* judgment of the Nepalese Supreme Court.[21] In such cases, the judiciary may consider international law to be a useful and fairly reliable (because internationally supported) tool to stand up to the political branches, or at least to rise above the political fray. The application of international law may therefore be seen as strengthening judicial independence – although a desire for independence does not necessarily go hand in hand with a need or willingness to apply international law, as the Iraqi experience demonstrates. If such uses of international law were isolated occurrences, it would be inappropriate to call them constitutional moments. However, this will be different if the courts have passed through the door, so to speak, towards a new mode of decision-making, and appear to have closed it behind them.

In some states, national courts have been given the power to apply all rules of international law, even when doing so would overrule pre-existing domestic law. For example, the Constitution of the Russian Federation introduced hierarchically superior international law, allowing the courts to review both executive and legislative power against international law, including the case law of the European Court of Human Rights (ECtHR);[22] the Croatian Constitution introduced supremacy of international treaties;[23] the Constitution of Bosnia and Herzegovina states the priority of all human rights inspired by the European Convention of Human Rights (ECHR), international agreements, and general principles of international law;[24] and the Constitution of Kosovo provides for the direct applicability and superiority of international treaties.[25]

Of particular relevance in a post-conflict society, of course, is the effect given to international human rights and international criminal law norms as agents of (transitional) justice. Indeed, in almost all the situations reviewed in this book, these bodies of law were at the center of attention, although there are also

21 See Wagle, *supra* note 5.

22 Cf Marochkin, *supra* note 6.

23 Constitution of Croatia, 1990, Art. 140.

24 Constitution of Bosnia and Herzegovina, eg Arts. II (2), II (7) and III(3)(b). See also Constitutional Court of Bosnia and Herzegovina, *Case of Abduladhim Maktouf*, Decision on Admissibility and Merits, AP-1785/06, para. 71 (ruling that a number of human rights and humanitarian law treaties 'have a status equal to that of constitutional principles and are directly applied in Bosnia and Herzegovina'). The same court held that the ICTY Statute contained general principles of international law which 'shall be an integral part of the law of Bosnia and Herzegovina and the Entities'. Id., para. 70.

25 Constitution of Kosovo 2008, Art. 19.

examples where this did not occur, as in Iraq and Afghanistan. It may be argued that the central role of human rights and international criminal law standards is supported by the fact that as these bodies of law are aimed directly at individuals, the international community and domestic courts can with relative ease draw on those bodies of law to override or circumvent the existing legal system of the state. The application of human rights law was for instance central in the situations in East-Timor,[26] Bosnia,[27] and Nepal.[28] Beyond the cases reviewed in this book, it can be observed that the strengthening of human rights law has become a central aim in post-conflict situations. It is central to much of the UN Security Council's actions when it establishes peace-keeping and peace-building operations,[29] as well as UN acts to strengthen the role of domestic courts, though in most such situations the UN is more concerned with getting the courts to function at all, than with the substantive laws they apply. International criminal law, for its part, was central to the transformation processes in Rwanda,[30] Serbia,[31] and Bosnia and Herzegovina.[32] The Security Council has also relied on international criminal law to transform a repressive political culture: it is no exaggeration to say that its referrals of the situations in Sudan and Libya to the International Criminal Court (ICC), and the ensuing ICC arrest warrants, may be understood as calls for regime and constitutional change in those countries.[33]

Obviously, merely making international law part of national law does not in itself guarantee that domestic courts will apply international law, especially not if the courts operate in a dualist system that precludes them from applying international law directly, if the invoked international norm lacks direct effect, or if the application of international law to a criminal case would violate the principle of legality. Nonetheless, domestic courts may find a way around those limitations, for instance by interpreting existing domestic law (such as offences or modes of liability) in the light of, or consistently with, international law.[34] It is conspicuous, but entirely understandable, that in such situations cases may be

---

26 See Ronen, *supra* note 4.

27 See Buyse, *supra* note 2.

28 See Wagle, *supra* note 5.

29 See notably UN Security Council Resolution 1674 (2006) on the protection of civilians in armed conflict, operational paragraph 16. See also the UN Security Council's resolutions on the rights of children in armed conflict: Resolutions 1539 (2004), 1612 (2005), setting up a monitoring and reporting mechanism, and 1882 (2009).

30 See Palmer, *supra* note 3.

31 See Weill and Jovanović, *supra* note 2.

32 See Uhlířová, *supra* note 2, and Popovic, *supra* note 2.

33 Respectively, UNSC Resolution 1593 (2005) and UNSC Resolution 1970 (2011). See also C. Gosnell, The Request for an Arrest Warrant in *Al Bashir*, 6 Journal of International Criminal Justice 841 (2008).

34 Cf, eg, Serbian War Crimes Chamber (interpretation in light of crimes against humanity and of the principle of command responsibility).

based on both domestic and international law.[35] Also, domestic courts may apply international law by nominally relying on a domestic law provision which refers directly to the application of international law (international law *renvoi*). Such provisions may have been on the statute books for a long time, but prosecutorial willingness to act upon them may have been lacking during the authoritarian regime in power, because of hostility to anything smacking of 'the international', or simply because of a lack of familiarity with international law, such as in the former Yugoslavia and Iraq.[36]

Post-*occupation* situations raise special questions as to the body of (international) law available to courts to apply. As the occupying power will often have enacted its own 'domestic' law, possibly without good reason, national courts may after the end of the occupation have to choose between continuing to give effect to this law, or to give effect to the law that applied before the occupation period. Indirectly, through the provisions of the Geneva Conventions[37] and the Hague Regulations[38] (which allow occupying powers to amend existing laws only in exceptional circumstances), such cases are relevant to international law and the rule of law. In fact, these cases sometimes pit one layer of international law against another, and thus require negotiation of different international interests: the international legal interest in the non-recognition of illegal acts of occupying powers, and the international human rights interest of protecting the legitimate expectations of individuals who engaged in acts and transactions during the period of occupation. Domestic courts may wish to consecrate a constitutional moment by refusing to give effect to certain legal acts, or even entire legal codes, of the occupant. In so doing, and summoning international law for support, they mark a clear break with the oppressive past, but because international law may insufficiently accommodate the acquired rights of persons who acted in good faith during the occupation, domestic courts may need to fine-tune this constitutional moment by acknowledging those 'human rights'. After all, constitutionalism is about protecting the rights and freedoms of individuals. Such a double-edged constitutional moment strengthens the international rule of law in two ways: it provides much-needed clarification of the application of the Geneva Conventions and the Hague Regulations in times of occupation, and it furthers the rights of individuals (including minorities) as enshrined in international human rights treaties.[39]

---

35 See eg the case of *Lekaj* in Serbia, as discussed in the chapter by Weill and Jovanović, *supra* note 2.

36 Cf. Article 142 of the Criminal Code of the Federal Republic of Yugoslavia, discussed in the chapter by Weill and Jovanović, *supra* note 2. In Iraq, treaties had become the law of the land also under Saddam Hussein, but the judiciary was not familiar with international law and only applied the national code: see Hamoudi, *supra* note 7.

37 1949 Geneva Conventions I-IV and Additional Protocols.

38 The Hague Conventions 1899 and 1907.

39 See E. Benvenisti and M. Saliternik, The Treatment of Occupation Legislation by Courts in Liberated Territories, in this volume at p. 269.

3. ACTORS

International constitutional moments may emerge bottom-up, through social and political processes that are unleashed once the weight of conflict or authoritarianism is lifted, as occurred in the former Soviet Union and in South Africa. But often this emergence is helped or even induced by international agents, a notable example being the strengthening of human rights in the Bosnian legal order through the Dayton Peace Agreement and in particular by the Human Rights Chamber.[40] Other examples are the use of hybrid models in the Bosnian War Crimes Chamber,[41] the operation of the hybrid UNTAET Special Panels for Serious Crimes in East Timor,[42] the contemplation of hybrid courts to deal with past atrocities in the Democratic Republic of the Congo (DRC),[43] and the internationally supervised case referrals from the ICTY and the ICTR to domestic courts in the former Yugoslavia and in Rwanda.[44] Other examples of the role of international institutions and/or foreign states in (attempted) internationalization of constitutions include Burundi,[45] Cambodia,[46] the DRC,[47] Peru,[48] Iraq, and Sudan.[49]

As these examples make clear, international 'norm penetration' and 'knowledge transfer' is especially facilitated where the international community and states in transition set up hybrid institutions with both an international and domestic component.[50] This is particularly apt in transitional situations where

40 See Buyse, *supra* note 2.

41 See Uhlířová, *supra* note 2.

42 See Ronen, *supra* note 4.

43 See Report of the UN Mapping Exercise documenting the most serious violations of human rights and international humanitarian law committed within the territory of the Democratic Republic of the Congo between March 1993 and June 2003, August 2010, p. 466–471.

44 In contrast, the initial adoption of the Organic Law in Rwanda shows a more diffuse influence of international institutions: this law was not so much initiated or facilitated by the international community, but was rather an attempt to take charge of prosecution in order to reduce or prevent the role of international institutions. See further Palmer, *supra* note 3.

45 Jackson and C.J. Kiiza, The Role of Third Party Intervention in Africa's Civil Conflicts: The Case of South Africa's Peace Mission in Burundi 199 (University of Witwatersrand Institutional Repository, 12 March 2008), available at http://hdl.handle.net/10539/4652 (visited 15 April 2010).

46 S.P. Marks, The New Cambodian Constitution: From Civil War to a Fragile Democracy, 26(45) Columbia Human Rights Law Review 45 (1994–1995).

47 J.T. Gathii, Popular Authorship and Constitution Making: Comparing and Contrasting the DRC and Kenya, 49(4) William & Mary Law Review 1115 (May 2008), available at http://ssrn.com/abstract=1397619.

48 O.B. Arewa and S. O'Rourke, Country Specific Legislation and Human Rights, 5 Harvard Human Rights Journal 183–192 (1992).

49 P. Dann and Z. al-Ali, The Internationalized Pouvoir Constituant – Constitution-Making Under External Influence In Iraq, Sudan and East Timor, 10 Max Planck Yearbook of United Nations Law 423–463 (2006).

50 Still, it should be borne in mind that the appointed international judges do not necessarily have a strong international law background; accordingly, knowledge transfer should not be taken for granted in such models.

the national judicial capacity to apply international law may have been destroyed – or lacking all along. In other words, strengthening the rule of law through empowering national courts may need to go hand in hand with the appointment of international judges, at least for the transition period, so as to compensate for reduced capacity, or political bias – possible or perceived – of national judges. In Bosnia, for instance, international judges filled the seats of the Bosnian Human Rights Chamber and the Bosnian War Crimes Chamber, alongside domestic judges,[51] and it is possible that the Ugandan High Court may follow this model. However, many states may consider such mixed courts as an affront to their sovereignty, or as the meddling of an international cabal in their internal affairs.[52]

As an alternative, the international community can in certain circumstances assist states in the setting up of domestic processes, and by monitoring and supervising them. The High Representative and the Organization for Security and Co-operation in Europe (OSCE) have done so in the case of the Bosnian Human Rights Court,[53] and the US Embassy, UN Development Program (UNDP), the ICTY, and local NGOs in the case of Serbia.[54] International institutions and NGOs similarly have assisted with atrocity trials in eastern DRC.[55] In case of NGO assistance, international NGOs tend to team up with grassroots NGOs, a process which weds international law with grassroots knowledge and thus strengthens both the legitimacy and the effectiveness of international intervention. In some cases, international legal assistance is not so much actively offered by the international community, but initiated bottom-up by states and domestic courts in the form of domestic laws implementing or giving effect to international law. Russia and South Africa are obvious examples here, though in the latter case it is difficult entirely to discount the more diffuse influence of the international community on the country's transition from apartheid.[56]

In the field of international criminal law, the examples of Serbia and Bosnia and Herzegovina show that national legislatures or courts may take the applicable

51 See Buyse, *supra* note 2, and Uhlířová, *supra* note 2.

52 Cf the rejection of a mixed Iraqi High Court with jurisdiction to try Saddam Hussein and his henchmen. See Hamoudi, *supra* note 7.

53 See Buyse, *supra* note 2.

54 See Weill and Jovanović, *supra* note 2.

55 See for empirical research E. Baylis, Reassessing the Role of International Criminal Law: Rebuilding National Courts Through Transnational Networks, 50 Boston College Law Review 1 (2009). See also the Mobile Gender Justice Court in the eastern DRC supported by the Open Society Justice Initiative and the Open Society Initiative for Southern Africa in partnership with the International Bar Association's Rule of Law Initiative. This DRC Court tries people charged with gender-based violence. Information available at www.soros.org/initiatives/justice/focus/international_justice/projects/gender-justice-court.

56 See Schmid, *supra* note 14, and the many condemnations of apartheid by the international community, in particular the mandatory arms embargo imposed on apartheid South Africa by UN Security Council Resolution 418 (1977).

law of international criminal tribunals as a model for domestic prosecutions of international crimes. This may occur on the basis of domestic statutes enacted to satisfy the transfer criteria of Rule 11*bis* of the ICTY and ICTR Rules of Procedure and Evidence. It may now also occur in states implementing the ICC Statute to fulfill the requirements of the complementarity principle.[57] A national legislature may draw inspiration from existing international criminal law procedures, without necessarily being bound by it, to carry out legal reform. Serbia, for instance, drew upon applicable ICTY law to push through some amendments to its national code of criminal procedure.[58] Engaging internationally does not preclude domestic actors to go beyond what is envisaged by the international processes. For instance, the Serbian War Crimes Prosecutor has issued indictments beyond the scope of the ICTY Rule 11*bis* referrals.[59]

A particular form of empowerment finally arises in post-occupation situations. Occupiers may, as in the case of Iraq (2003), use the occupation to try to partly entrench international law, in particular human rights, in the domestic legal order. As is evidenced in the chapters by Ronen and by Saliternik and Benvenisti, the question then is what lasting effect such 'transformative' intervention will have.[60]

4. LIMITATIONS

Despite the many modes of empowerment identified above, and the opportunities for applying international law, optimism may have to be tempered, as the willingness and ability of domestic courts to apply international law may be limited in various ways. The case studies show that limitations as to the effective application of international law by domestic courts may stem from the difficult relationship between the judiciary and the political branches, especially where the former censures the latter on international law grounds. The Nepalese judiciary's orders to the political branches to act on the basis of the UN Convention on Enforced Disappearances (to introduce appropriate legislation on the compensation of victims and the criminalization of enforced disappearances) serve to illustrate the gap between lofty judicial pronouncements on the requirements of international law, and the political reality of budgetary shortfalls and factional infighting. Faced with this reality, domestic courts may sometimes develop a practice of self-censorship and refuse to apply international law that is

57 Rome Statute of the International Criminal Court, Arts 1 and 17.

58 See Weill and Jovanović, *supra* note 2 (citing video-link hearings and assignment of protective measures to witnesses).

59 Weill and Jovanović, *supra* note 2.

60 See Ronen, *supra* note 4, and Benvenisti and Saliternik *supra* note 39, and see on transformative occupation A. Roberts, Transformative Military Occupation: Applying the Laws of War and Human Rights, 100 American Journal of International Law 580 (2006).

at loggerheads with domestic practices. In so doing, they avoid treading on the prerogatives of the political branches or rendering judgments that are not enforceable – a phenomenon that may also be discerned in Russia.

Other limitations may stem from inaccurate application of international law. An example of this is the *Lekaj* case in Serbia, where the domestic court considered that the alleged crimes had been committed in both an international armed conflict *and* a non-international armed conflict, applying law governing the former (Fourth Geneva Convention and Additional Protocol I), although the conflict was clearly a non-international conflict. Another example is the confusing use of the international law concept of joint criminal enterprise (JCE) in conjunction with the domestic law concept of co-perpetration by the Bosnian War Crimes Chamber to safeguard the principle of legality.[61]

Problems of domestic courts applying international law are of course compounded by the vagueness of international law itself. Unclear or open norms of international law may grant states too much leeway to decide what suits them, while allowing them to claim that they have upheld the rule of law. An example is the controversy within international law as to the proper 'control' standard for attributing one actor's conduct to another: is effective control required, or does overall control suffice?[62] Additionally, the use of international law by domestic courts may be complicated by the fact that different principles of international law are in tension with each other. An international criminal law principle may mandate the prosecution of international crimes, while an international human rights law principle may require that states live up to minimum due process standards when carrying out prosecutions. When discussing the Rwandan experience, the chapter by Palmer shows that it is not self-evident to superimpose the one rule of law principle on the other, when the former dovetails all too well with the policy interests of the state. Understandably, states – and their domestic courts are no exception – may tend to give priority to those international law obligations that are most favourable to them, placing into question the possibility of upholding the international rule of law in the local context.

Another limitation of international legal intervention in post-conflict societies is that the stabilization which internationally supported post-conflict constitutional moments may bring to an ethnically divided polity, comes at a

61 Article 180 of the Bosnian Criminal Code gives effect to international criminal law, arguably including the mode of liability known as JCE, in the domestic legal order, whereas Article 29 of the same code sets out the mode of co-perpetration. See for a discussion of relevant cases Uhlířová, *supra* note 2. In fact, a court should choose between those modes of liability, and cannot apply both at the same time.

62 See for the 'overall control' test: ICTY 15 July 1999, *Prosecutor v. Tadic*, Appeals Judgment, IT-94-1-A, para. 160, and for the 'effective control' test ICJ 26 February 2007, *Case Concerning the Application of the Convention on the Prevention and Punishment of the Crime of Genocide (Bosnia and Herzegovina v. Serbia and Montenegro)*, Judgment, paras 402–405. See for confusion as to the applicable standard in a domestic case, the *Scorpions* case before the Belgrade War Crimes Chamber, discussed in Weill and Jovanović, *supra* note 2.

price. Bosnia again is a good example. The internationally supervised peace negotiations which resulted in the 1995 Dayton Agreement – an international treaty which pacified Bosnia, and of which the Bosnian Constitution forms part[63] – did not include minority groups which had no role to play in the Bosnian conflict, such as Roma and Jews. As a result, these groups were excluded from the presidency of Bosnia, which the Constitution reserved for the three warring ethnic groups (Bosniaks, Croats, and Serbs). Faced with this discriminatory arrangement, in the case of *Sedjic and Finci v. Bosnia and Herzegovina* the European Court of Human Rights (ECtHR) could do little else than find it in violation of the ECHR.[64] It remains to be seen how Bosnia will respond to the ECtHR's findings. For many pundits, a revision of the sacrosanct guarantees of ethnic representation and stability may be a non-starter, although this appears to be precisely what the Court demands. At any rate, the case makes it clear, firstly, that internationally engineered constitutional moments may have serious rule of law flaws; secondly, that different rule of law values (stability and non-discrimination in this case) may be in tension with each other; and thirdly that the corrective intervention by international rule of law guardians such as the ECtHR may have very limited impact on the ground.

That said, not all international law is ambiguous, lends itself to self-serving application, or is rule of law deficient; its use by domestic courts often does have a stabilizing effect and contributes to the protection of rights. This book has mentioned many such examples, eg, South Africa, Rwanda, Serbia, and the practice of the Bosnian War Crimes Chamber. These cases show that domestic courts can give effect to international law and be open to foreign assistance, thereby breaking with a myopic past of legal autarky. But, then again, international actors specializing in spreading the international law gospel should not be deluded into assuming that simply because they are welcomed by domestic actors, those actors are necessarily interested in their transfer of international legal knowledge. Domestic courts may be interested in building capacity and developing practical skills rather than in acquiring specialized legal knowledge. As Weill and Jovanović show, the Serbian War Crimes Chamber and Prosecutor were apparently keener on learning practical skills, eg, relating to evidence-gathering, rather than on applying international law proper.[65] And as Palmer found in her work, Rwandan courts trying genocide suspects appeared more interested in developing judicial capacity than in implementing international

63 The Bosnian Constitutional Court even held that the Constitution could be interpreted on the basis of the relevant interpretation rules of the 1969 Vienna Convention on the Law of Treaties.

64 Ect.HR 22 December 2009, *Sejdic and Finci v. Bosnia and Herzegovina*, App. nos. 27996/06 and 34836/06. See also Uhlířová, *supra* note 2.

65 See Weill and Jovanović, *supra* note 2.

due process standards, given the huge backlog of cases which Rwandan courts had to deal with.[66]

International donors should realize that domestic courts in transitional societies may welcome international funding and infrastructure support, but may not necessarily be particularly keen on the application of international law. This stance is perfectly understandable in a post-conflict society where all infrastructure has been shattered and where the entire legal edifice has to be built up from scratch. Such societies may be primarily interested in effective, output-oriented, quantitative justice that provides a measure of accountability, rather than qualitative, input-oriented justice based on international due process standards. In this respect, it is observed that the rule of law also requires an *effective* administration of the law, and consequently that a focus of domestic courts on output is not necessarily at odds with the rule of law – although the question of 'at what cost' of course remains. In any event, patience will prove a virtue for international donors (and academic critics of international missions), who may wish to refrain from embarking on a vain quest for an immediate and perfect application of the full spectrum of rule of law values in post-conflict societies.

International donors should also guard against another major limitation of international rule of law entrenchment which has been described for some time in the law and development literature: the danger of international or donor legal transplants being effectively *rejected* by the recipient country after some time. We learned from the chapter by Uhlířová, for example, that the Bosnian WCC's initial concentration on international law may quickly be diluted after the departure of the internationals. Part of the reason being, 'that domestic actors did not participate in these changes to their legal system and they identify international law with international origins of law, as something that came from without, not within the state.'[67] As the failures of a blind transplantation of Western solutions in transitioning and developing countries gradually became apparent[68] and such solutions came to be seen as patronising and self-serving,[69] some authors have propounded that the success of rule of law entrenchment

66 See Palmer, *supra* note 3 (by 1999, the national courts had only heard 1,274 cases, ie merely one percent of the total number of detainees then held in custody).

67 Uhlířová, *supra* note 2, conclusion.

68 See eg R. Peerenboom, The Future of Rule of Law: Challenges and Prospects for the Field, 1 Hague Journal of the Rule of Law 5 (2009) ('The less than spectacular results of rule of law promotion efforts have called into question the role and influence of foreign actors, as well as the assumption that the best way for developing states to achieve rule of law is to base reforms on 'international best practices' and the transplantation of Euro-American institutions, values and beliefs.').

69 R. Peerenboom, What Have We Learned about Law and Development?: Describing, Predicting, and Assessing Legal Reforms in China, 27 Michigan Journal of International Law 823, 867 (2006) ('The patronizing conclusion that [developing states'] legal systems are backward then leads to well-intentioned efforts to export models not appropriate for the context, or less well-intentioned neo-imperialistic attempts to impose one's own contested

should be tied to incremental rule of law promotion and local ownership. Such an approach, termed 'cultural-historical', is more empirical and less ideological,[70] and 'recognizes a greater role and responsibility for target countries and is more open-ended and tolerant of institutional innovations and differences in norms, practices and outcomes'.[71] While it does not discount global norms and international best practices, this approach maintains that these norms and practices should only 'provide a normative basis and teleological orientation that informs and animates the reform process'.[72]

These insights draw attention to the fact that the interpretation of international norms by Western donor states and Western-dominated international institutions perhaps cannot and should not be transposed lock, stock and barrel to the domestic legal systems of countries in transition, including post-conflict societies, if rule of law entrenchment is to be successful. Courts in such countries may have to be allowed to mould and vernacularize international norms and practices so that they fit the local context, and take lasting root there.[73]

As regards local ownership of legal development and reform in post-conflict societies, however, the more specific, and often overlooked, question may arise as to who exactly can claim local ownership and invite international actors. In conflict-ridden countries, various groups may vie for political power and claim to represent the people. In the interest of stability and the long-term effectiveness of the application of international law by domestic courts in such countries, it is desirable that the international community involves itself with the group that embodies the will of the people most, and ideally have itself only invited after the most important rival groups have reached agreement. As Saul has usefully observed, while the vagueness of the law of self-determination leaves international actors a high level of discretion in this respect, they should refuse 'to initiate involvement on the basis of a request from a government with little claim to be an embodiment of the will of the people, unless there is strong contextual justification for such a course of action'.[74]

---

normative values on others and force them to adopt institutions that serve one's own economic and political interests.').

70 See eg, amongst many other publications by this author, R. Peerenboom, Between Global Norms and Domestic Realities: Judicial Reforms in China (May 2009), available at http://papers.ssrn.com/sol3/papers.cfm?abstract_id=1401232, p. 3–4 (discussing the agenda of the new president of the Supreme Court of China, Wang Shengjun).

71 Peerenboom, *supra* note 68, p. 5, 6.

72 Peerenboom, *supra* note 68, p. 11.

73 Peerenboom, *supra* note 69, p. 823, 827 ('Rather than merely being passive recipients, legal actors in the target state actively choose elements and reject others, interpret terms consistent with local perceptions and understandings, and modify or rework institutions, rules, or practices in light of domestic circumstances.').

74 M. Saul, Local Ownership of Post-Conflict Reconstruction in International Law: The Initiation of International Involvement, Journal of Conflict and Security Law 1, 40 (2011).

High-handed efforts by international actors to impose the application of international law on domestic courts without securing the support of groups considered as embodying the will of people will often backfire. The drafting of Article 23 of the Iraqi Transitional Administrative Law by the US Coalition Provisional Authority in Iraq may serve as a cautionary tale. This provision, which in its original version set out that Iraqi citizens enjoy 'the rights stipulated in international treaties and agreements, other instruments of international law that Iraq has signed and to which it has acceded, and others that are deemed binding upon it, and in the law of nations' was watered down and ultimately even deleted due to opposition by powerful Islamic groups taking issue with Western-style secular international law, and due to resistance against the US occupation of, or at least presence in, Iraq by major portions of the Iraqi population.

5. EFFECTS

A million dollar question (as indeed considerable amounts of funds are earmarked by international donors for rule of law development in post-conflict states) is whether the encouragement, assistance, legal expertise, and necessary funds offered by international actors to domestic courts applying international law has any lasting effects. Are these interventions not purely one-off acts tied to a moment of enhanced (but fleeting) international attention? Do they not merely effect cosmetic change in the domestic legal order? And, directly related to these questions, has the empowerment of national courts properly been embedded in a wider fabric of rule of law reforms?

At a more fundamental level, the question as to the lasting legacy of efforts to entrench international law in domestic court practice in transitional societies begs another question: can the rule of law really take root in such societies, which may lack the trappings of a strong legal community based on a system of reciprocal rights and responsibilities among its members?

In the absence of shared values, is the rule of law, or an international constitutional moment, not an alien construct engineered by foreign legal experts and artificially imposed on transitioning societies without much chance of success? Should community- or nation-building efforts (eg, through educational or art projects, such as theater, music, film, etc) not precede rule of law-promotion or constitution-making efforts? Or at the very least, other local transitional justice measures such as official investigations, truth telling, and other forms of debate and dialogue, to restore the national identity? Can the constitutional introduction of the rule of law, based on international law standards, in itself be expected to 'build' the community? A positive answer to the last question would likely be based on the argument that law has a social, community-building function in that it provides a common language which all members of a community, despite their differences, recognise, and adhere to out of a sense of 'constitutional patriotism', or civic nationalism.[75] Both Palmer and Popovic in their chapters advocated for more ethnographic and cultural research alongside the legal analysis in order to understand how Rwandan and Bosnian judges, respectively, have used and understood international law.[76]

To some extent, all these questions are not necessarily typical of transitional situations, or arise in all cases where national courts increase their use of international law. However, the fact that in situations of transition there often is a concerted effort by the UN, other international organizations, and NGOs, to empower courts to apply international law, and in particular the sheer importance of reinforcing the rule of law in such cases so as to prevent a re-emergence of lawlessness, makes these questions particularly pressing in situations of transition.

Questions on the ultimate effects of rule of law-building efforts and the strengthening of domestic courts are extremely difficult to answer. Not enough empirical research has been conducted in this field,[77] nor has the limited research that exists (which is often related to one specific country or region[78]) yielded conclusions or best practices that can be transposed to a range of similarly situated post-conflict or transitional societies. Some research has been done on the impact of the work of the international criminal tribunals on the societies where the atrocities over which they have jurisdiction took place,[79] or more generally on the impact of transitional justice mechanisms on peace and reconciliation, often on the basis of grassroots surveys.[80] But there has hardly

75 See J.W. Mueller, Constitutional Patriotism (Princeton University Press 2007).

76 See Palmer, *supra* note 3, introduction, and Popovic, *supra* note 2.

77 Although see eg A Nollkaemper, National Courts and the International Rule of Law (Oxford, 2008); J. Stromseth et al, Can Might Make Rights (Cambridge University Press, 2006).

78 See eg W. Mason, The Rule of Law in Afghanistan (Cambridge University Press, 2011); D.F. Haynes, Deconstructing the Reconstruction: Human Rights and Rule of Law in Postwar Bosnia and Herzegovina (Ashgate, 2008).

79 See on research done on the impact of the ICTY on Bosnia and Herzegovina: L.J. Nettelfield, Courting Democracy in Bosnia and Herzegovina: The Hague Tribunal's Impact in a Postwar State (Cambridge University Press, 2010). See generally on the effectiveness of international criminal tribunals: C. Ryngaert (ed.), The Effectiveness of International Criminal Justice (Intersentia, 2009). Research on the impact of international tribunals on domestic courts, such as international normative impact, judicial training and capacity-building, and procedural influences, has been conducted under the aegis of the 'DOMAC' project (Impact of International Courts on Domestic Criminal Procedures in Mass Atrocity Cases (www.domac.is), although this research did not delve specifically into rule of law issues.

80 Eg, in respect of Bosnia: S. Parmentier, M. Valinas and E. Weitekamp, How to Repair the Harm after Violent Conflict in Bosnia? Results of a Population-based Survey, 27 Netherlands Quarterly of Human Rights 27 (2009), in respect of Uganda: P. Pham and P.Vinck, Transitioning to Peace: a Population-Based Survey on Attitudes about Social Reconstruction and Justice in Northern Uganda (University of California, Berkeley: Human Rights Center, 2010); L. Gould and C. Ryngaert, The Interface Between Transitional Justice and Reconciliation in the Wake of Civil War: A Case Study of Northern Uganda', in: Liber Amicorum Bas de Gaay Fortman (Intersentia, forthcoming 2011).

been any research on the impact of *domestic courts* applying international law in post-conflict or transitional situations.

This volume has produced some evidence that in authoritarian states that had a legal tradition based on at least a 'thin' notion of the rule of law,[81] international rule of law-building efforts through domestic courts stand a greater chance of success. In South Africa, the new Bill of Rights – which mirrored international human rights law – may perhaps only have been possible because South Africa had a long legal tradition, and once the malignancy of apartheid had been excised, that legal tradition was ready to embrace international law as a normative source. Accordingly, during the transitional process, actors from both sides shared a belief in the centrality of law and considered judicial decision-making as a source of legitimacy.

The example of South Africa is also remarkable for showing that changes concerning the place and effect of international law may occur *in the absence of* meaningful international intervention (except for the role of foreign experts informing the domestic debates). South Africa thus shows that significant rule of law changes can be made purely by domestic actors and processes. In fact, in light of the danger of foreign legal transplants being rejected by a local judiciary, a process that is seen to be 'owned' by a post-conflict society is likely to produce more lasting effects than an internationally-driven process. In South Africa, at least, it was precisely the domestic nature of the actors and processes which helped confer legitimacy on the new Bill of Rights, and the process incidentally involved a broad social movement and cultural awakening through art, music, public debate and national soul-searching. This bottom-up mandate empowered the South African Constitutional Court not to hesitate to use its powers in the realm of economic and social rights.

In most other societies studied in this volume, shared beliefs in the legitimacy of the law may not have been present to the same extent as in South Africa. In many formerly totalitarian states, the law had historically been used as an instrument of control rather than emancipation. In addition, even if there existed a semblance of a rule of law-based culture in those states, the occurrence of armed conflict had devastating effects on the legal profession and on the material infrastructure of the judiciary. After the genocide in Rwanda, few lawyers were left. In the Balkans, notably in Bosnia, legal professionals were killed and many court facilities were destroyed during the campaign of ethnic cleansing. Faced with infrastructure and personnel shortages, the priority in these societies of having their courts up and running again through international capacity-building was not necessarily tantamount to a desire or commitment to have those courts, once restored, start to apply international law in all its technical nuances.

---

[81] 'Thin' here meaning a rule of law that is not informed by considerations of human rights and substantive justice.

In states that historically lacked a strong legal tradition, and that are traditionally opposed to applying 'culturally alien' norms and institutions – Afghanistan being a case in point – it is *a fortiori* doubtful whether a rule of law undertaking, even if supported by the international community, can bear any fruit.[82] Afghanistan, in any event, does not provide us with a very uplifting account. Lacking functioning political and judicial institutions and respect for any normative (ie, non-power-based) commitments or judicial dispute-settlement, constitutional changes incorporating international law may simply be cosmetic, and attempts at advancing the international rule of law further down the legal system may be condemned to failure.

In almost all the societies studied in this volume, there is a discernible gap between the endorsement of international law by the political branches, and the impact of this law on the practice of the courts. Lip service may be paid to international law in various legal texts and political declarations, but there is no guarantee that the formal availability of international law will ineluctably lead to a wider application of international law by domestic courts. For instance, Iraq's support for international law in general at the inter-state level, evidenced by its willingness to enter into treaties after the overthrow of Saddam Hussein, was not matched by increased openness to the application of international law by domestic courts.[83]

In any event, modest expectations of the effects of rule of law building efforts may be called for. Perhaps the most lasting positive effect of the international community's interventions in transitional societies' domestic courts is located at the very material level of having built courtrooms, trained police, and provided computers and software. As was already noted above, domestic courts may in the end be more interested in developing judicial capacity and acquiring practical skills rather than applying international law that has not come to them through the normal law-making process and is recognizable as a rule of law process rather than as a means to an end. Understandably, however, the international community – eager to promote peace and security and prevent impunity for serious crimes and gross human rights violations – may not want to settle for such a modest outcome, aiming rather for the entrenchment of international law in domestic courts. This, however, requires sustained training and support by the international community, also once it no longer has an operational presence in the post-conflict region.

Herein lies a 'Catch 22': an international intervention can only have lasting effects if it is wound down as soon as practicable. It is difficult for domestic actors to acquire ownership of their own legal process in the continuous presence of

82 See E. Afsah, Constitutionalism without Governance: International Standards in the Afghan Legal System, in this volume, and W. Mason, The Rule of Law in Afghanistan. Missing in Inaction (Cambridge University Press, 2010).

83 Cf Hamoudi, *supra* note 7.

international actors, and it is this local ownership that is key to successful rule of law-building in a post-conflict society. International assistance should therefore ideally create the legal-institutional conditions for the rule of law to blossom. This assistance should be inherently transitional in nature and should not create dependence of the post-conflict society on international donors or the presence of international organizations. Thus, in the interest of the emancipation of such societies, international intervention should be phased out and the domestic institutions should take over. Fine examples of this process are provided by the 'international' Bosnian Human Rights Chamber, which was integrated into the Bosnian legal structure when it became part of the Constitutional Court, and the ICTY/ICTR 'Rule 11*bis*' policy of referring atrocity cases from the international to the local level.

While the phasing out should begin as soon as possible, it should be designed as a gradual process that ensures the proper transfer of international know-how: the process of rule of law-building could fall flat if international actors were to pull out abruptly without transitional arrangements having been put in place. The 'internationalized' Bosnian War Crimes Chamber serves as a good example of the importance of securing continuity in rule of law-building. The Bosnian WCC was established with a five-year mandate in 2005, and it was thus expected that the international engagement would be phased out at the end of 2009. As of 2009, however, it became apparent that local judges and prosecutors were not yet fully up to the task of prosecuting and adjudicating war crimes. Eventually an intervention of the international Office of the High Representative in Bosnia was required to extend the mandate of international judges and prosecutors in the WCC until the end of 2012. In so doing, it overruled the Bosnian Parliament, which claimed full local ownership of the prosecutorial process. Whether or not the Bosnian side was up to the task may remain an open question, but this account makes it clear that the international side is often not without leverage to secure its continued presence in a post-conflict society in consultation with local actors. Only rarely, however, will it have as much leverage as it did in Bosnia, where the High Representative had the legal power of overruling decisions of elected local representatives.

At one point, of course, the international community will have to leave in the face of local pressure, even in the absence of perfect local capacity-building or knowledge acquisition that ensures the proper application of international law in domestic courts (but then, which stable country can truly boast of having a perfect relationship with international law?). In some situations, the departure of internationals may, perhaps somewhat counter-intuitively, lead to a greater acceptance of international law. This will especially be the case when changes to the domestic legal system, inspired by international law, were not accepted in the transitional period, because they were perceived as foreign or imperialist impositions, but once the foreign intervener leaves, the international origins of those changes may fade with the passing of time. There is some hope, for instance, that international law may come to play a greater role, naturally or organically, in Iraqi courts after the US leaves Iraq.

One of the greatest challenges, finally, for rule of law-building efforts in post-conflict societies concerns the *internalization* of the fundamental rule of law values underpinning international law, such as fairness and non-discriminatory application of international law. As Uhlířová points out, even top-level international negotiators may conclude peace agreements such as the Dayton Agreement more for the purpose of ending a war than as a legal basis a functioning state.[84] There is a real danger that domestic courts in post-conflict societies demonstrate knowledge of international law and willingness to apply it in concrete cases, but that the application of international law *in fact* benefits only one group (eg, the victorious party to the conflict, or those who ousted the autocrat). This is scarcely the legacy that the international community wants to leave in post-conflict countries. One-sided application of international law that does not firmly entrench the rule of law, and even clashes with the self-same rule of law principles it seeks to impart, may exacerbate tensions within a transitional society. It can hamper national reconciliation and discredit international law as arbitrary and result-oriented in the eyes of the disadvantaged party and its popular support base if the result sought is something other than simply the rule of law. For example, prosecutions based on international law which single out only the rebel forces and leave the government forces untouched, or ethnically composed courts that disproportionately target ethnic adversaries, should be shunned.[85] Such prosecutions make a mockery of the rule of law, as they presume guilt before conviction, benefit persons belonging to a (new) majority or powerful group, and sideline minorities or groups with an anti-systemic agenda. No matter how universally vilified the losing parties in such cases may be, domestic courts need to strike a balance between being more open towards new norms, and being stalwarts against political pressures – whether from within or from the outside. For example, international advocacy groups whose goals, however noble, may be to vindicate a victimized group, may be impatient with rule of law reforms and see them more as procedural and legalistic hindrances.

Admittedly, it could be argued that it constitutes progress in itself if international law is at least invoked in some cases, albeit selectively and in a discriminatory manner, and that an imperfect rule of international law is to be preferred over the utter absence of any semblance of the rule of law. But what are the limits of such imperfection? What margin of appreciation should international law leave to domestic courts in applying international norms? These questions all raise the issue of whether international law can or should

84 See Uhlířová, *supra* note 2, section 2.3.

85 Cf the ethnic composition of Bosnian cantonal and district courts, as described in Popovic, *supra* note 2.

accept a certain heterogeneity, and whether it may countenance slight deviations from accepted rule of law models.

Both Teitel and Beaulac have pointed to the need for a compromise as to the application of rule of law values in light of the extraordinary nature of transitional justice situations. Which values can or should precisely be compromised will normally depend on the context of the transition. Since every transition from authoritarianism to democracy is unique in its own right, no one-size-fits-all solution can simply be imposed. Beaulac therefore recommends what he calls an '*à la carte*' model that provides for some 'wholesale' and 'piecemeal' adjustments to the rule of law. When discussing the macro-adjustments that might be applicable across the wide range of transitional situations in spite of their irreducible differences, in our view he rightly warns against the temptation to implement a supposedly 'neutral' formal conception of the rule of law that is robbed of substantive human rights content. Such a thin conception may limit the symbolic 'watershed' effect of the constitutional moment which the application of international law marks after all; it may sap popular support for the rule of law and ultimately impede societies' shedding of their authoritarian past and the effectiveness of international law.[86] Therefore, substantive rule of law standards of procedural fairness, equity, and judicial review should govern domestic procedures, aside from such obvious principles as accountability, formal legality (including the prohibition of retroactive application of the law), and the limitation on the discretionary exercise of power.[87] This theoretical approach does not answer acute questions as to what precisely those rule of law standards mean at the micro-level in domestic court proceedings in transitional societies. The suggested standards are open-textured and amenable to widely varying interpretations. Reasonable people can reasonably differ as to what these standards mean in a concrete court case. The precise scope of the standards may be informed by the imperatives of other laudable policies, such as the reduction

86 Cf S. Beaulac, Lost in Transition? Domestic Courts, International Law and Rule of Law '*À la Carte*', in this volume at p. 17 (emphasising the performative role of the law and submitting that 'too thin an account of the rule of law, with no basic human rights content for instance, can be counter-productive as the reforming measures may lack apparent legitimacy and, as a result, might be considered unsatisfactory by people in transition societies.').

87 As far as the prohibition of retroactivity as an element of the rule of law is concerned, it is submitted that prosecution of genocide and crimes against humanity should not necessarily be based on the existing *domestic* penal code. It is allowed to base such prosecutions on *international* criminal law, which may have outlawed these crimes for a very long time. Cf. Art. 7.2 ECHR and Art 15.2 of the International Covenant on Civil and Political Rights (ICCPR) ('Nothing in this article shall prejudice the trial and punishment of any person for any act or omission which, at the time when it was committed, was criminal according to the general principles of law recognised by the community of nations.'). See for a domestic provision of a post-conflict state in this respect Article 3 of the Criminal Code of Bosnia and Herzegovina (stating that 'no punishment or other criminal sanction may be imposed on any person for an act which, prior to being perpetrated, has not been defined as a criminal offense by *law or international law*, and for which a punishment has not been prescribed by law') (emphasis added).

of the prison population, the countering of national security threats, or the swift delivery of justice, as is and was the case in Rwanda. Too strict an application or 'transplantation' of rule of law values may at times fail to solve wider societal problems with which post-conflict societies have to cope. As far as Rwanda is concerned, the ICTR and human rights NGOs may have paid insufficient heed to the local context in which domestic courts in Rwanda operate, in particular in the context of the Rule 11*bis* referrals,[88] and they may have demanded unreasonably – albeit understandably, in light of the shocking atrocities and the international community's failure to prevent the genocide – strict and 'thick' due process guarantees.[89] And in Iraq, foreign advisers should possibly have espoused a less 'revolutionary' approach of allowing the invocation of international law, in particular international human rights. As Hamoudi notes in his chapter, this could have soothed Islamists' concerns that the Sharia would be sidelined in favour of secular rights interpretations. In the end, incremental change may be the path to tread, although it may run counter to both international juridical instincts that international rights should not be compromised through 'flexible' contextual interpretations, and the international civil society's steep demands for swift justice and accountability.

It is submitted here, on the basis of the insightful case studies in the preceding chapters, that adaptation of rule of law standards in transitional societies need not necessarily mean a *relaxation* of standards. Under certain well-defined circumstances, it may well be that an interpretation of rule of law standards in a *more* human rights-protective manner is called for, and that domestic courts in post-conflict countries may want to go further than courts in countries enjoying peace and stability. This policy will often be informed by the special characteristics of a post-conflict country, but it is not to be excluded that it can set the stage for new, progressive interpretations of rule of law values that may be applicable in other situations as well.

A good example of 'protective' flexibility is provided by the case law of the Bosnian Human Rights Chamber. This Chamber gave a much wider interpretation of substantive ECHR rights than the ECtHR, eg by affirming positive obligations relating to the right to respect for the home, and also by including occupancy rights and rental agreements in the notion of 'possessions'.[90]

---

88 From a rule of law perspective these referrals may have been questionable *ab initio*: these referrals appeared to be informed by the desire to get rid of cases at the international level as a result of the completion strategy mandated by the UN Security Council (requiring that the ICTR close shop in due course) rather than by the desire to strengthen the capacity of domestic courts to adequately apply international law.

89 Cf. the statement of the Rwandan Prosecutor General, in Palmer, *supra* note 3: 'Justice in this country has been contextual. What they call double standards is justice in a contextual environment'. See also Palmer's interview with another justice actor in Rwanda at p. 171: 'We have done a lot to accommodate the practice of the ICTR, they also need to adapt to the national system. It is a matter of law and legal tradition'.

90 See in respect of the Bosnia Human Rights Chamber Buyse, *supra* note 2.

Such 'protective' flexibility will typically be tailor-made for post-conflict situations where the state system and the rule of law has collapsed. Still, novel interpretations espoused in such a context may make their way to the international level, thereby strengthening the international rule of law.[91]

Another example of this feedback loop is the direct influence of the South African Constitutional Court's interpretation of the principle of reasonableness in the application of economic and social rights on the wording of a new international instrument, the Optional Protocol to the International Covenant on Economic, Social and Cultural Rights.[92]

The application of international law by domestic courts may thus, through a sort of bottom-up feedback loop, strengthen the protection of the rule of law at the international level; after all, the rule of law quality of the international institutions that are instrumental in empowering national courts to apply international law may sometimes be questionable (remedies against these institutions may be lacking, and a democratic deficit may be apparent). This is what Beaulac calls 'reflexive' complementarity, or the 'mutually self-perfecting relationship', between on the one hand the internationalization of the rule of law (ie, the exportation of rule of law values from one jurisdiction to another), often by means of a somewhat biased interpretation of vaguely defined international human rights and good governance principles, and on the other hand the rule of law internationalized (ie, the rule of law as it is given shape at the level of international institutions such as courts and intergovernmental organizations). Indeed, international institutions come under more intense pressure to carry out internal rule of law reforms when even the most unstable post-conflict states carry out, more or less successfully, such reforms domestically.

The effectiveness of the application of international law by domestic courts in post-conflict or transitional situations may thus also be a function of the *international* rather than the domestic impact of such courts' development of legal basis practices. It remains no less true, however, that the long-term sustainability of international law-inspired legal reform, and the improvement of the lot of the local population whom the norms of international human rights and criminal law are supposed to protect, should be at the centre of the effectiveness analysis. From our study it can be gleaned that in most post-conflict societies studied in this volume, except perhaps Iraq and Afghanistan, domestic courts continue to rely on international law after its initial introduction. Unfortunately, however, there is as yet an absence of empirical data on the true

91 Also, interpretations of international law that are tailor-made for particular problems arising in post-conflict states may become of general application in those states, also with respect to issues that bear no specific relationship to the conflict. A fine example is the application in the general law of criminal procedure of Serbia of such legal tools as video link hearing and witness protection, which were originally designed for war crimes prosecutions, and were inspired by the law and practice of the ICTY. See Weill and Jovanović, *supra* note 2.

92 See Schmid, *supra* note 14.

effectiveness *on the ground* of the application of international law: to what extent has the situation of the local population been improved as a result of international (law) intervention? Answering this question is, in fact, mainly a task for social scientists rather than the legal scholars who contributed to this volume. But, ultimately, the legitimacy and *raison d'être* of the international community's efforts to promote the international rule of law depend on finding an answer to it.

www.ingramcontent.com/pod-product-compliance
Ingram Content Group UK Ltd.
Pitfield, Milton Keynes, MK11 3LW, UK
UKHW051912100926
8556IPUK00006B/863

9 781780 68041